Artificial Intelligence and Taxation Law

This book identifies how artificial intelligence (AI) systems can be used as part of decision processes within international tax and transfer pricing disputes.

The issue of double taxation and its impact on economic development continues to escalate as globalization causes states to interact on a growing scale. In recent years, AI applications have shown potential to solve this issue, particularly in reference to the length of time taken to resolve cases of double taxation in the field of transfer pricing. These cases can typically take at least two or more years to resolve, resulting in high cost to taxpayers and tax administrations. The book identifies the current legal frameworks available to prevent and solve tax and more specific transfer pricing disputes and details their advantages and disadvantages. Providing an analysis of what AI can offer to different legal principles, it shows how this can challenge existing rules, and the changes this requires within the legal framework. The book provides an overview of the challenges and opportunities that lie at the intersection of AI systems and the domain of international law, providing case studies to demonstrate its practical applications. It asks and answers the fundamental question: Can AI, or more specifically machine learning (ML), replace human decisions within the resolution of international tax and transfer pricing disputes?

The book will be of interest to researchers in the field of tax law, data protection law, consumer protection law, intellectual property law and artificial intelligence.

Enrico Gallo is a tax lawyer and holds a master's degree in law from LUMSA University and an LLM in international and European business law from Vienna University of Economics and Business (WU). He defended his PhD thesis, *Artificial Intelligence in the Resolution of Transfer Pricing Disputes*, at the University of Alicante in 2024. He worked as an international tax advisor in international consulting firms and in in-house roles in Italy and Austria. He is currently working as a tax manager in a multinational company.

Routledge Research in Tax Law

Tax Avoidance and the Law
Selina Keesoony

Tax Avoidance and European Law
Redesigning Sovereignty Through Multilateral Regulation
Mihaela Tofan

Social Media and Tax Law
Alara Efsun Yazıcıoğlu

Public Sector Performance, Corruption and State Capture in a Globalized World
Edited by Susan Rose-Ackerman

Artificial Intelligence and Taxation Law
Double Taxation Dispute Resolution
Enrico Gallo

Artificial Intelligence and Taxation Law

Double Taxation Dispute Resolution

Enrico Gallo

Routledge
Taylor & Francis Group
LONDON AND NEW YORK

First published 2026
by Routledge
4 Park Square, Milton Park, Abingdon, Oxon OX14 4RN

and by Routledge
605 Third Avenue, New York, NY 10158

Routledge is an imprint of the Taylor & Francis Group, an informa business

British Library Cataloguing-in-Publication Data
A catalogue record for this book is available from the British Library

ISBN: 978-1-032-97816-1 (hbk)
ISBN: 978-1-032-98654-8 (pbk)
ISBN: 978-1-003-59981-4 (ebk)

DOI: 10.4324/9781003599814

Typeset in Times New Roman
by Apex CoVantage, LLC

Contents

Preface

This monograph derives from the PhD that this author, Dr. Enrico Gallo, successfully defended the 9th of February 2024 at the premises of the Faculty of Law of the University of Alicante (Spain), before an evaluation committee chaired by Dr. María Teresa Soler Roch, Emeritus Full Professor of Tax Law, together with Dr. Cristina García-Herrera Blanco, Associate Professor of Tax Law at Complutense University of Madrid (Spain), Head of Studies of the Institute for Fiscal Studies of the Spanish Ministry of Finance; and Dr. Alesandro Turina, Academic Fellow at Bocconi University (Milan, Italy), Principal Associate at IBFD (Amsterdam, The Netherlands). The PhD was unanimously qualified as Excellent cum laude and received the International Doctorate Mention. It was supervised by the two undersigning professors: Dr. Aurora Ribes Ribes and Dr. Marina Serrat Romaní.

There is a sweet story behind the supervision of this PhD that deserves to be told. Dr. Gallo and Dr. Serrat were classmates during their studies for a master's degree in international tax law at the University of Economics and Business of Vienna (Austria). Despite parting ways after the completion of their PhDs, they remained in contact. Years after, Dr. Gallo contacted and transmitted to Dr. Serrat his aim to develop a PhD thesis about a particular topic he had already been thinking about—the application of AI on tax and transfer pricing disputes resolution. This main idea of research was the outcome of years of experience working on the tax and transfer pricing area, combined with the curiosity awakened by the progressive infiltration of new digital technologies, AI and particularly machine learning, in the legal field.

Due to the speciality of the topic, Dr. Serrat approached Dr. Ribes, who had done previous extensive work in the field of dispute resolutions and transfer pricing issues, and Dr. Ribes rapidly agreed to supervise the interesting proposal. As a manifested polyglot, Dr. Gallo—Italian living in Austria—did not hesitate to pursue a PhD thesis at a Spanish University, in both languages, Spanish and English. Au contraire! It was an appealing challenge for him, one that he successfully achieved. The development of the thesis did not happen in the most ideal of the circumstances, as we were navigating through the turbulences of the COVID pandemic and each of us was living in different countries at that time. However, digital technology—the same that Dr. Gallo was analysing in his PhD—allowed us to be in touch.

Despite the bumps on the road, we were able to have pleasant and fruitful discussions and guide him throughout the process of development of the PhD. In this sense, we must openly say that it was a pleasure for us to accompany Enrico Gallo during the three years of elaboration of his thesis, which was finally named "Artificial Intelligence in the Resolution of Transfer Pricing Disputes". The shaping of the content led him to analyse common international taxation issues, as the dispute resolutions are, but with the innovative character of digital technologies. A good closing-of-the-circle that defines the remarkable international character of both the PhD and this author.

This monograph, however, does not include all the original content of the PhD. It has been reshaped for publication, after the lively and substantive academic debate that took place during the defence. Therefore, it is the result of applying all the suggestions and recommendations received—that we are thankful for—from the members of the evaluation committee, lightening a part of the original manuscript that made reference to more general concepts of international taxation and focusing on the most relevant ones for answering the following question: Can artificial intelligence (AI), or more specifically machine learning (ML), replace human decisions within the mutual agreement procedures? More specifically transfer pricing (TP) mutual agreement procedures (MAPs)?

Allan Turing, the father of modern computer science, formulated the question "Can machines think?" in his well-known paper "Computer Machinery and Intelligence", published in 1950 in the journal *Mind*.[1] Since then, a lot of water has gone under the bridge, and now we are even able to train algorithms, making learning machines able to transform input data duly encoded to obtain a particular outcome. Besides, machine learning has been proven useful in practically all sectors of society, including the legal one. Legal reasoning is based on the interpretation of the law; however, legal questions can have more than one answer, depending on the case facts and the different approaches provided by guidelines, making legal terms susceptible to interpretation on multiple factors, including the passing of time. Being a legal point of view not static, but it evolves according to the evolution and the needs of the society, an automated answer to the legal (tax) issues can be provided with difficulty by a machine-learning model. Despite the difficulties present in the legal field for AI algorithms, there have been attempts to develop software useful for different legal purposes.

In recent years, there have been several developments in AI software to predict the identification of case law and doctrine in order to help legal practitioners support their arguments and angles of defence. In the legal field, these types of software have also been developed to help judges identify similar case law to those cases currently in process. Even though the software is not perfect, it is proven to be useful and helpful in the preparative tasks of judges, legal practitioners and advisors. If it is useful in terms time saving and streamlining the resolution of procedures, why not to apply it in other legal areas?

Within this context, Enrico Gallo dared to explore the possibility of introducing algorithms and mathematical calculations into the murky territory of valuations,

1 Turing, A., Computer Machinery and Intelligence, *Mind*, Vol. 59(236), 1950, pp. 433–460.

negotiations and legal interpretations that mutual agreement procedures and transfer pricing entail. It seems a difficult match, something so rigid taking decisions over case facts full of nuances. Maybe this is the main reason why no one has yet implemented or even studied the implementation of disruptive technology in cases of MAP or even arbitration. Nevertheless, Dr. Gallo, using a truly innovative methodology for a legal PhD, showed that it is possible that predictive models based on AI algorithms can be developed to issue MAP decisions, yet within a set of clear rules. Enrico Gallo's method of analysis consists of a mix of classical legal exposition and analysis of the international tax norms and conflicts that MAP normally deal with combined with a case study or proof of concept, typical of a science PhD thesis, trying to proof how AI software processes the legal texts on TP to reach conflict solutions.

In his findings, Dr. Gallo found that it is possible to use AI on MAP, yet within a very clear-cut set of rules. On the one hand, the background of the cases to be solved within a MAP needs to be identical to past cases. On the other hand, the set of tax provisions—normally tax treaty provisions when dealing with MAP—also need to be identical in both the negotiated case and in past cases, with which it matches the pattern. Finally, the competent authorities involved in the case should also ideally be identical as to minimize mistakes, algorithms need precise matching patterns. The more the merrier: legislation analysed, case facts, competent authorities involved. This set of rules greatly reduces the chances that a software can be as efficient as possible in reaching a fair solution. The further the patterns are from past cases, the more possibilities of failure in the predictability of the software, since their capacity of learning is not that developed so far. For this reason, it is important for such software to access the information. Whenever relevant data are classified under the secrecy of information, making them unavailable, it keeps machine learning unapplicable. Consequently, while AI can identify patterns from past rulings, it still lacks the capacity to autonomously make the necessary analogies for understanding the effect of different variable from past cases, which is a natural human capacity.

These main issues still prevent AI from being fully functional in the legal field. For this reason, Dr. Gallo insists on the importance of trying to improve not only the codification of AI and machine learning models for the interpretation of international treaties, but he also shows a particular concern regarding human rights. Particularly, the most important issues and threads of AI's predictive models in the legal field have taken place when human and fundamental rights where directly or indirectly involved. In that sense, on a more political ground, there have been attempts by governments to use AI to predict cases of potential tax and public subsidy fraud as well as target potential profiles of fraudsters.[2] However, machine learning has failed resoundingly due to the violations on human rights produced by its predictions (outcome). Therefore, Dr. Gallo insists that there is a need to boost

2 See, Rechtbank Den Haag, C-09-550982-HA ZA 18-388, 06-03-2020, available at https://uitspraken.rechtspraak.nl/details?id=ECLI:NL:RBDHA:2020:1878.

the development of these new technologies that benefit daily activities, but in a proper legal environment where human rights play a fundamental role.

This monograph transcends the classical manuscripts one finds in the legal field, making it unusual and creative, and it reflects the interdisciplinary character of the author, capable of navigating complex legal concepts as well as plunging into informatics concepts necessary to understand and develop the case studies. His exhaustive and detailed analysis makes this book worth reading for all those practitioners, political scientists and even IT experts dealing with the challenging crossroads of Law and Technology.

Aurora Ribes Ribes (University of Alicante)
Marina Serrat Romaní (University of Barcelona)
November 22, 2024

Acknowledgements

This monograph, being the final act of the PhD journey undertaken and concluded at the University of Alicante, would not have been possible without the support of a number of wonderful people—my thanks and appreciation to all of them for being part of this journey and making this work possible. I would first like to express my sincere gratitude to my PhD supervisors—Prof. Dr. Aurora Ribes Ribes and Prof. Dr. Marina Serrat Romaní—for their insightful comments, encouragement and commitment, which helped me identify the right steps to be undertaken when performing my research and topics analysis.

I express my warmest gratitude also to the University of Alicante and the Tax Law Department colleagues for their friendship and support, and for creating a cordial working environment. My greatest gratitude also goes to Prof. Dr. Michael Lang and Prof. Dr. Mario Grandinetti for giving me the opportunity to join their research teams respectively at WU University (Vienna University of Economics and Business) and at Turin University. This granted me access to research resources as well as participation in conferences, seminars, doctoral meetings and courses, all of which helped my research.

Furthermore, I would like to express my gratitude and appreciation to the members of the Tribunal, in the persons of Prof. Dr. Maria Teresa Soler Roch, Prof. Dr. Cristina García-Herrera Blanco and Prof. Dr. Alessandro Turina, for the observations and suggestions they addressed to me that helped me in writing this monograph.

I want to extend my gratitude to my partner in life Gudrun and our two children, Laetitia and Matteo, from whom I have taken precious time that I will never be able to make up for. I also thank them for their affection in moments where I was not able to be present to put up with my worries and my absences. They patiently and kindly supported me during this journey.

I would like to thank my parents, the transmitters of the values that have made me the person I am today, for their unconditional support and for promoting and inspiring the decisions I have made in my life. Thanks are also due to my brother Edoardo, to be always present when support is needed.

Finally, a big thank you goes to Dr. Félix Iglesias Vázquez, a real friend that invested his personal time with an enormous amount of patience to support me along the tortuous path of trying to get me into the AI world. His knowledge is boundless, but his heart is even bigger.

Abbreviations

AI	Artificial Intelligence
AIGO	OECD Working Party on Artificial Intelligence Governance
ANN	Artificial Neural Networks
ANP	Attention Network-Based Prediction
APA	Advance Pricing Agreement
ARL	Analogical Legal Reasoning
ASSYST	Applied Sentencing System
BAPA	Bilateral Advance Pricing Agreement
BOE	Boletín Oficial del estado
CABARET	Case-Based Reasoning Tool
CEPEJ	Commission for the Efficiency of Justice
CFA	OECD Committee of Fiscal Affairs
CMS	Case Management System
CPS	Cyber-Physical System
DBSCAN	Density-Based Spatial Clustering of Applications with Noise
DT	Decision Tree
DTC	Double Tax Convention
ECHR	European Convention on Human Rights
ETACA	European Trust and Cooperation Approach
EU	European Union
FTA	Forum on Tax Administration
GDPR	General Data Protection Regulation
G-LDA	Native algorithm implemented in the Gensim package
IBP	Issue-Based Prediction
ICAP	International Compliance Assurance Programme
IKBS	Intelligent Knowledge-Based System
KNN	K-Nearest Neighbours
LDA	Latent Dirichlet Allocation
LOF	Local Outlier Factor
MAP	Mutual Agreement Procedure
ML	Machine Learning
M-LDA	Collapsed Gibbs Sampling

MLI	Multilateral Instrument
MNE	Multinational Enterprise
MOMA	Multilateral Mutual Agreement Procedures and Advance Pricing Arrangements
MTC	Model Tax Convention
NB	Naive Bayes
NLP	Natural Language Processing
OECD	Organisation for Economic Cooperation and Development
PCA	Principal Component Analysis
RF	Random Forest
RLR	Rule-Based Legal Reasoning
S.P.A.	Societá per Azioni
SVM	Support Vector Machine
TCF	Tax Control Framework
TPG	OECD Transfer Pricing Guidelines 2022
TRM	Tax Risk Management
t-STNE	t-distributed Stochastic Neighbour Embedding
UDHR	Universal Declaration of Human Rights
UK	United Kingdom
UMAP	Uniform Manifold Approximation and Projection
UN	United Nations
US	United States
VAEs	Variational Auto Encoders
VJAP	Value Judgement Formalism System

1 International double taxation

Methods to solve it and their ineffectiveness

1 Introduction to international double taxation

The tax system as it is known today is based on the concepts of residence and source. The current tax system provides that individuals and entities are taxed in their state of residence on all income received irrespective of the place of receipt (worldwide income).[1] By contrast, non-residents are taxed according to the territoriality principle (i.e., source taxation).[2] These concepts and their effects, in identifying which state has the right to tax through income or wealth taxes, have been analysed over the years, and mainly since 1928 with the League of Nations, in line with increased globalization, cross-border transactions and international investments. The set of tax rules of one country has collided with tax rules of another country (i.e., rules of the country of the investor and rules of the country of investment) and has led to cases of double taxation,[3] that is, situations where the same person is taxed twice on the same taxable matter, or where two different persons are taxed on the same income or wealth (these cases are identified as juridical double taxation[4] and economic double taxation[5] respectively).

1 Instituto de Estudios Fiscales, Documentos de trabajo 7/2018, I.S.S.N.: 1578–0244, p. 325 that can be found at https://www.ief.es/docs/destacados/publicaciones/documentos_trabajo/2018_07.pdf and Adonnino, V. P., voce "Doppia imposizione" in *Enciclopedia Giuridica Treccani*, vol. XII.

2 Instituto de Estudios Fiscales, Documentos de Trabajo 7/2018, I.S.S.N.: 1578–0244, p. 325 that can be found at https://www.ief.es/docs/destacados/publicaciones/documentos_trabajo/2018_07.pdf.

3 OCDE Model Tax Convention (2017), Introduction, p. I and EU Commission Staff Working Document, Impact Assessment Accompanying the Document Proposal for a Council Directive on Double Taxation Dispute Resolution Mechanism in the European Union, SWD(2016) 343 final 5 (25 Octubre 2016). See also Article 2, p. I, of the EU Directive (UE) 2017/1852 10 of October 2017 and Panta Trelles, J. A., Análisis de la interpretación de los convenios para evitar la doble imposición internacional, *IUS ET VERITAS*, Vol. 45, 2012, p. 358.

4 Lang, M., *Introduction to the Law of Double Taxation Conventions*, Linde, 2010, pp. 23–24 y Simón Acosta, E., La doble imposición jurídica como obstáculo para la internacionalización de las empresas: el papel de las convenciones fiscales nacionales, *Nueva Fiscalidad*, Nr. 3, Julio–Septiembre 2018, p. 23. See also Carli, C. C., voce Cooperazione Internazionale Tributaria, in *Enciclopedia Giuridica Treccani*, vol. IX.

5 Kofler, G. and Potgens, F., *—Article 23—Methods for Elimination of Double Taxation*, IBFD, 2020, p. 5. See also Lang, M., *Introduction to the Law of Double Taxation Conventions*, Linde, 2010, p. 25 and Finnerty, C., Merks, P., Petriccione, M. y Russo, R., *Fundamentals of International Tax Planning*, IBFD, 2007, p. 9.

DOI: 10.4324/9781003599814-1

Double taxation is directly related to globalization and the opening of markets, where business networks have developed between companies and individuals located in different and interrelated countries.[6] The phenomenon of globalization[7] has been booming in the 20th and 21st centuries, affecting not only trade per se but also taxation.[8] The increase in foreign direct investment and the parallel opening of new economies to foreign investors has led to more difficulties in the relationship of legal and tax systems between countries.[9] Therefore, with the globalization of trade, legal tax systems have had to face this evolution of the economic system as never before and, considering that their purpose is to protect the economic interests of their own states, double taxation phenomena have intensified due to the overlapping of rules.[10]

Therefore, for double taxation to exist, the following are necessary: (i) the identity or similarity of the tax, that is, that there are two or more taxes imposed by two or more states in which the taxable events are identical or similar, which means that the phenomenon giving rise to the tax liability must coincide; (ii) identity of the period or timing of the taxable event in the taxes imposed by two or more states; and (iii) identity of the taxable person on whom the tax is imposed.[11]

One of the most frequent cases of economic double taxation occurs in the application of transfer pricing rules and more specifically when the arm's length principle has to be applied. In a world where the economy is becoming increasingly globalized and the growing importance of multinational groups plays a fundamental role in its development, there is a need to implement methods to avoid tax base erosion and profit shifting. In this regard, the arm's length principle has been provided under Article 9 of the OECD Model Tax Convention (MTC), providing that prices charged for transactions between related parties have to be comparable to prices that would have been agreed between unrelated parties in similar circumstances.

6 Ring, D. M., *International Tax Relations: Theory and Implications*, Boston College Law School, Legal Studies Research Paper Series, 2006, p. 3.

7 Council of Europe, *Resolution of the Executive Committee of the European Confederation of the Social Dimension of the Globalization*, 2005, available at https://www.coe.int/es/web/compass/globalisation.

8 Kofler, G. and Potgens, F., *—Article 23—Methods for Elimination of Double Taxation*, Global Topics IBFD, 2020, p. 4.

9 Bagaria, S., *The Nature and Purposes of Double Taxation Agreements and the Issues Which the Interpretation of Such Agreements May Give Rise*, 2012, p. 3, available at https://papers.ssrn.com/sol3/papers.cfm?abstract_id=2018859.

10 Rixen, T., Bilateralism or Multilateralism? The Political Economy of Avoiding International Double Taxation, *European Journal of International Relations*, Vol. 16, 2010, p. 589 y OECD, What Is a Competitive Tax System, *OECD 50th Anniversary Challenges in Designing Competitive Tax Systems*, Paris, 30 June 2011, p. 4.

11 Panta Trelles, J. A., Análisis de la interpretación de los convenios para evitar la doble imposición internacional, *IUS ET VERITAS*, Vol. 45, 2012, p. 358.y Ismer, R. y Ruß, J., What's International Double Taxation?, *Intertax*, Vol. 28, 2020, p. 556 and Fantozzi, A., and Vogel, K., voce Doppia Imposizione Internazionale, in Digesto delle discipline privatistiche – sezione commerciale, p. 181 and OECD Model Tax Convention, 2017, p. 10.

The arm's length principle, based on the comparison between arm's length prices and prices used in activities and transactions between members of multinational groups, provides that price adjustments are possible in case of discrepancies. In other words, if tax administrations recognize that intra-group prices do not respect the prices that would have been charged in arm's length transactions, they may adjust the prices charged so that they are in conformity with the market. Thus, where the arm's length principle is respected, there is no need to perform adjustments and if adjustments are necessary, they should not exceed what is required under the arm's length principle.

The types of adjustments are multiple and can be identified as primary, corresponding, secondary and compensatory adjustments. The OECD Transfer Pricing Guidelines describe them in the Glossary.

Therefore, in order to avoid double taxation, it is necessary that where there is a challenge by a jurisdiction that recognizes, through a primary adjustment, a redefinition of income in accordance with the arm's length principle, an adjustment of the same amount, but with a different sign, of the taxable income of the counterparty to the transaction in the other jurisdiction is made through a corresponding adjustment. Consequently, where one jurisdiction makes a primary adjustment and the other jurisdiction does not make a corresponding adjustment, or the same taxpayer does not make a secondary adjustment, economic double taxation cases could occur.

It is important to note that, even if the OECD Model Tax Convention identifies the corresponding adjustments as methods to avoid double taxation, there is no explanation for how this objective is to be achieved. In other words, it is left to the competent authorities to consult and determine the corresponding adjustments, identifying as the sole modality that of Article 25 of the OECD Model Tax Convention. Thus, if in the case of juridical double taxation, Articles 23A and 23B identify clear methods to achieve the reduction or elimination of double taxation, in the case of economic double taxation—and with greater reference to transfer pricing cases—everything is left to a consultation procedure between financial administrations.

2 Methods to prevent international double taxation

In general terms, different methods have been developed to reduce or eliminate double taxation, both at unilateral and at international levels (according to double tax conventions).

2.1 Unilateral methods to prevent international double taxation

When dealing with international double taxation issues, unilateral measures play an important role. Although, the use of double taxation treaties is very extensive, not all cross-border transactions are covered by treaties between two or more states. Therefore, to reduce or avoid cases of double taxation, where treaty measures are lacking, states also use unilateral measures.

Even if there are different cases and applications, in line with the different legal-tax systems of each country, three types of measures can be identified: (i) the exemption of income generated abroad (full or with progression), (ii) the tax credit granted for taxes paid abroad on income generated there and (iii) the deduction from the tax base of taxes paid on income generated abroad.[12]

2.2 Double tax conventions to prevent international double taxation

The work of the League of Nations contributed to the development of standardized model tax conventions. In the years between World Wars I and II, the League of Nations produced several model tax conventions which gained importance in the negotiations of bilateral tax conventions between states and left their mark on the later work of other international organizations. The OEEC, and later the OECD, continued the work of the League of Nations. In 1963, 1977 and 1992, the OECD published model tax conventions in the area of taxes on income and on capital. These agreements were further developed in 1994, 1995, 1997, 2000, 2002, 2005, 2008, 2010, 2014 and 2017.

The methods for eliminating double taxation are found in Articles 23A (exemption) and 23B (imputation or credit) of the OECD Model Tax Convention (OECD MTC) and in the same articles in the United Nations (UN) MTC.[13] The methods identified here, as the commentaries to the Model Agreements explain in their first paragraph, refer to methods for resolving juridical double taxation, while in the second paragraph, with reference to the issue of economic double taxation, states are required to resolve these issues between themselves, mainly bilaterally.

In general, the Model Tax Convention proposes a division of taxing powers that attributes a limited power to the source state and an unlimited power to the state of residence. In cases where both the state of residence and the source state retain the right to tax income, the MTC provides that it is the state of residence that guarantees the exemption or credit for taxes paid in the source state.[14]

Therefore, if in the case of juridical double taxation Articles 23A and 23B identify clear methods to achieve the reduction or elimination of double taxation, in the case of economic double taxation—and with greater reference to transfer pricing cases—everything is left to a consultation procedure between tax administrations with a consequence of tax uncertainty for the taxpayer.

3 Instruments to prevent tax and transfer pricing disputes

The causes of disputes can be different and mainly derive from the unclear set of rules that could generate a high amount of uncertainty in the taxpayer–tax

12 Lang, M., *Introduction to the Law of Double Taxation Conventions*, Linde, 2010, p. 26.

13 Tarigo, P., *Trattati Fiscali Italiani e Limiti Quantitativi del Foreign Tax Credit, Rivista di Diritto Finanziario e Scienza delle Finanze*, Giuffré Francis Lefebvre, 2020, p. 461.

14 Lang, M. y Owens, J., *The Role of Tax Treaties in Facilitating Development and Protecting the Tax Base*, WU International Taxation Research Paper Series, No. 2014–03, p. 5.

administration relationship. There are several reasons a taxpayer can start a dispute: (i) the consideration that the tax administration has applied, in a concrete case, a law provision that brings unfair results; (ii) the fact that the tax administration has wrongly interpreted or qualified a law provision; or (iii) the tax systems itself is unfair and blurry, and it harms the taxpayers' interests.[15]

It should be noted that, over the last two decades, many governments moved towards tax systems that are more business-friendly and encourage entrepreneurship.[16] Different instruments have been developed, at an international level, to prevent disputes between the parties. The procedures are the ones that provide the possibility to find an agreement/solution between the taxpayers and the tax authorities before reaching the local courts, or the MAP (mutual agreement procedure)—that is, the latter being tax dispute resolution mechanisms.

3.1 Overview of the current status of the tax disputes

To understand the magnitude of the disputes, here is a general overview of the status of disputes to show the extent of the issue related to the number and the time needed to solve disputes when they arise.

The Report on Action 14: Making Dispute Resolution Mechanisms More Effective (2015 Action 14 Report) was approved by the OECD Committee of Fiscal Affairs (CFA) in September 2015 and presented to the OECD Council and endorsed by the G20 Finance Ministers on October 8, 2015. This report contained a commitment by the countries engaged in the work to the implementation of a minimum standard to ensure that they resolve treaty-related disputes in a timely, effective and efficient manner (average time frame of 24 months), and to have their compliance with the minimum standard reviewed by their peers—that is, the other members of the Forum on Tax Administration MAP Forum (FTA MAP Forum). To achieve that objective, jurisdictions are required to provide timely and complete reporting of MAP statistics, pursuant to the agreed reporting framework.[17]

Following this approach, more agreements have been attempted and reached between tax administrations during the MAP phase. The data provided by the OECD on MAPs statistics with respect to the increase on open MAPs proves the

15 Herrera Molina, P. M., *Justicia y claridad de las normas: la mejor estrategia global para prevenir la conflictividad en materia tributaria*, en Documento de Trabajo 11/2019–VII Encuentro de Derecho Financiero y Tributario, Una estrategia global al servicio de la reducción de la conflictividad en materia tributaria, coordinado por Cristina García Herrera Blanco, pp. 188–189.

16 Owens, J., Tax Administrators, Taxpayers and Their Advisors: Can the Dynamics of the Relationship Be Changed? *Bulletin for International Taxation*, September 2012, p. 516.

17 See MAP Statistics Reporting Framework, p. 1. All members of the Inclusive Framework on BEPS (IF) commit to the implementation of the Action 14 minimum standard, which includes timely and complete reporting of Mutual Agreement Procedure (MAP) statistics pursuant to an agreed reporting framework.

All cases*	2023 Start Inventory	Cases started in 2023	Cases closed in 2023	2023 End Inventory
Cases received prior to 1 January 2016 or of year of joining the BIPS Inclusive Framework	1042	0	213	813
Cases received on or after 1 January 2016 or of year of joining the BIPS Inclusive Framework	5413	2336	2388	5362

Figure 1.1 All cases under MAP.

Transfer pricing cases*	Start Inventory	Cases started	Cases closed	End Inventory
Cases received prior to 1 January 2016 or of year of joining the BIPS Inclusive Framework	529	0	107	420
Cases received on or after 1 January 2016 or of year of joining the BIPS Inclusive Framework	2869	979	1078	2770

Figure 1.2 TP cases under MAP.

increase of the agreements.[18] In 2023, as shown in the Figures 1.1[19] and 1.2,[20] there were a total of 2,336 new MAPs, out of which 979 corresponded to transfer pricing procedures.

The OECD identified, as depicted in Figure 1.3[21] the MAP outcomes in 2023. At this stage, the OECD also identified the time needed to close MAPs related to transfer pricing and non-transfer pricing issues. Indeed, the average time needed to close transfer pricing issues is 32.01 months, while for other tax-related issues the time is relatively shorter and quantified in 23.36 months.

The long steps in the procedure, due to the complexity of the cases, leads to a long time required to solve the cases and to a risk that the double taxation situation will not be resolved. Consequently, the taxpayer will always face the risk of not only having to bear significant costs during the ongoing procedure but also to

18 OECD, *Mutual Agreement Procedure Statistics for 2023*, available at https://www.oecd.org/en/data/datasets/mutual-agreement-procedure-statistics.html.

19 OECD, *Mutual Agreement Procedure Statistics for 2023*, available at https://www.oecd.org/en/data/datasets/mutual-agreement-procedure-statistics.html.

20 OECD, *Mutual Agreement Procedure Statistics for 2023*, available at https://www.oecd.org/en/data/datasets/mutual-agreement-procedure-statistics.html.

21 OECD, *Mutual Agreement Procedure Statistics for 2023*, available at https://www.oecd.org/en/data/datasets/mutual-agreement-procedure-statistics.html.

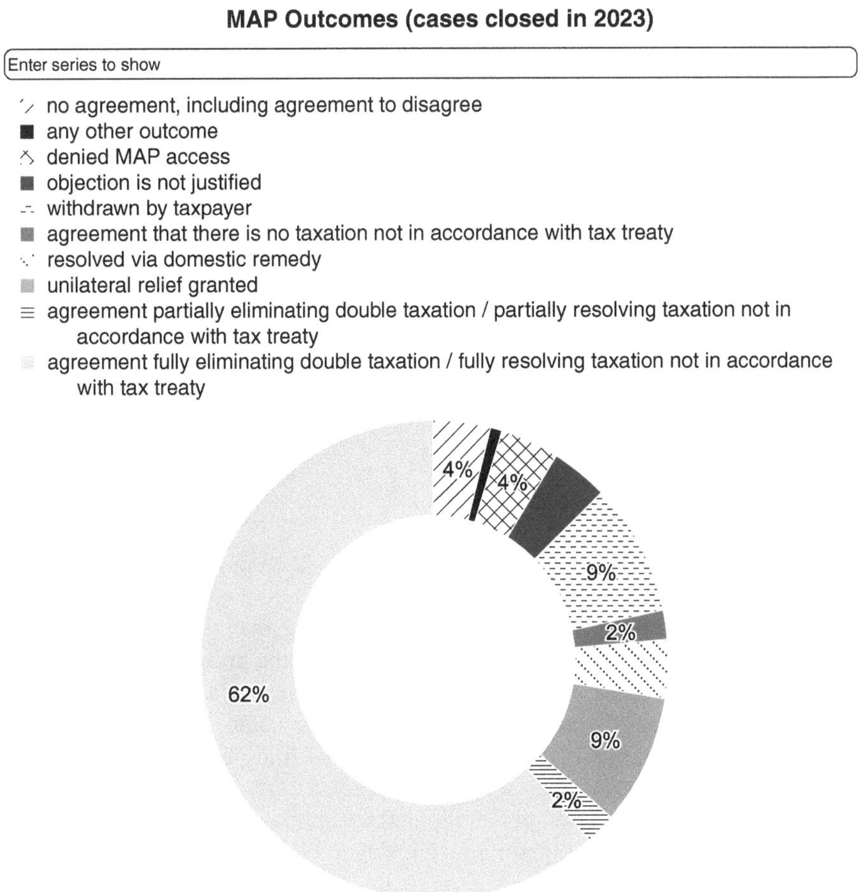

Figure 1.3 MAP outcomes.

having the double taxation problem not solved. Therefore, a preventive solution could be welcomed from both the parties involved, as it could generate both cost savings and time efficiency.

3.2 Methods to prevent tax dispute resolutions

Tax certainty for taxpayers is an important component of investment decisions and can have significant impacts on economic growth.[22] Double taxation is an increas-

22 2019 Progress Report on Tax Certainty, IMF/OECD Report for the G20 Finance Ministers and Central Bank Governors, June 2019, p. 6.

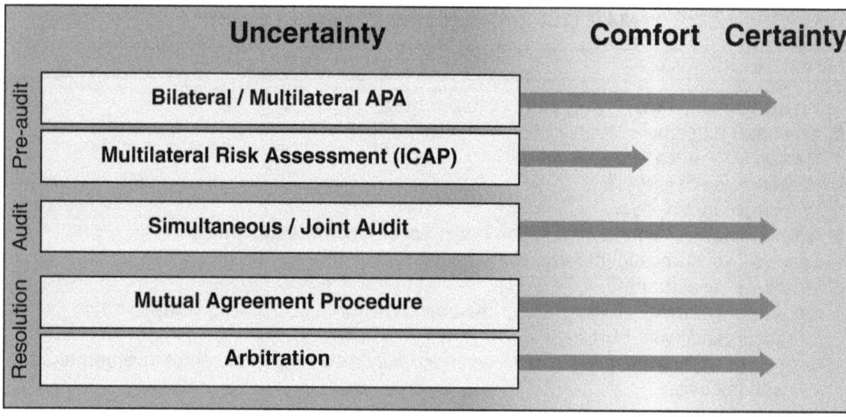

Figure 1.4 Level of tax certainty per instrument

ing matter of concern for the coming years, and it will be important to find a way to eliminate it, especially in the transfer pricing field.

As a consequence, at international and EU levels there is a need to build proper legislative solutions that grant the right to tax the profits generated in its territory, and cooperative mechanisms that allow identification and prevent the increase of tax disputes while always considering the balance between a proper tax system administration (i.e., tax certainty and tax transparency) and the need to protect a country's revenue base. In this respect, a quick resolution to possible disagreements between tax administrations that can give rise to double taxation situations is one of the most important elements to be considered when speaking about tax certainty as to taxpayers running their businesses with less or nil tax implications.

In this sense, under the umbrella of a cooperative compliance relationship that, according to who writes it, is the basis to try to avoid further disputes, we can identify the following methods: (i) Advance Pricing Agreement (APA), (ii) safe harbours, (iii) joint audits and (iv) International Compliance Assurance Programme (ICAP). On the other side, dispute resolution methods are (i) MAP and (ii) arbitration.[23] One of the main purposes of the international taxation discussion today is to grant certainty to the relationship between tax administrations and taxpayers; therefore, before analysing the different instruments currently available, it is interesting to identify the level of certainty that they can provide. Figure 1.4[24] provides an overview per instrument.

23 2017 Tax Certainty, IMF/OECD Report for the G20 Finance Ministers and Central Bank Governors, March 2017, p. 7.

24 OECD, *International Compliance Assurance Programme—Handbook for Tax Administrations and MNE Groups*, Paris, 2021, p. 9.

The purpose of the following paragraphs is to identify and describe methods that have been developed at the international level to solve double taxation cases at an early stage, that is, before reaching a dispute.

3.3 Cooperative compliance

Tax compliance activities, especially at the international level, can create quite high burdens both at tax administration and taxpayer levels. Tax administrations can either fully trust the taxpayers when providing their tax returns or performing intercompany transactions or they can be suspicious and continuously check the taxpayers' behaviours. To overcome the constant mistrust between tax administrations and taxpayers, a scheme of cooperative compliance has been created that aims to create a relationship of trust in order to solve any tax issue in a preliminary phase before a dispute arises.

Tax administrations have been provided in recent years with new compliance instruments that allow them to exchange tax rulings and country-by-country reports and also to automatically exchange information. However, the amount of information can create a paralysis in terms of using such information, therefore reducing the applicability of such instruments.[25] Therefore, due to the need to grant tax certainty in the relationship between tax administrations and taxpayers, the new paradigms in the tax field point towards cooperation and cooperative compliance.[26] While tax administrations have strengthened tax audits, they also try to offer alternative tools, as part of voluntary processes, to address tax issues with taxpayers before they launch any formal audit.[27] The aim of these processes is to create a climate of collaborative cooperation between taxpayers and tax administrations in addressing tax issues.

This new approach moves away from the previous view where the state is the creditor, and the taxpayer is a mere debtor. Indeed, according to the original dogmatic approach, tax administration's position was one of *potentior persona*, which brings the relationship on a path of inequality.[28] Indeed, in the latter half of the 20th century, the approach of tax administrations could have been seen as a military analogy where the target (evaders) was identified and taken out (in other words tax administrations were the "cops").[29] In this old approach neither "side" had

25 Bronzewska, K. and Majdańska, A., The New Wave of Cooperative Compliance Programmes and the Impact of New Technology, *European Taxation*, February/March 2019, p. 99.

26 Pablos Mateos, F., De las relaciones cooperativas al cumplimento cooperativo: las propuestas previas de tributación en el País Vasco, en *Documento de Trabajo 11/2019—VII Encuentro de Derecho Financiero y Tributario "Una estrategia global al servicio de la reducción de la conflictividad en materia tributaria"*, coordinado por Cristina García_Herrera Blanco, p. 223, 2019.

27 Daluzeau, X. and Pasquier, C., *Emerging Tax Compliance Programs*, Linde, TPI 1/2020.

28 Soler Roch, M. T., Forum: Tax Administration versus Taxpayer—A New Deal? *World Tax Journal*, October 2012, p. 283.

29 Owens, J., The Role of Tax Administrations in the Current Political Climate, *Bulletin for International Taxation*, March 2013, p. 156.

sufficient confidence in their relationship to engage in a dialogue, and the relationship itself was characterized by confrontation and mistrust.[30]

In the recent past, and especially through the implementation of the BEPS project, it has been of fundamental importance to identify proper coordinated means and fiscal policies aiming to obtain the right tax payment in each jurisdiction where the multinational enterprises were operating.[31] Indeed, all revenue authorities are generally required to achieve as good as compliance outcome as possible (i.e., to maximize the overall level of compliance with the tax laws[32]). Therefore, it is necessary to combine the tax compliance of the taxpayers with the services that tax administrations should provide to the former. In this respect, through the OECD, on July 2002, the Forum on Tax Administration (FTA) was created as an independent body under the Committee on Fiscal Affairs. The FTA's purpose is to increase efficiency and equality in the organization and operating functioning of the tax administrations as well as decrease the costs for the taxpayers when complying with tax law requirements.[33]

After its creation, the FTA started to meet annually[34] to discuss different topics such as (i) the way and the level of communication between tax administrations and taxpayers, (ii) the importance of tax risk management by the tax administration, (iii) strategies to obtain an equilibrium between the provision of services to taxpayers and the application of the rules and (iv) the deal with the intermediaries to improve tax compliance.[35]

Out of all the meetings, the one that took place in 2008 in Cape Town, with the final report "Study into the Role of Tax Intermediaries" (2008 Study), could be identified as the one where the cooperative compliance concept, that initially was named "enhanced relationship", was conceived. Then, in 2013, the OECD published a document[36] where the "enhanced relationship" term was replaced by "cooperative compliance" due to some constraints that the former term encompasses, especially in relation to inequality in tax treatment and equality before the law.[37] Therefore, the concept of cooperative compliance is intended to deliver

30 Owens, J., The "Enhanced Relationship": A Challenge for Revenue Bodies and Taxpayers, *European Taxation*, July 2008, p. 351.

31 Calderón Carrero, J. M., Quintas Seara, A., Introducción al modelo del cumplimento tributario cooperativo: estudio de los trabajos de la OCDE y principales experiencias internacionales, *Revista Española de Derecho Financiero*, Vol. 167, Julio–Septiembre 2015, p. 77.

32 OECD, *Compliance Risk Management: Managing and Improving Tax Compliance (Guidance Note)*, Paris, 2004, p. 6.

33 The purpose of the FTA can be identified in the OECD, *Programs to Reduce the Administrative Burden of Tax Regulations (Follow-Up Report)*, Paris, 2010, p. 4.

34 The first meeting took place in Sevilla in January 2004.

35 Calderón Carrero, J. M. and Quintas Seara, A., Introducción al modelo del cumplimento tributario cooperativo: estudio de los trabajos de la OCDE y principales experiencias internacionales, *Revista Española de Derecho Financiero*, Vol. 167, 2015, p. 78.

36 OECD, *Co-operative Compliance: A Framework—from Enhanced Relationship to Co-operative Compliance*, Paris, 2013.

37 OECD, *Co-operative Compliance: A Framework—from Enhanced Relationship to Co-operative Compliance*, Paris, 2013, p. 16.

quality compliance in the sense that the taxes should be paid on time in an efficient and effective manner within a context of trust between the parties, especially regarding the ability of the tax administrations to behave predictably and with a provision of certainty regarding the taxpayers' tax positions.[38]

3.3.1 The functioning of the cooperative compliance and its benefits

The OECD study, while underlining that the enhanced relationship is based on establishing and sustaining mutual trust between taxpayers and revenue bodies, also sets the behaviours that should be followed by the parties.[39]

The cooperative compliance goal can be achieved through a compliance risk strategy.[40] A first definition of the compliance risk management concept can be found in the Compliance Risk Management Guide,[41] where it is identified as

> a systematic process in which a revenue body makes substantiated choices on which interventions could be used to effectively stimulate compliance and prevent non-compliance, based on the knowledge of the behaviour of all taxpayers and related to the available capacity.

Further, the OECD, in its 2013 document, described the scope of the Tax Risk Management (TRM) as

> the internal control of all process and transactions with possible tax consequences. This means that the specific requirement to be "in control" of all tax issues—able to detect, document and report any relevant tax risks to the revenue body in a timely way—needs to be extend to all processes in scope of the ICF (Internal Control Framework).[42]

Further to this first identification of the importance of the TRM was the need to clarify how to design such a system and define its value. In this sense, the 2013 OECD report provided recommendations on how to set up and use the tax control framework (TCF).

38 Van der Enden, E. and Bronzewska, K, The Concept of Cooperative Compliance, *Bulletin for International Taxation*, October 2014, p. 567.

39 OECD, *Co-operative Compliance: A Framework—from Enhanced Relationship to Co-operative Compliance*, Paris, 2013, p. 15 and OECD, *Study into the Role of Tax Intermediaries*, Paris, 2008, p. 40. See also Romaní Sancho, A., La nueva relación Hacienda-contribuyente auspiciada por la OECD: la relación cooperativa. El Foro de Grandes Empresas y el Código de Buenas Prácticas Tributarias, *Cuadernos de Formación 4/10*, Vol. 11, 2010, pp. 278–279.

40 OECD, *Co-operative Compliance: A Framework—From Enhanced Relationship to Co-operative Compliance*, Paris, 2013, p. 29.

41 European Commission, *Compliance Risk Management Guide for Tax Administrations*, European Union, 2010, p. 5.

42 OECD, *Co-operative Compliance: A Framework—From Enhanced Relationship to Co-operative Compliance*, Paris, 2013, p. 59.

The corresponding activities of the taxpayer, to the suggested behaviours in order to grant the tax certainty, are then the implementation of a proper TRM/TCF. In fact, it is properly this last step that grants the maximum grade of tax certainty. Therefore, in countries where a cooperative compliance programme has been implemented, taxpayers who want to apply for such a programme need to offer disclosure and transparency, and therefore go beyond their statutory obligations, via implementation of the TCF system of internal controls. This will ensure that tax returns submitted to the revenue bodies are accurate and that transactions or positions giving rise to material tax uncertainty are disclosed. In turn, revenue bodies will assess the monitoring, electronic business and accounting systems of the taxpayer to form an opinion on the effectiveness of its TCF.[43]

3.3.2 EU Cooperative Compliance Programme

Also, the European Commission presented an Action Plan in July 2020[44] for fair and simple taxation supporting the recovery strategy and announced plans to introduce an EU Cooperative Compliance Programme. The aim of this programme is to facilitate and promote tax compliance on greater cooperation, trust and transparency between taxpayers and tax administrations as well as among tax administrations.[45]

The initiative covers (i) small- and medium-sized enterprises and (ii) large multinational enterprises.

3.3.2.1 SMALL- AND MEDIUM-SIZED ENTERPRISES

For the small- and medium-sized enterprises, a Fiscalis Project Group (small and medium enterprises) was set up in September 2020 with the aim to discuss and develop a possible programme to allow tax administrations to solve together, in a preventive manner, cross-border tax issues faced by small and medium enterprises within the EU. According to the information gathered at the moment of writing, a pilot project was planned to be launched in 2022, but no further information is available.[46]

3.3.2.2 LARGE MULTINATIONALS

A Fiscalis Project Group was also established for large multinationals, and in October 2021 the Guidelines European Trust and Cooperation Approach (ETACA)

43 OECD, *Co-operative Compliance: A Framework—From Enhanced Relationship to Co-operative Compliance*, Paris, 2013, p. 61.

44 European Commission, An Action Plan for Fair and Simple Taxation Supporting the Recovery Strategy, Brussels 15.7.2020, COM(2020) 312 final.

45 European Commission, *EU Cooperative Compliance Programme*, available for consultation at https://taxation-customs.ec.europa.eu/eu-cooperative-compliance-programme_en.

46 European Commission, *EU Cooperative Compliance Programme*, available athttps://taxation-customs.ec.europa.eu/eu-cooperative-compliance-programme_en.

were released as a basis for the pilot project. The programme aims to bring together tax administrations and taxpayers in a transparent environment to stimulate a preventive dialogue leading to the performance by the tax administrations of a high-level risk assessment of the transfer pricing policy adopted by the Multinational Enterprise (MNE) groups.[47]

3.4 Advance pricing agreement (APA)

An advance pricing agreement (APA) is "an arrangement that determines in advance of controlled transactions an appropriate set of criteria for the determination of the transfer pricing for those transactions over a fixed period of time".[48] Therefore, an APA can be identified as an instrument that could be able to grant, in relation to cross-border transaction, a tax certainty due to the previous agreement reached with the respective tax authorities of the countries involved.

3.4.1 APA's overview and historical development

The definition of APA can be found in the OECD Transfer Pricing Guidelines (TPG) where it is described as an arrangement that determines, in advance of controlled transactions, an appropriate set of criteria for the determination of the price for those transactions over a fixed period and with the aim to supplement the traditional administrative, judicial and treaty mechanisms for resolving transfer pricing issues.[49] In other terms, APA refers to a procedural arrangement between a taxpayer or taxpayers and a tax administration intended to resolve potential transfer pricing disputes in advance.[50] Therefore, in the APA process, the taxpayers and the tax authorities involved can agree in advance which is the best approach to define the pricing of a specific transaction or more types of transactions for a given period.[51]

An APA grants the possibility to determine transfer pricing issues before the performance of questionable transactions in a collaborative manner that engages both actors—that is, tax authorities and taxpayers.[52] The role of the APA can usually be limited to the transfer pricing field[53] for questions that are related to profit

47 European Commission, *Guidelines European Trust and Cooperation Approach (ETACA)*, pp. 2–3, available at https://taxation-customs.ec.europa.eu/eu-cooperative-compliance-programme/european-trust-and-cooperation-approach-etaca-pilot-project-mnes_en.

48 OECD, *OECD Transfer Pricing Guidelines for Multinational Enterprises and Tax Administrations*, 2017, para. 4.134.

49 OECD Transfer Pricing Guidelines 2017, Chapter IV, paragraph 4.134, p. 214.

50 OECD Transfer Pricing Guidelines 2017, Annex II to Chapter IV, paragraph 13, p. 475.

51 Valente, P., *Manuale del Transfer Pricing*, Ipsoa, 2012, p. 168.

52 Valente, P., Advance Pricing Agreements; Optimal Tool—Optimal Framework?, *Intertax*, Vol. 48, 2020, p. 67.

53 OECD Transfer Pricing Guidelines 2017, Annex II to Chapter IV, paragraph 35, p. 485.

attributions to permanent establishments (PEs) and profit allocation according to Articles 7 and 9 of the OECD MTC.[54]

The decision to set up an APA comes from the taxpayers and there are different types of APAs—that is, unilateral, bilateral, or multilateral. The bilateral and multilateral types have been recognized to provide an increased level of certainty, hence they are preferable when it comes to double taxation cases.[55] That statement demonstrates the importance that the APA instrument, especially bilateral and multilateral, has acquired as one of the methods that could really be helpful in preventing dispute resolutions and could bring a high level of cooperation between tax authorities and taxpayers.

In this respect and to boost the use of bilateral APA, on September 28, 2022, the OECD FTA released a detailed manual on bilateral advance pricing agreements (BAPAs)[56] with the intention to create a guide to tax administrations and taxpayers for streamlining the BAPA process through increased transparency and collaboration between competent authorities and taxpayers and mitigating delays created by differences in individual jurisdiction's BAPA processes.[57]

Furthermore, the OECD, on February 1, 2023, released a Manual on the Handling of Multilateral Mutual Agreement Procedures and Advance Pricing Arrangements (MoMA, or the Manual) aiming at defining the procedure to be followed to prevent disputes on a multilateral level.[58] The basis for the release of such a document was the recognition that jurisdictions enter into tax treaties bilaterally with the consequence that disputes on their interpretation or application are also bilateral in nature, and this could cause legal difficulties in cases of the application of multiple tax treaties (this is particularly the case of MNE, which may simultaneously have presence in multiple jurisdictions, and the transactions can be covered by multiple tax treaties[59]).

54 OECD Model Tax Convention on Income and Capital 2017 and Valente, P., Nuovo Interpello Internazionale e Rapporti con le Verifiche Fiscali in Corso, il fisco n. 42, pp. 1–4055.

55 OECD/G20 Base Erosion and Profit Shifting Project, Making Dispute Resolution Mechanisms More Effective, Action 14: 2015 Final Report, p. 30.

56 OECD Forum on Tax Administration—Publications, *Bilateral Advance Pricing Arrangement Manual*, available at https://www.oecd.org/en/publications/bilateral-advance-pricing-arrangement-manual_4aa570e1-en.html.

57 OECD Forum on Tax Administration, *Bilateral Advance Pricing Arrangement Manual*, 2022, p. 3, available at https://www.oecd-ilibrary.org/taxation/bilateral-advance-pricing-arrangement-manual_4aa570e1-en;jsessionid=7ADISZUV5VPCST14wjOg-y4yxNkd42s5p8Zo0F3T.ip-10–240–5–139.

58 OECD, *Manual on the Handling of Multilateral Mutual Agreement Procedures and Advance Pricing Arrangements—Enhancing Tax Certainty*, 1 February 2023, available at https://www.oecd-ilibrary.org/taxation/manual-on-the-handling-of-multilateral-mutual-agreement-procedures-and-advance-pricing-arrangements_f0cad7f3-en.

59 OECD, *Manual on the Handling of Multilateral Mutual Agreement Procedures and Advance Pricing Arrangements—Enhancing Tax Certainty*, 1 February 2023, p. 12, available at https://www.oecd-ilibrary.org/taxation/manual-on-the-handling-of-multilateral-mutual-agreement-procedures-and-advance-pricing-arrangements_f0cad7f3-en.

The favour of bilateral and multilateral APAs, against the unilateral APAs, is supported and strengthened, at the EU level, by the application of EU state aid rules[60] that bought under scrutiny, for ethical reasons, many tax rulings as possible illegal state aid.[61] Indeed, according to the European Commission, all the measures used to obtain a reduction of a tax burden could be qualified as state aid.[62]

3.4.2 APAs' main characteristics

If generally an APA can set the price methodology for a future transaction, it is also true that the factual assumptions can be the basis not only for the definition of an APA for the future years but, in case of bilateral or multilateral APA, they can also be used to resolve similar transfer pricing issues in open prior years[63] (rollback).

In general, independently, if the APA should be set for the future and also for the past, it does not settle all the details as to how the transaction will be taxed but simply establishes the basic framework by which the transactions will be analysed.[64] The structure of an APA depends mainly on how the different jurisdictions have implemented such an instrument. Indeed, an APA could cover the full range of transfer pricing transactions related to the business of a taxpayer or specific transactions out of the overall business.[65] Therefore, the two main characteristics of an APA that make it differ from a classical ruling procedure are (i) the requirement from one side of a detailed overview and a verification of the factual assumptions before determining the legal consequences applicable to the transaction(s) and (ii) a continual monitoring of the factual assumptions about the validity of the APA.[66] The constant monitoring of the factual assumptions is performed by tax authorities either (i) requiring taxpayers to file an annual report demonstrating compliance with the relevant assumptions or (ii) during the regular audit cycle but with no re-evaluation of the price methodology set in the APA.[67]

Because of the importance of maintaining transparency in the taxpayer–tax administration relationship, in case during the monitoring phase, the tax administration is faced with the case where a taxpayer has fraudulently or incorrectly interpreted the information provided during the negotiation, the APA could be subject

60 According to Article 107(1) TFUE (Treaty of the Functioning of the European Union).

61 Van der Enden, E. and de Groot, J., Two Missing Links: A Move Towards an Auditing Standard Specifically for the Tax Control Framework, *Bulletin for International Taxation*, September 2015, p. 503.

62 Commission notice on the application of the state aid rules to measures relating to direct business taxation (98/C 384/03), par. 9, available at https://eur-lex.europa.eu/legal-content/EN/TXT/PDF/?uri=CELEX:31998Y1210(01)&from=EN.

63 OECD Transfer Pricing Guidelines 2017, Chapter IV, paragraph 4.147, p. 217.

64 Owens, J., *Resolving International Tax Disputes: The Role of the OECD*, OECD Observer No. 243, 2004, p. 45, available at https://www.oecd-ilibrary.org/economics/oecd-observer_15615529.

65 OECD Transfer Pricing Guidelines 2017, Chapter IV, paragraph 4.147, p. 217.

66 OECD Transfer Pricing Guidelines 2017, Chapter IV, paragraph 4.143, p. 216 and Annex II to Chapter IV, paragraph 3, p. 472.

67 OECD Transfer Pricing Guidelines 2017, Chapter IV, paragraph 4.148, p. 218.

to termination or cancellation with a proper reasoned notification provided to the taxpayers.

3.4.3 Advantages and disadvantages of APA

The APA programme seems to be recognized as an important tool to prevent tax disputes. Indeed, from one side, the Minimum Standard of BEPS Action 14 is to strengthen the effectiveness and efficiency of the mutual agreement procedure (MAP), and on the other side, as mentioned earlier, it has recommended the countries to implement the bilateral APA (BAPAs). It is therefore useful to clearly identify the overall advantages and disadvantages of the APA.

According to the OECD TPG 2017,[68] the main advantages can be identified as follows:

1. Assisting tykuoplaxpayers by eliminating uncertainty through enhancing the predictability of tax treatment in international transactions;
2. Possibility of extension of the agreed treatment as well as renegotiation;
3. Close consultation and cooperation between taxpayers and the tax authorities involved, bringing to a closer relation and the possibility to discuss about complex topics in a non-adversarial spirit;
4. Preventing costly and time-consuming examinations and litigations for the parties involved;
5. Bilateral and multilateral APAs substantially reduce or eliminate the possibility of juridical or economic double or non-taxation since all the relevant countries participate;
6. Improvement of knowledge from the tax authorities of the business models.

Even if the advantages in successfully starting and concluding an APA could bring a certain degree of certainty and transparency between taxpayers and tax administrations, remember that there are also several disadvantages or difficulties in positively concluding an APA process. As mentioned, in case of unilateral APA the protection granted will be only a one side protection against audit risk, as the rule established in the APA should be accepted by all the tax authorities of the countries involved in the cross-border transaction.[69] Moreover, in case one tax authority, not part of a unilateral APA, would not allow corresponding adjustment in considering the APA inconsistent with the arm's length principle, a case of double taxation can easily arise.[70]

68 OECD Transfer Pricing Guidelines 2017, Chapter IV, paragraphs 4.153–4.157, pp. 219–221. See also Valente, P., *Manuale del Transfer Pricing*, Ipsoa, 2012, p. 169.

69 Markham, M., Are Advanced Pricing Agreements Experiencing a Renaissance as a Dispute Resolution Mechanism in the Era Following the OECD/G20's Base Erosion and Profit Shifting Initiative? *Bulletin for International Taxation*, January 2020, p. 4.

70 OECD Transfer Pricing Guidelines 2017, Chapter IV, paragraph 4.159, p. 221.

Another aspect to be considered are the costs and the resources, both economical and personnel, that taxpayers and tax authorities should invest in an APA process. From one side, tax authorities should decide if and how many resources are needed to shift from normal audit activities to an APA programme, while, on the other side, taxpayers should involve not only internal personnel but also external advisors to support the process.[71] Together with this element, the time needed to conclude an APA could affect the decision to embark, at least from the taxpayer side, on an APA process. The lack of knowledge of the duration of the process is still a limit on the use of the instrument, and it could be the case that the long time required to define the elements of a cross-border transaction would make the APA useless as the market conditions have already changed during the discussion.[72]

Lastly, due to the amount of information and documents that the taxpayers should provide in an APA process, there is a risk of misuse of this process by the tax authorities, especially in cases where an APA is not finalized. Therefore, it is important that this information and the documents are kept confidential and that they will not be used during a future tax audit. A different approach would undermine the trust and the spirit of cooperation that is the basis of an APA and in general of a fruitful relationship between taxpayer and tax authority.

3.5 Safe harbours

A safe harbour is a provision that applies to a defined category of taxpayers or transactions and that relieves eligible taxpayers from certain obligations otherwise imposed by a country's general transfer pricing rules.[73] Therefore, we can identify the safe harbour rules as applicable, provided that certain predetermined criteria are met, to certain categories of taxpayers or transactions performed.

3.5.1 Definition and characteristics of safe harbour rules

According to the OECD TPG 2017, a safe harbour is described as

> a provision that applies to a defined category of taxpayers or transactions and that relieves eligible taxpayers from certain obligations otherwise imposed by a country's general transfer pricing rules. A safe harbour substitutes simpler obligations for those under the general transfer pricing regime.[74]

These rules are exceptions to the application of the arm's length principle, as there is an automatic presumption of appropriateness of the prices and, therefore, of conformity

71 OECD Transfer Pricing Guidelines 2017, Chapter IV, para. 4.161, pp. 221–222.

72 See also OECD Forum on Tax Administration, *Bilateral Advance Pricing Arrangement Manual*, 2022, p. 17, available at https://www.oecd-ilibrary.org/taxation/bilateral-advance-pricing-arrangement-manual_4aa570e1-en.

73 OECD, OECD Transfer Pricing Guidelines 2017, para. 4.102.

74 OECD Transfer Pricing Guidelines 2017, Chapter IV, paragraph 4.102, p. 205.

with the arm's length principle, in the event those prices comply with predefined margins.[75] In the context of safe harbour rules, it is possible to identify between safe harbour rules based on transaction types and others based on taxpayer type.[76]

Usually, safe harbour rules are applied to smaller taxpayers and/or to less complex transactions which involve low transfer pricing risks. An important feature is that such rules must be carefully targeted and prescribed,[77] hence reducing the risk of misinterpretation and misapplication while strengthening the tax certainty, even if, being implemented unilaterally, it leaves open the risk that it is not recognized by the other state.[78]

3.5.2 Challenges and limits of safe harbour rules

The OECD TPG[79] also identifies concerns. First, there is the risk of approximation to the arm's length principle, or, in other words, the taxable income could not be in accordance with the arm's length principle. In addition, the application of safe harbour rules could lead to issues of double or non-taxation, especially when a unilateral rule is provided or such rules can be used for an inappropriate tax planning and also risks of uniformity and equity could arise. The price divergence from the arm's length principle derives mainly from the fact that safe harbour rules involve a trade-off between strict compliance with the arm's length principle and administrability. A possible solution to this is collecting, collating and frequently updating a pool of information regarding prices and pricing developments in respect to the relevant types of transactions between uncontrolled parties of a relevant nature.[80] Another way to avoid such a risk is the option of either choosing the safe harbour or the general transfer pricing rules, where obviously the conditions of such an option are properly identified.

Another concern that has been identified is the possibility to pursue an inappropriate tax planning scheme. This could happen when, in case of safe harbour rules applied to small transactions, taxpayers break it down to make the safe harbour rules applicable. Another case is identifiable when safe harbour rules are based on industry average, and taxpayers with better than average profitability shift the remaining percentage profitability to a lower tax jurisdiction. The same solution, bilateral or multilateral rules could be still the solution to such an issue.

Lastly, the equitable treatment of similar taxpayers and transactions could be jeopardized using safe harbour rules. In case of unclear criteria regarding the type

75 Maisto, G., DAC 6 and Transfer Pricing: The Hallmark Concerning Unilateral Safe Harbours, *Kluwer International Tax Blog*, 11 June 2020, available at https://kluwertaxblog.com/2020/06/11/dac-6-and-transfer-pricing-the-hallmark-concerning-unilateral-safe-harbours/.

76 Capristano Cardoso, G. and Kovacs, D., Using Safe Harbors to Simplify the Application of the Arm's Length Principle, *Tax Notes International.—Falls Church*, Vol. 101(6), 2021, p. 728.

77 OECD Transfer Pricing Guidelines 2017, Chapter IV, paragraph 4.97, p. 204.

78 OECD Transfer Pricing Guidelines 2017, Chapter IV, paragraph 4.96, pp. 204–206 and OECD Transfer Pricing Guidelines 2017, Annex I to Chapter IV, Introduction, p. 449.

79 OECD Transfer Pricing Guidelines 2017, Chapter IV, paragraph 4.110, p. 208.

80 For example, the possibility to yearly use the benchmark tools to set the funding prices could help the maintenance of the safe harbour rules with a lower effort required to tax administrations.

of transactions or taxpayers to whom the rules apply, inequality and non-uniformity can easily arise. Therefore, it is desirable to have clear and carefully designated criteria when identifying transactions involved and taxpayers that can benefit from such a treatment.

3.6 Joint tax audit: functioning and challenges

A joint tax audit should be understood as two or more tax administrations joining together to examine an issue(s)/transaction(s) of one or more related taxable persons (both legal entities and individuals) with cross-border business activities, proceeding in a pre-agreed and coordinated manner and including the presence of officials from the other tax administration where the tax administrations jointly engage with the taxpayer, enabling the taxpayer to share information with them jointly and the teams include competent authority representatives from each tax administration for the exchange of information.[81]

The main steps of a joint audit can be identified in (i) case selection, (ii) case preparation and initiation, (iii) conducting the audit, (iv) audit completion and (v) evaluation. A joint audit starts with the identification of the situations/cases that should fall under it, and the selection can follow a top-down approach (a jurisdiction defines the criteria a case should meet to be suggested for a joint audit) or a bottom-up approach (the selection is done by auditors that decide which cases are suitable to be treated in a joint audit[82]). The conclusion phase is the release of a final joint audit report.

3.7 International Compliance Assurance Programme (ICAP)

ICAP is a voluntary programme for MNE groups and tax administrations to work together in a cooperative risk assessment and assurance process. It is designed to provide MNE groups willing to engage actively, openly and in a fully transparent manner with increased tax certainty with respect to certain of their activities and transactions. ICAP, however, does not provide an MNE group with legal certainty as may be achieved, for example, through an advance pricing agreement (APA). It does, however, give comfort and assurance where tax administrations participating in an MNE group's risk assessment consider covered risks to be low risk.[83]

3.7.1 Overview and historical developments

ICAP, as a complement to other instruments such as domestic tax audit, bilateral/multilateral APAs and joint/simultaneous audit or MAP available to tax

81 OECD, Forum on Tax Administrations, Joint Audit 2019—Enhancing Tax Co-operation and Improving Tax Certainty, Implementation Package, 28 March 2019, p. 21.

82 OECD, *Joint Audit 2019—Enhancing Tax Co-operation and Improving Tax Certainty—Forum on Tax Administration*, Paris, 2019, pp. 57–59. In this respect, the report identifies a series of possible criteria which can lead to the use of a joint audit.

83 OECD, Forum on Tax Administration, *International Compliance Assurance Programme—FAQs*, February 2021, p. 1.

administrations to improve tax certainty,[84] was developed under the framework of the FTA Large Business and International Programme, sponsored by the Canada Revenue Agency, and has been tested through two pilots. The first began in 2018 with eight participating tax administrations (Australia, Canada, Italy, Japan, the Netherlands, Spain, the United Kingdom and the United States). The initial process was construed as a four-stage process involving taxpayers (i.e., MNEs), the lead tax administrations and the other tax administrations.[85]

After the first pilot[86] phase, a second one has started the beginning of 2019 with 19 participating tax administrations, and a second Handbook has been released based on the first one, reporting the increased experience gained by the other countries involved.[87] In 2021, a further Handbook[88] was released incorporating the experience of the two previous pilots. It was kept in the form of a "working document" so as to capture the countries' experiences in the coming years. With the release of this document, the OECD stated also that the ICAP programme for the first time is being run as a full programme (i.e., a permanent programme) open to all of the current 22[89] FTA member tax administrations.[90]

3.7.2 ICAP: process, benefits and rights of taxpayers

ICAP, being a collaborative process for the multilateral risk assessment and assurance of an MNE, provides active participation of the MNE in planning and conducting an ICAP risk assessment.[91] The taxpayer direct involvement grants, from one side, the tax administrations to gain a full overview and understanding of the internal taxpayers' processes and intercompany transactions, and from the other

84 OECD, *International Compliance Assurance Programme Pilot Handbook 2.0*, Paris, 2019, p. 9.

85 Daluzeau, X. and Pasquier, C., *Emerging Tax Compliance Programs—From ICAP to French Domestic Initiatives*, Linde, TPI 1/2020, p. 7 and Russo, R. and Martini, M. H. The International Compliance Assurance Programme Reviewed: The Future of Cooperative Tax Compliance, *Bulletin for International Taxation*, September 2019, p. 453.

86 OECD, *International Compliance Assurance Programme Pilot Handbook—Working Document*, Paris, 2018. The first ICAP pilot was launched in Washington DC in January 2018.

87 OECD, *International Compliance Assurance Programme Pilot Handbook 2.0*, Paris, 2019. The second ICAP Pilot (ICAP 2.0) was announced at the OECD Forum on Tax Administration Plenary in Santiago del Chile and the participating jurisdictions have increased to 19 (Australia, Austria, Belgium, Canada, Denmark, Finland, France, Germany, Ireland, Italy, Japan, Luxembourg, the Netherlands, Norway, Poland, Russia, Spain, the United Kingdom and the United States).

88 OECD, *International Compliance Assurance Programme—Handbook for Tax Administrations and MNE Groups*, 18 February 2021.

89 The full list of participating tax administration to ICAP can be found at the dedicated ICAP webpage: OECD, *OECD International Compliance Assurance Programme (ICAP)*, available at https://www.oecd.org/tax/forum-on-tax-administration/international-compliance-assurance-programme.htm.

90 OECD, Forum on Tax Administration, Leading tax administrations release details of the ICAP multilateral tax risk assurance programme to provide early certainty for tax administrations and MNEs, section news on 18.02.2021. available at https://www.oecd.org/tax/forum-on-tax-administration/news/leading-tax-administrations-release-details-of-the-icap-multilateral-tax-risk-assurance-programme-to-provide-early-certainty-for-tax-administrations-and-mnes.htm.

91 OECD, *International Compliance Assurance Programme Pilot Handbook 2.0*, Paris, 2019, p. 37.

side, taxpayers can benefit from a direct and immediate analysis of the goodness of their businesses from a tax point of view. Indeed, when only one tax administration is involved—that is, a unilateral process—there could be several misunderstandings on the processes and the transactions' delineation as the investigation and the questions posed are separate from one each other.[92] Instead, ICAP includes a commitment from MNE groups and tax administrations to work together through the ICAP risk assessment and assurance process in a transparent, open and cooperative manner. As a result of participation in the programme, a relationship of mutual trust based on reciprocal openness and good faith may be generated.[93] In fact, the different steps in which the ICAP is structured grant a higher level of participation and interaction between the tax administrations and the taxpayers.[94]

The ICAP mechanism, as it has been built, should be considered a more cooperative and collaborative risk assessment and assurance of MNE groups and should improve how tax administrations understand the perception and treatment of transactions by other tax administrations, providing the opportunity for tax administrations to discuss transactions at the risk assessment stage, before differing views are adopted and become entrenched, leaving the taxpayers with the only solution to proceed with a MAP process.[95]

4 International tax disputes: methods to solve them and their deficiencies

However, if the means of cooperation fail to find a solution to international double taxation cases, or if the domestic judicial systems themselves fail to reach a resolution, this will lead to international disputes in which two or more financial administrations claim rights to taxes arising from one or more transactions.

The need to find methods to solve double taxation issues was also underlined by the former director of the OECD's Centre for Taxation and Administrative Policy, Jeffrey Owens, who said

> Unresolved International tax disputes can undermine co-operation and discourage investment, and so become a serious impediment to global Development. Clearly, we must try to help ensure that such disputes do not arise and, if they do, provide procedures for resolving them.[96]

92 Majdanska, A. and Leigh-Premberton, J., *The OECD's International Assurance Programme (Part II)*, Linde, TPI, 4/2018, p. 181.

93 OECD Forum on Tax Administration, *International Compliance Assurance Programme—FAQs*, February 2021, p. 2.

94 OECD, *International Compliance Assurance Programme Pilot Handbook 2.0*, Paris, 2019, pp. 37–38.

95 OECD Forum on Tax Administration, *International Compliance Assurance Programme—FAQs*, February 2021, p. 2.

96 Owens, J., *Resolving International Tax Disputes: The Role of the OECD*, OECD Observer, May 2004, observer-v2004-2-en.pdf (oecd-ilibrary.org), see also the Opinion of Advocat General Colomer, 26 October 2004, C-376/03, para. 85, and Bettge, T. D., et al., Mutual Agreement Procedure: Progress Without Perfection, *Tax Notes International*, Vol. 110, 2023, p. 468.

To counteract these situations, methods have been identified at both the conventional and the European levels. Under double taxation treaties, the instrument identified for settling disputes between two or more states is the mutual agreement procedure (MAP), which may be followed, as an integral part of the same procedure, by an arbitration procedure.

At the European level, a proposal for a directive to eliminate double taxation in connection with adjustments between associated enterprises started in 1976[97] and the "Convention on the Elimination of Double Taxation in Connection with the Adjustment of Profits of Associated Enterprises" was developed in the early 1990s.[98] In 2017, to improve the system implemented by the 1990 Convention and to align all European states, Directive 2017/1852 was adopted.[99] It pertains to tax dispute resolution mechanisms in the European Union.

As a consequence of the massive increase in international tax disputes,[100] which entails a possible risk of undermining the rights of taxpayers to obtain effective justice within a reasonable time frame,[101] here is provided a brief review of the instruments that have been developed at international (OECD and UN) and EU levels to address the issue of international double taxation once it has manifested itself, by analysing its evolution, scope of application, functioning and its critical aspects.

4.1 Mutual agreement procedure and the arbitration process under Article 25 of the OECD Model Tax Convention

To counteract international double taxation judicial measures, unilateral administrative measures and bilateral convention measures have been developed to try to prevent this phenomenon. In the early 1970s, with the enactment of the first Model Convention adopted by the OECD, an attempt was made to incorporate a mechanism—called a mutual agreement procedure (or MAP)—into bilateral agreements to mutually resolve international tax disputes without recourse to the courts of each state involved.[102] This procedure can be found in Article 25 of the OECD MTC and of the UN Model Convention.[103] It is relevant to mention here that in February 2007 in the report "Improving the Process for Resolving International

97 Proposal for a Council Directive on the elimination of double taxation in connection with the adjustment of transfers of profits between associated enterprises (arbitration procedure), COM(76)611 final, 25 November 1976.

98 BOE, Convenio relativo a la supresión de la doble imposición en caso de corrección de los beneficios de empresas asociadas 90/436/EEC, fecha de la firma: 23/07/1990 en Bruselas.

99 Directive 2017/1852 of 10 October 2017.

100 Mooij, H., Chapter 14: MAP Arbitration in Tax Treaty Disputes, in *Flexible Multi-Tier Dispute Resolution International Tax Disputes* (eds. P. Pistone and J. J. P. de Goede), IBFD, 2021, p. 274.

101 Pistone, P., Chapter I: General Report, in *Tax Treaty Arbitration Section 1.3* (eds. M. Lang, et al., WU—Tax Law and Policy Series), IBFD, 2020, pp. 4–5.

102 Bantekas, I., The Mutual Agreement Procedure and Arbitration of Double Taxation Disputes, *ACDI*, Vol. 1, 2018, p. 184.

103 Article 25 of the UN MC has slight differences with the OECD MC.

Tax Disputes", the OECD provided a binding arbitration procedure as a complementary mechanism to the mutual agreement procedure for settling disputes.[104] This addition has caused a major change in the structure of Article 25, which has been recognized in the 2008 OECD Model Convention.[105]

4.1.1 Relevant aspects of the mutual agreement procedure

The MAP is a procedure that has a particular character, in the sense that it goes beyond national law and is a supplementary mechanism to solve double taxation problems not resolved in other treaty provisions. Above all, it is a mechanism for administering treaty benefits that identifies three types of MAP: (i) double taxation is contrary to the convention itself (or expected to be, hence the MAP will be "in motion" (Article 25(1) and (2)); (ii) difficulties of interpretation or application of the Convention (Article 25(3), first sentence); and (iii) elimination of double taxation in cases not provided for in the treaty (Article 25(3), second sentence).[106]

Accordingly, taxpayers who are affected by an inconsistent interpretation or application of the Convention (i.e., who consider that the assessment(s) of one or both tax authorities of the states gives rise to double taxation or taxation not in accordance with the Convention) may refer the case to the competent authority of either contracting state. If the competent authorities have not resolved the dispute within two years, the taxpayer has the possibility to request arbitration, but only for specific issues.[107]

What is relevant for our purposes is the procedure concerning the MAP as provided for in Article 25(1)(2) of the OECD Model, whereas in regard to the MAP as provided for in Article 25(3) a mention has been previously made.

Article 25(1)(2) provides a mutual agreement procedure to taxpayers, without depriving them of ordinary local remedies. It is aimed at resolving disputes through

104 OECD, *Improving the Process for Resolving International Tax Disputes* (Report adopted by the Committee on Fiscal Affairs on 30 January 2007), 2007, pp. 4–5.

105 Hadari, Yitzhak, *Compulsory Arbitration in International Transfer Pricing and Other Double Taxation Disputes*, October 6, 2009, p. 6, available at https://papers.ssrn.com/sol3/papers.cfm?abstract_id=1483621. See also Ferroni, B., La nuova Direttiva UE per la risoluzione delle controversie fiscali, *il fisco*, n. 5, 2018, p. 3.

106 Martín Jiménez, A. J., Procedimiento Amistoso, en Convenios fiscales internacionales y fiscalidad de la Unión Europea / coord. por Néstor Carmona Fernández, *José Manuel Calderón Carrero*, CISS, 2006, p. 505 y Groen, G., The Nature and Scope of the Mandatory Arbitration Provision in the OECD Multilateral Convention (2016), *Bulletin for International Taxation*, Vol. 71(11), 2017, p. 609.

107 Artículo 25(5) del MCOCDE. See also Castagna, S., Essential Elements of Taxation—Investment Protection and Dispute Settlement, in *International Arbitration and EU Law* (eds. J. R. Mata Dona and N. Lavranos), Elgar Arbitration Law and Practice Series, 2021, p. 437. See also Para. 8 OECD MTC: Commentary to Article 25 (2017), p. 202 and Valente, P., Procedure amichevoli, procedure arbitrali e rapporti Fisco-contribuente, *il fisco*, n. 5, 2017, p. 1.

an agreement between the competent authorities.[108] This procedure can be applied to cases of both juridical and economic international double taxation.[109]

In relation to transfer pricing, paragraphs 10 to 12 of the OECD MTC Commentary to Article 25 identifies that MAP could be used to solve cases related to profit allocation according to Article 9(1) of the OECD MTC and in cases related to transfer pricing adjustments under Article 9(2) of the OECD MTC.

The MAP is divided into two phases: (i) the first phase is the submission of the application to competent authority of either contracting state; and (ii) the second phase takes place between the contracting states and consists of the mutual agreement procedure.[110] The submission of the application should occur within three years from the notification to the taxpayer of the act that results for him in taxation not in accordance with the provisions of this Convention.[111] With reference to the time requirement, it is important to note that this time limit continues to run if the taxpayer has decided to resort to domestic remedies earlier to resolve the dispute.[112]

In the first phase, the taxpayer may, within three years from notification of the act, submit an application to the competent authority of either contracting state, which must assess the correctness of the application itself and, if all the necessary conditions are met, act unilaterally (i.e., by granting the tax adjustment or relief) or by involving the competent authority of the other contracting state. With this second step begins the second phase of the mutual agreement procedure, which is an activity exclusively between the competent authorities.[113]

At this early stage, the discretion on the part of competent authorities in justifying the admissibility of an application has been discussed, but no definitive solution seems to have been found. The 2014 OECD Commentary clarifies that a competent authority cannot reject an application without good reasons, but without specifying what is meant by "good reasons".[114] The 2017 OECD Commentary does not seem to have improved this situation, because it continues to leave the decision as to what is a justifiable application in the hands of the authorities, further underlining the discretionary nature of the decision.[115]

108 Valente, P., Procedure amichevoli, procedure arbitrali e rapporti Fisco-contribuente, *il fisco*, n. 5, 2017, p. 1.

109 OECD MTC Commentary to Article 25 (2017). Paragraphs 8 to 11. See also Valente, P., Alagna, C., y Mattia, S., *Controversie internazionali: procedure amichevoli e gestione delle relazioni*, IPSOA, 2013, p. 68

110 OECD MC Commentary, para. 7: (2017), p. 202 and Biçer, R., The Effectiveness of Mutual Agreement Procedures as a Means for Settling International Transfer Pricing Disputes, *International Transfer Pricing Journal*, Vol. 21(2), 2014, p. 79.

111 Para. 16 OECD MTC: Commentary to Article 25 (2017).

112 Para 25 OECD MTC: Commentary to Article 25 (2017).

113 Luchena Mozo, G.Mª., The Prevention and Resolution of Tax Conflicts within the Framework of International Exchange of Information, *European Taxation*, Vol. 52(5), 2012, pp. 228–229.

114 Para. 34 OECD MTC: Commentary to Article 25 (2014) and Groen, G., The Nature and Scope of the Mandatory Arbitration Provision in the OECD Multilateral Convention (2016), *Bulletin for International Taxation*, Vol. 71(11), 2017, p. 609.

115 Artículo 25(2) MLI OCDE y D'Alessandro, V. P., Improving the Resolution of International Tax Disputes, *Tax Notes International*, Vol. 55(13), 2009, p. 1154.

An important aspect to be analysed with reference to the filing of the application is the relationship between the MAP and the remedies provided by domestic rules. The Commentary clarifies that the commencement of the MAP is independent of the remedies granted by domestic law and, if an appeal is pending before the competent authority of the state of residence, there will not have to be a final decision on the case, but rather an assessment of whether the assumptions for commencing a MAP exist and, if so, an assessment of whether it can be resolved independently or whether the authorities of the other state should be involved.[116]

It is also possible that, once a decision has been reached through a domestic appeal, the taxpayer may file an application for a MAP. In this case, some states allow deviation from the decision of the domestic courts, while in others the competent authorities are obliged to accept the domestic decision, still with the possibility of submitting the case to the competent authorities of the other state and requesting that double taxation avoidance measures be taken.[117]

The authorities are required to attempt to negotiate but are not obliged to find a solution,[118] that is, it is not required to reach a solution.[119] This last point involves different scenarios. If a solution has been reached by the competent authorities, it can be accepted by the taxpayer and will be implemented regardless of whether there are time limits in the contracting states; or, if the taxpayer does not accept it, it can pursue domestic remedies. It happens that a solution is not always reached by the competent authorities, so if a decision has not been reached within the two-year period, recourse may be had to arbitration in the conventions that have implemented them, or always to the domestic remedies of each state.

4.1.2 Arbitration and the alternative dispute resolution systems

The possibility of using arbitration was already on the agenda of WorkingParty 6 of the OECD Committee on Fiscal Affairs in the early 1990s, but this approach was only activated in 2003 with the creation of a joint working group of WorkingParty 6 and WorkingParty 1 delegates, who in January 2007 delivered the final text on arbitration with their Commentary to the OECD Committee on Fiscal Affairs.[120]

These changes to the OECD MTC were inserted in the 2008 update of the OECD MTC by the approval of the OECD Council on July 17, 2008,[121] whereas

116 Para 34 OECD MTC: Commentary to Article 25 (2017).

117 Para. 35 MLI OCDE: Commentary to Article 25 (2017).

118 Para. 37.1 MLI OCDE: Commentary to Article 25 (2017).

119 Martín Jiménez, A. J., *Procedimiento Amistoso, en Convenios fiscales internacionales y fiscalidad de la Unión Europea / coord. por Néstor Carmona Fernández*, José Manuel Calderón Carrero, CISS, 2006, p. 512.

120 Biçer, R., The Effectiveness of Mutual Agreement Procedures as a Means for Settling International Transfer Pricing Disputes, *International Transfer Pricing Journal*, Vol. 21(2), 2014, p. 79.

121 Ault, H. J., and Sasseville, J., 2008 OECD Model: The New Arbitration Provision, *Bulletin International Taxation*, Vol. 63(5), 2009, p. 209.

in the case of the UN MTC the arbitration procedure was introduced slightly later, in 2011, based on Article 25(5) of the OECD MTC. Thus, the OECD has decided to complement the MAP with mandatory and binding arbitration by adopting the fifth paragraph to Article 25 of the MCOCDE. It has to be considered that arbitration was conceived as an integral part of the MAP and not as an alternative to it.[122] However, this solution was introduced with the aim of contributing to improving the effectiveness of the dispute resolution mechanism. Nevertheless, it has been unevenly received by the states, considering the period between 2008 and 2013, without generally achieving the intended objective, that is, the protection of taxpayers.[123] In fact, in international tax arbitration, taxpayers are not entitled to participate, as arbitration is a matter to be settled between states.[124]

According to this provision, if the competent authorities of the contracting states do not reach a solution eliminating the double taxation within two years, the taxpayer has the option of submitting the unresolved case, provided that a local or administrative court has not decided on the case, or submitting to an Arbitration Commission to issue a decision on how to eliminate the double taxation.[125] On the functioning of the arbitration procedure, according to the last sentence of Article 25(5) and the Commentary to paragraph 85, it is left to the competent authorities of the contracting states, which will mutually agree on the modalities of how to implement the fifth paragraph. The important point, as stressed in the Commentary, is that whatever the form of the agreement, the decision of the arbitrators will be binding on both states.[126]

The rules of procedure are set out in the Commentary, where the taxpayer (or the competent authorities in the UN MTC) can initiate the procedure by sending a written request to one of the competent authorities after a period of two years (three years under the UN MTC) that begins on the date when all the information required for both competent authorities in order to address the case has been provided to both of them.[127]

122 Lieb, J. P., Chapter I—Introduction: Taking the Debate Forward, in *International Arbitration in Tax Matters, WU—Tax Law and Policy Series* (ed. Lang, M.), Jeffrey Owens, 2016, IBFD, p. 3.

123 Ribes Ribes, A., La resolución de los conflictos tributarios en el ámbito internacional en la era post BEPS, en *Medios alternativos de solución de controversias en materia fiscal* (eds. G. Cotero, J. de Jesús, B. Rivera and L. José). Thomson Reuters, 2019, p. 153 y Markham, M., Litigation, Arbitration and Mediation in International Tax Disputes: An Assessment of Whether This Results in Competitive or Collaborative Relations, *Contemporary Asia Arbitration Journal*, Vol. 11(2), 2018, p. 288.

124 Dourado, A. P., Post-BEPS International Tax Arbitration, *Intertax*, Vol. 42(8&9), 2019, p. 671.

125 Valente, P., Procedure amichevoli, procedure arbitrali e rapport Fisco-contribuente, *il fisco*, n. 5, 2017, p. 2 y Hadari, Y., *Compulsory Arbitration in International Transfer Pricing and OtherDoubleTaxation Disputes*, 6 October 2009, p. 6, available at https://papers.ssrn.com/sol3/papers.cfm?abstract_id=1483621.

126 Para. 85 MLI OCDE: Commentary to Article 25 (2017).

127 Garbarino, C., and Lombardo, M., *Arbitration of Unresolved Issues in Mutual Agreement Cases: The New Paragraph 5*, Art. 25 OECD Model Convention, A Multi-Tiered Dispute Resolution Clause, Bocconi Legal Studies Research Paper No. 1628765, 2010, p. 16.

There are two main approaches that can be followed when designing the arbitration process that will be used to supplement the mutual agreement procedure: "last best offer" or "final offer", where each competent authority would be required to give to the arbitration panel a proposed resolution of the issue involved. The arbitration panel would then choose between the two proposals which were presented to it and "independent opinion" where the arbitrators would be presented with the facts and arguments by the parties based on the applicable law, and would then reach their own independent decision, which would be based on a written, reasoned analysis of the facts involved and applicable legal sources.[128]

Once a decision is reached, it is communicated to the competent authorities, which within six months will implement the resolution through the MAP. The decision is binding on both contracting states, while the taxpayer may not accept the agreement involving the arbitration decision, thus allowing the taxpayer the possibility of using domestic remedies to settle the case.

4.1.3 Criticisms of the MAP and arbitration procedure

To some extent, each jurisdiction has developed a domestic consultation system, an audit procedure and the possibility of access to courts. In addition, many states have signed double taxation treaties with MAP clauses, but not all apply them regularly and few have an arbitration clause that can definitively settle an international dispute.[129]

However, despite the wide recognition of the MAP as a flexible and efficient instrument in the interpretation, application and development of tax treaties, there are many criticisms of it.[130] Indeed, the MAP has undisputed advantages for both taxpayers and competent authorities, but it cannot be considered a fail-safe dispute resolution mechanism.[131] As a consequence—irrespective of the high probability of success—there are some drawbacks to initiating a MAP, which are identified

128 Monsenego, J., Designing Arbitration Provisions in Tax Treaties: Reflections Based on the US Experience, *Intertax*, Vol. 42(3), 2014, pp. 165–166 y Devillet, C., The Text of and the Commentary on Article 25—Round-up of the Charges and Their Significance, *Bulletin for International Taxation*, Vol. 66(11), 2012, p. 616.

129 Del Campo, C., Dispute Resolution Procedures in International Taxmatters, *IFA General Report*, Madrid, 2016, Cahier 101a, p. 21 and UN, Coordinator's Rep. on Work of the Subcommittee on the Mutual Agreement Procedure—Dispute Avoidance and Resolution, Comm. of Experts on Int'l Cooperation in Tax Matters, Rep. on Its Twelfth Session, par. 3.1.1, p. 63, U.N. Doc. E/C.18/2016/CRP.4 (11 October 2016), que se encuentra al siguiente enlace: https://www.un.org/esa/ffd/wp-content/uploads/2016/10/12STM_CRP4_Disputes.pdf.

130 Ribes Ribes, A., Compulsory Arbitration as a Last Resort in Resolving Tax Treaty Interpretation Problems, *European Taxation*, Vol. 42(9), 2002, p. 400.

131 Roy Rohatgi on International Taxation—Volume 1: Principles, Part 4: Interpretation and Application of Tax Treaties—Chapter 26: Tax Treaties and Dispute Resolution (eds. Ola Ostaszewska and BelemaObuoforibo), IBFD, 2018, p. 465. See also Lindencrona, G., and Mattsson, N., Arbitration in Taxation: AnIntroduction, *Intertax*, Vol. 42(3), 2014, p. 161 and Altman, Z., *Dispute Resolution under Tax Treaties, Chapter 5: Current Procedures and the Need for Change*, On-Line Books IBFD, 2005, p. 257.

as follows:[132] (i) lack of obligation of the competent authorities to reach an agreement, (ii) slowness and excessive length of the procedure, (iii) possible absence of independence,[133] (iv) lack of uniformity with regard to the publication of the adopted agreement, (v) lack of means to ensure the implementation of the adopted agreement and (vi) little information on its functioning and general lack of interest of states in the MAP.

With reference to the preceding points, it is important to remember that competent authorities often fail to reach an agreement or, if they do reach an agreement,[134] do not eliminate the double taxation of the taxpayer,[135] and the relatively long time for a decision to be reached also creates uncertainty in the intervening period where the disputed taxes may have to be paid in advance or interest may accrue on the taxes, so that the capital of the company involved is affected by these costs.[136]

The procedure and its outcome remain fully confidential in that both are protected from public knowledge,[137] and these aspects further underline the lack of centrality of the taxpayer who does not take part in the discussions between the competent authorities and remains a marginal player.[138]

Finally, on the one hand, the arbitrary nature of its enforcement which, as Article 25(2) identifies, is left to the states themselves and their domestic legislation, with the risk that its implementation is not always guaranteed, and, on the other hand, the fact that the procedure is not always sufficiently well known, so that taxpayers are not always informed about how it works,[139] continues to show how the states and their authorities can handle the entire procedure at will. It has been commented that the MAP, being a mechanism that moves in the logic of international relations and is characterized by the criterion of taxing power, may entail a detriment to the rules of law and above all to the protection of the taxpayer.[140]

132 RibesRibes, A., La resolución de los conflictos hermenéuticos en los convenios para evitar la doble imposición internacional, *Revista de Contabilidad y Tributación*, no. 235, 2002, pp. 33–36 y Koch, K., Mutual Agreement—Procedure and Practice, IFA, *Cahiers de droit fiscal International*, Vol. 66a, 1981, pp. 118–121.

133 Protto, C., Mutual Agreement Procedures in Tax Treaties: Problems and Needs in Developing Countries and Countries in Transition, *Intertax*, Vol. 42(3), 2014, p. 177.

134 Lang, M., and Wiman, B., Conference on Arbitration in Tax Treaty Law—Uppsala University—22 August 2013, *Intertax*, Vol. 42(3), 2014, p. 202.

135 Ault, H. J., Improving the Resolution of International Tax Disputes, *Florida Tax Review*, Vol. 7(3), 2005, p. 139.

136 Vroemen, E., Solving Double Taxation outside the Realm of Mutual Agreement Procedure, *International Transfer Pricing Journal*, Vol. 26(2), 2019, p. 114.

137 Christians, A., Take MAP With a Grain of Salt: *Sifto* and the Legal Nature of Competent Authority Agreements, *Tax Notes International*, Vol. 86, 2017, p. 81.

138 Bantekas, I., The Mutual Agreement Procedure and Arbitration of Double Taxation Disputes, *ACDI*, Vol. 1, 2018, p. 203.

139 Ribes Ribes, A., La resolución de los conflictos hermenéuticos en los convenios para evitar la doble imposición internacional, *Revista de Contabilidad y Tributación*, no. 235, 2002, pp. 33–36.

140 Dominici, R., Le regole per la risoluzione dei conflitti in materia di doppia imposizione internazionale, in AA. VV., *Corso di diritto tributario internazionale, a cura di V. Uckmar*, CEDAM, 2002, p. 149 and Perrou, K., The Ombudsman and the Process of Resolution of International Tax Disputes—Protecting the "Invisible Party" to the MAP, *World Tax Journal*, Vol. 10(1), 2018, p. 100.

It can often be argued that, while there are cases where the interests of states and taxpayers may coincide, there are many cases where the rights of the taxpayer are at the same time opposable to the interests of the two contracting states.[141] Thus, taxpayer protection cannot be automatically assumed in relations between states.[142]

In the case of arbitration, it is found that similar to the doctrine of diplomatic protection, a tax dispute is conducted only by the two states involved and the private party is excluded from the procedure so that it is the state that determines how to allocate the tax rights of the taxpayer in dispute.[143] Furthermore, the secrecy of arbitration has been criticized, that is, the lack of publication of the award, with the consequence that it continues to be perceived as an instrument that lacks transparency and is disconnected from public accountability.[144] Indeed, the publication of arbitral decisions would bring benefits such as dispute prevention, help the consistency of decisions and raise awareness of arbitration, encouraging its use.[145]

On these points it is now interesting to analyse whether and to what extent the BEPS Project, in its Actions 14 and 15, has succeeded in bringing improvements to the amicable procedure and arbitration.

4.2 BEPS Actions 14 and 15

The development of the BEPS Plan is based on the recognition that base erosion is a serious risk to tax revenues, tax sovereignty and tax fairness in many countries, and identifies profit shifting abroad as one of the most significant sources of erosion. The rules, as they were defined, allowed profit manipulation based on artificial legal structures and intangible rights and obligations through the legal treatment of intra-group risks, with the consequence of reducing profits where productive activities took place. Consequently, it was necessary to review the existing rules and align them with developments in the global economy, thus

141 Perrou, K., *Taxpayer Participation in Tax Treaty Dispute Resolution—Part II: Private Parties in International Disputes: The Case of International Tax Disputes—Chapter 3: International Double Taxation Disputes as Disputes between the State(s) and the Taxpayer(s)*, IBFD Doctoral Series, 2014, p. 75.

142 Züger, M., *Arbitration under Tax Treatiesc, Chapter 1: The Lack of Legal Protection in International Tax Law*, On-Line Books IBFD, Doctoral Series 5, 2001, p. 11.

143 Foucard, A., and Grandfond, L., Arbitration of International Tax Disputes: A Move Towards Democratization?, in *Contemporary Issues in International Arbitration and Mediation: The Fordham Papers 2014* (ed. Arthur W. Rovine), BRILL, 2015, p. 435.

144 Lieb, J. P., Chapter I—Introduction: Taking the Debate Forward, in *International Arbitration in Tax Matters, WU—Tax Law and Policy Series* (eds. Michael Lang and Jeffrey Owens), IBFD, 2016, pp. 5–6.

145 Avery Jones, J. F., Arbitration and Publication of Decisions, in *International Arbitration in Tax Matters* (eds. Michael Lang and Jeffrey Owens), IBFD, 2015, p. 367 y Dourado, A. P., and Pistone, P., Some Critical Thoughts on the Introduction of Arbitration in Tax Treaties, *Intertax*, Vol. 42(3), 2014, p. 160 and Mooij, H., Chapter 14: MAP Arbitration in Tax Treaty Disputes, in *Flexible Multi-Tier Dispute Resolution International Tax Disputes* (eds. P. Pistone and J. J. P. de Goede), IBFD, 2021, p. 283.

ensuring that profits are taxed where economic activities take place and where value is created.[146]

The BEPS Plan, with the aim of improving certainty and predictability for economic operators, identified 15 actions around three main pillars: (i) bringing coherence to domestic rules dealing with cross-border activities, (ii) strengthening substance requirements in current international standards and (iii) improving transparency and legal certainty for businesses that do not take an aggressive stance.[147] For our purposes, out of the 15 BEPS actions, Action 14 (Making Dispute Resolution Mechanisms More Effective) and Action 15 (Multilateral Instrument) will be the objects of our analysis.

4.2.1 BEPS Action 14: making dispute resolution mechanisms more effective

The same 2015 final report identifies that the OECD Model Convention, in Article 25, provides a mechanism, independent of legal actions and/or remedies under domestic law, through which the competent authorities of the contracting states can resolve differences or overcome obstacles in cases of interpretation or application of the Convention on the basis of a consensual approach and ensures that none of the contracting states subjects taxpayers to taxation not in accordance with the provisions of the Convention to which the benefits of the Convention apply.[148]

In line with Action 14, it addresses the need for states to adopt measures to ensure that the mutual agreement procedures provided for in double tax treaties are operational and effective.

By adopting the final report, countries have agreed to change their attitudes to dispute settlement; this is achieved through the development of a minimum standard regarding the resolution of conflicts of interpretation and application of conventions.[149] Proper implementation will ensure effective, efficient and timely resolution of tax treaty disputes, which is further ensured by peer monitoring, the results of which will be regularly reported by the G20 Committee on Fiscal Affairs (CFA).[150] The implementation of the minimum standard relies on a monitoring

146 Saint-Amans, P., y Russo, R., The BEPS Package: Promise Kept, *Bulletin for International Taxation*, Vol. 4(2), 2016, p. 236.

147 OCDE, *Proyecto OCDE/G20 sobre la Erosión de la Base Imponible y el Traslado de Beneficios, Informes Fiscales 2015*, Resumen Informativo, p. 3.

148 OCDE, *Hacer más efectivos los mecanismos de resolución de controversias*, Informe final, 2015, p. 9.

149 OCDE, *BEPS, Hacer más efectivos los mecanismos de resolución de controversias*, Acción 14: Informe final 2015, p. 9.

150 Pires de Oliveira, P. T., Action 14 of the OECD/G20 Base Erosion and Profit Shifting Initiative: Making Dispute Resolution More Effective—Did Action 14 "Piggyback" on the Initiative? *Bulletin for International Taxation*, Vol. 71(1), 2017, p. 7.

mechanism and the BEPS paper discusses the framework for the development of a monitoring mechanism.

4.2.2 *Analysis of figures, cases and resolutions based on public data*

According to the following 2023 OECD MAP statistics, it could be identified that the procedure is a long step one due to the complexity of the cases and leads to a long time required to solve the cases. Indeed, in the 2023 OECD MAP statistics it has been shown that the average time needed to close a TP case is still 32.01 months, while for other cases it is 23.36 months. Costs, time needed, and the uncertainty of the final solution added to the need to identify methods that could prevent or accelerate disputes in an atmosphere of cooperation.

Figures 1.5,[151] 1.6[152] and 1.7[153] present the cumulative evolution of the total number of MAP cases from 2016 to the end of 2023 with the relative subdivision between transfer pricing cases and other cases.[154]

At first glance, we see that (i) approximately 10% more MAP cases were closed in 2023 than in 2022 and more cases were closed in 2023 than in any previous year; (ii) the number of new MAP cases opened in 2023 decreased (over –6%) compared to 2022; (iii) approximately three-quarters of both transfer pricing and other cases concluded in 2023 with their issues fully resolved through an agreement to eliminate double taxation, the grant of unilateral relief or resolution through a domestic remedy (similar to 73% for transfer pricing cases and other cases in 2022). Approximately 4% of MAP cases were closed with no agreement in 2023, two percentage points more than in 2022; (iv) on average, the MAP cases closed in 2022 took 32 months for transfer pricing cases (an increase from 29 months in 2022) and approximately 23.4 months for all cases (compared to 22.2 months in 2022). The average time to close all types of cases was 27.3 months, which is above the OECD's recommended target of 24 months; and (v) the 2023 MAP statistics also include a new data point regarding the age of cases in MAP inventory. Approximately 52% of open MAP cases are less than two years old and 24% are between two and four years old.[155]

151 OECD, *Mutual Agreement Procedure Statistics 2023—Inventory Trends*, available at https://www.oecd.org/en/data/datasets/mutual-agreement-procedure-statistics.html.

152 OECD, *Mutual Agreement Procedure Statistics 2023—Inventory Trends*, available at https://www.oecd.org/en/data/datasets/mutual-agreement-procedure-statistics.html.

153 OECD, *Mutual Agreement Procedure Statistics 2023—Inventory Trends*, available at https://www.oecd.org/en/data/datasets/mutual-agreement-procedure-statistics.html.

154 OECD, *Mutual Agreement Procedure Statistics 2023—Inventory Trends*, available at https://www.oecd.org/en/data/datasets/mutual-agreement-procedure-statistics.html.

155 EY, *OECD's 2023 Mutual Agreement Procedure Statistics Show Continued Strength in the US Program*, 2024, available at https://globaltaxnews.ey.com/news/2024-2149-oecds-2023-mutual-agreement-procedure-statistics-show-continued-strength-in-the-us-program

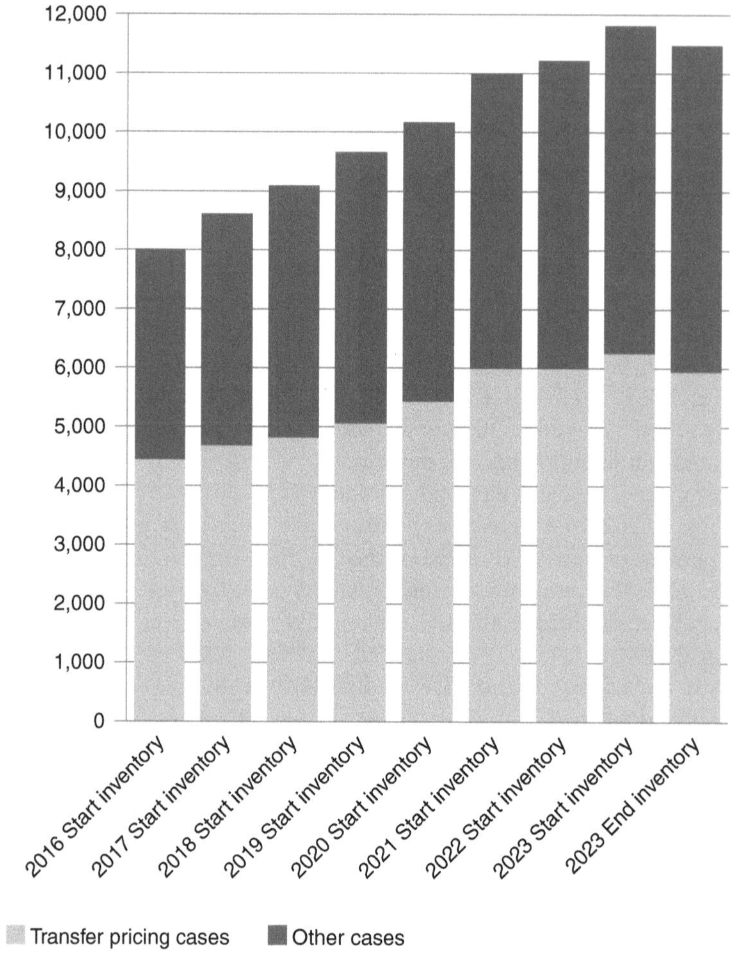

Figure 1.5 MAP inventory evolution (all cases).

4.2.3 OECD multilateral instrument: implementation and main features

The objective of Action 15 is to streamline the implementation of the BEPS Plan measures.[156] Since the OECD saw an urgency to implement the new and modified provisions developed under the BEPS Project in the Double Tax Conventions (DTCs), the multilateral instrument (MLI) was developed under the auspices

156 Saint-Amans, P., y Russo, R., The BEPS Package: Promise Kept, *Bulletin for International Taxation*, Vol. 4(2), 2016, p. 240.

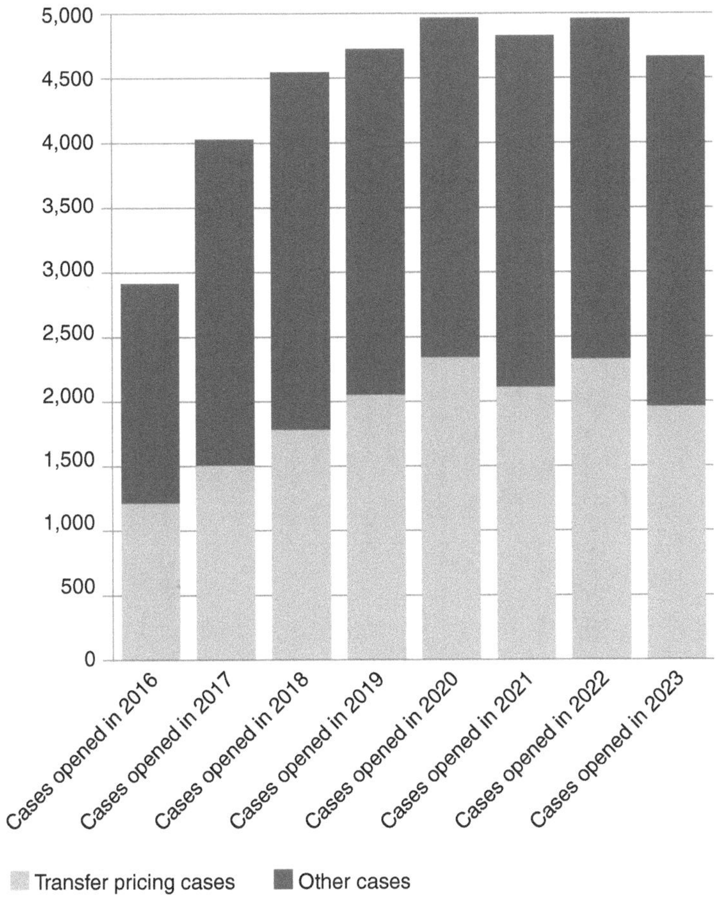

Figure 1.6 Evolution of cases opened (all cases).

of the OECD (BEPS Action 15).[157] The MLI is a multilateral convention which swiftly modifies the application of existing bilateral tax treaties without the need to renegotiate each such treaty individually.[158] It does not replace the existing tax treaties, but rather changes their content, hence the current bilateral system is not

157 OECD, *Action 15 Multilateral Instrument*, p. 11, available at https://www.oecd.org/en/topics/beps-multilateral-instrument.html.

158 OECD, *Action 15 Multilateral Instrument*, available at https://www.oecd.org/en/topics/beps-multilateral-instrument.html. Véase también Berbari, A., The OECD/G20 Base Erosion and Profit Shifting (BEPS) Initiative and the Multilateral Convention to Implement Tax Treaty Related Measures to Prevent BEPS, *Bulletin for International Taxation*, Vol. 71(10), 2017, p. 539.

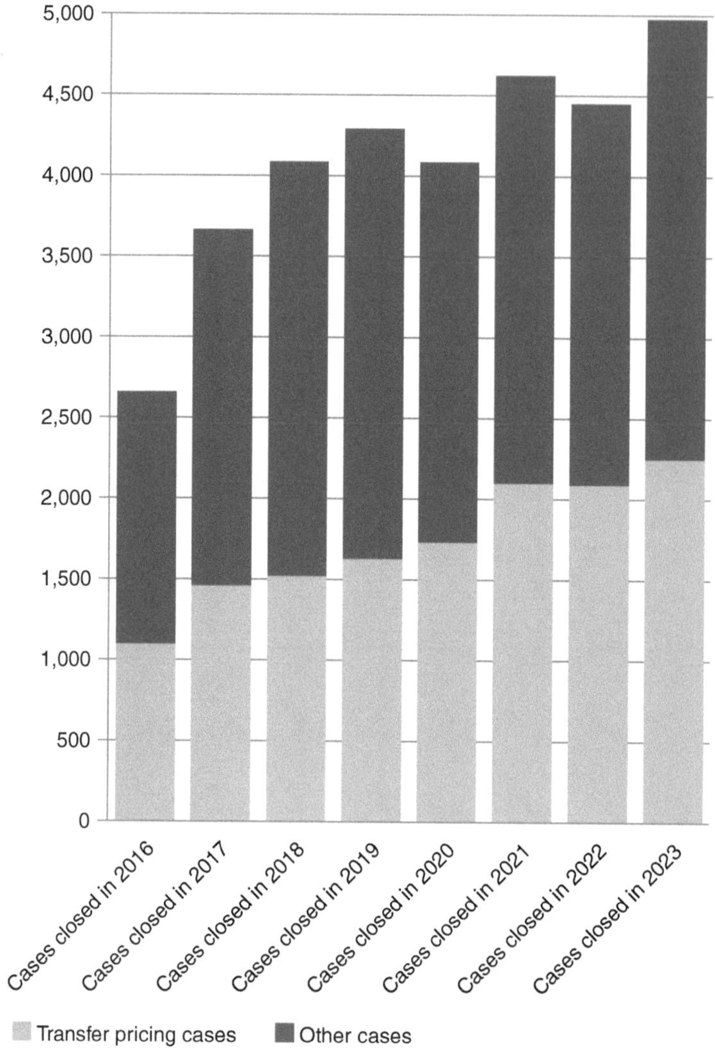

Figure 1.7 Evolution of cases closed (all cases).

abandoned, but rather the current conventions are modified, leaving the structure of the tax system as bilateral.[159]

159 Confédération Fiscale Européenne, Opinion Statement FC 15/2014 on Developing a Multilateral Instrument to Modify Bilateral Tax Treaties (BEPS Action 15), *European Taxation*, Vol. 55(4), 2015, p. 157 y Antón, R. G., The 21st Century Multilateralism in International Taxation: The Emperors's New Clothes? *World Tax Journal*, Vol. 8(2), 2016, p. 11.

The MLI was finalized in November 2016 and a first signing ceremony was held in Paris on June 6, 2017. A total of 76 jurisdictions signed the MLI in this first ceremony. In the meantime, the MLI covers almost 100 jurisdictions.[160]

In general, three advantages of using the multilateral convention have been identified: (i) it addresses and involves a multitude of subjects; (ii) it makes it possible to amend in a synchronized manner bilateral treaties with reference to BEPS issues without needing to amend each convention in a network with more than 3,000 treaties; and (iii) it makes it possible to reduce the abuses identified by the BEPS Plan with governments, which can immediately pursue their international tax policies without fear of violating bilateral treaties (which could have occurred if unilateral or uncoordinated measures had been employed for the implementation of BEPS[161]).

4.2.4 Improving dispute resolution under the MLI: the mutual agreement procedure and the implementation of Article 9(2) of the OECD MTC

The MLI aims to speed up and simplify the implementation of BEPS measures and the amendment of bilateral treaties in the framework of BEPS provisions. It has identified the need to develop effective solutions to ensure the resolution of international tax disputes and to strengthen the mutual agreement procedure, as defined in Article 25 of the OECD CM. Consequently, in developing the structure of the MLI, Part V of the MLI has been devoted to describing the mechanisms useful for resolving disputes as set out in the BEPS Action 14 report. In this regard, Articles 16 and 17 of the MLI seek to achieve the objective of embedding minimum standards and good practices in the tax treaties covered.

With reference to the harmonization of the MAP procedure, Article 16, which concerns the mutual agreement procedure, requires the parties to amend their covered tax treaties by incorporating Article 25(1) to (3). Article 16 is divided into operative clauses, compatibility clauses, reservation clauses and notifications. The first three clauses of Article 16, which are of an operational nature, represent a minimum standard and have to be applied directly to the covered tax treaties, unless the latter do not contain provisions with solutions equal to those contained in the MLI. Their function is to improve the mutual agreement

160 OECD, *Action Plan on Base Erosion and Profit Shifting*, 2013, p. 11. Serrano Antón, F., La Era Post BEPS o la Ejecución de su Plan de Acción: Convenio Multilateral vs. Implementación Unilateral, *Quincena Fiscal*, Vol. 12, junio 2016, p. 133 and Dourado, A. P., and Kostić, S., The MLI in Action, *Intertax*, Vol. 49(10), 2021, p. 753. Jiménez Vargas, P. J., El Nuevo Convenio Multilateral: un Paso a delante de la OCDE en la Armonización Fiscal en Contra de la Evasión y la Elusión Fiscal, *Quincena Fiscal*, Vol. 19, Noviembre 2018, p. 22 y OECD, *Multilateral Convention to Implement Tax Treaty Related Measures to Prevent Base Erosion and Profit Shifting*, Multilateral Instrument, Information Brochure, May 2020, que se puede encontrar al enlace: https://www.oecd.org/content/dam/oecd/en/topics/policy-sub-issues/beps-mli/multilateral-instrument-beps-tax-treaty-information-brochure.pdf.

161 OECD, *Developing a Multilateral Instrument to Modify Bilateral Tax Treaties*, Action 15: 2015 Final Report, p. 16.

procedure under Article 25 of the OECD MTC, and they have to be read together with the fourth clause, which describes how the new provisions should be introduced in a manner compatible with those already existing in Article 25 of the different bilateral conventions, which will be modified in accordance with the minimum standard.[162]

Specifically in relation to transfer pricing corresponding adjustment, the minimum standard element of the Action 14 final report also states that jurisdictions provide access to the MAP in transfer pricing cases and implement agreements resulting from the MAP through adjustments to taxes. In line with this need, Article 17 of the MLI requires the implementation of Article 9(2) of the OECD MTC in all covered tax treaties, unless already present.[163]

4.2.5 Criticisms and unresolved issues

Despite the work of the OECD, the development of the MAP under BEPS Action 14 does not involve new aspects in that the provisions of the MLI tend to be aligned with Article 25 of the OECD MLI.[164] As a consequence, some fundamental issues that would surely have favoured the use of the MAP have been left unresolved, such as (i) the guarantee that double taxation would be resolved at the end of the MAP; (ii) a period of time within which the MAP would have to be completed irrespective of whether states have opted for arbitration; (iii) taxpayer participation through hearings, remedies through domestic provisions to remedy cases of inaction by the authorities involved in the MAP; and (iv) the suspension of domestic collection procedures until the conclusion of the MAP.[165]

In these cases, it is possible to highlight that a broader participation in the taxpayer's procedure could certainly help in the resolution of the cases in a phase prior to a possible arbitration. It has been pointed out that the taxpayer must become a substantial party and not be limited only to helping the competent authorities,

162 Lombardo, M., Il miglioramento della risoluzione delle controversie fiscali internazionali, *Bollettino Tributario*, Vol. 6, 2021, pp. 453–454.

163 OECD, *Explanatory Statement to the Multilateral Convention to Implement Tax Treaty Related Measures to Prevent Base Erosion and Profit Shifting*, 2016, pp. 53–54.

164 Ribes Ribes, A., La resolución de los conflictos tributarios en el ámbito internacional en la era post BEPS, en *Medios alternativos de solución de controversias enmateria fiscal* (coords., Gómez Cotero, José de Jesús; Béjar Rivera, and Luis José). Thomson Reuters, 2019, p. 160, Schoueri, L. E., y Tomazela, R., The Influence of the BEPS Multilateral Instrumento in Tax Treaties Concluded by Non-signatory Countries, *Intertax*, Vol. 49(10), 2021, p. 838 y Pistone, P., and Čičin-Šain, N., Chapter 1: The Implementation and Lasting Effects of the Multilateral Instrument: General Report, in *The Implementation and Lasting Effects of the Multilateral Instrument* (eds., M. Lang, et al., WU—Tax Law and Policy Series), IBFD, 2021, pp. 27–28.

165 Govind, S., y Turcan, L., The Changing Contours of Disputes Resolution in the International Tax World: Comparing the OECD Multilateral Instrument and the Proposed EU Arbitration Directive, *Bulletin for International Taxation*, Vol. 71(3/4), 2017, p. 2 and also Govind, S., and Monsenego, J., Chapter 11: Multilateralism in Dispute Resolution: Some Thoughts on the OECD Multilateral Instrument and the EU Dispute Resolution Directive, in *International and EU Tax Multilateralism: Challenges Raised by the MLI* (eds. Ana Paula Dourado, GREIT Series), 2020, p. 299.

having, in general terms, all the rights enjoyed by the competent authorities in MAP procedures and of arbitration. As an example, the taxpayer must be able not only to initiate the MAP by submitting a request to the competent authorities but also (i) have full access to the documents in the file that concerns their case; (ii) participate in MAP meetings and, in general, in all procedures, either through oral hearings or by submitting written observations; (iii) draft the Terms of Reference in collaboration with the competent authorities; and (iv) have an active role in the selection and appointment of arbitrators.[166]

In addition to what was mentioned, there is still a specific requirement for the publication of the MAP decision, so the latter can still be classified as a "black box" that lacks transparency since its decisions are not published and are not exposed to criticism,[167] at the same time, they cannot be used as a guide or as a precedent for future cases.

Regarding transfer pricing, it should be noted that the new provision of Article 17(1) does not add any novelty to what is contained in Article 9(2)[168] of the OECD MTC of 2017, that is to say, there is still an automatic obligation to grant the relief as a consequence of a corresponding adjustment in the other state and the identification of a deadline for making the corresponding adjustment is still missing. This means that the MLI can be recognized as a missed opportunity to resolve the interpretative issues raised by the corresponding adjustment clause in Article 9(2) of the 2017 OECD MTC.[169]

Also in relation to the arbitration, notwithstanding that the MLI in Part VI, according to Articles 18 to 26, reflects the work of the subgroup that has focused on arbitration with the intention to develop provisions for mandatory and binding arbitration in cases of MAP procedures,[170] it is important to highlight that the reservation for the application of Part VI is optional, in other words, a jurisdiction and those with which the former has bilateral agreements must expressly opt for the adoption of arbitration clauses.[171] Indeed, not only are there general

166 Perrou, K., *Taxpayer Participation in Tax Treaty Dispute Resolution—Part IV: Summary and Conclusions—Chapter 8: Redesigning the International Tax Dispute Resolution Mechanism*, IBFD Doctoral Series 28, 2014 p. 227.

167 De Ruiter, M., Supplementary Dispute Resolution, *European Taxation.*, Vol 48(9), 2008, p. 493 y Connors, J., y Delputte, B., Alternative Dispute Resolution in International Tax Law—The View of Business, in *International Arbitration in Tax Matters* (eds., M. Lang and J. P. Owens), IBFD, 2016, p 80.

168 Hinnekens, L., The Tax Arbitration Convention. Its Significance for the EC Based Enterprise, the EC Itself, and for Belgian and International Tax Law, *EC Tax Review*, 1992/2, p. 76.

169 Navarro, A., The Multilateral Instrument (MLI) and Transfer Pricing, *Intertax*, Vol. 49(10), 2021, pp. 812–813.

170 OECD, *Explanatory Statement to the Multilateral Convention to Implement Tax Treaty Related Measures to Prevent Base Erosion and Profit Shifting*, 2016, p. 7 and Del Federico, L., La tutela del contribuente nell'evoluzione del diritto tributario internazionale: dagli accordi amministrativi fra autoritá fiscali alle procedure arbitrali, *Rivista Semestrale di Diritto*, N. 2/2020, p. 143.

171 Pit, H. M., Arbitration under the OECD Multilateral Instrument: Reservations, Options and Choises, *Bulletin for International Taxation*, Vol. 71(10), 2017, p. 571 y OECD, FAQs, July 2017, p. 7.

reservations but also the possibility for the parties to make their own reservations with reference to the cases to which the arbitration procedure will be applied, considering that in the latter case the reservations must also be accepted by the other party.[172]

Even if the MLI provisions aim to harmonize the arbitration procedure, there are still open issues that have not been solved. The MLI arbitration procedure, as provided for by the MLI itself, is not considered, as in the provision contained in Article 25(5) of the OECD Model Convention, an autonomous procedure, but rather an extension of the MAP procedure. In fact, it is constructed as a procedure executed by the most competent tax authorities, with limited participation of taxpayers.[173]

Note that the flexibility granted, broader than in other parts of the MLI, could create a risk of asymmetries due to the use of reservations with a consequent implementation of the arbitration instituted very limited or even stopped, as in the case of Article 23(3) of the MLI. In short, with reference to the form of the arbitration process, considering the two options—"final proposal"/"best offer" (baseball/last final offer) or "independent opinion"—the default use of the first could go against the principles of legality, certainty and equality, as it allows deciding only based on a monetary evaluation. This could lead to identical cases in one country being decided in different ways, generating risks of judicial challenges to arbitration awards.[174]

4.3 European Arbitration Convention 90/436/EEC and directive 2017/1852

Within the European Union, two avenues of appeal have been designed to counteract international double taxation: (i) the European Arbitration Convention (90/436/EEC) (also called the Convention), relating to the elimination of double taxation in case of correction of the profits of associated companies, and (ii) Directive 2017/1852, relating to tax dispute resolution mechanisms in the European Union.

172 Articulo 28(2)(a)(b) de la Convención Multilateral para aplicar las medidas relacionadas con los tratados fiscales para prevenir la erosión de las bases imponibles y el traslado de beneficios, OCDE y Explanatory Statement to the Multilateral Convention to Implement Tax Treaty Related Measures to Prevent Base Erosion and ProfitShifting, p. 7. See also Bravo, N., Interpreting Tax Treaties in the Light of Reservations and Opt-Ins under the Multilateral Instrument, *Bulletin for International Taxation*, Vol. 74 (4/5), 2020, p. 232.

173 Groen, G., The Nature and Scope of the Mandatory Arbitration Provision in the OECD Multilateral Convention (2016), *Bulletin for International Taxation*, Vol. 71(11), 2017, p. 610. See also Groen, G., The Nature and Scope of the Mandatory Arbitration Provision in the OECD Multilateral Convention (2016), *Bulletin for International Taxation*, Vol. 71(11), 2017, p. 611.

174 Govind, S., y Turcan, L., The Changing Contours of Disputes Resolution in the International Tax World: Comparing the OECD Multilateral Instrument and the Proposed EU Arbitration Directive, *Bulletin for International Taxation*, Vol. 71(3/4), 2017, p. 3.

4.3.1 European Arbitration Convention (90/436/EEC)

The European Arbitration Convention came into force in 1995.[175] The purpose of the agreement is the elimination of the economic double taxation that is generated when the taxable income of a company increases because of an adjustment, according to the principle of fair price, without a corresponding adjustment made to the company's income associated in the other state. In this way, the Convention provides a mechanism to eliminate double taxation, but only in relation to adjustments of profits between associated companies with reference to income taxes.[176] As a result of the adoption of this agreement, the European Joint Transfer Pricing Forum was created in 2002 to promote the adequate resolution of disputes under this instrument.[177] The discussions of this body with reference to the interpretation and application of the Convention were published as a guide and clarification,[178] for its practical application, a Code of Conduct of the Council of the European Union and its revision.[179]

In general terms, the application of the Convention is based on two stages: (i) a typical MAP and (ii) binding arbitration when a solution has not been reached in the previous phase. The first phase begins with the taxpayer who initiates the procedure with the proposal of a request to the competent authority in his state of residence within three years from the notification of the act[180] that has given rise or may give rise to double taxation[181] and regardless of the resources provided for by the national legislation of the states involved.[182]

175 Pistone, P., The Settlement of Cross-Border Tax Disputes in the European Union, in *European Tax Law—Part 2—B. Terra & P. Wattel* (eds. Peter J. Wattel, Otto Marres and Hein Vermeulen), Wolters Kluwer, 2018, pp. 177–178, Hinnekens, L., Different Interpretations of the European Tax Arbitration Convention, *ECTaxReview*, 1998/4, p. 249 y Beretta, G., La giurisdizione sul diniego di acceso alla procedura arbitrale in tema di transfer pricing, *il fisco*, n. 1, 2016, p. 3.

176 Valente, P., Procedure amichevoli, procedure arbitrali e rapporti Fisco-Contribuente, *il fisco*, n. 5, 2017, p. 2.

177 Navarro Ibarrola, A., La eliminación de la doble imposición en la Unión Europea: el antiguo art. 293, competencias de la Unión y aspectos controvertidos de la Directiva de Arbitraje, 2018, p. 496 J. M. Almudí Cid et al. eds., La armonización de las normas contra la elusión fiscal relativas a la fiscalidad directa en la Unión Europea (Thomson Reuters Aranzadi).

178 CFE Fiscal Committee, OpinionStatement FC 4/2017 on the Proposed Directive on Double Taxation Dispute Resolution Mechanisms in the European Union, *European Taxation*, Vol. 57(8), 2017, p. 351 y Mattarelli, F., La sospensione del processo tributario: influenza del nuovo art. 39, D.Lgs. n. 546/1992 sulle procedure amichevoli internazionali in materia di transfer pricing, *Rassegna Tributaria*, n. 1, 2017, p. 138.

179 Diario Oficial de la Unión Europea C 322, 30 diciembre 2009, 2009/C 322/01 Código de conducta revisado para la aplicación efectiva del Convenio relativo a la supresión de la doble imposición en caso de corrección de los beneficios de empresas asociadas.

180 Este puede entenderse como un acto de liquidación o equivalente. Véase el Código de Conducta, artículo 4.

181 EU Arbitration Convention 90/436/CEE, Article 6(1).

182 EU Arbitration Convention 90/436/CEE. Article 7(1).

4.3.2 Controversial issues

Although this instrument has been one of the most used and powerful in the EU to resolve transfer pricing adjustment issues, some deficiencies have been identified. First, the lack of a sanction's mechanism has been recognized if member states do not comply with their obligations under the Convention.[183] A first element arises in the case of procedural aspects that can be found in the two years necessary to resolve the controversy amicably and until the advisory commission must be appointed.[184] This is due to the different interpretation that member states make on when this period should be calculated and also on the time necessary to establish the advisory committee. In practice, this can be a problem and require more time than necessary.[185]

Furthermore, the procedure identified by Article 7 of the Convention appears to lack a very important aspect due to the independence credentials of some members.[186] Another element that must be considered is the fact that the taxpayer is not part of the procedure.[187] That is, the solution and discussion of the case remains exclusively in the hands of the two competent administrations involved.[188]

Finally, the issue of tax collection and interest collection during the procedure is also relevant. The Code of Conduct recommends and allows states to adopt all necessary measures to guarantee the suspension of collection under the same terms as provided for in internal procedures.[189] This last aspect can generate a problem if this guarantee is not granted in the internal procedures, or if subsequent guarantees are required to grant it to cover the state's credit, thus further aggravating the financial situation of the taxpayer.[190]

183 Pit, H. M., *Dispute Resolution in the EU—The EU Arbitration Convention and the Dispute Resolution Directive—Chapter 19: Improving the Governance of the EU Arbitration Convention*, IBFD Doctoral Series 42, 2018, p. 963.

184 Huibregtse, S. B., and Offermanns, R. H. M. J., What is the future of the EU Arbitration Convention? *International Transfer Pricing Journal*, Vol. 11(2), 2004, p. 81.

185 Van Vlem, X., et al., The EU Arbitration Convention: Reinforcing the Procedure to Cope with an Expected Flood of Double Taxation Disputes, *International Transfer Pricing Journal*, Vol. 21(4), 2014, p. 232 and EU JTPF, JTPF/007/2002/REV1/EN, par. 30 y Pit, H. M., *Dispute Resolution in the EU—Chapter 20: Improving the Functioning of the EU Arbitration Convention*, IBFD Doctoral Series 42, 2018, p. 1003.

186 Bantekas, I., The Mutual Agreement Procedure and Arbitration of Double Taxation Disputes, *ACDI*, Vol. 1, 2018, p. 198 y Pit, H. M., Improving the Arbitration Procedure under the EU Arbitration Convention (1), *ECTaxReview*, 2015/1, p. 21.

187 CFE Fiscal Committee, Opinion Statement FC 4/2017 on the Proposed Directive on Double Taxation Dispute Resolution Mechanisms in the European Union, *European Taxation*, Vol. 57(8), 2017, p. 351.

188 Pit, H. M., Improving the Arbitration Procedure under the EU Arbitration Convention (2), *ECTaxReview*, Vol. 24(2), 2015, p. 81.

189 Codeo of Conduct, Article 8(1)(a) and Di Cesare, F., How to Revitalize the EC Arbitration Convention: The New Recommendations of the Joint Transfer Pricing Forum, *International Transfer Pricing Journal*, Vol. 17(4), 2010, p. 279.

190 Article 3 Law 99/1993.

4.3.3 Directive 2017/1852

In the session of May 23, 2017, an agreement was reached, after which the Council of the European Union published Directive 2017/1852 on October 10, 2017. The objective was to improve the mechanisms for resolving double taxation disputes.[191] The directive, as structured, sets out some innovative methods to ensure that disputes are resolved using multiple levels and options of protection and falls within the scope of EU law.[192] The fundamental element of the directive in the European single market has been recognized in that it establishes a stable regulatory framework in the resolution of disputes and introduces into the European legal system the minimum standards and best practices of Actions 14 and 15 of the BEPS.[193]

Due to its nature, the Convention was not interpreted and applied in the same way by all member states, thus lacking the integration character that is typical of a directive.[194] The mechanisms of the bilateral agreements and the Convention are not always effective—given, for example, the deficiencies that we have shown in relation to access to the procedure, the duration and its effective conclusion.[195] At the European level, the need has been perceived to develop another instrument that can definitively guarantee the resolution of disputes regarding double taxation.[196]

With the introduction of the directive, it has been recognized that the improvement of the dispute resolution mechanism should be based on existing systems in the EU, including the Arbitration Convention, but the scope of application of the directive is broader than that of the Arbitration Convention, which is limited exclusively to disputes regarding transfer pricing and the attribution of profits to permanent establishments. This means that this directive should apply to all taxpayers

191 Directive 2017/1852, Article 23. See also Noticias de actualidad, Nuevo sistema de resolución de litigios de doble imposición en el seno de la UE, Carta Tributaria, *Revista de Opinión*, Número 29–30, 2017, p. 94 and Zeyen, G., When Taxation Meets Arbitration: Recent Initiatives to Introduce and PromoteArbitration in International and EuropeanTaxation, *Intertax*, Vol. 45(1), 2017, p. 729.

192 Lang, M., ECJ and Mutual Agreement Procedures, *Intertax*, Vol. 42(3), 2014, p. 172.

193 Ferroni, B., La nuova Direttiva UE per la risoluzione delle controversie fiscali, *il fisco*, n. 5, 2018, p. 8.

194 Directive 2017/1852, Para. 1 in the introduction. See also Terra, B. J. M., and Wattel, P. J., European Tax Law, *Kluwer Law International—Wolters Kluwer*, 2012, p. 711 and also Luchena Mozo, G.Mª., A Collaborative Relationship in the Resolution on International Tax Disputes and Alternative Measures for Dispute Resolution in a Post-BEPS Era, *European Taxation*, Vol. 58(1), 2018, p. 24 y Govind, S., and Turcan, L., The Changing Contours of Dispute Resolution in the International Tax World: Comparing the OECD Multilateral Instrument and the Proposed EU Arbitration Directive, *Bulletin for International Taxation*, Vol. 71(3/4), 2017, p. 5.

195 Valente, P., L'art. 25 del Modello di Convenzione OCSE: la procedura di composizione delle controversie internazionali, *il fisco*, n. 9, 2004, p. 863.

196 Pit, H. M., Commission Initiative to Improve Dispute Settlement Mechanisms within the European Union—The EU Arbitration Convention (90/436), *European Taxation*, Vol. 56(11), 2016, p. 519 y Proposal for a Council Directive on Double Taxation Dispute Resolution Mechanisms in the European Union, COM(2016) 686 final, 25 October 2016, Cerioni, L., The Commission's Proposal for a Directive on Double Taxation Dispute Resolution Mechanisms: Overcoming the Final Hurdle of Juridical Double Taxation within the European, *European Taxation*, Vol. 57(5), 2017, p. 186, 189.

subject to income and wealth tax[197] covered by bilateral tax treaties and the EU Arbitration Convention.[198]

The aim of the directive is "dispute resolution between Member States where such disputes arise out of the interpretation and application of agreements and conventions providing for the elimination of double taxation".[199] That is to say, the scope of application of the directive is determined by that of the instrument to which it applies, whether a bilateral treaty, the MLI or the Arbitration Convention, thus identifying its alternative nature with reference to dispute resolution mechanisms characteristic of these instruments.[200]

Furthermore, the directive not only fits in with existing solutions by identifying specific provisions for resolving disputes but also has managed to increase the powers of taxpayers, especially when competent authorities are inert.[201] A final important aspect of progress in the directive lies in the fact that it also covers disputes in triangular and multi-triangular situations, which is often a risk area for unresolved double taxation cases.[202]

The directive, based on the Arbitration Convention, finds an implementation like this one with a procedure divided into three phases: (i) claim phase (Articles 3–5), (ii) phase of the friendly procedure (Article 4) and (iii) conflict resolution phase (Articles 5–16).[203]

However, even if the directive has an innovative character with respect to the existing dispute resolution mechanisms, there are still some controversial issues which are briefly described next.

4.3.4 Controversial issues

Although the directive guarantees dispute resolution the necessary strength to make it more effective than unilateral procedures,[204] there are still controversial aspects and room for improvement. Indeed, it has been pointed out that, although

197 Kofler, G., EU Tax Dispute Resolution Directive: The Deathblow to Double Taxation in the European Union, *EC Tax Review*, 6/2019, p. 267–268.

198 Directive 2017/1852, Para. 7 of the introduction and CFE Fiscal Committee, Opinion Statement FC 4/2017 on the Proposed Directive on Double Taxation Dispute Resolution Mechanisms in the European Union, *European Taxation*, Vol. 57(8), 2017, p. 351.

199 Directiva 2017/1852, artículo 1.

200 Govind, S., and Turcan, L., Cross-Border Tax Disputes Resolution in the 21st Century: A Comparative Study of Existing Bilateral and Multilateral Remedies, *Derivatives & Financial Instrument*, Vol. 19(5), 2017, p. 9.

201 Ferroni, B., La nuova Direttiva UE per la risoluzione delle controversia fiscali, *il fisco*, n. 5, 2018, p. 454 y Iannacone, A., Doppia imposizione internazionale: approvata la Direttiva sui meccanismi di risoluzione delle controversia, *Corriere tributario*, n. 4, 2018, IPSOA, p. 273.

202 Directive 2017/1852, Article 2(1)(c). See also Kofler, G., EU Tax Dispute Resolution Directive: The Deathblow to Double Taxation in the European Union, *EC Tax Review*, Vol. 28(6), 2019, p. 268.

203 Kotha, A. P., Baseball Arbitration Option under the EU Dispute Resolution Directive: How Well Does It Fare against the Objectives? *World Tax Journal*, Vol. 13(2), 2021, p. 255 y 258.

204 Govind, S., The New Face of International Tax Dispute Resolution: Comparing the OECD Multilateral Instrument with the EU Dispute Resolution Directive, *EC Tax Review*, Nr. 6, 2018, p. 323.

the introduction of the directive has led to an increase in the protection of taxpayer rights, the fundamental structure of the dispute resolution mechanisms, as provided for by the Arbitration Convention (90/436) and the 2017 OECD MTC,[205] has not changed, so taxpayer participation in the procedure is still lacking. This means that the alternative of overcoming the premise between administration and taxpayer is no longer fulfilled.[206]

Indeed, the recognition of the fundamental rights of taxpayers in the directive procedure must be analysed starting from the fact that the form of implementation of the procedure through a directive guarantees not only the intervention of the European Court of Justice for the correct interpretation of the EU law but also potentially entails the application of the Charter of Fundamental Rights of the European Union (also called simply the Charter) in accordance with its Article 51.[207] Consequently, what still remains an unsolved issue is the correct understanding of how the right to effective judicial protection and an impartial judge, recognized in Article 47, could be applied to the directive.[208]

In fact, the different decisions provided by the European Court of Justice on the topic related to what could be considered as "tribunal" leave many open questions about the possibility to insert in this definition the dispute resolution bodies identified in the directive with the risk that, according to these conflicting ECJ decisions, taxpayers cannot have their fundamental rights respected if these are violated during the MAP phase pursuant to the directive.[209]

Therefore, the directive gives taxpayers some additional powers with respect to the OECD/UN Article 25 and Arbitration Convention procedures and strengthens the time limits to speed up the process. Despite this, as we have mentioned, there are still gaps and room for improvement, especially with reference to the independence of the arbitrators (with the still open question if these bodies could be considered as "tribunal") and the role of the taxpayer, which should/could be more active. Finally, one positive aspect is the obligation to publish the final decision or an abstract of it even if the decision does not set a precedent.

5 Summary

The issue of double taxation, whether of juridical nature (same income taxed several times against the same person) or economic (when the same income is taxed

205 De Carolis, D., The EU Dispute Resolution Directive (2017/1852) and Fair Trial Protection under Article 47 of the EU Charter of Fundamental Rights, *European Taxation*, Vol. 58(11), 2018, p. 496.

206 Luchena Mozo, G.Mª., Procedimientos de resolución de controversias tributarias internacionales: Entre BEPS y la UE, *Aranzadi*, 2017, p. 143.

207 EU Charter of Fundamental Rights, Article 51(1).

208 EU Charter of Fundamental Rights, Article 47. See also Debelva, F., and Luts, J., The European Commission's Proposal for Double Taxation Dispute Resolution: Turning the Tide? *Bulletin for International Taxation*, Vol. 71(5), 2017, p. 5.

209 FRA, *European Union Agency for Fundamental Rights, Access to Justice in Europe: An Overview of Challenges and Opportunities*, Luxembourg: Publications Office of the European Union, 2011, p. 14. García Antón, R., Cecin'est pas une Pipe: The Notion of Tax Court Under Article 267 of the TFUE, *European Taxation*, Vol. 55(11), 2015, pp. 515–516.

several times on different subjects), entails not only difficulties in economic development and trade, but once it has manifested itself, it implies an increase in the expenses of taxpayers, who will have to interact with the different tax administrations to find a solution or reach an agreement to eliminate or limit the effects of double taxation.

To counteract this phenomenon, which could cost years of uncertainty and affect the business of taxpayers, different tools have been developed with the aim to prevent tax disputes granting tax certainty or at least a tax comfort and can definitely be of great help in the prevention of disputes. These instruments, which can be used in all tax fields (i.e., from direct to indirect taxes), bring, in certain cases, tax certainty (bilateral/multilateral APA, simultaneous/joint audits), while others bring comfort in the relationship between the parties (Multilateral Risk Assessment—ICAP). On the other side, even if part of the preventive instruments category, some other instruments described, such as safe harbour (unless in a bilateral or multilateral form) or unilateral APA, can help in avoiding the litigation phase; but neither certainty nor comfort can be provided as there is a lack of consensus among the parties involved in the transaction analysis.

However, if available, these instruments do not always grant an intensive participation of taxpayers nor are they affected from the length of time required to get a final result; the taxpayer is then left with the possibility to find a solution to double taxation locally or through the MAP process. With respect to the latter, on the one hand, the importance of the MAP procedure is recognized, which gives the taxpayer an alternative to the national tax litigation phase, which normally must take place in both states to reach a resolution of double taxation and usually generates a lot of uncertainty. On the other hand, it must be recognized that the current framework is not without criticism. Likely, the insertion of the arbitration clause, which is mandatory, brings some advantages, although there are still some disadvantages and gaps to should be resolved.

Finally, at the European level, there is the coexistence of the European Arbitration Convention and of the European Directive 2017/1852, where the second tried to improve the inefficiencies present in the first document but still left space for doubts and open issues that could yet jeopardize the developed procedures.

From the analysis carried out so far, it may be clear that, despite the multitude of existing instruments at the international level aimed at solving international tax disputes, there is still uncertainty around bringing double taxation cases before the bodies designated to resolve them. Often, in practice, multinational groups do not trust that cases will be resolved or think that the time needed for a possible solution may affect the smooth running of their businesses, thus opting for negotiation solutions with the authorities.

Thus, in the described constantly changing scenario, it is interesting to study how and whether new technologies—more specifically AI and its subfield machine learning—can help in the resolution of international tax disputes, mainly in relation to the decision phase, either by the competent authorities or the arbitrators.

2 Artificial intelligence

Introduction, types, common application, ethical issues and analogies in the disputes field

1 Introduction

During the Second World War, technology took a leap forward as a result of scientists developing instruments and systems aimed at counteracting the enemies. In the 1950s, Alan Turing set the standard for what could be regarded as a "thinking machine"—what some might call artificial intelligence (AI) today.[1] He suggested the imitation game test whereby a computer would have to be indistinguishable from a human.[2] AI was initially developed at a rapid pace in the 1950s and the 1960s,[3] however, disappointing progress led to an AI winter from the 1970s to the 1990s.[4] Afterwards, renewed interest in AI and machine learning (ML), from both researchers and businesses, has led to a dramatic increase in funding and investment.[5]

1 Turing, A. M., The Word Problem in Semi-Groups with Cancellation, *Annals of Mathematics Second Series*, Vol. 52(2), 1950, pp. 491ss, and Smith, C., et al., *The History of AI, History of Computing*, University of Washington, 2006, p. 5, available at http://courses.cs.washington.edu/courses/csep590/06au/projects/history-ai.pdf.

2 Gutiérrez Tapia, A., Inteligencia Artificial, *Manual formativo de ACTA*, n. 60, 2011, p. 32.

3 Quintarelli, S., et al., Intelligenza artificiale—cos'è davvero, come funziona, che effetti avrà, A cura di Claudia Giulia Ferrauto, *Bollati Boringhieri*, 2020, p. 29.

4 Somers, J., The Man Who Would Teach Machines to Think, *The Atlantic*, 2013, available at https://www.theatlantic.com/magazine/archive/2013/11/the-man-who-would-teach-machines-to-think/309529/ (accessed 20 December 2022). See also Katz, Y., *Manufacturing and AI Revolution*, Harvard Medical School; Berkman Klein Center for Internet & Society, 2017, pp. 1–2, available at SSRN: https://ssrn.com/abstract=3078224 or http://doi.org/10.2139/ssrn.3078224.

5 History of Data Science, AI Winter: The Highs and Lows of AI, *Blog*, 9 September 2021, available at https://www.historyofdatascience.com/ai-winter-the-highs-and-lows-of-artificial-intelligence/ (accessed 20 December 2022). See also Dick, S., Artificial Intelligence, *Harvard Data Science Review*, Issue 1.1, 2 July 2019, available at https://hdsr.mitpress.mit.edu/pub/0aytgrau/release/3 (accessed 15 December 2022).

DOI: 10.4324/9781003599814-2

However, as recently pointed out, currently AI systems can replace humans in some low-level pattern recognition skills, but they are still missing, at a cognitive level, any creativity and they are just imitating humans.[6] In other words,

> for the foreseeable future, computers will not be able to match humans in their ability to reason abstractly about real-world situations. We will need well-thought-out interactions of humans and computers to solve our most pressing problems. And we will want computers to trigger new levels of human creativity, not replace human creativity.[7]

The graphic in Figure 2.1[8] provides an overview of the evolution of AI over the years.

In the last two decades, the development and use of artificial intelligence (AI) schemes and models has grown exponentially. Information is being produced and stored at an unprecedented rate, with the corresponding promise that the "big data"[9] revolution could provide answers to the fundamental questions of businesses, governments and social sciences.[10] Indeed, data is the new oil,[11] and it is through AI systems and architectures that data can be tamed. The aim of this chapter is to provide an introduction and a general overview of the development of AI, and more specific of ML algorithms, with a specific focus on such developments in the field of law/tax law and more specifically in relation to dispute resolutions. The chapter will also analyse the ethical and legal issues and the risks related with the implementation of AI, especially with reference to existing human rights as recognized at the international level.

6 Pretz, K., Stop Calling Everything AI, Machine-Learning Pioneer Says, *IEEE Spectrum*, 31 March 2021, available at https://spectrum.ieee.org/stop-calling-everything-ai-machinelearning-pioneer-says (accessed 20 December 2022).

7 Jordan, M. I., AI—The Revolution Hasn't Happened Yet, *Harvard Data Science Review*, Issue 1 January 2019, available at https://hdsr.mitpress.mit.edu/pub/wot7mkc1/release/9 (accessed 12 December 2022).

8 OECD, AI in Society, 2019, p. 20. See also Anyoha, R., The history of AI, *Harvard University Graduate School of Arts and Sciences Blog*, 28 August 2017, available at http://sitn.hms.harvard.edu/flash/2017/historyartificial-intelligence/ (accessed 12 December 2022).

9 Krishnamachari, R. T., *Big Data and AI Strategies ML and Alternative Data Approach to Investing*, J.P. Morgan, 2017, p. 10.

10 Grimmer, J., We Are All Social Scientists Now: How Big Data, ML, and Causal Inference Work Together, *PS: Political Science & Politics*, Vol. 48(1), January 2015, p. 80 and Kolanovic, M., and Krishnamachari, R. T., *Big Data and AI Strategies ML and Alternative Data Approach to Investing*, J.P. Morgan, 2017, p. 9. See also Iacoviti, G., How Technology Influences Information Gathering and Information Spreading, *Church, Communication and Culture*, Vol. 7(1), 2022, p. 77.

11 Marr, B., *Here's Why Data Is Not The New Oil*, 5 March 2018, available at Here's Why Data Is Not The New Oil (forbes.com) (accessed 11 December 2022). See Hern, A., Partnership on AI Formed by Google, Facebook, Amazon, IBM and Microsoft, *The Guardian*, 28 September 2016, available at https://www.theguardian.com/technology/2016/sep/28/google-facebook-amazon-ibm-microsoft-partnership-on-ai-tech-firms (accessed 11 December 2022).

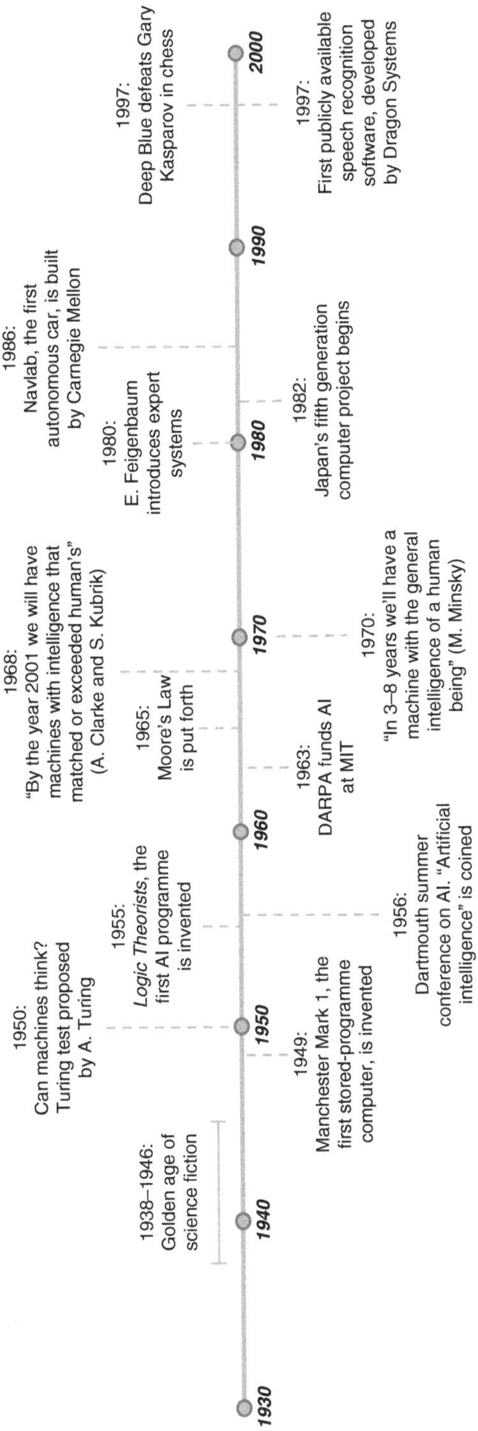

Figure 2.1 Timeline of early AI development.

2 Architecture and objectives of AI

The objectives and goals of AI can be viewed partly as engineering and partly as science:

- The engineering goal of AI is to solve real-world problems using AI as an armamentarium of ideas about representing knowledge, using knowledge, and assembling systems.
- The scientific goal of AI is to determine which ideas about representing knowledge, using knowledge, and assembling systems explain various sorts of intelligence.[12]

According to a philosophical view, AI can be divided in (i) weak AI, that is, when machines are made to act as if they are intelligent, hence machines have the capability to perform activities that could only be expected of the human brain (e.g., playing chess[13]), and (ii) strong AI (also known as general AI), which is that machines can be made to think or could represent the human mind (i.e., machines can work like humans and have similar or even superior human intelligence).[14] In respect to the latter, no machines with self-sustaining long-term goals and intent have been developed, nor are they likely to be developed in the near future.[15] However, it has been recognized that until now progress has been made according to three types of capabilities: (i) systems have the ability to learn in a self-supervised or self-motivated way, (ii) a single AI system is able to continually learn to solve problems coming from different domains with less need to retrain it and (iii) the ability of AI systems to adapt their knowledge and skills acquired for one task to new situations with less or no additional training.[16]

12 Winston, P., *Artificial Intelligence*, Addison-Wesley Publishing Company, 1992, p. 6, available at https://courses.csail.mit.edu/6.034f/ai3/rest.pdf (accessed 10 December 2022).

13 Mohssen, M., et al., *ML: Algorithms and Applications*, CRC Press, 2017, introduction, where there is a reference to Deep Blue chess machine, designed in 1997 by IBM that defeated Garry Kasparov, the world chess champion.

14 Borana, J., Applications of AI& Associated Technologies, *IDL—International Digital Library of Educational Research*, Vol. 1(6), 2017, p. 64 and Flowers, J., *C., Strong and Weak AI: Deweyan Considerations*, AAAI Spring Symposium: Towards Conscious AI Systems, 2019, pp. 1–2, available at http://ceur-ws.org/Vol-2287/paper34.pdf. and Six, P., Ethics, Regulation and the New Artificial Intelligence, Part I: Accountability and Power, *Information Communication and Society*, Vol. 4(2), 2001, pp. 199–229, available at https://www.tandfonline.com/doi/abs/10.1080/713768525.

15 Stanford University, *One Hundred Year Study on AI (AI100)*, AI and Life in 2030, 2016 Report, p. 4, available at https://ai100.stanford.edu/sites/g/files/sbiybj18871/files/media/file/ai100report-10032016fnl_singles.pdf.

16 Stanford University, Gathering Strength, *Gathering Storms: The One Hundred Year Study on Artificial Intelligence (AI100)*, 2021 Study Panel Report, p. 30, available at https://ai100.stanford.edu/gathering-strength-gathering-storms-one-hundred-year-study-artificial-intelligence-ai100-2021-studyand Venkatachalam, S., Why 2017 Is The Year of Artificial Intelligence, *Forbes*, 27 February 2017, available at https://www.forbes.com/consent/ketch/?toURL=https://www.forbes.com/councils/forbestechcouncil/2017/02/27/why-2017-is-the-year-of-artificial-intelligence/.

In general terms, AI can be classified as a branch of computer science where machines are programmed in a way that they can think and mimic actions like living beings.[17] In other words, "AI is thus considered a branch of science and engineering that focuses on simulating a wide range of issues and functions in the field of human intellect".[18] However, a common definition of AI is missing. At first, AI was described as "AI is that activity devoted to making machines intelligent, and intelligence is that quality that enables an entity to function appropriately and with foresight in its environment".[19] In addition to that, both the high-level expert group on AI established by the EU and the OECD's AI Experts Group (AIGO) provided a definition of AI:

> AI refers to systems designed by humans that, given a complex goal, act in the physical or digital world by perceiving their environment, interpreting the collected structured or unstructured data, reasoning on the knowledge derived from this data and deciding the best action(s) to take (according to pre-defined parameters) to achieve the given goal.[20]

In a later document, AIGO explained that an AI system is

> a machine-based system that is capable of influencing the Environment by making recommendations, predictions or decisions for a given set of Objectives. It does so by utilizing machine and/or human-based inputs/data to: i) perceive real and/or virtual environments; ii) abstract such perceptions into models manually or automatically; and iii) use Model Interpretations to formulate options for outcomes.[21]

17 Johnson, D., Difference Between Deep Learning and ML vs AI, *Guru99, Blog*, 2023, that can be found https://www.guru99.com/machine-learning-vs-deep-learning.html (accessed 11 May 2023). See also Meya, M., La inteligencia artificial, *Revista Española de Lingüística*, Vol. 10(1), 1980, p. 135.

18 Sarker, I. H., AI-Based Modeling: Techniques, Applications and Research Issues Towards Automation, Intelligent and Smart Systems, *SN Computer Science*, Vol. 3, 2022, pp. 1–20.

19 Nilsson, N. J., *The Quest for AI: A History of Ideas and Achievements*, Cambridge: Cambridge University Press, 2010, p. 13.

20 European Commission, Artificial Intelligence for Europe, Brussels, COM(2018) 237 final, p. 1 and European Commission, High-Level Expert Group on Artificial Intelligence, A Definition of AI: Main Capabilities and Scientific Disciplines, Definition developed for the purpose of the deliverables of the High-Level Expert Group on AI, 2018, p. 7, available at https://eur-lex.europa.eu/legal-content/EN/TXT/?uri=COM%3A2018%3A237%3AFIN. See also Dempsey, J. X., AI: An Introduction to the Legal, Policy and Ethical Issues, *Berkeley Centre for Law & Technology*, 2020, p. 3, available at https://imgsvr.edgereg.net/ERImg/02/91/24/LegalIssues-AI-April2019.pdf where some other definitions of AI are provided.

21 OECD, *Scoping the OECD AI Principles—Deliberation of the Expert Group on AI at the OECD (AIGO)*, OECD Digital Economic Papers, n. 291, 2019, p. 7.

This could be better explained as follows:

> An AI system is composed of two main elements—an agent and its surrounding environment. An agent can be either a human or a machine. An agent can be anything that can perceive its environment through sensors and act upon that environment through effectors. The intelligence of agents is calculated by their ability to create goals and achieve them.[22]

The definition, as showed in Figure 2.2,[23] can be read together with the structure of a generic AI system where the three main elements of such a system are (i) sensors, (ii) operational logic and (iii) actuators.[24]

In order to obtain a result while running an AI system, it is necessary to have in mind the following steps, visible also in Figure 2.3[25], which are part of the AI system life cycle: (i) design, data and models, which is a context-dependent sequence encompassing planning and design, data collection and processing, as well as model building; (ii) verification and validation; (iii) deployment; and (iv) operation and monitoring.[26]

Data and input are the data and the expert input with which an AI model builds a representation of the context or environment, while an AI model can be identified as

> a computational representation of all or part of the external environment of an AI system—encompassing, for example, processes, objects, ideas, people and/or interactions that take place in that environment. AI models use data and/or expert knowledge provided by humans and/or automated tools to represent, describe and interact with real or virtual environments.[27]

Figure 2.4[28] represents a view of an AI model.

22 Microsoft, *Fundamentals of AI—Student Guide Module 1*, 2020, available at https://news.microsoft.com/wp-content/uploads/prod/sites/93/2020/04/Student-Guide-Module-1-Fundamentals-of-AI.pdf#:~:text=Artificial%20Intelligence%20is%20an%20attempt%20to%20make%20a,tries%20to%20solve%20problems%20or%20execute%20a%20task. (accessed 2 December 2022) and Kovač, M, *Judgement-Proof Robots and AI—A Comparative Law and Economics Approach*, Springer Nature, 2020, p. 54 and Skilton, M., and Hovsepian, F., *The 4th Industrial Revolution—Responding to the Impact of Artificial Intelligence on Business*, Palgrave Macmillan, 2018, p. 100, where agent is identified as "an autonomous entity, which has the ability to sense its environment through the use of its sensors, and acts on the environment through the use of its actuators".

23 OECD, *Scoping the OECD AI Principles—Deliberation of the Expert Group on AI at the OECD (AIGO)*, OECD Digital Economic Papers, n. 291, 2019, p. 6.

24 OECD, *Scoping the OECD AI Principles—Deliberation of the Expert Group on AI at the OECD (AIGO)*, OECD Digital Economic Papers, n. 291, 2019, p. 7.

25 OECD, *Scoping the OECD AI Principles—Deliberation of the Expert Group on AI at the OECD (AIGO)*, OECD Digital Economic Papers, n. 291, 2019, p. 13.

26 OECD, *AI in Society*, 2019, p. 15.

27 OECD, *OECD Framework for The Classification of AI Systems—OECD Digital Economy Papers*, n. 323, 2022, p. 20.

28 OECD, *OECD Framework for The Classification of AI Systems—OECD Digital Economy Papers*, n. 323, 2022, p. 42.

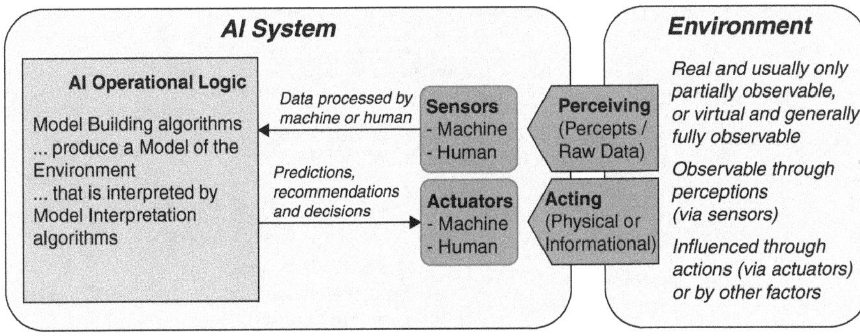

Figure 2.2 A high-level conceptual view of an AI system.

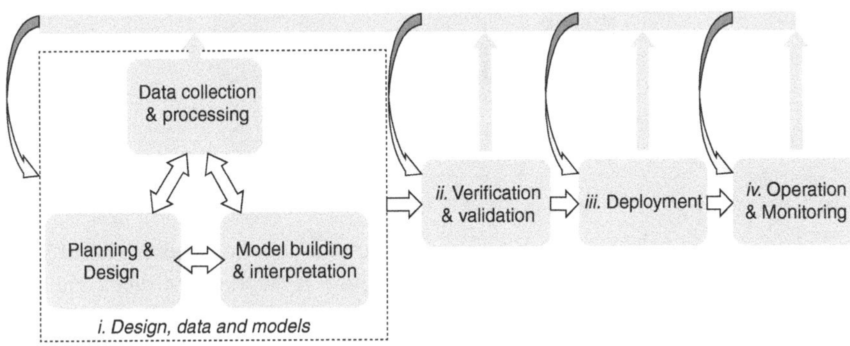

Figure 2.3 A high-level conceptual view of an AI system.

The AI models can be divided in three categories: (i) symbolic AI models, which derive a conclusions from a set of constraints using logical representations (i.e., machines arrive to human-like decisions based on a detailed human-understandable decision structure created by humans); (ii) statistical AI models, where machines induce a trend of patterns based on data rather than expert human knowledge (e.g., genetic algorithms, neural networks[29] and deep learning); and (iii) hybrid AI models, where the two previous models are combined in one system.[30]

The next step is that, once the knowledge has been modelled, there is a need to reason with it (e.g., making inferences, planning and scheduling activities, searching through a large solution set and optimizing among all possible solutions to a

29 Gubelmann, R., and Hongler, P., *Natural Language Processing—A Game Changer for Normative Reasoning in the Legal Discipline?*, IFF-HSG Working Papers, Working Paper No. 2021-7, 2021, p. 12.

30 OECD, *OECD Framework for The Classification of AI Systems—OECD Digital Economy Papers*, n. 323, 2022, p. 44 and OECD, *Artificial Intelligence in Society*, 2019, p. 27.

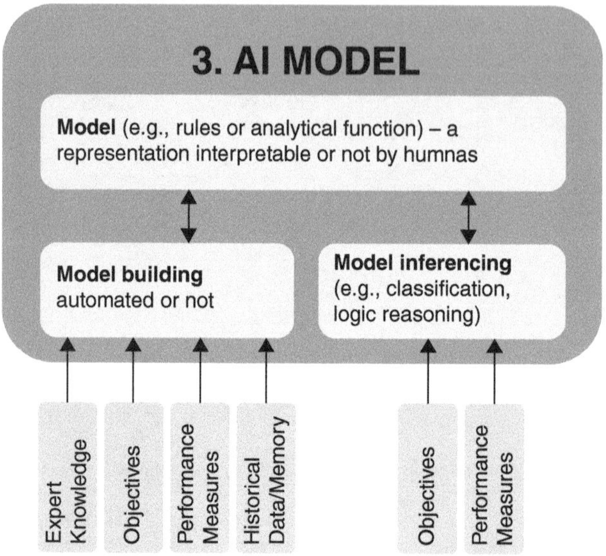

Figure 2.4 Detailed conceptual view of an AI model.

problem). On the other side, when we approach the learning phase, we refer to techniques that include, among others, ML, neural networks, deep learning and decision trees. These techniques enable an AI system to learn how to solve problems that cannot be accurately specified, or whose solution methods cannot be described by symbolic reasoning rules.[31]

The relation of the different AI systems is described in Figure 2.5.[32]

Thus, we can infer that AI has much potential and different types of AI can serve and be used in today's world. As pointed out by Sarker, the various types of AI can be summarized as follows: (i) Analytical AI, which refers to the process of identifying, interpreting and communicating meaningful patterns of data with the aim to discover new insights, patterns and relationships or dependencies in data and to assist in data-driven decision-making. (ii) Functional AI, which works similarly to analytical AI but executes actions rather than making recommendations. For instance, a functional AI model could be useful in robotics and Internet of Things (IoT) applications to take immediate actions. (iii) Interactive AI, which typically enables efficient and interactive communication automation. For instance, it is used to build chatbots and smart personal assistants in interactive AI. (iv) Textual

31 European Commission, *A Definition of AI: Main Capabilities and Scientific Disciplines*, Definition Developed for the Purpose of the Deliverables of the High-Level Expert Group on AI, 2018, p. 4.

32 OECD, *Artificial Intelligence in Society*, 2019, p. 27 and European Commission, *A Definition of AI: Main Capabilities and Scientific Disciplines, Definition Developed for the Purpose of the Deliverables of the High-Level Expert Group on AI*, 2018, p. 6.

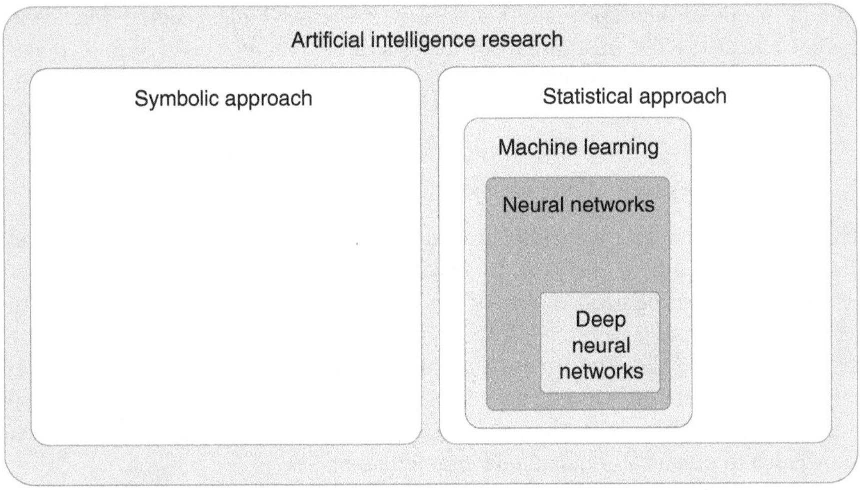

Figure 2.5 A high-level conceptual view of an AI system and sub-disciplines.

AI, which typically covers textual analytics or natural language processing through which businesses can enjoy text recognition, speech-to-text conversion, machine translation as well as content generation capabilities (e.g., answering consumers' queries). (v) Visual AI, which is typically capable of recognizing, classifying and sorting items, as well as converting images and videos into insights.[33]

The boom in high generation and availability of data has made the use of AI possible in many different areas, for example, transportation, healthcare, education, public safety and security, law, entertainment, finance and networking. The use of AI systems in production processes in many different industries can be constantly monitored, especially in the pharmacy industry, where it is used in preclinical stages or in drug discovery; in the aerospace industry, where it can be used for the identification in production problems or for the air traffic, especially in fuel and cabin crew optimization; in the oil industry, where AI can detect small fissures in pipelines; in the mining industry, where AI is quite useful for the exploration of mineral deposits or to operate autonomous drills; and in construction, where AI can optimize building shapes and layouts and link scheduling information to each building component.[34]

Given a brief introduction to the evolution of AI and according to the fact that AI systems have to be intended as a wrapper for different techniques that are based on the AI concept (i.e., machines can learn and mimic humans), the following paragraphs will provide a general overview of some of the most relevant AI techniques

33 Sarker, I. H., AI-Based Modeling: Techniques, Applications and Research Issues Towards Automation, Intelligent and Smart Systems, *SN Computer Science*, Vol. 3, 2022, pp. 1–20.

34 OECD Science, *Technology and Innovation Outlook*, 2018, p. 53.

with the scope of their applicability to real-world issues with specific reference to the law and tax field.[35] In addition, an analysis of the potential risks of implementing AI systems in our society is provided to describe the limits of such systems in regard to human rights.

3 Big data analysis and machine learning

This section provides a general introduction to the importance of big data and the way data should be analysed. In a second step, machine learning will be presented, it being recognized as one of the most important evolving parts of AI in recent years. Before starting, it is important to mention that AI systems involve the distinction among data, information and knowledge; they are put in a hierarchical structure where an AI system understands the world by aggregating data into information, then processing information to extract knowledge and then using that knowledge to direct subsequent data interpretation.

3.1 Big data analysis

The great evolution of AI systems is mainly due to the availability of a large amount of data that are used to develop and train algorithms.[36] Before delving into the subject, it is good to dwell on the definition of an algorithm, as this is a basic element in ML development. According to Tarleton Gillespie,

> algorithms need not be software: in the broadest sense, they are encoded procedures for transforming input data into a desired output, based on specified calculations. The procedures name both a problem and the steps by which it should be solved.[37]

Algorithms are thus perceived as "a series of steps undertaken in order to solve a particular problem or accomplish a defined outcome".[38]

The improvement of ML and the algorithms related to its use benefits from the higher availability of data so that scientists can constantly train machines to get new results. Indeed, with this sort of countless amounts of data, machines (computers) can investigate the data and try to find elements and patterns that would be nearly impossible for human minds to accomplish. The relation between AI and big

35 Baeldung, What Is the Difference Between Labeled and Unlabeled Data? *Blog*, 5 May 2023, available at https://www.baeldung.com/cs/ml-labeled-vs-unlabeled-data (accessed 11 May 2023).

36 Boyd, D., and Crawford, K., Critical Questions for Big Data, *Information, Communication & Society*, Vol. 15(5), 2012, pp. 662–679, https://doi.org/10.1080/1369118X.2012.678878.

37 Gillespie, T., The Relevance of Algorithms, in *Media Technologies: Essays on Communication, Materiality, and Society* (eds. T. Gillespie, P. J. Boczkowski and K. A. Foot), Cambridge, MA: MIT Press, 2014, p. 167.

38 Diakopoulos, N., Algorithmic Accountability, *Digital Journalism*, Vol. 3(3), 2015, p. 400.

data is bi-directional: AI, through ML, needs a vast amount of data to learn, and in the other direction, big data uses AI techniques to extract value from big data sets.[39]

Big data characteristics can be categorized as follows: (i) volume, meaning that the essence of "big data" is that it is composed of large data sets, that is, an extremely high number of data samples whose management entails a technological challenge; (ii) variety, that is, data can come from different formats and have different sources; (iii) velocity, meaning that new data is expected to be quickly generated and, commonly, also promptly processed; (iv) value, meaning that data is intrinsically relevant, must be transformed into "information" and have a strong connection with a real-life need and application; and (v) veracity, meaning that data is, in principle, not corrupted, biased or distorted, and represents with reliability and authenticity a phenomenon or a set of phenomena to which it corresponds.[40]

It is worth emphasizing that data needs to be transformed into something useful or, in other words, data is by itself useless and needs experts (scientists) in order make it available in a "readable" and "understandable" way in current human life. In this sense, data can come in three forms: structured, unstructured and semi-structured. Structured data is normally present in databases and already classified in fields (e.g., names, account numbers, date of birth, place of living, etc.). Unstructured data is data coming from different sources that is not initially identified in a specific field (e.g., spam emails, photographs, surveillance data, text messages, etc.) and the semi-unstructured data is not stored in databases but contains organizational properties that facilitate its analysis (e.g., GTML, XML).[41] On top of this three-party differentiation there is a fourth category called metadata, which could be defined as "data about data", where the same data describes the relevant data information (e.g., author, file, size, keywords to define a document).[42]

39 European Data Protection Supervisor (EPDS), Artificial Intelligence, Robotics, Privacy and Data Protection, Room document for the 38th International Conference of Data Protection and Privacy Commissioners, October 2016, p. 4, Curry, E., et al., *The Elements of Big Data Value* (eds. Edward Curry, Andreas Metzger, Sonja Zillner, Jean-Christophe Pazzaglia and Ana García Robles), Springer, 2021, pp. 5–8 and Suthaharan, S., *ML Models and Algorithms for Big Data Classification—Thinking with Examples for Effective Learning*, Integrated Series in Information Systems 36, Series Editors: Ramesh Sharda · Stefan Voß, Springer, 2016, p. 21.

40 Hurley, R., *Data: A Guide to Big Data Trends, AI, ML, Predictive Analytics, Internet of Things, Data Science, Data Analytics, Business Intelligence, and Data Mining*, Ationa Publications, 2019, p. 9, Mohankumar, P., BIG Data Analytics: A Framework for Unstructured Data Analysis, *International Journal of Engineering and Technology (IJET)*, Vol. 5(1), 2013, p. 155 and Knoblock, C. A., and Szekely, P., Exploiting Semantics for Big Data Integration, *AI Magazine*, Vol. 36(1), 2015, pp. 25–38.

41 Eberendu, A. C., Unstructured Data: An Overview of the Data of Big Data, *International Journal of Emerging Trends & Technology in Computer Science*, Vol. 38(1), pp. 46–50. It has been recognized that the unstructured data accounts for more than 90% of the digital universe. See Gantz, J., and Reinsel, D., Extracting Value from Chaos, *IDCIVIEW*, June 2011, pp. 1–12, available at https://pdf4pro.com/view/idc-i-v-i-e-w-extracting-value-from-chaos-dell-emc-5a42d1.html (accessed 25 November 2022).

42 Sarker, I. H., Machine Learning: Algorithms, Real-World Applications and Research Directions, *SN Computer Science*, Vol. 2, 2021, p. 3.

To examine and find patterns in big data processes, data mining[43] and/or ML are used, which, despite not being the same, use the same methods and algorithms and are commonly taken as synonyms. ML and its application are studied in the next paragraphs.

To process big data, it is important to control the following aspects: (i) methods to obtain data; (ii) warehouse (data storage) and (iii) computer processing power. These three elements can then be used together with ML algorithms to produce predictive models.[44] In this sense, big tech companies like Google, Facebook and Amazon basically operate with data and base their existence on the ability to collect, store and make data usable.

3.2 Machine learning

ML derives from the intersection between computer science and statistics and can be classified as an application of AI that aims to build computer systems that automatically improve with experience, focusing on the development of computer programs that can access data and use it to learn from themselves.[45] We can establish two primary task categories: prediction and data exploration/description.[46] According to the doctrine,

> ML is not a specific research tool: it is a catch-all term that refers to any method that features learning by a machine about quantitative data. A unifying feature of these methods is that they leverage (ever increasing) computational power to apply (even more complicated) techniques of statistical inference to (even larger) dataset.[47]

Initially, computer science had the issue of defining how to manually program computers, whereas with ML, the objective is to define how the computer programs itself and "what computational architectures and algorithms can be used to

43 Fleur, J., Data Mining as Global Governance, in *The Oxford Handbook of Law, Regulation and Technology* (eds. Roger Brownsword et al.), Oxford University Press, 2017, pp. 776–798.

44 Hurley, R., *Data: A Guide to Big Data Trends, AI, ML, Predictive Analytics, Internet of Things, Data Science, Data Analytics, Business Intelligence, and Data Mining*, Ationa Publications, 2019, pp. 46–48.

45 Mitchell, T. M., *The Discipline of ML, CMU-ML-06-108*, School of Computer Science Carnegie Mellon University, July 2006, p. 1, that can be found http://www.cs.cmu.edu/~tom/pubs/MachineLearning.pdf., Harfoush, F. A., *From Big Data to Intelligent Data—An Applied Perspective*, Springer Cham, 2021, p. 64 and Cummings, M. L., and Stimpson, A., Identifying Critical Contextual Design Cues Through a ML Approach, *AI Magazine*, Vol. 40(2), 2019, pp. 28–39.

46 Nay, J., Natural Language Processing for Legal Texts, in *Legal Informatics* (eds. D. M. Katz, R. Dolin and M. Bommarito), Cambridge University Press, 2018, p. 3, available at SSRN: https://ssrn.com/abstract=3438276 or http://doi.org/10.2139/ssrn.3438276.

47 Copus, R., et al., *Credible Prediction: Big Data, ML and the Credibility Revolution, Forthcoming in Law as Data: Computation and the Future of Legal Analysis*, SFI Press, 2018, p. 2, available at SSRN: https://ssrn.com/abstract=3156795.

most effectively capture, store, index, retrieve and merge these data, how multiple learning subtasks can be orchestrated in a larger system, and questions of computational tractability".[48]

In recent years, the field of ML has achieved the capability to build applications that retrieve their power from data, examples and experiences, which allows the systems to be trained on a large pool of examples.[49] ML algorithm efficiency highly relies on the goodness of the representation of the input data—bad data representation often leads to low performance[50]—and on the performance of the learning algorithms (it is important to select the learning algorithm that better suits the target application).[51] In fact, ML involves algorithms that are able to produce outcomes (also called predictions, responses or dependent variables, and commonly identified with *Y*) according to patterns found in data. Variables that help predict, guess or model outcomes are commonly called "predictors" or "input variables", which are ideally expected to be "independent variables" and are usually identified with the letter *X*. We can say that ML delegates the statistical learning process to the algorithms that aims to generate the best descriptions, models or predictions possible through a provided data set.[52]

The ML goal is to build new or leverage existing algorithms to learn from data, and to build models that can give accurate predictions, or to find patterns, especially with new and unseen data.[53] Therefore, the process of learning begins with observations of data, such as examples, direct experience, or instruction, to look for patterns in data and make decisions in the future based on examples that have been provided.[54] Thus, it can be said that ML implements data mining, pattern recognition and natural language processing by using self-learning algorithms that are

48 Mitchell, T. M., *The Discipline of ML, CMU-ML-06-108*, School of Computer Science Carnegie Mellon University, July 2006, p. 1 and 5, that can be found http://www.cs.cmu.edu/~tom/pubs/MachineLearning.pdf.

49 Herrera, F., et al., Advances in AI, *18th Conference of the Spanish Association for AI, CAEPIA 2018 Granada, Spain, October 23–26, 2018 Proceedings*, Springer, 2018, p. 24.

50 Pouyanfar, S., et al., A Survey on Deep Learning: Algorithms, Techniques, and Applications, *ACM Computing Surveys*, Vol. 51(5), 2018, p. 2.

51 Sarker, I. H., ML: Algorithms, Real-World Applications and Research Directions, *SN Computer Science*, Vol. 2, 2021, p. 2.

52 Copus, R., et al., *Credible Prediction: Big Data, ML and the Credibility Revolution, Forthcoming in Law as Data: Computation and the Future of Legal Analysis*, SFI Press, 2018, p. 4, available at SSRN: https://ssrn.com/abstract=3156795 and Alikhademi, K., et al., *A Review of Predictive Policing from the Perspective of Fairness*, Springer, 2021, p. 2.

53 Sagwan, S., The Discipline of ML, *Medium, Blog*, 24 October 2017 that can be found https://medium.com/@shashis890/the-discipline-of-machine-learning-8d09e6b5b966 (accessed 20 November 2022) and Copus, R., et al., *Credible Prediction: Big Data, ML and the Credibility Revolution, Forthcoming in Law as Data: Computation and the Future of Legal Analysis*, SFI Press, 2018, p. 13, available at SSRN: https://ssrn.com/abstract=3156795.

54 Copus, R., et al., *Credible Prediction: Big Data, ML and the Credibility Revolution, Forthcoming in Law as Data: Computation and the Future of Legal Analysis*, SFI Press, 2018, p. 2, available at SSRN: https://ssrn.com/abstract=3156795.

devised to mimic the way the human brain works.[55] Some examples include: a self-driving car "learns" initially from human drivers and then it reinforces its learning itself by using a test environment, a set of given constraints and a mechanism to award or penalize its performance; "smart" finance prescription works being fed with historical patterns from which it establishes a model and detects a forecast outcome based on the samples.[56]

AI systems are more and more using ML, where machines, through the use of patterns and interfaces, rather than through human instructions, are able to learn either by using many examples provided by the researchers or according to trial-and-error mechanisms starting from an initial set of rules.[57] ML can be used to detect anomalies in certain processes or frauds; it can be the basis to develop self-driving cars and trucks or in the law environment it can be used to identify terrorists or the propensity to commit a crime.[58]

4 Fundamental aims of ML: description/interpretation, prediction, prescription

As we previously saw, currently our society is flooded with data and that needs to be analysed to identify both its meaning and its use once an outcome of the analysis is available. In this respect, it is fundamental to have a strong analytic environment that allows an understanding and classification of the data, according to needs.

To a large extent, the predictive analysis is a process that encompasses different stages: (i) definition of the problem; (ii) identification of the best data source to tackle and solve the problem (i.e., data selection); (iii) identification of the best algorithm to solve the problem and produce the expected result; (iv) training of the subsets of data (learning phase), where the system, according to the data, will seek out for patterns, correlations and trends; (v) final results analysed by data scientists until they are satisfied with the performance; and (vi) deployment of the models in real time.[59] Thus, the ML process can be summarized in

55 Marr, B., What Everyone Should Know About Cognitive Computing, *FORBES*, 23 March 2016, available at https://www.forbes.com/sites/bernardmarr/2016/03/23/what-everyone-should-know-about-cognitive-computing/?sh=a928df950884 (accessed 20 October 2022).

56 Kolanovic, M., and Krishnamachari, R. T., *Big Data and AI Strategies ML and Alternative Data Approach to Investing*, J.P. Morgan, 2017, p. 11 and Sarker, I. H., ML: Algorithms, Real-World Applications and Research Directions, *SN Computer Science*, Vol. 2, 2021, p. 5.

57 OECD, *AI in Society*, 2019, pp. 27–28, and Copus, R., et al., *Credible Prediction: Big Data, ML and the Credibility Revolution, Forthcoming in Law as Data: Computation and the Future of Legal Analysis*, SFI Press, 2018, p. 2, available at SSRN: https://ssrn.com/abstract=3156795.

58 Hurley, R., *Data: A Guide to Big Data Trends, AI, ML, Predictive Analytics, Internet of Things, Data Science, Data Analytics, Business Intelligence, and Data Mining*, Ationa Publications, 2019, pp. 58–60 and Identifying Critical Contextual Design Cues Through a Machine Learning Approach, *AI Magazine*, Vol. 40(4), 2019, pp. 28–39.

59 Hurley, R., *Data: A Guide to Big Data Trends, AI, ML, Predictive Analytics, Internet of Things, Data Science, Data Analytics, Business Intelligence, and Data Mining*, Ationa Publications, 2019, pp. 33–34.

three main phases: (i) training, where parameters of a machine learning model are estimated, approximated and optimized using a labelled data set, the domain characteristics and the class characteristics; (ii) validation (that includes also cross-validation and early stopping), where an algorithm validates the effectiveness of the model using another data set not used in the training phase; and (iii) testing, that provides an algorithm to test if the trained and cross-validated model works using another data set, which was not used in the training or validation phases.[60]

All these steps could be included likewise in the three main categories: descriptive analytic, predictive analytic and prescriptive analytic.

Therefore, a possible classification of data analysis based on analysis purposes is (i) descriptive analytic, which uses data aggregation and data mining to provide a view of the past and answers the question "what has happened" (with the aim to know the data underlying the schemes); (ii) predictive analytic, which aims to understand the future using statistical models and forecasting techniques and provide an answer to the question "what could happened" (with the aim to carry out prognoses based on the knowledge accumulated in the past); and (iii) prescriptive analytic, through which the use of algorithms advise on possible outcomes, answering the question "what should we do" (it could be defined as a subpart of predictive applications in which the scope is to make the best decision based on the knowledge accumulated in the past).[61]

The first form of analytics (descriptive) is generally used to retrieve historical data and then collect, organize and present the data in an intelligible way. Being the fact that this form of analytics is based only on data from the past, it is not used to create predictions or inferences, and its scope is more related to creating a basis (i.e., a ready set of data) to perform further analysis. Its functioning is based on two methods: (i) data aggregation, which allows collecting and organizing the data, and (ii) data mining (DM), which is a process of discovering patterns in large data sets involving methods at the intersection of ML, statistics and database systems. DM has an overall goal to extract information (through the application of intelligent methods) from a data set and transform such information into a comprehensible structure for further use.[62]

60 Suthaharan, S., *ML Models and Algorithms for Big Data Classification—Thinking with Examples for Effective Learning*, Integrated Series in Information Systems 36, Series Editors: Ramesh Sharda · Stefan Voß, Springer, 2016, p. 21.

61 Logility, Descriptive, Predictive and Prescriptive Analytics Explained, *Blog*, 13 March 2020, available at https://www.logility.com/de/blog/descriptive-predictive-and-prescriptive-analytics-explained/ (accessed 10 October 2022) and Datapred, Prediction and Prescription—Continuous Intelligence Twins (Part 1/2), *Blog*, 23 September 2019, available at https://www.datapred.com/blog/prediction-and-prescription-continuous-intelligence-twins-part-1 (accessed 22 March 2022).

62 UNSW, Descriptive, Predictive & Prescriptive Analytics: What Are the Differences?, *Blog*, 29 January 2020, available at https://studyonline.unsw.edu.au/blog/descriptive-predictive-prescriptive-analytics#:~:text=If%20descriptive%20analytics%20tells%20you,you%20what%20should%20be%20done%20((accessed 22 March 2022).

The second form of analytics (predictive) could be defined as the next phase—that is, when the data set is ready, predict future trends according to the data patterns and trends from the past. The base of such analysis is the probabilities to attempt to forecast possible outcomes in the future. The activity is performed through different techniques, that is, DM, statistical modeling and ML algorithms (such as classification, regression and clustering).[63] The basis of predictive analytics is "capturing and exploiting relationships between explanatory variables and predicted variables from previous events to predict the unknown outcome".[64] Supervised classification, understood as "guessing" a class/type based on a set of characteristic features or a data sample, can be interpreted as equivalent or included in "predictive" analysis.

The last form of analytics (prescriptive) is the last stage and, as already shown, has the aim to guide in the next steps to be undertaken. Starting from what has been learned in the descriptive and predictive analysis, prescriptive analytics recommend and address on the best courses and actions to be followed in the future.[65]

5 Types of machine learning

As stated in the previous section, ML is a system used to identify patterns among a large amount of data. However, before using the developed system in reality, it needs to be properly configured and adjusted. Based on how the system uses historical or past data to tune its responses and models, ML methods can be classified in the following groups:

- Supervised learning. This consists of inferring a classification or regression from labelled training data.
- Unsupervised learning. This approach does not use labels and performs its outputs by only using the intrinsic geometrical and topological properties of data spaces.
- Semi-supervised learning. In this case, both labelled and unlabelled[66] data are combined. This learning paradigm is a combination of supervised and unsupervised learning.

63 UNSW, Descriptive, Predictive & Prescriptive Analytics: What Are the Differences?, 29 January 2020, available at https://studyonline.unsw.edu.au/blog/descriptive-predictive-prescriptive-analytics#:~:text=If%20descriptive%20analytics%20tells%20you,you%20what%20should%20be%20done%20 (accessed 24 April 2022).

64 Sarker, I. H., ML: Algorithms, Real-World Applications and Research Directions, *SN Computer Science*, Vol. 2, 2021, p. 15.

65 UNSW, Descriptive, Predictive & Prescriptive Analytics: What Are the Differences?, 29 January 2020, available at https://studyonline.unsw.edu.au/blog/descriptive-predictive-prescriptive-analytics#:~:text=If%20descriptive%20analytics%20tells%20you,you%20what%20should%20be%20done%20 (accessed 22 March 2022).

66 Baeldung, What Is the Difference Between Labeled and Unlabeled Data?, *Blog*, 5 May 2023, available at https://www.baeldung.com/cs/ml-labeled-vs-unlabeled-data (accessed 23 May 2023).

- Reinforcement learning. Here, combining and confronted algorithms take sequences of actions in an environment to maximize cumulative rewards.[67]

In the following paragraphs each technique will be briefly discussed with a general perspective of the possible real-world application.

5.1 Supervised learning: classification and regression

Supervised learning is the ML task of learning a function or model that maps an input to an output based on example input–output behaviours.[68] In other words, the system imitates the human ability to extract patterns from known examples and uses the insight to create a repeatable outcome (trying to find a rule which can be used to predict a variable).[69] In supervised learning, given an input variable (or predictors or independent variable) (X) and an output (dependent) variable (Y), using an algorithm it is possible to learn the mapping function from the input to the output Y = f(X). It infers a function from labelled training data consisting of a set of training examples.[70] A supervised learning model is composed of a training data set to derive the model, and a testing data set to validate the model predictability.[71]

In supervised learning each example is a pair consisting of an input object (typically a vector) and a desired output historical value, from which, after collecting a high enough number of training examples, an algorithm infers a model (a relationship that has the best predictive power for out-of-sample data) that can be used for mapping new examples.[72] The key point of supervised learning is that the system learns (i.e., generalizes) from already solved examples (i.e., the system is provided with labelled data, that is data whose outcome is already known).[73]

The most common supervised learning tasks are classification and regression: (i) classification is a process of finding a function that helps in dividing the data

67 Lavet, F. V., et al., An Introduction to Deep Reinforcement Learning, *Foundations and Trends in ML*, Vol. 11(3–4), 2018, p. 6 and Mohssen, M., et al., *ML: Algorithms and Applications*, CRC Press, 2017, p. 7.

68 European Commission, *A Definition of AI: Main Capabilities and Scientific Disciplines*, Definition Developed for the Purpose of the Deliverables of the High-Level Expert Group on AI, 2018, p. 4.

69 Theobald, O., *ML for Absolute Beginners: A Plain English Introduction* (Third Edition), Independently Published, 2021, p. 18.

70 Copus, R., et al., *Credible Prediction: Big Data, ML and the Credibility Revolution, Forthcoming in Law as Data: Computation and the Future of Legal Analysis*, SFI Press, 2018, p. 5, available at SSRN: https://ssrn.com/abstract=3156795.

71 Harfoush, F. A., *From Big Data to Intelligent Data—An Applied Perspective*, Springer Cham, 2021, p. 65.

72 Kolanovic, M., and Krishnamachari, R. T., *Big Data and AI Strategies ML and Alternative Data Approach to Investing*, J.P. Morgan, 2017, p. 18.

73 Suthaharan, S., *ML Models and Algorithms for Big Data Classification—Thinking with Examples for Effective Learning*, Integrated Series in Information Systems 36, Series Editors: Ramesh Sharda · Stefan Voß, Springer, 2016, p. 8, where a definition of supervised learning is provided as "In supervised learning, the classes are known and class boundaries are well defined in the given training) data set, and the learning is done using these classes (i.e., class labels)".

set into classes based on different parameters (a data set is trained to be able to categorize data in different classes), while (ii) regression is the process of finding the correlation between dependent and independent variables (e.g., weather prediction).[74] The main difference between supervised classification and regression is that classification tries to figure out the category (label) that corresponds to a given set of feature values, whereas regression tries to discover a numerical value. In the case of regression, the set of feature values commonly corresponds to input random variables that form a function together. The most important algorithms used to solve such problems are described in Section 7.

5.1.1 Classification

As mentioned earlier, classification links input data to one or more classes that represent a category, a class, or an event; in other words, it refers to a predictive modeling problem where a class label is predicted for a given example of input data (there is a data separation).[75]

With classification, the scope is to allocate data in bins, as the problem identifying which set of categories (sub-populations) a new observation belongs to, based on a training set of data containing observations (or instances) whose category membership is known.[76] Usually, classification is used to identify features from unstructured data, such as, for example, assigning a given email to the "spam" or "non-spam" class or assigning a diagnosis to a given patient based on observed characteristics of the patient himself (sex, blood pressure, presence or absence of certain symptoms, etc.).[77]

74 The main difference between classification and regression is that the regression algorithms are used to predict continuous values such as price, salary, age, and so on, while classification is used to predict/classify the discrete values such as male and female, true or false, and so on. See Point, J. T., Support Vector Machine Algorithm, *Blog*, available at https://www.javatpoint.com/regression-vs-classification-in-machine-learning (accessed 6 June 2022) and Han, J., et al., *Data Mining: Concepts and Techniques* (Third Edition), Elsevier, 2011, par. 1.4.3.

75 Quintarelli, S., et al., Intelligenza artificiale—cos'è davvero, come funziona, che effetti avrà, A cura di Claudia Giulia Ferrauto, *Bollati Boringhieri*, 2020, p. 39 and Suthaharan, S., *ML Models and Algorithms for Big Data Classification—Thinking with Examples for Effective Learning*, Integrated Series in Information Systems 36, Series Editors: Ramesh Sharda · Stefan Voß, Springer, 2016, p. 8.

76 McKinsey Global Institute, *Notes from the AI Frontier Insights from Hundreds of Use Cases*, 2018, p. 5, available at https://www.mckinsey.com/west-coast/~/media/McKinsey/Featured%20Insights/Artificial%20Intelligence/Notes%20from%20the%20AI%20frontier%20Applications%20and%20value%20of%20deep%20learning/Notes-from-the-AI-frontier-Insights-from-hundreds-of-use-cases-Discussion-paper.pdf.

77 Sarker, I. H., ML: Algorithms, Real-World Applications and Research Directions, *SN Computer Science*, Vol. 2, 2021, p. 3. The author identify among: (i) binary classification, that refers to the classification tasks having two class labels such as "true and false" or "yes and no", (ii) multiclass classification, that are those classification tasks having more than two labels and examples are classified belonging to one class, and (iii) multi-label classification, where an example is associated with several classes or labels, for example in cases where classes involved in the problem are hierarchically structured and each example may simultaneously belong to more than one class in each hierarchical level.

5.1.2 Regression

In statistical modeling, regression analysis is a set of statistical processes for estimating the relationships between a dependent variable or "outcome variable" and one or more independent variables, "predictors" or "features". The most common form of regression analysis is linear regression (or in case of more than one independent variable, the multiple linear regression) in which a researcher finds the line (or a more complex linear combination) that most closely fits the data according to a specific mathematical criterion, or, in other words, this technique predicts an unknown variable using results that are known (the output is related to several input variables).[78] We can identify regression as a sort of adjustment in order that given certain inputs data, the outcome will be the one desired (i.e., the machine learns the parameters involved in the relationship between input/output data).[79] An example here would be to determine how changes in certain assumptions or drivers of business will impact revenues or expenses in the future (i.e., there may be a very high correlation between the number of salespeople employed by a company, the number of stores they operate, and the revenue the business generates).[80]

Regression analysis is primarily used for two conceptually distinct purposes. First, regression analysis is widely used for prediction and forecasting. Second, in some situations, regression analysis can be used to infer causal relationships between independent and dependent variables. Importantly, regression by itself only reveals relationships between a dependent variable and a collection of independent variables in a fixed data set. To use regression for prediction or to infer causal relationships, respectively, a researcher must carefully justify why existing relationships have predictive power for a new context or why a relationship between two variables has a causal interpretation. The latter is especially important when researchers hope to estimate causal relationships using observational data.

78 Theobald, O., *ML for Absolute Beginners: A Plain English Introduction* (Third Edition), Independently Published, 2021, p. 52. Linear regression can be described according to the following example: let's take a sitcom as the basis data with the following variables where season number as the x coordinate and the number of viewers per season as the y coordinate. From the data set it is seen that there is an upward trend in viewers starting at season 4 with a peak at season 9. From this point we set the dependent variable as the number of viewers per season (what should be predict) and the season number as the independent variable. Inserting a line (call hyperplane) in the graphic where the points express in the abscissa and ordinate are represented it is possible to determine the aggregate distance of each point that equates to the smallest possible distance to the hyperplane. This could help in predict how many viewers there will be in the tenth seasons.

79 Imagine that, according to court decisions, there is the interest to understand if there is a correlation with the reverse of court decisions when the members of a panel are with majority of a right or left party. Regression is then used to identify which role the party element plays in the decision given an initial function that was originally set only to detect the result of court decisions. See, Copus, R., et al., *Credible Prediction: Big Data, ML and the Credibility Revolution, Forthcoming in Law as Data: Computation and the Future of Legal Analysis*, SFI Press, 2018, pp. 6–7, available at SSRN: https://ssrn.com/abstract=3156795.

80 Taylor, S., Regression Analysis, Corporate Finance Institute, *Blog*, 2 May 2023, available at https://corporatefinanceinstitute.com/resources/data-science/regression-analysis/ (accessed 22 May 2023).

5.2 Unsupervised learning: clustering and anomaly detection

Unsupervised learning looks for previously undetected patterns in a data set with no pre-existing labels and with a minimum of human supervision and it is generally used for grouping the data.[81] In contrast to supervised learning, which usually makes use of human-labelled data, unsupervised learning allows for modeling of probability densities over inputs enabling the discovery of unknown patterns in the data and granting further analysis once new groups are identified (as the machine does not know which are the independent and dependent variables).[82]

The main difference between supervised and unsupervised learning is that unsupervised learning is not guided by external features that contain labels (classification) or expected values (regression) for the training data. It only accounts for the intrinsic internal characteristics of the data itself. Indeed, data samples are grouped based on their similarity, in a way that similar data is considered part of the same group and inserted in the same cluster.[83] It should be noted, however, that being that the output is unknown, a strict validation of the model is not possible, and the results are more subjective and ambiguous than in supervised learning.

5.2.1 Clustering

Cluster analysis, or clustering, is the task of grouping a set of objects in such a way that objects in the same group (a cluster) are more similar (in some sense) to each other than to those in other groups (other clusters).[84] Indeed, data is divided/stored in clusters based on the fact that it shares certain characteristics, and in this sense the data clustering facilitates the finding of similarities among data.[85]

Clustering is a main task of exploratory data mining, and a common technique for statistical data analysis, used in many fields, including pattern recognition, image analysis, information retrieval, bioinformatics, data compression, computer graphics and ML.[86] Cluster analysis itself is not one specific algorithm, but the

81 Pretz, K., Stop Calling Everything AI, Machine-Learning Pioneer Says, *IEEE Spectrum*, 31 March 2021, available at https://spectrum.ieee.org/stop-calling-everything-ai-machinelearning-pioneer-says.

82 Theobald, O., *ML for Absolute Beginners: A Plain English Introduction* (Third Edition), Independently Published, 2021, p. 20 and Kolanovic, M., and Krishnamachari, R. T., *Big Data and AI Strategies ML and Alternative Data Approach to Investing*, J.P. Morgan, 2017, p. 18.

83 Quintarelli, S., et al., *Intelligenza artificiale—cos'è davvero, come funziona, che effetti avrà, A cura di Claudia Giulia Ferrauto*, Bollati Boringhieri, 2020, p. 39 and Suthaharan, S., *ML Models and Algorithms for Big Data Classification—Thinking with Examples for Effective Learning*, Integrated Series in Information Systems 36, Series Editors: Ramesh Sharda · Stefan Voß, Springer, 2016, p. 8.

84 Han, J., et al., *Data Mining: Concepts and Techniques* (Third Edition), Elsevier, 2011, chapter. 10.

85 Hurley, R., *Data: A Guide to Big Data Trends, AI, ML, Predictive Analytics, Internet of Things, Data Science, Data Analytics, Business Intelligence, and Data Mining*, Ationa Publications, 2019, p. 50 and Suthaharan, S., *ML Models and Algorithms for Big Data Classification—Thinking with Examples for Effective Learning*, Integrated Series in Information Systems 36, Series Editors: Ramesh Sharda · Stefan Voß, Springer, 2016, p. 9.

86 Iglesias Vazquez, F., et, al, Clustering Refinement, *International Journal of Data Science and Analytics*, Vol. 12(4), 2021, pp. 333–353.

general task to be solved. It can be achieved by various algorithms that differ significantly in their understanding of what constitutes a cluster and how to efficiently find them. The appropriate clustering algorithm and parameter settings (including parameters such as the distance function to use, a density threshold or the number of expected clusters) depend on the individual data set and intended use of the results. However, cluster analysis as such is not an automatic task, but an iterative process of knowledge discovery or iterative multi-objective optimization that involves trial and failure. It is often necessary to modify data processing and model parameters until the result achieves the desired properties.

5.2.2 Anomaly/outlier detection

In data analysis, anomaly detection (also outlier detection) is the identification of rare items, events or observations which raise suspicions by differing significantly from most of the data.[87] Typically, the anomalous items will translate to some kind of problem, such as bank fraud, a structural defect, medical problems or errors in a text. Anomalies are also referred to as outliers, novelties, noise, deviations and exceptions.

In the context of abuse and network intrusion detection, the interesting objects are often not rare objects, but unexpected bursts in activity.[88] This pattern does adhere to the common statistical definition of an outlier as a rare object, and many outlier detection methods (unsupervised methods) will fail on such data, unless it has been aggregated appropriately. Instead, a cluster analysis algorithm may be able to detect the micro-clusters formed by the patterns.[89]

5.3 Semi-supervised learning

This is a technique that makes use of both labelled and unlabelled examples when learning a model where the labelled examples are used to learn class models and the unlabelled examples are used to refine boundaries between classes.[90] In fact, the target of this method, considering that labelled data is scarce while unlabelled data is present in large quantities, is to learn a model that predicts classes of future-tested data better than from the model generated by using the labelled data alone (e.g., initially a child is provided with unlabelled data from the environment and the labelled data could be seen as a parent teaching the child with names (labels) of objects by pointing them out and saying the names of a selection of representa-

87 Han, J., et al., *Data Mining: Concepts and Techniques* (Third Edition), Elsevier, 2011, par. 13.3.4.

88 Berge, E., Introducing Anomaly/Outlier Detection in Python with PyOD, *Blog*, 27 December 2021, available at https://towardsdatascience.com/introducing-anomaly-outlier-detection-in-python-with-pyod-40afcccee9ff (accessed 7 July 2022).

89 Iglesias Vazquez, F., et al., Outlier Detection Based on Low Density Models, in *Proceedings of the 18th IEEE International Conference on Data Mining Workshops, ICDMW Vol. 2018-November* (eds. J. Yu, Z. Li, H. Tong and F. Zhu), IEEE Press, 2018, pp. 970–979.

90 Han, J., et al., *Data Mining: Concepts and Techniques* (Third Edition), Elsevier, 2011, par. 1.5.2.

tive samples. Hence, the child must infer how to extend the labels to the rest of the samples by applying similarity or distance criteria).[91] Semi-supervised learning is commonly understood as a combination of supervised and unsupervised learning.

5.4 Reinforcement learning

The theory of reinforcement learning (RL) provides a normative account, deeply rooted in psychological and neuroscientific perspectives on animal behaviour; namely, how agents may optimize their control of an environment.[92] However, to use reinforcement learning successfully in situations approaching real-world complexity, agents are confronted with a difficult task: they must derive efficient representations of the environment from high-dimensional sensory inputs and use these to generalize past experience to new situations.[93]

Reinforcement learning is the problem faced by an agent that must learn behaviour through trial-and-error interactions with a dynamic environment to maximize the notion of cumulative reward (the agent receives virtual rewards or punishments).[94] Indeed, "the usual way to use reinforcement learning to solve a problem is to reward the agent according to its success in solving the problem".[95] The main idea is that an artificial agent may learn by interacting with its environment and using the experience gathered; the artificial agent should be able to

91 Mohssen, et al., *ML: Algorithms and Applications*, CRC Press, 2017, p. 11.

92 An intelligent agent is an entity that collects information about its environment from sensors and then processes that information to decide how to respond to its environment. See Tegmark, M., *Life 3.0 Being Human in the Age of AI*, New York: Alfred A. Knopf, 2017, p. 84.

93 Mnih, V., et al., Human-Level Control Through Deep Reinforcement Learning, *Nature International Journal of Science*, Vol. 518, 2015, p. 529 and Gronauer, S., and Diepold, K., Multi-Agent Deep Reinforcement Learning: A Survey, *AI Review*, Vol. 55(6), 2022, pp. 1–49 where the authors pointed out the importance not only to use the single-agent systems but also the utility of the multi-agent systems. Indeed, when using these systems "Each agent seeks to accomplish an assigned goal for which a broad set of skills might be required to build intelligent behavior. Depending on the task, an intricate interplay between agents can occur such that agents start to collaborate or act competitively to excel opponents".

94 Pack Kaelbling, L., et al., Reinforcement Learning: A Survey, *Journal of AI Research*, Vol. 4, 1996, p. 237 and McKinsey Global Institute, *Notes from the AI Frontier Insights from Hundreds of Use Cases*, 2018, p. 4, available at https://www.mckinsey.com/west-coast/~/media/McKinsey/Featured%20Insights/Artificial%20Intelligence/Notes%20from%20the%20AI%20frontier%20Applications%20and%20value%20of%20deep%20learning/Notes-from-the-AI-frontier-Insights-from-hundreds-of-use-cases-Discussion-paper.pdf and Taylor, M. E., and Stone, P., An Introduction to Intertask Transfer for Reinforcement Learning, *AI Magazine*, Vol. 32(1), 2011, pp. 15–34, and Toro Icarte, R., et al., Reward Machines: Exploiting Reward Function Structure in Reinforcement Learning, *Journal of AI Research*, Vol. 73, 2022, pp. 173–208.

95 Sutton, R. S., and Barto, A. G., *Reinforcement Learning: An Introduction* (Second Edition), Cambridge, MA and London: The MIT Press, 2017, p. 386 and Edelkamp, S., and Lomuscio, A., Model Checking and AI—4th Workshop, *MoChArt IV Riva del Garda*, Italy, 29 August 2006 Revised Selected and Invited Papers, Lecture Notes in AI, Edited by J. G. Carbonell and J. Siekmann, Subseries of Lecture Notes in Computer Science, Springer, p. 86.

optimize some objectives given in the form of cumulative rewards.[96] Therefore, its focus is finding a balance between exploration (of uncharted territory) and exploitation (of current knowledge).

To understand it better, analogously to a video game player that improves her knowledge of the field of play every time she reaches a new step/level (i.e., through learning and experience the player's behaviours are influenced during the game), reinforcement learning algorithms are set to train the model based on continuous learning, according to measurable performance criteria where outputs are graded.[97]

Usually, four elements are contained in an RL algorithm:

1. A model of the environment mimics the behaviour of the environment, or more generally, that allows inferences to be made about how the environment will behave (agent-environment relationship).
2. A policy defines the learning agent's way of behaving at a given time (way on how the agent decides).
3. A reward signal, that is, the RL problem goal. On each time step, the environment sends to the reinforcement learning agent a single number called the reward. The agent's sole objective is to maximize the total reward it receives over the long run. The reward signal thus defines what the good and bad events are for the agent. In a biological system, we might think of rewards as analogous to the experiences of pleasure or pain.
4. A value function specifies what is good in the long run. The value of a state is the total amount of reward an agent can expect to accumulate over the future, starting from that state.[98]

The steps of the RL activity can be summarized as follows: (i) start of the learning with an agent that takes an initial action selected from the first state in the environment and the environment returns a reward and the next state to the agent; (ii) the agent's decision is defined through the policy that describe how it makes decisions or chooses actions within a state or, in other words, it allows the agent to advance through the environment to maximize the reward; (iii) the reward of the agent is designed by a designer (the designer judges the agent's performance by criteria that he or she is attempting to translate into reward signals so that the agent's goal matches his or her own).

96 Lavet, F. V., et al., An Introduction to Deep Reinforcement Learning, *Foundations and Trends in ML*, Vol. 11(3–4), 2018, p. 2. See also Barto, A. G., Reinforcement Learning: Connections, Surprises, Challenges, *AI Magazine*, Vol. 40(1), 2019, pp. 3–15.

97 Theobald, O., *ML for Absolute Beginners: A Plain English Introduction* (Third Edition), Independently Published, 2021, p. 24.

98 Sutton, R. S., and Barto, A. G., *Reinforcement Learning: An Introduction* (Second Edition), Cambridge, MA and London: The MIT Press, 2017, p. 5 and Barto, A. G., and Fragkiadaki, K., *Deep Q Learning*, Carnegie Mellon University, 2018, available at https://www.cs.cmu.edu/~katef/DeepRLFall2018/lecture_DQL_katef2018.pdf.

The use of this system is generally made in recommendation systems (i.e., when consumers are suggested by system what to buy) or in marketing[99] or in the law field (e.g., to predict citations in a document from its semantic content and to predict the search results generated by human users[100]).

6 Common application of AI

AI systems have many fields of application and areas of development such as large-scale ML, deep learning, reinforcement learning, robotics, computer vision and natural language.[101] Based on this first identification of AI applications, in the following section more insight will be provided on the potential use of AI and its techniques.

6.1 Modeling, pattern and image detection

To perform data analytics, it is necessary to create analytic models that allow finally retrieving information from the huge amount of data currently available. AI modeling is

> a tool or algorithm which is based on a certain data set through which it can arrive at a decision—all without the need for human interference in the decision-making process. An AI model is a program or algorithm that utilizes a set of data that enables it to recognize certain patterns. This allows it to reach a conclusion or make a prediction when provided with sufficient information, often a huge amount of data.[102]

The term "modeling" should be understood as a mathematical and statistical data modeling aiming at developing a parametrized mapping between the data domain

99 European Commission, A Definition of AI: Main Capabilities and Scientific Disciplines, Definition developed for the purpose of the deliverables of the High-Level Expert Group on AI, 2018, p. 5, Alpaydin, E., *Lecture Slides for—Introduction to ML* (Third Edition), available at https://www.cmpe.boun.edu.tr/~ethem/i2ml3e/3e_v1-0/i2ml3e-chap18.pdf and Sutton, R. S., and Barto, A. G., *Reinforcement Learning: An Introduction* (Second Edition), Cambridge, MA and London: The MIT Press, 2018, p. 37

100 Susskind, R., *Tomorrow's Lawyers—An Introduction to Your Future* (Second Edition), Corby Northants: Oxford University Press, 2017, p. 11, Dadgostari, F., et al. Modeling Law Search as Prediction, *AI and Law*, Vol. 29, 2021, pp. 3–34, and Delgado Guevara, B., and Leiva García, Y., El conocimiento jurídico. Una propuesta tecnológica para su gestión, *Revista Internacional de Gestión del Conocimiento y la Tecnología*, Vol. 1(1), 2013, pp. 1–12.

101 Stanford University, One Hundred Year Study on AI (AI100), *AI and Life in 2030*, 2016 Report, p. 9, available at https://ai100.stanford.edu/sites/g/files/sbiybj18871/files/media/file/ai100report10032016fnl_singles.pdf and Kreutzer, R. T., and Sirrenberg, M., *Understanding AI—Fundamentals, Use Cases and Methods for a Corporate AI Journey*, Springer, 2020, p. 23.

102 Klingler, N., The Ultimate Guide to Understanding and Using AI Models (2023), *viso.ai, Blog*, available at https://viso.ai/deep-learning/ml-ai-models/, (accessed 24 June 2023).

and the response set, where the mapping learns the characteristics of a system from the input data.[103]

The model creation gives rise to the possibility, using the algorithms (a model creation could be based on one or more algorithms), to recognize patterns and regularities in data as texts, images, sounds or any other definable qualities (e.g., the capability of a system to classify emails as "spam" or "not spam"). Pattern recognition could be performed, (i) in case of supervised learning, through data classification based on statistical information or knowledge gained from samples and their representation, that is, the system learns independently from a completely predefined data set to recognize the relevant explanatory patterns, or (ii) in case of unsupervised learning, where no target values are predefined, the AI system must recognize similarities and thus patterns in the data independently, hence the algorithm is in charge of recognizing them independently.[104]

The set-up of a model for pattern finding plays an interesting role in the image detection activity, as the image classification is deemed as a classical problem of image processing, computer vision and ML fields where the former came into existence for decreasing the gap between the computer vision and human vision through the training of a computer with data.[105] Indeed, computers can be used to handle images in two different ways: (i) image analysis to obtain quantitative data or (ii) image understanding.[106] Image recognition (also called tagging) commonly corresponds to processing images or videos and classifying the results of training an algorithm with hundreds of thousands of images that show different objects and are provided with corresponding labels. This can be performed either directly over images or videos, or on vectorized data sets that represent their characteristics.[107]

6.2 Detection of failures and frauds

Failure and fraud detection is an area where the use of AI has developed and can be used in different situations. Indeed, it can be used to look for characteristics of tax returns, loan applications and card payments and indicate identity theft or any

103 Suthaharan, S., *ML Models and Algorithms for Big Data Classification—Thinking with Examples for Effective Learning*, Integrated Series in Information Systems 36, Series Editors: Ramesh Sharda · Stefan Voß, Springer, 2016, p. 7 and Klügl, F., and Bazzan, A. L. C., Agent-Based Modeling and Simulation, *AI Magazine*, Vol. 33(3), 2012, p. 30 where the authors define the modeling as "Modeling Is the Development of a Model as a Representative of a System".

104 Kreutzer, R. T., and Sirrenberg, M., *Understanding AI—Fundamentals, Use Cases and Methods for a Corporate AI Journey*, Springer, 2020, p. 7.

105 Krishna, M. M., et al., Image Classification Using Deep learning, *International Journal of Engineering & Technology*, Vol. 7(2.7), 2018, pp. 614–617.

106 Bengtsson, E., Image Processing and Its Hardware Support Analysis vs Synthesis—Historical Trends, in *Image Analysis. SCIA 2017. Lecture Notes in Computer Science* (eds. P. Sharma and F. Bianchi), vol. 10269, Cham: Springer, available at https://link.springer.com/chapter/10.1007/978-3-319-59126-1_1.

107 Kreutzer, R. T., and Sirrenberg, M., *Understanding AI—Fundamentals, Use Cases and Methods for a Corporate AI Journey*, Springer, 2020, p. 31.

other type of fraudulent activity.[108] In general, expert systems, decision tree–based models, neural networks, Bayesian networks, evolutionary algorithms, Markov models, support vector machines and density and/or distance-based models are all AI solutions that can be used to detect fraud.[109]

Fraud detection is generally viewed as a data mining classification problem, where the objective is to correctly classify the credit card transactions as legitimate or fraudulent.[110] Card frauds have increased very quickly, amounting to 1.87 billion euro in 2019.[111] A credit fraud materializes when a payment has been recognized as unauthorized, in which case the transaction needs to be reviewed. Such non-genuine transactions are identified through is a sequence of events or arrangement of transactions that criminals follow for a particular fraud vector, and through automated methods it is possible to recognize these common elements and discriminate the transactions.[112]

In the tax field, the implementation of supervised ML is of great importance. Tax administrations can aggregate huge amounts of data because of tax submissions by taxpayers, and once this data is available and labelled, auditing departments can use it to identify and focus on fraudulent submissions instead of relying on human experience only.[113]

6.3 Natural language processing (NLP)

Will a computer program ever be able to convert a piece of English text into a data structure that unambiguously and completely describes the meaning of the natural language text?[114] Natural language processing (NLP) is a sub-field of com-

108 Hurley, R., *Data: A Guide to Big Data Trends, AI, ML, Predictive Analytics, Internet of Things, Data Science, Data Analytics, Business Intelligence, and Data Mining*, Ationa Publications, 2019, p. 36.

109 Ryman-Tubb, N., and Krause, P. J., How AI and ML Research Impacts Payment Card Fraud Detection: A Survey and Industry Benchmark, *Engineering Applications of AI*, Vol. 76, 2018, p. 135. See also Ramaki, A. A., et al., Credit Card Fraud Detection Based on Ontology Graph, *International Journal of Security, Privacy and Trust Management (IJSPTM)*, Vol. 1(5), 2012, p. 1–12, available at https://idc-online.com/technical_references/pdfs/data_communications/CREDIT%20CARD.pdf.

110 Bhatia, S., et al., Analysis of Credit Card Fraud Detection Techniques, *International Journal of Science and Research (IJSR)*, Vol. 5(3). 2016, p. 1302.

111 European Central Bank, *Seventh Report on Card Fraud*, 2019, p. 2, available at https://www.ecb.europa.eu/press/cardfraud/html/ecb.cardfraudreport202110~cac4c418e8.en.html.

112 Ryman-Tubb, N., and Krause, P. J., How AI and ML Research Impacts Payment Card Fraud Detection: A Survey and Industry Benchmark, *Engineering Applications of AI*, Vol. 76, 2018, pp. 132–133.

113 Adamov, A., ML and Advanced Analytics in Tax Fraud Detection, *2019 IEEE 13th International Conference on Application of Information and Communication Technologies (AICT)*, 2019, p. 4, available at file:///C:/Users/Gallo/Downloads/MachineLearningandAdvancedAnalyticsinTaxFraudDetection.pdf.

114 Collobert, R., et al. Natural Language Processing (Almost) from Scratch, *The Journal of ML Research*, Vol. 122(1), 2011, p. 2493.

puter linguistics, computer science and AI that is concerned with the interactions between computers and human language, in particular how to program computers to process and analyse large amounts of natural language data. (In other words, computers operate on the foundation of if/then logic statements, whereas natural human language systems do not; NLP endeavours to bridge this by enabling a computer to analyse what a user said (input speech recognition) and process what the user meant.)[115] In a few words, NLP is a series of algorithms and techniques that mainly focus on teaching computers to understand the human language.[116]

According to this definition, through NLP a computer is capable of "understanding" the contents of documents, including the contextual nuances of the language within them. Therefore, the technology can accurately extract information and insights contained in the documents as well as categorize and organize the documents themselves, and there is considerable commercial interest in the field because of its application to automated reasoning, machine translation, question answering, newsgathering, text categorization, voice-activation, archiving and large-scale content analysis.[117]

The great improvement in this technique, the fact that its development needs a huge amount of data (i.e., the more an NLP system knows about a user's individual manner of speech, frequently used words, habits, social connections, physiological state and other information, the better it can process the user's natural language utterances), can create problems in relation to privacy and security.[118] Indeed, it is a fact that the so-called "personal digital assistants such as Apple's Siri, Amazon's Alexa, Google's Google Now and Microsoft's Cortana can be always on and listen constantly to the user's speech.[119] This continuous transfer of data is not based on the user's consent, and this unconscious transfer of private data can jeopardize the privacy of millions of users.[120]

115 Peng, L. L., Natural Language Processing, *Georgetown Law Technology Review*, Vol. 1(98), 2016, p. 98.

116 Pouyanfar, S., et al., A Survey on Deep Learning: Algorithms, Techniques, and Applications, *ACM Computing Surveys*, Vol. 51(5), 2018, p. 14.

117 Stanford University, *Gathering Strength, Gathering Storms: The One Hundred Year Study on AI (AI100)*, 2021 Study Panel Report, p. 13, available at https://ai100.stanford.edu/gathering-strength-gathering-storms-one-hundred-year-study-artificial-intelligence-ai100-2021-study. See also Bommarito, J. M., et al., *LexNLP: Natural Language Processing and Information Extraction for Legal and Regulatory Texts*, 2018, pp. 1–7, available at https://ssrn.com/abstract=3192101 or http://dx.doi.org/10.2139/ssrn.3192101 and Pujara, J., et al., Using Semantics and Statistics to Turn Data into Knowledge, *AI Magazine*, Vol. 36(1), 2015, pp. 65–74.

118 Peng, L. L., Natural Language Processing, *Georgetown Law Technology Review*, Vol. 1(98), 2016, p. 103.

119 Komando, K., 3 Gadgets That Are Always Listening and How to Stop Them, *USA Today*, 2015, available at https://eu.usatoday.com/story/tech/columnist/komando/2015/10/02/3-gadgets-always-listening-and-how-stop-them/73191644/ (accessed 15 July 2022).

120 Gray, S., *Always On: Privacy Implications of Microphone-Enabled Devices*, Future of Privacy Forum, 2016, pp. 3–10, available at https://fpf.org/blog/always-privacy-implications-microphone-enabled-devices/.

Natural-language understanding (NLU) or natural-language interpretation (NLI) is a subtopic of natural-language processing in AI that deals with machine reading comprehension.[121] Its main focus is to make machines (i) interpret the natural language, (ii) derive meaning, (iii) identify context and (iv) draw insights.[122]

Some authors pointed out that the choice of still using the word "processing" is very deliberate and should not be replaced with "understanding". Initially the NLP field was referred to as "natural language understanding" (NLU), but based on the development that has occurred so far, even if the goal of NLP is true NLU, that goal has not yet been accomplished. To obtain a full NLU system all of the following four elements should be present: (i) paraphrase an input text, (ii) translate the text into another language, (iii) answer questions about the contents of the text and (iv) draw inferences from the text. While NLP has made serious inroads into accomplishing the first three goals, the fact that NLP systems cannot, by themselves, draw inferences from text, keeps NLU as a far goal of NLP.[123]

6.3.1 Text categorization

Text categorization, or text classification, is a problem in library science, information science and computer science.[124] It can be identified as a three steps issue (preliminary tasks, learning and classification[125]) related to classification task, where a process is established to assign one or some of the predefined categories to each text (i.e., to derive high-quality information from text).[126]

The task to assign a document to one or more classes or categories can be done "manually" or algorithmically. The intellectual classification of documents has mostly been the realm of library science, while the algorithmic classification of documents is mainly in information science and computer science. Documents to be classified may be texts, images, music and so on. Each kind of document processing has its special classification problems. Documents may be classified according to their subjects or according to other features (such as document type, author, printing year, etc.). The use of algorithms in this field can be useful to reach, among other goals, semantic information, text summarization, classification and clustering.[127]

121 Haney, B. S., Applied Natural Language Processing for Law Practice, *Boston College Intellectual Property and Technology Forum*, 2020, p. 3, available at https://ssrn.com/abstract=3476351 or http://doi.org/10.2139/ssrn.3476351.

122 Kidd, K., and Saxena, B., NLP vs NLU: What's the Difference?, *ML& Big Data Blog*, available at https://www.bmc.com/blogs/nlu-vs-nlp-natural-language-understanding-processing/.

123 Liddy, E. D., Natural Language Processing, in *Encyclopedia of Library and Information Science* (Second Edition), New York: Marcel Decker, Inc, 2001, p. 3.

124 Murugan, A., et al., *Practical Text Analytics: Maximizing the Value of Text Data*, Springer International Publishing: Imprint: Springer, 2019, p. 2.

125 Taeho, J., *Text Mining: Concepts, Implementation, and Big Data Challenge*, ed. Springer International Publishing AG, 2018, ProQuest Ebook Central, p. 80.

126 Murugan, A., et al., *Practical Text Analytics: Maximizing the Value of Text Data*, Springer International Publishing: Imprint: Springer, 2019, p. 2 and Taeho, J., *Text Mining: Concepts, Implementation, and Big Data Challenge*, ed. Springer International Publishing AG, 2018, ProQuest Ebook Central, p. 79.

127 Bolasco, D. M., et al., Understanding Text Mining: A Pragmatic Approach, in *Knowledge Mining*, Heidelberg: Springer, 2005, pp. 31–50.

6.3.2 Machine translation

Machine translation, sometimes referred to by the abbreviation MT is a sub-field of computational linguistics that investigates the use of software to translate text or speeches from one language to another.[128]

6.3.3 Question answering

Question answering (QA) is a computer science discipline within the fields of information retrieval and NLP which is concerned with building systems that automatically answer questions posed by humans in a natural language, hence an automatic question-and-answering system should be able to interpret a natural language question and use reasoning to return an appropriate reply.[129] Thus, a question-answering system, whose essential task is information extraction, searches a large text collection and finds a short phrase or sentence that precisely answers a user's question.[130] In this sense, it worthwhile to mentioned IBM's Watson machine, which is able to answer questions posed in natural language and is recognized as one of the milestones of the AI used today.[131]

6.4 Robotics and cyber-physical systems

Robotics involves design, construction, operation and use of robots to help and assist humans. A robot is a machine, especially one programmable by a computer, that is capable of carrying out a complex series of actions automatically (in this case we can say that AI is "in-action" in the physical world, aka embodied AI).[132] Robots, with the help of ML are fast developing and can grab things, roll on the floor to clean it, jump (e.g., Atlas robot),[133] run (e.g., Cassie the bipedal robot)[134] and execute movements and manoeuvres that could be considered quite complex. In other terms, as explained by some experts:

> AI and robotics, they are two separate fields of technology and engineering. However, when combined, you get an artificially intelligent robot where AI

128 Bower, L., and Buitrago, C. J., *Machine Translation and Global Research: Towards Improved Machine Translation Literacy in the Scholar Community* (First Edition). Bingley: Emerald Publishing, 2019, p. 38.

129 Pouyanfar, S., et al., A Survey on Deep Learning: Algorithms, Techniques, and Applications, *ACM Computing Surveys*, Vol. 51(5), Article 92, 2018, p. 16.

130 Haney, B. S., Applied Natural Language Processing for Law Practice, *Boston College Intellectual Property and Technology Forum*, 2020, p. 23, available at SSRN: https://ssrn.com/abstract=3476351 or http://doi.org/10.2139/ssrn.3476351.

131 Mohssen, M., et al., *ML: Algorithms and Applications*, CRC Press, 2017, p. 31.

132 European Commission, *A Definition of AI: Main Capabilities and Scientific Disciplines*, Definition Developed for the Purpose of the Deliverables of the High-Level Expert Group on AI, 2018, p. 5.

133 Raibert, M., Turing Lecture: Building Dynamic Robots—Marc Raibert, *Boston Dynamics*, available at https://www.bing.com/videos/search?q=Turing+Lecture%3a+Building+dynamic+robots+-+Marc+Raibert%2c+Boston+Dynamics&docid=603529285505845955&mid=96D99820A3562066110796D99820A35620661107&view=detail&FORM=VIRE, (accessed 16 July 2022).

134 Heater, B., Cassie the Bipedal Robot Runs a 5k, *World Economic Forum*, 2021, available at https://www.weforum.org/stories/2021/08/cassie-the-bipedal-robot-runs-a-5k/ (accessed 2 August 2022).

acts as the brain, and the robotics acts as the body to enable robots to walk, see, speak, smell, and more.[135]

A cyber-physical system (CPS) is a computer system in which a mechanism is controlled or monitored by computer-based algorithms (i.e., integration of computation with physical processes[136]). In cyber-physical systems, physical and software components are deeply intertwined, able to operate on different spatial and temporal scales, exhibit multiple and distinct behavioural modalities and interact with each other in ways that change with context. Examples of CPS include smart grids, autonomous automobile systems, medical monitoring, industrial control systems, robotic systems and automatic pilot avionics.[137]

7 Main algorithms, methods and architectures

This section briefly analyses the most popular ML algorithms,[138] methods and architectures of algorithms that can be classified according to their functionalities, even if some of them can be used in different ways. In principle, we can differentiate algorithms based on whether they are used for classification, regression, or clustering.

Before moving to the following analysis, it is worthwhile to mention that the use of algorithms fosters multiple opportunities for analysis, however, the functioning of each algorithm depends mainly on the types of data that are used, that is, unlabelled or labelled[139] (i.e., some algorithms work better with labelled data, while others perform just as well with unlabelled data).

7.1 Classification analysis

Classification is a supervised learning ML method that analyses data and extracts models describing important data classes. Such models are called classifiers and predict or guess categorical class labels.[140] In other words, a class label is predicted/

135 Kovač, M., *Judgement-Proof Robots and AI—A Comparative Law and Economics Approach*, Springer Nature, 2020, p. 57.

136 Lee, E. A., and Seshia, S. A., *Introduction to Embedded Systems, A Cyber-Physical System Approach* (Second Edition). MIT Press, 2017, p. ix (preface).

137 Taha, W. M., *Cyber-Physical Systems: A Model-Based Approach* (First Edition). Cham: Springer International Publishing: Imprint: Springer, 2021, p. 5.

138 Suthaharan, S., *ML Models and Algorithms for Big Data Classification—Thinking with Examples for Effective Learning*, Integrated Series in Information Systems 36, Series Editors: Ramesh Sharda · Stefan Voß, Springer, 2016, p. 7 and also Dempsey, J. X., AI: An Introduction to the Legal, Policy and Ethical Issues, *Berkeley Center for Law & Technology*, 2020, p. 6, available at https://www.law.berkeley.edu/wp-content/uploads/2020/08/Artificial-Intelligence-An-Introduction-to-the-Legal-Policy-and-Ethical-Issues_JXD.pdf.

139 Blasch, E., et al., Methods of AI for Multimodal Sensing and Action for Complex Situations, *AI Magazine*, Vol. 40(4), 2019, pp. 50–56.

140 Han, J., et al., *Data Mining: Concepts and Techniques* (Third Edition), Elsevier, 2011, par. 8.

guessed for a given example.[141] In the following paragraphs the most common algorithms that tackle such types of analysis are described.

7.1.1 Naive Bayes

Naive Bayes (NB) is a supervised ML method that uses a training data set with known target classes to predict the future or any incoming instance of class value. The method is designed for supervised induction tasks, where the performance goal is to accurately predict the class of test instances and where the training instances include class information.[142]

Naive Bayes methods assume that the presence or absence of any attribute of a class variable is not related to the presence or absence of any other attributes (a Naive Bayes classifier assumes that the presence of a particular feature in a class is unrelated to the presence of any other feature or that all these properties have independent contributions to the probability).[143] To explain the assumption of independence among features we can resort to the example of fruit classification. Some fruit is commonly identified on the basis of colour, shape and taste, for example, then, a red, spherical and sweet fruit is recognized as an apple, hence each feature individually contributes to identify what an apple is, under the assumption that there is no dependency among colour, shape and taste that can affect the classification.[144]

Bayesian networks are also known as belief networks, and a Bayesian network is a type of AI programming that uses a variety of methods to create layers of belief. By using supervised learning, Bayesian networks can process data as needed, without experimentation, and are very effective for modeling situations where some information is already known, and incoming data is uncertain or partially unavailable (this information or belief is used for pattern identification and data classification).[145]

7.1.2 Logistic regression

Logistic regression is a statistical method for analysing a data set in which there are one or more independent variables that determine an outcome where the goal is to find the best fitting model to describe the relationship between the dichotomous characteristic of interest (dependent variable = response or outcome variable) and

141 Sarker, I. H., ML: Algorithms, Real-World Applications and Research Directions, *SN Computer Science*, Vol. 2, 2021, p. 5.

142 John, G. H., and Langley, P., Estimating Continuous Distributions in Bayesian Classification, in *Proceedings of the Eleventh Conference on Uncertainty in AI*, Morgan Kaufmann, 1995, p. 339.

143 Sidana, M., Types of Classification Algorithms in ML, *MEDIUM, Blog*, 2022, available at https://medium.com/sifium/machine-learning-types-of-classification-9497bd4f2e14 (accessed 15 July 2022).

144 Java T Point, *Support Vector Machine Algorithm*, available at https://www.javatpoint.com/machine-learning-support-vector-machine-algorithm (accessed 20 July 2022).

145 Bhatia, S., et al., Analysis of Credit Card Fraud Detection Techniques, *International Journal of Science and Research (IJSR)*, Vol. 5(3), 2016, p. 1304.

a set of independent (predictor or explanatory) variables (i.e., it can predict the class of the dependent variable from the set of given independent variables).[146] Its purpose is to classify cases into the most likely category.[147]

It relies on the concept of the "odds" of the event, which is a probability of an event occurring divided by the probability of an event not occurring, which weights, associated with dimensions of input data, are, contrary to linear regression, in an exponential relationship with the output of the model (the "odds").[148] Indeed, it is used to predict for a binary outcome or state, such as *yes/no*, *success/failure* and *will occur/won't occur.*[149]

7.1.3 K-nearest neighbour (KNN)

The k-nearest-neighbours algorithm is a supervised classification technique that uses proximity as a proxy for "sameness", where it takes a bunch of labelled points and uses them to learn how to label other points. In other words, to label a new point, it looks at the labelled points closest to that new point (those are its nearest neighbours).[150]

The KNN technique is a simple algorithm which stores all available instances and then it classifies any new instances based on a similarity measure (i.e., it works on the assumption that similar things (data) exist near each other).[151] The KNN algorithm is an example of an instance-based learner (in contrast with model-based learners). In the nearest neighbour classification method, each new instance is compared with existing instances by using a distance metric, and the closest existing instance is used to assign the class to the new one.[152] It is quite robust to noisy training data, and its accuracy depends on the data quality.[153]

146 Sidana, M., Types of Classification Algorithms in ML, *MEDIUM*, 10 May 2022, available at https://medium.com/sifium/machine-learning-types-of-classification-9497bd4f2e14 (accessed 15 July 2022) and Klingler, N., Deep Learning—What Is an AI Model? Here's What You Need to Know, *viso.ai, Blog*, 2023, available at https://viso.ai/deep-learning/ml-ai-models/ (accessed 15 July 2023).

147 Olson, D. L., and Wu., D., *Predictive Data Mining* (Second Edition), Springer, 2020, p. 99.

148 Bartosik, A., and Whittinghamb, H., Chapter 7: Evaluating Safety and Toxicity, in *The Era of AI, ML, and Data Science in the Pharmaceutical Industry* (ed. Stephanie Kay Ashenden), Elsevier Science Publishing Co Inc, 2021, p. 119.

149 Seufert, E. B., Chapter 3: Quantitative Methods for Product Management, in *Freemium Economics—Leveraging Analytics and User Segmentation to Drive Revenue*, Morgan Kaufmann, 2014, pp. 47–82.

150 Sidana, M., Types of Classification Algorithms in ML, *MEDIUM*, 10 May 2022, available at https://medium.com/sifium/machine-learning-types-of-classification-9497bd4f2e14 (accessed 15 July 2022).

151 Klingler, N., Deep Learning—What Is an AI Model? Here's What You Need to Know, *Blog*, 2023, available at https://viso.ai/deep-learning/ml-ai-models/ (accessed 16 July 2022).

152 Bhatia, S., et al., Analysis of Credit Card Fraud Detection Techniques, *International Journal of Science and Research (IJSR)*, Vol. 5(3), 2016, p. 1305.

153 Sarker, I. H., ML: Algorithms, Real-World Applications and Research Directions, *SN Computer Science*, Vol. 2, 2021, p. 6 and see also Brodley, C. E., et al., Challenges and Opportunities in Applied ML, *AI Magazine*, Vol. 33(1), 2012, pp. 11–24 and Java T Point, *Support Vector Machine Algorithm*, available at www.javatpoint.com/machine-learning-support-vector-machine-algorithm (accessed 2 September 2022).

The algorithm assumes the similarity between the new data inputs and the old data and allocates the new data in the category that is the closest to the already available categories. The main drawback of KNN is that, whereas the training is non-existent or negligible, computational costs during application times can be expensive, as for every new point the algorithm must search the k-closest neighbours in the historical/past data. Sampling techniques or temporal windows can be used in order to severely alleviate such costs.

7.1.4 Support vector machine (SVM)

SVM is a supervised ML algorithm that excels in analysing limited amounts of data and it is mainly applicable for classification problems, outlier detection and regression problems.[154] SVMs apply a simple linear method to the data but in a high-dimensional feature space, and it separates the different classes of data by hyper-planes corresponding to the decision functions. The optimal hyper-plane is the one with the maximal margin of separation between two classes (i.e., the greater the margin, the lower the classifier's generalization error).[155]

Hence, the SVM algorithm finds the closest points to the separation boundary from both classes (called support vectors) and the distance to such boundary (called margin). Such class boundaries are computed to maximize the margin (i.e., the hyperplane for which the margin is maximum is the optimal hyperplane[156]).

7.1.5 Decision tree (DT)

Decision trees (DTs) reach an inference model based on data and past decisions by creating a tree-like conditional structure. A DT builds classification or regression models where data is broken down into smaller and smaller subsets while at the same time an associated decision tree is incrementally developed. The result is a tree with decision nodes and leaf nodes. A decision node has two or more branches, and a leaf node represents a classification or decision.[157] To classify the data through a decision tree, the steps are as follows: (i) it puts all training exam-

154 Klingler, N., Deep Learning—What Is an AI Model? Here's What You Need to Know, *Blog*, available at https://viso.ai/deep-learning/ml-ai-models/ (accessed 30 August 2022).

155 Karatzoglou, A., et al., *Support Vector Machines in R, Research Report Series/Department of Statistics and Mathematics, 21*. Department of Statistics and Mathematics, WU Vienna University of Economics and Business, Vienna, 2005, pp. 1–25 and Sarker, I. H., ML: Algorithms, Real-World Applications and Research Directions, *SN Computer Science*, Vol. 2, 2021, p. 6 and Java T Point, *Support Vector Machine Algorithm*, available at www.javatpoint.com/machine-learning-support-vector-machine-algorithm (accessed 15 August 2022).

156 Pupale, R., Support Vector Machines(SVM)—An Overview, *Towardsdatascience, Blog*, 2018, available at https://towardsdatascience.com/https-medium-com-pupalerushikesh-svm-f4b42800e989 (accessed 15 August 2022).

157 Sidana, M., Types of Classification Algorithms in ML, *MEDIUM*, 10 May 2022, available at https://medium.com/sifium/machine-learning-types-of-classification-9497bd4f2e14 (accessed 15 July 2022) and Klingler, N., Deep Learning—What Is an AI Model? Here's What You Need to Know, *Blog*, available at https://viso.ai/deep-learning/ml-ai-models/ (accessed 15 July 2022).

ples to a root; (ii) it divides training examples based on selected attributes; (iii) it selects attributes by using some statistical measures; and (iv) recursive partitioning continues until no training example remains, or until no attribute remains or the remaining training examples belong to the same class.[158]

By sorting down the tree from the root to some leaf nodes, DT classifies the instances by checking the attribute defined by that node, starting at the root node of the tree and then moving down the tree branch corresponding to the attribute value.[159] DTs are one of the most interpretable ML algorithms.

7.1.6 Random forest (RF)

Random forest is an ensemble learning model[160] useful for solving both regression and classification problems. It operates using multiple decision trees and makes the final prediction using the bagging method (i.e., it builds a "forest" with multiple decision trees, each trained on different data subsets, and merges the results together to come up with more accurate predictions).[161]

RF predictor is a tree-based algorithm that uses a voting rule to determine the predicted class of each observation (i.e., RF is a combination of tree predictors such that each tree depends on the values of a random vector sampled independently and with the same distribution for all trees in the forest).[162]

Compared to a plain DT, an RF is substantially more robust and accurate, but, on the other hand, the human interpretation of the model becomes considerably harder. RF is one of the best general-purpose solutions for ML that can be applied in almost any field and obtain acceptable results (whenever the data scenario is suitable for modeling).

158 Mohssen, M., et al., *ML: Algorithms and Applications*, CRC Press, 2017, p. 37 and Akinbo, R. S., and Daramola, O. A., *Chapter 4—Ensemble ML Algorithms for Prediction and Classification of Medical Images*, IntechOpen Book Series, Edited by Jaydip Sen, Vol. 7, 2021, p. 70.

159 Sarker, I. H., ML: Algorithms, Real-World Applications and Research Directions, *SN Computer Science*, Vol. 2, 2021, p. 6 and Olson, D. L., and Wu., D., *Predictive Data Mining* (Second Edition), Springer, 2020, p. 107.

160 Akinbo, R. S., and Daramola, O. A., *Chapter 4—Ensemble ML Algorithms for Prediction and Classification of Medical Images*, IntechOpen Book Series, Edited by Jaydip Sen, Vol. 7, 2021, p. 68.

161 Sidana, M., Types of Classification Algorithms in ML, *MEDIUM*, 10 May 2022, available at https://medium.com/sifium/machine-learning-types-of-classification-9497bd4f2e14 (accessed 15 July 2022) and Klingler, N., Deep Learning—What Is an AI Model? Here's What You Need to Know, *Blog*, available at https://viso.ai/deep-learning/ml-ai-models/ (accessed 15 July 2022) and Sarker, I, H., Data Science and Analytics: An Overview from Data Driven Smart Computing, Decision Making and Applications Perspective, *SN Computer Science*, Vol. 2, 2021, p. 9, available at https://www.researchgate.net/publication/353198951_Data_Science_and_Analytics_An_Overview_from_Data-Driven_Smart_Computing_Decision-Making_and_Applications_Perspective.

162 Basuchoudhary, A., et al., *Machine-learning Techniques in Economics—New Tools for Predicting Economic Growth*, Springer, 2017, p. 25 and Breiman, L., Random Forest, *ML*, Vol. 45(1), 2001, p. 5.

7.2 Regression analysis

As we have identified in Section 5.1, regression algorithms are used to predict continuous quantity. To cite some examples, it fits applications such as financial forecasting, prediction of cost estimation, trend analysis, marketing and so on. Some of the most used algorithms are described here.

7.2.1 Linear regression and multiple regression

In general terms, regression can be a linear or simple regression that involves finding the "best" line to fit two attributes (or variables) so that one attribute can be used to predict the other. Linear regression algorithms are used in modeling relationships between observed (dependent) and design (independent) variables, while multiple linear regression is an extension of linear regression, where more than two attributes are involved and the data is fit to a multidimensional surface.[163] In other words, it is assumed that there is a direct correlation between the two variables and the straight line represents such relationship (i.e., higher the experience, higher the salary).

7.3 Clustering

Clustering is an unsupervised learning technique that tries to group objects having the same or similar characteristics. Some of the most important and used cluster methods are reported here.

7.3.1 K-means clustering

The most traditional clustering technique is called k-means and its application is divided into several steps: (i) determination of the number of cluster to be sought (i.e., the parameter *k*); (ii) assigning the instances to their closest cluster centre (centroid); (iii) next, calculate the distance of all data points to the centroids (this is the "means" part); (iv) assign data points to the closest cluster; (v) find the new centroids of each cluster by taking the mean of all data points in the cluster; and (vi) finally, the whole process is repeated with the new cluster centres until cluster centres are stable and all data points have been processed.[164] Therefore, the parti-

163 Han, J., et al., *Data Mining: Concepts and Techniques* (Third Edition), Elsevier, 2011, par. 3.4.5. and Sarker, I. H., ML: Algorithms, Real-World Applications and Research Directions, *SN Computer Science*, Vol. 2, 2021, p. 8 and Java T Point, *Regression Analysis in ML*, available at www.javatpoint.com/regression-analysis-in-machine-learning (accessed 15 July 2022).

164 Witten, I. H., et al. *Data Mining—Practical ML Tools and Techniques* (Third Edition), Morgan Kaufmann, 2011, p. 139 and Yildirim, S., K-Means Clustering—Explained, *Towardsdatascience, Blog*, 2020, available at https://towardsdatascience.com/k-means-clustering-explained-4528df86a120 (accessed 18 July 2022) and Kalla, A., K Means Clustering, *Medium Blog*, 2019, available at https://medium.datadriveninvestor.com/k-means-clustering-4a700d4a4720 (accessed 15 July 2022) and Zhang, M. H. and WU, J., Implementation of Rough Fuzzy K-Means Clustering Algorithm, in *Matlab, 2010 International Conference on ML and Cybernetics*, 2010, pp. 2084–2087.

tion of the objects into groups, or clusters, brings that objects within a cluster are "similar" and "dissimilar" to objects in other clusters.[165]

7.3.2 Hierarchical clustering

Hierarchical clustering aims at building cluster hierarchy such as in a tree structure by a dichotomous step-by-step process, that is, it groups samples by establishing pairs at different levels. There are two main strategies: (i) Agglomerative, that is, a "bottom up" approach in which samples are paired based on similarity and form small subsets, then such subsets are paired again into subsets of a higher level. This process is repeated until it is not possible to establish more pairs. (ii) Divisive, which is considered a "top down" approach directing from the root to the leaves. All observations are initially considered as one cluster and then splits are performed recursively as one moves down the hierarchy.[166]

The key benefit of hierarchical clustering is that the created tree-structure hierarchy is more informative than an unstructured set of flat clusters.[167] If hierarchical clustering is indeed more accurate than k-means clustering and less prone to local maxima problems, it is also more computationally demanding.

Both k-means and hierarchical clustering share the drawback of requiring the number of clusters *k* given as an external parameter.

7.3.3 Density-based methods

Usually, it is possible to identify distinct groups or clusters in a data space when there is contiguous region of high point density isolated by other groups or clusters by contiguous regions of low point density (where a point is not associated to a cluster it is called "noise").[168] Some algorithms have been developed, such DBSCAN (Density Based Spatial Clustering of Applications with Noise) and

165 Han, J., et al., *Data Mining: Concepts and Techniques* (Third Edition), Elsevier, 2011, par. 3.4.7.

166 Zhang, Z., et al, Hierarchical Cluster Analysis in Clinical Research with Heterogeneous Study Population: Highlighting Its Visualization with R., *Annals of Translational Medicine*, Vol. 5(4), 2017, p. 75, https://doi.org/10.21037/atm.2017.02.05 and Zolfaghari, F., Hierarchical Cluster Analysis to Identify the Homogeneous Desertification Management Units, *PLoS ONE*, Vol. 14(12), 2019, p. 5, https://doi.org/10.1371/journal.pone.0226355 and Sarker, I. H. ML: Algorithms, Real-World Applications and Research Directions. *SN Computer Science*, Vol. 2(160), 2021, p. 9, https://doi.org/10.1007/s42979-021-00592-x.

167 Sarker, I. H., Data Science and Analytics: An Overview from Data-Driven Smart Computing, DecisionMaking and Applications Perspective, *SN Computer Science*, Vol. 2, 2021, p. 10, available at https://www.researchgate.net/publication/353198951_Data_Science_and_Analytics_An_Overview_from_Data-Driven_Smart_Computing_Decision-Making_and_Applications_Perspective.

168 Sarker, I. H., ML: Algorithms, Real-World Applications and Research Directions. *SN Computer Science*, Vol. 2(160), 2021, p. 9, https://doi.org/10.1007/s42979-021-00592-x.

OPTICS, the latter being an evolution of the former, according to the idea that a point belongs to a cluster if it is close to many other points of a given cluster (hence it is possible and important to be able to discover clusters of different shapes and sizes and noises in a spatial database without the need to provide the algorithm with the number of clusters present in a given database; i.e., it can find them by itself[169]).

When using such algorithms that can clean or remove noise, detected clusters of points become purer, therefore increasing the accuracy to find out suitable descriptions of classes that are well delimited by its concentration or density areas.

7.4 Algorithms for anomaly detection

Anomaly detection, or outlier analysis, is a data mining technique that aims to identify/detect abnormal points, that is, samples that deviate from a normal behaviour of a data set; in other words, objects that are different from most other objects.[170] The meaning of "outlier" has a strong dependency on the final application, and it covers different interpretations, such as anomaly (i.e., interesting exception), noise (i.e., uninteresting, annoying deviation) or novelty (i.e., case not seen before that might be introducing a context change or a new class/cluster). Hence, the clear definition of "outlier" within the intended application is a key step to reach a successful performance. Some algorithms that are used for the anomaly detection have been already described in the preceding categories, such as k-nearest neighbours, cluster analysis and SVM.

However, very popular algorithms used for outlier detection are the local outlier dactor (LOF) and isolation forests. LOF uses the distance between the k-nearest neighbours to estimate the density and compares the local density of an item to the local densities of its neighbours (in such a situation it can determine areas of similar

169 Ram, A., et al., A Density based Algorithm for Discovering Density Varied Clusters in Large Spatial Databases, *International Journal of Computer Applications*, Vol. 3(6), 2010, pp. 1–4, available at https://www.researchgate.net/publication/44250717_A_Density_Based_Algorithm_for_Discovering_Density_Varied_Clusters_in_Large_Spatial_Databases#:~:text=DBSCAN%20is%20a%20base%20algorithm%20for%20density%20based,the%20local%20density%20variation%20thatexists%20within%20the%20cluster, Ester, M., et al., A Density-Based Algorithm for Discovering Clusters in Large Spatial Databases with Noise, (*KDD)*, Vol. 96, 1996, pp. 226–231, available at https://cdn.aaai.org/KDD/1996/KDD96-037.pdf and Ankerst, M., et al., OPTICS: Ordering Points to Identify the Clustering Structure, *ACM Sigmod Record*, Vol. 28(2), 1999, pp. 49–60, https://dl.acm.org/doi/10.1145/304182.304187.

170 Sarker, I. H., Data Science and Analytics: An Overview from Data-Driven Smart Computing, DecisionMaking and Applications Perspective, *SN Computer Science*, Vol. 2(377), 2021, p. 12, available at https://link.springer.com/content/pdf/10.1007/s42979-021-00765-8.pdf. The author explains that "anomalies are usually referred to as outliers, abnormalities, novelties, noise, inconsistency, irregularities, and exceptions". Sandhya Madhuri, G., and Usha Rani, M., Statistical Approaches to Detect Anomalies, *SSRN Electronic Journal*, 2018, p. 1, available at https://www.researchgate.net/publication/325191790_Anomaly_Detection_Techniques.

density and items that have a significantly lower density than their neighbours—hence the outliers).[171]

Isolation forests are built based on decision trees. They explicitly identify anomalies instead of profiling normal data points. They build ensembles of iTrees for a given data set, then anomalies are those instances which have short average path lengths on the iTrees.[172] In these trees, partitions are created by first randomly selecting a feature and then selecting a random split value between the minimum and maximum value of the selected feature (outliers are less frequent than regular observations and are different from them in terms of values).[173]

Points lie further away from the regular observations in the feature space, hence, when a forest of random trees collectively produces shorter path lengths for some points, then they are highly likely to be anomalies.[174]

7.5 Neural networks and deep learning

Nowadays, the most popular ML infrastructure is based on neural networks.[175] Artificial neural networks (ANN) were inspired by information processing and distributed communication nodes in biological systems (even if still some differences exist as neural networks tend to be static and symbolic, while the biological brain of most living organisms is dynamic) and it has become a dominant ML approach due to the improvement of computational power and speed.[176] The base

171 Valcheva, S., 5 Anomaly Detection Algorithms in Data Mining (With Comparison), *Intellspot, Blog*, available at https://www.intellspot.com/anomaly-detection-algorithms/ and Bhadri Naarayanan, P., et al., Comparing the Performance of Anomaly Detection Algorithms, *International Journal of Engineering Research & Technology (IJERT)*, Vol. 9(2), 2020, p. 1103, available at https://www.intellspot.com/anomaly-detection-algorithms/ and Varma, A., Local Outlier Factor, *GeeksforGeeks, Blog*, 2022, available at https://www.intellspot.com/anomaly-detection-algorithms/ (accessed 3 September 2022).

172 Liu, F. T., et al., Isolation Forest, *ICDM'08. Eighth IEEE International Conference on Data Mining*, 2008, pp. 413–422, available at https://cs.nju.edu.cn/zhouzh/zhouzh.files/publication/icdm08b.pdf.

173 Bhadri Naarayanan, P., et al., Comparing the Performance of Anomaly Detection Algorithms, *International Journal of Engineering Research & Technology (IJERT)*, Vol. 9(2), 2020, p. 1103, available at https://www.ijert.org/research/comparing-the-performance-of-anomaly-detection-algorithms-IJERTV9IS070532.pdf and Liu, F. T., et al., Isolation Forest, *ICDM'08. Eighth IEEE International Conference on Data Mining*, 2008, pp. 413–422, available at https://cs.nju.edu.cn/zhouzh/zhouzh.files/publication/icdm08b.pdf.

174 Bhadri Naarayanan, P., et al., Comparing the Performance of Anomaly Detection Algorithms, *International Journal of Engineering Research & Technology (IJERT)*, Vol. 9(2), 2020, p. 1103, available at https://www.ijert.org/research/comparing-the-performance-of-anomaly-detection-algorithms-IJERTV9IS070532.pdf and Liu, F., T., et al., Isolation Forest, *ICDM'08. Eighth IEEE International Conference on Data Mining*, 2008, pp. 413–422, available at https://cs.nju.edu.cn/zhouzh/zhouzh.files/publication/icdm08b.pdf.

175 Kelleher, J. D., and Tierney, B., *Data Science*, Cambridge, MA: The MIT Press, Knowledge Serie, 2018, p, 121.

176 Theobald, O., *ML for Absolute Beginners: A Plain English Introduction* (Third Edition), Independently Published, 2021, p. 102.

for this mechanism is the neuron, which through axons and synapses, communicates with the close neurons transmitting electric impulses and therefore the inputs contribute in a different way in the information provision.[177] To sum up, ANN in its architecture tries to emulate the biological brain with the aim to reproduce its parallel and highly interconnected structure. Indeed, the maturation of ML should be linked to the rise of a digital economy (i.e., the large quantity of data available) and the empirical success of ANN which can be trained with huge data sets and large-scale computing (known as "deep learning").[178]

The starting point of ANN is the perceptron invention made by Frank Rosenblatt in 1958. The perceptron[179] is a single processing unit that receives weighted input and produces a rule-based thresholder output.[180] ANN is a technique for data analysis through a network of decision layers consisting of interconnected decision functions (nodes) which interact with each other through axon-like (edges). The nodes are separated in layers: input layer, output layer and some hidden layers in between of connected neurons.[181] The input layer is fed with data (such as numeric values, text, image pixel or sound) which is unequally shared among nodes/neurons and later propagated into subsequent layers with modifications until information finally reaches the output layer.[182]

The implementation derives using sums of multiplications where to each channel that receive an input data is linked a weight (a numeric value) that represents the importance of this input/data to the overall final value (activation function) and, if reached, then activates the next layer.[183] The network is then trained, and it learns to build a probabilistic model that describes the learned data and, at the end of the study, can allocate a probability to belong to a cluster/class per each input analysed.[184]

177 MCculloch, W. S., and Pitts, W., A Logical Calculus of the Ideas Immanent in Nervous Activity, *Bulletin of Mathematica Biology*, Vol. 52(1/2), 1990, p. 99.

178 Stanford University, One Hundred Year Study on AI (AI100), *AI and Life in 2030*, 2016 Report, p. 9, available at ai100report10032016fnl_singles.pdf (stanford.edu).

179 Franklin Rosenblatt built the first modern neural network model called the Perceptron and showed that the weights in the McCulloch-Pitts model could be calibrated using the available data set; in essence, he had invented what we now call a learning algorithm. See Kolanovic, M., and Krishnamachari, R. T., *Big Data and AI Strategies ML and Alternative Data Approach to Investing*, J.P. Morgan, 2017, p. 252 and Graben, P., and Wright, J., From McCulloch–Pitts Neurons Toward Biology, *Bulletin of Mathematical Biology*, Vol. 73, 2011, pp. 261–265.

180 Suliman, A., and Zhang, Y., A Review on Back-Propagation Neural Networks in the Application of Remote Sensing Image Classification, *Journal of Earth Science and Engineering*, Vol. 5, 2015, p. 53.

181 Alpaydin, E., *ML*, The MIT Press, Essential Knowledge Series, 2016, p. 100.

182 Theobald, O., *ML for Absolute Beginners: A Plain English Introduction* (Third Edition), Independently Published, 2021, p. 102.

183 Rosenblatt, F., The Perceptron: A Probabilistic Model for Information Storage and Organization in the Brain, *Psychological Review*, Vol. 65(6), 1958, pp. 386–408.

184 Quintarelli, S., et al., *Intelligenza Artificiale—cos'è davvero, come funziona, che effetti avrà, A cura di Claudia Giulia Ferrauto*, Bollati Boringhieri, 2020, pp. 43–44 and Theobald, O., *ML for Absolute Beginners: A Plain English Introduction* (Third Edition), Independently Published, 2021, p. 102.

Deep learning can be considered as a family of ML methods. It is based on artificial neural networks (ANNs) and, in contrast to traditional shallow learning, consists of analysing data in multiple layers of learning.[185] Some authors define this technique as

> deep-learning methods are representation-learning methods with multiple levels of representation, obtained by composing simple but non-linear modules that each transform the representation at one level (starting with the raw input) into a representation at a higher, slightly more abstract level . . . which key aspect is that these layers of features are not designed by human engineers: they are learned from data using a general-purpose learning procedure.[186]

In this process, neural networks commonly learn from a large amount of data by a brute force, bombarding learning procedure.[187]

Deep-learning architectures such as deep neural networks, deep belief networks, recurrent neural networks, convolutional neural networks and generative adversarial networks[188] have been applied to fields including computer vision, machine vision, speech recognition, natural language processing, audio recognition, social network filtering, machine translation, bioinformatics, drug design, medical image analysis, material inspection and board game programs, where they have produced results comparable to and in some cases surpassing human expert performance.[189]

However, this technique has a downside that derives from the difficulties to trace its decision structure that brings to the final outcomes. Indeed, it is difficult to understand how the specific variables influence its decision (i.e., the model is unable to specify the relationship between independent variables and dependent variables).[190]

Deep learning is built on ANNs with many internal layers, thus the word "deep", and where the machine is able to create maps in which abstractions are formed and stored to achieve the desired learning. In other words, deep learning is able to make machines abstract and synthesize a given context, enabling them to make precise descriptions, predictions and recommendations starting from a training with huge sets of labelled

185 European Commission, Communication from the Commission to the European Parliament, the European Council, the Council, the European Economic and Social Committee and the Committee of the Regions on AI for Europe, Brussels, COM(2018) 237 final, p. 10.

186 LeCun, Y., et al., Deep Learning, *Nature*, Vol. 521(7553), 2015, p. 436.

187 Haney, B. S., The Perils and Promises of Artificial General Intelligence, *Journal of Legislation*, Vol. 45(2), 2019, p. 157.

188 Stanford University, *Gathering Strength, Gathering Storms: The One Hundred Year Study on Artificial Intelligence (AI100)*, 2021 Study Panel Report, p. 12, available at Gathering Strength, Gathering Storms: The One Hundred Year Study on AI (AI100) 2021 Study Panel Report | One Hundred Year Study on AI (AI100) (stanford.edu).

189 Macpherson, T., et al., Natural and AI: A Brief Introduction to the Interplay Between AI and Neuroscience Research, *Neural Networks*, Vol. 144, 2021, pp. 603–613 available at https://www.sciencedirect.com/special-issue/1017VB2Z2R5.

190 Theobald, O., *ML for Absolute Beginners: A Plain English Introduction* (Third Edition), Independently Published, 2021, p. 104.

data based on which machines are later able to label unseen objects and situation themselves (e.g., a deep learning algorithm that has been trained to identify people in images should be able to abstract a feature that corresponds to the concept "face").[191]

The idea of training neural networks with multiple layers, as previously identified, was discovered many years ago, however, the importance and the use of deep learning rose in 2012 due to an increase in computational power and data. It plays a leading role in domains such as speech recognition, image recognition and language translation with regard to ML approaches.[192] Until the implementation of the DL architecture, ML usually used shallow-structured architectures that typically contained a single layer, lacking multiple layers (even if these architectures could be helpful to solve simple or well-constrained problems, they were not fit to solve more complex real-world problems involving signals such as human speech, natural sound and language, and natural image and visual scenes).[193]

The functioning of deep learning, whose typical mission is to decide which of a set of categories a given input belongs to, can be easily clarified considering that in speech recognition a neural network learns a mapping between a set of speech sounds and set of labels (such as words) or, in the case of object recognition, the neural network learns a mapping between a set of images and a set of labels (e.g., pictures of cars are labelled as cars).[194] Deep learning is highly used in the financial sector, particularly in partially automated lending decisions for lenders, in the trading function where high-frequency trading relies on a combination of models that help to inform better decisions and for personal finance advice in relation to financial planning activity.[195]

8 Law and AI: evolution and interrelation

De facto, technologies developed in the field of justice can be grouped in three categories: (i) basic technologies such as desktop computers, word processing,

191 Montesinos López, O. A., et al., *Multivariate Statistical Machine Learning Methods for Genomic Prediction*, Springer, 2022, pp. 383–384, available at https://link.springer.com/chapter/10.1007/978-3-030-89010-0_10, and Tao, S., *ML, Optimization, and Data Science, 5th International Conference*, LOD 2019 Siena, Italy, September 10–13, 2019 Proceedings, Eds. Giuseppe Nicosia, PanosPardalos, Renato Umeton, Giovanni Giuffrida, and Vincenzo Sciacca, Springer, 2019, pp. 1–13 and Dertat, A., Applied Deep Learning—Part 1: Artificial Neural Networks, *Towardsdatascience, Blog*, 2017, available at https://towardsdatascience.com/applied-deep-learning-part-1-artificial-neural-networks-d7834f67a4f6 (accessed 30 July 2022).

192 Gary, M., *Deep Learning: A Critical Appraisal*, Ithaca, NY: Cornell University, 2018, p. 2, available at https://arxiv.org/abs/1801.00631.

193 Deng, L., A Tutorial Survey of Architectures, Algorithms, and Applications for Deep Learning, *APSIPA Transactions on Signal and Information Processing*, Vol. 3(e2), 2014, p. 2.

194 Gary, M., *Deep Learning: A Critical Appraisal*, Ithaca, NY: Cornell University, 2018, p. 5, available at https://www.cs.cmu.edu/~katef/DeepRLFall2018/lecture_DQL_katef2018.pdf.

195 Stanford University, *Gathering Strength, Gathering Storms: The One Hundred Year Study on AI (AI100)*, 2021 Study Panel Report, p. 17, available at https://ai100.stanford.edu/gathering-strength-gathering-storms-one-hundred-year-study-artificial-intelligence-ai100–2021-study.

spreadsheets and both internal and external email for judges and administrative personnel; (ii) applications used to support the administrative personnel of the court, which include automated registers and case management systems; and (iii) technologies used to support the activities of the judges, such as law and case law electronic libraries and sentencing support systems.[196] Here, we are interested in the third category, especially in relation to the area of decision-making.

Computers and their capabilities lead legal academics to dream of the replacement of lawyers and judges, mainly due to the enthusiasm of computer scientists when trying to develop a general AI that could replicate the human mind.[197] However, as previously mentioned, the evolution of AI has not reached the level of so-called "strong" AI yet, although it is able to do many activities, some of them even better than humans.

Nevertheless, the domain of law is driven by language, logic and conceptual relationships,[198] and this way of reasoning might create considerable obstacles in the automatic application of AI systems to the law field.[199] In short, law is not neat and clean, and it should be considered as an abstraction created by the human mind with many interrelated subjective nuances.[200]

Based on this general statement, and considering the legal reasoning scheme as facts (given), rules (given) and certain legal consequence(s),[201] the hurdles of the application of AI to law can be summarized as follows:[202]

1. Legal reasoning is rule-guided, rather than rule-governed.[203]
2. Legal terms are open textured (i.e., legal interpretation of facts).

196 Velicogna, M., Justice Systems and ICT-What Can Be Learned from Europe, *Utrecht Law Review*, Vol. 3(1), 2007, p. 131.

197 Fagan, F., Natural Language Processing for Lawyers and Judges, *Michigan Law Review*, Vol. 119(6), 2021, p. 1399.

198 Bommarito, M. J., et al., LexNLP: Natural Language Processing and Information Extraction For Legal and Regulatory Texts, *SSNR*, 2018, Available at https://papers.ssrn.com/sol3/papers.cfm?abstract_id=3192101.

199 Mandel, G. N., Legal Evolution in Response to Technological Change, in *The Oxford Handbook of Law, Regulation and Technology* (ed. Roger Brownsword), Oxford University Press, 2016, pp. 225–245.

200 See Loevinger, L., Jurimetrics—The Next Step Forward, *Minnesota Law Review*, Vol. 33(5), 1949, pp. 462 and 468, available at https://scholarship.law.umn.edu/cgi/viewcontent.cgi?article=2795&context=mlr. See also Ribes Ribes, A., La Inteligencia Artificial al Servicio del "Compliance Tributario", *Revista Española de Derecho Financiero*, Vol. 188, 2020, pp. 147–148.

201 Verheij, B., Artificial Intelligence as Law—Presidential Address to the Seventeenth International Conference on AI and Law, *AI as Law*, Vol. 28(3), 2020, p. 188 and also Tuzet, G., Assessment Criteria or Standards of Proof? An Effort in Clarification, *AI and Law*, Vol. 28(2), 2020, pp. 91–109.

202 Rissland, E., Book Review. An AI Approach to Legal Reasoning, *Harvard Journal Law Technology*, Vol. 1(Spring), 1988, pp. 224–225.

203 Verheij, B., Formalizing Value-Guided Argumentation for Ethical Systems Design, *AI and Law*, Vol. 24(4), 2016, p. 390 and Gubelmann, R., and Hongler, P., Natural Language Processing—A Game Changer for Normative Reasoning in the Legal Discipline?, *IFF-.-HSG Working Papers*, Working Paper No. 2021-7, 2021, p. 4–5. See also Ződi, Z., Algorithmic Explainability and Legal Reasoning, *The Theory and Practice of Legislation*, Vol. 10(1), 2022, pp. 67–92.

3. Legal questions can have more than one answer.[204]
4. The answers to legal questions can change over time.[205]

According to this list, predictive and causal inferences of legal outcome are susceptible to changing circumstances and the changing behaviour of the parties (i.e., law's causal effect is accurate only to the extent that the future resembles the past).[206] These elements of legal reasoning and the environment have led to the initial focus, in the first 25 years of research on the application of information technology to law, on the development of legal information retrieval systems (e.g., FLITE, Westlaw or LexisNexis), where users operate through a terminal and, having initially executed various preliminary instructions in order to gain access to the systems, they enter one or more keywords, relevant for their inquiry, and then the computer compares the keywords provided with the full-text of the database. Users can then search over the collection of information outputted by the query system.[207]

However, although these systems have a goal to achieve speedy, accurate and reliable information retrieval to free up time for proper legal research and logical thought,[208] they don't provide answers to any legal problems but merely provide a set of information from which to start dealing with the legal problem.

Due to the need to improve these systems, that is, the systems that go beyond simply providing legal information, intelligent knowledge-based systems (IKBS) have been developed. They aim—through the representations of knowledge to be

204 See also Viola, L., Giustizia predittiva non equivale a Ia, *ItaliaOggi7*, Lunedì 24 Ottobre 2022, p. 3.

205 Valiant, L., *Probably Approximately Correct*, Basic Books, 2013, pp. 61–62 and Liebwald, D., On Transparent Law, Good Legislation and Accessibility to Legal Information: Towards an Integrated Legal Information System, *AI and Law*, Vol. 23(3), 2015, pp. 301–314 and Vozza, A., Intelligenza artificiale, giustizia predittiva e processo tributario, *il fisco*, n. 32, 2019, pp. 1–3154, and Prakken, H., and Sartor, G., Law and Logic: A Review from an Argumentation Perspective, *AI*, Vol. 227, 2015, pp. 214–245.

206 Fagan, F., Natural Language Processing for Lawyers and Judges, *Michigan Law Review*, Vol. 119(6), 2021, p. 1402. See also Surden, H., AI and Law: An Overview, *Georgia State University Law Review*, Vol. 35(4), 2019, p. 1306 and Jirakunkanok, P., et al., Dynamic Epistemic Logic of Belief Changes in Legal Judgments, *AI and Law*, Vol. 26(3), 2018, pp. 201–249.

207 Susskind, R. E., Expert Systems in Law: A Jurisprudential Approach to AI and Legal Reasoning, *Modern Law Review*, Vol. 49, 1986, pp. 168–169. See also Mehl, L., Automation in the Legal World: From the Machine Processing of Legal Information to the "Law Machine". *Mechanisation of Thought Processes Proceedings of a Symposium Held at the National Physical Laboratory*, 24–27 November 1958 (1959, vol. II, Her Majesty's Stationery Office, London), pp. 755–787 and Hyman, H., et al., A Process Model for Information Retrieval Context Learning and Knowledge Discovery, *AI and Law*, Vol. 23(2), 2015, pp. 103–132, Mandal, A., et al., Unsupervised Approaches for Measuring Textual Similarity between Legal Court Case Reports, *AI and Law*, Vol. 29(1), 2021, pp. 1–35.

208 Dymitruk, M., Borderlands of the Law and Technology: From Digital Machines to LegalTech, in *Legal Tech: Information Technology Tools in the Administration of Justice* (eds. Dariusz Szostek and Mariusz Załucki), Nomos VerlagsgesellschaftmbH& Co. KG, 2021, pp. 65–78.

deployed—to solve legal problems.[209] The development of such techniques coincided with the emergence of the data-centric approach where all the cases of a given court or all the rules of a given jurisdiction provide a new perspective on the properties of legal systems, such as the graph topologies of citation networks, the evolution of legal doctrines, and the probability of decisions or the outcomes of other cases.[210]

With this in mind, and according to the logic of argumentation[211] of the law reasoning (i.e., where different hypothetical perspectives are constructed and evaluated until a good answer is found), AI systems have been built.[212] Challenges here emerged when trying to develop logic-based systems,[213] which are mainly focused on representing, efficiently and in a verifiable manner, legal texts in the form of logic expressions and when evaluating legal predicates from facts expressed in the language of ordinary discourse. Indeed, current machines are limited, and legal terms are mostly vague verbalization, the choice of a legal term not being constrained as lawsuit are not decided by formal logics or well-delimited unambiguous procedures.[214]

Based on the aforementioned characteristics of the process driving the law reasoning, the starting point regarding the use of AI, when dealing with law decisions, is to determine if it is possible to identify a good prediction, or, in other words, if a system can perform good prediction of cases. The problem—in the opinion of who writes—is to identify if it is possible to define a "good decision", considering that "human" judges provide mainly heterogeneous decisions.[215]

In fact, judges are usually under an obligation to justify their final decisions, in a way that criteria behind final judgements need to be: (i) justificatory, in the sense that it is articulated in expressing the arguments on the basis of which the judgement should appear valid, reliable and reasonable, and (ii) dialogical, where

209 Susskind, R. E., Expert Systems in Law: A Jurisprudential Approach to AI and Legal Reasoning, *Modern Law Review*, Vol. 49, 1986, p. 172.

210 Branting, K., Data-Centric and Logic-Based Models for Automated Legal Problem Solving, *AI Law*, Vol. 25, 2017, p. 6.

211 Dung, P. M., On the Acceptability of Arguments and Its Fundamental Role in Non-Monotonic Reasoning, Logic Programming and N-Person Games, *AI*, Vol. 77(2), 1995, pp. 321–357 and Bench-Capon, T. J. M. and Dunne, P. E., Argumentation in Artificial Intelligence, *Artificial Intelligence*, Vol. 171(10–15), 2007, pp. 619–641.

212 Verheij, B., Presidential Address to the Seventeenth International Conference on AI and Law, *AI as Law*, Vol. 28(3), 2020, pp. 190–191.

213 Branting, K., Data-Centric and Logic-Based Models for Automated Legal Problem Solving, *AI Law*, Vol. 25, 2017, p. 5.

214 Loevinger, L., Jurimetrics—The Next Step Forward, *Minnesota Law Review*, Vol. 33(5), 1949, p. 472, available at https://scholarship.law.umn.edu/cgi/viewcontent.cgi?article=2795&context=mlr. See also Holmes, O. W., The Path of Law, *Harvard Law Review*, Vol. 110(5), 1997, pp. 991–1009, Dadgostari, F., et al. Modelling Law Search as Prediction, *AI and Law*, 29, 2021, pp. 3–34. See also Branting, K., Data-centric and Logic-Based Models for Automated Legal Problem Solving, *AI Law*, Vol. 25, 2017, p. 7.

215 Castellano, P. S., Inteligencia Artificial Y Valoración de la Prueba: las Grantías Jurídico-Constitucionales del Órgano de Control, *THĔMIS-Revista de Derecho*, Vol. 79, 2021, p. 288.

the final judgement is somehow an answer to the parties and in doing so judges are required to set forth the reasons grounding their own choices.[216]

The complexity, variability, flexibility and discretion that are typical of judicial decisions are not easily tackled by computer automated systems.[217] Judges' predictions rely on many informative features that are usually unobservable to an algorithm because they cannot be part of a data set.[218] Consequently, with the need to co-mingle law and AI, in the 1960s what was called "legal computing" started,[219] that is, the transition from jurisprudence (intended as a mere speculation about law) to jurimetrics (intended as the scientific investigation of legal problems).[220] This led to the creation of AI systems and database technology that have been used in server allege-scale information systems, generally referred to as "sentencing information systems", and being implemented in a variety of jurisdictions and used on a practical day-to-day basis to support the sentencing process.[221]

In recent years, NLP is the one of the most used methods of AI in the practice of law.[222] It can be very useful for reviewing a huge amount of case law and figuring out similarities (if any) to the disputed case (so-called summarization).[223] In addition to that, AI can assist with making predictions about future outcomes, as

216 Taruffo, M., Judicial Decisions and AI, *AI and Law*, Vol. 6, 1998, pp. 311–324.

217 Copus, R., and Hübert, R., *Detecting Inconsistency in Governance*, SSRN, 2017, p. 1, available at SSRN-id2812914.pdf (ryanhubert.com).

218 Lakkaraju, H., et al., The Selective Labels Problem: Evaluating Algorithmic Predictions in the Presence of Unobservables, *KDD*, 2017, p. 275, https://doi.org/10.1145/3097983.3098066.

219 Nissan, E., Digital Technologies and AI's Present and Foreseeable Impact on Lawyering, Judging, Policing and Law Enforcement, *AI & Society*, Vol. 32(3), 2017, pp. 441–464.

220 Loevinger, L., Jurimetrics—The Next Step Forward, *Minnesota Law Review*, Vol. 33(5), 1949, p. 483, available at https://scholarship.law.umn.edu/cgi/viewcontent.cgi?article=2795&context=mlr. See Loevinger, L., Jurimetrics: The Methodology of Legal Inquiry, *Law and Contemporany Problems*, Vol. 28(1), Duke University School of Law, 1963, p. 8, available at https://scholarship.law.duke.edu/lcp/vol28/iss1/2/.

221 Tata, C., The Application of Judicial Intelligence and 'Rules' to Systems Supporting Discretionary Judicial Decision-Making, *AI and Law*, Vol. 6(2), 1998, pp. 207–208. See also McGinnis, J. O., and Pearce, R. G., The Great Disruption: How Machine Intelligence Will Transform the Role of Lawyers in the Delivery of Legal Services, *Fordham Law Review*/edited by Fordham Law Students, Vol. 82(6), 2014, p. 3052.

222 Haney, B. S., Applied Natural Language Processing for Law Practice, *Boston College Intellectual Property and Technology Forum*, 2020, p. 3, available at https://papers.ssrn.com/sol3/papers.cfm?abstract_id=3476351. See also Ash, E., The Making of International Tax Law: Empirical Evidence from Natural Language Processing, UC Irvine School of Law Research Paper No. 2019-02, 2019, pp. 1–46, available at SSRN: https://papers.ssrn.com/sol3/papers.cfm?abstract_id=3314310.

223 Bell, K., et al., The Recon Approach: A New Direction for ML in Criminal Law, *Berkeley Technology Law Journal*, Vol. 37, 2021, p. 104. Available at SSRN: https://papers.ssrn.com/sol3/papers.cfm?abstract_id=3834710. See also Rohan, N., et al., Unsupervised and Supervised Text Similarity Systems for Automated Identification of National Implementing Measures of European Directives, *AI and Law*, Vol. 27(2), 2019, pp. 199–225.

AI systems have the ability to reason about the long-term effects of a decision (i.e., forecasting or risk scoring).[224]

By using ML models, it is possible to identify how one judge decides compared to another, that is, after comparing the decisions of two judges, the model was able to say whether the outcome of each specific case in the data set is more consistent with one or the other judges' decision, independently of the reasons behind such decisions.[225] Therefore the model can identify elements and patterns that are common between the data set and the judges' decisions but cannot go behind the reasoning of a judge when deciding. Another example on how computer applications could support the judicial activity is the development of ASSYST (applied sentencing system) based on simple algorithms/decision paths/calculator.[226] The starting point was that "judges have had a great deal of latitude in their sentencing decisions" that could "introduce inconsistent sentencing decisions", thus, with ASSYST judges, prosecutors, defence attorneys, probation officers and other key members of the federal criminal justice system could easily compute, record, archive and examine the implications of guidelines promulgated by the United States Sentencing Commission.[227]

Notwithstanding, it seems that the current AI systems should be considered complementary to human activities in such a way that there is a cooperation between machines and humans as long as AI technologies still show some limiting weaknesses. The judiciary is in the early stages of a transformation in which AI technology will help to make the judicial process faster, cheaper and more predictable, without compromising the integrity of judges' discretionary reasoning rather than aiming at the hardly possible dream (or nightmare) of building an automatic judge.[228] AI researchers are producing tools to support judicial activities, including programs for intelligent document assembly, case retrieval and support for discretionary decision-making; and developing new analytical tools for understanding and modeling the judicial process, such as case-based reasoning[229] and formal models of dialectics, argumentation and negotiation.[230]

224 Stanford University, *Gathering Strength, Gathering Storms: The One Hundred Year Study on AI (AI100)*, 2021 Study Panel Report, p. 48, available at https://ai100.stanford.edu/gathering-strength-gathering-storms-one-hundred-year-study-artificial-intelligence-ai100-2021-study.

225 Copus, R., et al., *Credible Prediction: Big Data, ML and the Credibility Revolution, Forthcoming in Law as Data: Computation and the Future of Legal Analysis*, SFI Press, 2018, p. 21 and 30, available at SSRN: https://ssrn.com/abstract=3156795.

226 Simon, E., et al., *ASSYST—Computer Support for Guideline Sentencing*, ICAIL, Association for Computing Machinery, 1989, pp. 198–199, https://doi.org/10.1145/74014.74039.

227 Simon, E., et al., *ASSYST—Computer Support for Guideline Sentencing*, ICAIL, 1989, p. 195.

228 Contini, F., and Cordella, A., *Law and Technology in Civil Judicial Procedures* (eds. Roger Brownsword et al.), 2017, pp. 246–268.

229 Ashley, K. D., An AI Model of Case-Based Legal Argument from a Jurisprudential Viewpoint, *Artificial and Law*, Vol. 10(1–3), 2002, pp. 163–2018.

230 Sartor, G., and Branting, L., Introduction: Judicial Applications of AI, *AI and Law*, Vol. 6, 1998, pp. 105–110.

When dealing with justice and with the solution to a controversy, we can consider that, in general terms, there are no right or wrong decisions, hence, what matters is not the search for the exact decision, but for that decision that can be explained and argued by means of logical reasoning, based not only on the rules in force but also on the analysis of the case considering elements other than the mere application of a logical system of law. Indeed, who can establish whether a behaviour is right or wrong? What may be right for one may be wrong for another since nature is made of variability and the idea of perfection as well as precision is itself a wrong idea.[231]

Therefore, a machine that applies the law systematically without a full analysis of the circumstances of the individual case runs the risk of flattening decisions by not considering the subjective elements of each individual case.[232] In fact, it has been pointed out that it is possible to predict an event, but a judicial decision is not derived from a mechanical process, as the facts are always different, or at least they present significant elements of diversity that need to be constantly adapted to the rule applied and determined in the precedent fact.[233]

Even if there are tentative to develop algorithms that can be applied to the different law fields, this still seems far from being completely possible, mainly due to two factors: (i) the development of computer systems that, although they have reached a surprising level in recent years, are still unable to fully reproduce the levels of complexity inherent to the human brain, and (ii) the complexity of the law itself, which clashes with the purely deductive nature of machines.[234] In fact, law cannot be based on the invariance assumption,[235] as we can never be certain that the world will not change so that future examples will be from a very different distribution from those in the past—that is, past performance is not

231 Quintarelli, S., et al., *Intelligenza Artificiale—cos'è davvero, come funziona, che effetti avrà, A cura di Claudia Giulia Ferrauto*, Bollati Boringhieri, 2020, p. 70.

232 In this sense see Spiekermann, S., *Ethical IT Innovation: A Value-Based System Design Approach*, Auerbach Publications, 2015, p. 283.

233 Patroni Griffi, F., La decisione robotica e il giudice amministrativo, Intervento al Convegno "Decisione robotica", organizzato nell'ambito dei Seminari 'Leibniz' per la teoria e la logica del diritto—Roma, *Accademia dei Lincei*, 5 luglio 2018, p. 2, available at https://www.avvocatibf.eu/wp-content/uploads/2018/09/Patroni-Griffi-La-decisione-robotica-e-il-giudice-amministrativo-28-agosto-2018.pdf and Fazi, B. M., Can a Machine Think (Anything New)? Automation Beyond Simulation, *AI & Society*, Vol. 34(3058), 2019, pp. 813–824.

234 Noto La Diega, G., Against the Dehumanisation of Decision-Making—Algorithmic Decisions at the Crossroads of Intellectual Property, Data Protection, and Freedom of Information, *JIPITEC—Journal of Intellectual Property, Information Technology and E-Commerce Law*, Vol. 9(1), 2018, pp. 3–34.

235 Cutting, J. E., Four Assumptions about Invariance in Perception, *Journal of Experimental Psychology Human Perception & Performance*, Vol. 9(2), 1983, pp. 10–17 and Cheng, P., et al., Humans' Invariance Assumption: Should Statistics and AI Adopt It?, *The Brain Blog*, 2021, available at https://philosophyofbrains.com/2021/10/28/humans-invariance-assumption-should-statistics-and-ai-adopt-it.aspx.

necessarily indicative of future results.[236] Indeed, if we consider the possibility that a positive legal system characterized by closed and well-defined cases would exist, the natural incompleteness of the law provisions would still entail the need of analogy with the intrinsic need to evaluate this logic procedure and if from this abstract model we move to the concrete experience it is easy to recognize how the existing provisions suffer, due to the interaction with the system and the relevant interests, a heterogenies of ends, hence an ongoing change in the intrinsic sense of their wording.[237]

This last concept can be better understood from reading the interpretation of Kurt Gödel's incompleteness theorems by the philosopher John R. Lucas and the physicist Roger Penrose. Gödel's theorem recognizes that a system of consistent (i.e., non-contradictory) rules is itself incomplete, that is, there are truths that cannot be proved (here meaning that they cannot be derived automatically) by the axioms of the system itself.[238] Hence, a computer that reproduces by means of its circuits logical rules of thought is an incomplete system insofar as it cannot automatically derive the truth value of each statement, whereas men know things that cannot be derived automatically, that is, humans can understand truth and construct axioms.[239] From this it can be derived that "The human mind is capable of reasoning, in a similar way to a computer, about questions that are formulated algorithmically, but it is also capable of performing other functions that some authors consider impossible to simulate by a machine".[240] Indeed, a case can be counted under a certain law provision but due to some exceptions it can then fall outside the law application as recognized by Schulz and Dankert who clarify how "normative rules provide an idea of what should be 'normal' (meaning potentially benefiting a society), but they only come into actual effect whenever a discrepancy of the actual and desired behaviour occurs".[241]

236 Valiant, L., *Probably Approximately Correct—Nature's Algorithms for Learning and Prospering in a Complex World*, Basic Books, 2013, p. 85.

237 Passagnoli, G., Il diritto civile al tempo dell'intelligenza artificiale: spunti per una problematizzazione, in *Il ragionamento giuridico nell'era dell'intelligenza artificiale, a cura di Stefano Dorigo*, Pacini Giuridica Srl, 2020, p. 73.

238 Francesconi, E., Intelligenza artificiale e Diritto: tra scienza e fantascienza, in *Il ragionamento giuridico nell'era dell'intelligenza artificiale, a cura di Stefano Dorigo*, Pacini Giuridica Srl, 2020, p. 10 and Ostalé García, J., Lucas y Penrose sobre los teoremas de Gödel, *Acontecimiento: órgano de expresión del Instituto Emmanuel Mounier*, no. 120, 2016, pp. 38–42, que se encuentra en el enlace https://www.academia.edu/28396765/Lucas_y_Penrose_sobre_los_teoremas_de_G%C3%B6del.

239 Francesconi, E., Intelligenza artificiale e Diritto: tra scienza e fantascienza, in *Il ragionamento giuridico nell'era dell'intelligenza artificiale, a cura di Stefano Dorigo*, Pacini GiuridicaSrl, 2020, p. 10.

240 Suay Belenguer, J. M., La mente mecánica, Naturaleza y Libertad, *Revista de estudios interdisciplinares*, no. 1, 2012, pp. 139–169.

241 Schulz, W., and Dankert, K., 'Governance by Things' as a Challenge to Regulation by Law, *Internet Policy Review*, Vol. 5(2), 2016, pp. 1–28, available at https://policyreview.info/articles/analysis/governance-things-challenge-regulation-law.

The current evolution of the interaction between law and AI seems to demonstrate that trying to rewrite legal rules with code might not be the right approach; indeed it has been pointed out that

> both lawmakers and regulators should be cautious as they attempt to code legal obligations into software. While computer code and human language both enable forms of communication, the affordances offered by each are distinct and, in many respects, mutually exclusive. Code seeks to eliminate the forms of ambiguity and flexibility characteristic of much language, including legal language. Just as quests to replace all standards with rules have failed, so too will most efforts to rewrite legal rules as code.[242]

In the present situation, an "intelligent artificial judge" seems still too far away to be implemented. However, we must acknowledge that AI systems have already entered predominantly into the law domain, especially in assisting with decision-making and as it will be further examined, models have been developed with the aim of assisting judges in predicting cases' outcomes.

8.1 Elements of AI that present direct analogies with the dispute resolutions

In the preceding paragraphs, we have provided an overview of the development of AI and, more specifically, of the ML and the algorithms in the core of AI systems. In recent years, there have been several attempts to develop systems to predict decisions that can be somehow used to recommend attorneys to identify useful cases and support their defence opinions—also, systems that support judges by providing similar cases to help perform the final decisions on a given case.

These systems are within the category of recommender systems. These can be understood as a type of information filtering system where, by nourishing from huge data sets, the system's algorithm is able to pinpoint accurate user preferences; in other words, once the systems are aware of users' preferences, profiles and requirements, they can recommend new relevant content.[243] A common application of a recommender system generally works as follows: it tries to find similarities between users, hence suggesting items seen in similar profiles that users might find difficult to discover by themselves due to the high number and diversity of options (e.g., when a user searches for cat videos on YouTube, the user might be

242 Pasquale, F., A Rule of Persons, Not Machines: The Limits of Legal Automation, *George Washington Law Review*, Vol. 87(1), 2019, p. 3.

243 Severt, N., An Introduction to Recommender Systems, (+9 Easy Examples), *Blog*, 2018, available at https://www.iteratorshq.com/blog/an-introduction-recommender-systems-9-easy-examples/ and Isinkaye, F. O., et al., Recommendation Systems: Principles, Methods and Evaluation, *Egyptian Informatics Journal*, no. 16, 2015, p. 262, available at https://reader.elsevier.com/reader/sd/pii/S1110866515000341?token=0E34EAB4E01301A448911C602C4E70132736E5B8A06B6546ED03F318C80173D0B5118D21E163626798A8E8FDE23C2073&originRegion=eu-west-1&originCreation=20220420154416.

recommended more cat videos).[244] Therefore, in this case systems accomplish two tasks: from one side they help users to cope with information overload, and, on the other side, companies can benefit from a system that better fits users' necessities and potential desires, being also able to seduce them, increase their satisfaction and extend their permanence as clients.[245]

Recommender systems can be used in much broader ways than just for videos, music and marketing, and can be used to assist legal professionals in finding relevant literature for supporting their cases.[246] Indeed, the research in the use of these systems encompasses a wide variety of AI techniques, including, among others, ML, data mining, user modeling, case-based reasoning and constraint satisfaction.[247]

Finding relevant sources of law that discuss a specific legal issue and support a favourable decision is an onerous and time-consuming task, and by using recommendation systems, it should be possible to extract legal arguments.[248] As stated by Winkels, in the legal world there is the constant need to have easily accessible legal-related documents and, especially judges, to explain and justify their verdicts—that is, applying the law in practice. This indicates that the cited sources are somehow related, therefore a legal recommender system can be built for users of a legislative portal to receive suggestions of other relevant sources of law.[249] The importance of recommendation systems can also be seen in case law retrieval. Indeed, through

244 Nelen, J. W., *A Recommender System for a Legal Search Engine*, Delft University of Technology—Bachelor Thesis, 2021, p. 5, available at https://repository.tudelft.nl/record/uuid:233bbbb8-7c15-4a7d-aab3-1df4416eed17, Jannach, D., et al., Recommender Systems: Past, Present, Future, *AI Magazine*, Vol. 42(3), 2021, pp. 3–6 and Burke in Burke, R., et al., Recommender Systems: An Overview, *AI Magazine*, Vol. 32(3), 2011, pp. 13–18.

245 Martin, F. J., et al., The Big Promise of Recommender Systems, *AI Magazine*, Vol. 32(3), 2011, pp. 19–27 and also Lanzing, M., Strongly Recommended Revisiting Decisional Privacy to Judge Hypernudging in Self-Tracking Technologies, *Philosophy & Technology*, Vol. 32(4), 2019, pp. 549–568, where the author recognized that "The rise of Big Data practices adds more worries to the nudging debate", where hyper-nudging has been described as "the algorithmic real-time personalization and reconfiguration of choice architectures based on large aggregates of (personal) data" and Isinkaye, F. O., et al., Recommendation Systems: Principles, Methods and Evaluation, *Egyptian Informatics Journal*, no. 16, 2015, p. 264, available at https://reader.elsevier.com/reader/sd/pii/S1110866515000341?token=0E34EAB4E01301A448911C602C4E70132736E5B8A06B6546ED03F318C80173D0B5118D21E163626798A8E8FDE23C2073&originRegion=eu-west-1&originCreation=20220420154416 and Burke, R., et al., Recommender Systems: An Overview, *AI Magazine*, Vol. 32(3), 2011, pp. 13–18 X.

246 Ostendorff, M., et al., Evaluating Document Representations for Content-based Legal Literature Recommendations, *Conference: ICAIL '21: Eighteenth International Conference for AI and Law*, Association for Computing Machinery, 2021, p. 109.

247 Burke, R., et al., Recommender Systems: An Overview, *AI Magazine*, Vol. 32(3), 2011, pp. 13–18.

248 Merine, T., Quick Check: A Legal Research Recommendation System, published in NLLP@KDD 2020, *Law, Computer Science*, 2020, p. 1, available at https://www.semanticscholar.org/paper/Quick-Check%3A-A-Legal-Research-Recommendation-System-Thomas-Vacek/3387e73583d17230bfe3d0bc137e66f4c46cea4f.

249 Winkels, R., et al., Towards a Legal Recommender System, Legal Knowledge and Information Systems: JURIX 2014: The Twenty-Seventh Annual Conference, *Frontiers in AI and Applications*, 2014, pp. 169–178 and Huang, Z., et al., Context-Aware Legal Citation Recommendation Using Deep Learning, *ICAIL '21: Proceedings of the Eighteenth International Conference on AI and Law*, Association for Computing Machinery, 2021, pp. 79–88.

different methods—among which the most used are Boolean retrieval, vector space retrieval and probabilistic retrieval—case law can be retrieved.[250]

Furthermore, recommendation systems are not only useful for the retrieval of case records, judgement and law sources recommendations, they can be also helpful to identify *a priori* legal proceedings and contextualize the insights to a given user profile. Template-based recommendation systems have been created based on users' profiles and insights obtained from similar past cases using natural language processing techniques. This consists of parsing the relevant text to create user-specific legal insights and to use these insights to populate a template and provide the final recommendations to the user.[251]

In principle, the model generates statistical insights from historical case data in a semi-automated manner, and the recommendation system provides the user with a set of instructions populated from the statistical insights. In the next section some of the most relevant decision predictor models based on algorithms are reported.

8.2 Modeling

Before entering in the modeling evolution in the law field, it is worth mentioning the fact that discussions on decision theory, intended as a framework to formalize the question of how to qualify and compare decisions whose consequences are not completely known, started in 1968.[252] The general decision theory concept—that is, how decisions are taken and what drives the decisions—has been identified as

> put in its most abstract form, the typical decision-theory problem involves the proper course of action to be taken by a decision-maker who may gain or lose by taking action upon certain data that inconclusively support or discredit differing hypotheses about the state of the real but nonetheless unknowable world,

250 Locke, D., Case Law Retrieval: Accomplishments, Problems, Methods and Evaluations in the Past 30 Years, *ACM Computing Surveys*, Vol. 1(1), Article 1, 2022, pp. 1–37, available at https://arxiv.org/pdf/2202.07209. See also Shulayeva, O., at al., Recognizing Cited Facts and Principles in Legal Judgments, *AI and Law*, Vol. 25(4), 2017, pp. 107–126 where the authors developed a system that apply ML methodology in order to automatically identify legal principles and facts associated with case citations (i.e., automated identification of legal principles and facts embedded within common law citation).

251 Saxena, K., et al., Towards Recommendations from User-specific Insights Based on Historical Legal Cases, in *14th Innovations in Software Engineering Conference (Formerly Known as India Software Engineering Conference) (ISEC 2021)*, 25–27 February 2021, Bhubaneswar, Odisha: ACM, New York, p. 1, available at https://www.researchgate.net/publication/350007811_Towards_Recommendations_from_User-specific_Insights_based_on_Historical_Legal_Cases and Saxena, K., et al., Towards Recommendations from User-specific Insights Based on Historical Legal Cases, in *14th Innovations in Software Engineering Conference (Formerly Known as India Software Engineering Conference) (ISEC 2021)*, 25–27 February 2021, Bhubaneswar, Odisha: ACM, New York, p. 2, available at https://www.researchgate.net/publication/350007811_Towards_Recommendations_from_User-specific_Insights_based_on_Historical_Legal_Cases.

252 Biedermann, A., et al., Normative Decision Analysis in Forensic Science, *AI and Law*, Vol. 28, 2020, p. 10.

however,

> although we are in most legal areas far away from a useable quantification of our problems, the effort of thinking through the abstract quantitative relations among different variables turns out to provide a host of insights into the workings of our legal system.[253]

Keeping this in mind, and starting from a definition of what models are, we will try to identify the current developments that have tried to solve the need for connecting the series of data available with the provision of legal decisions.

An AI model is a program/software or algorithm that utilizes a set of data that enables it to recognize certain patterns.[254] AI models use decision-making algorithms to learn from the training and data and apply such learning to achieve specific predefined objectives.[255] These models have been developed "to reflect aspects of how humans build, exchange, analyze, and use arguments in their daily lives to deal with a world where the information may be controversial, incomplete, or inconsistent".[256]

In the law field, to understand human reasoning, two approaches—analogical legal reasoning (ARL) and rule-based legal reasoning (RLR)—can be used by judges or a decision body when performing activity that also depends on the legal system—that is, common or civil law. ARL involves reasoning directly from prior cases to the case at hand, thus the judge evaluates the similarities and differences between the previous cases and the one at hand with the decision that is based on the principle that similar cases should be treated alike. Instead, the rule-based legal reasoning (RLR) involves reasoning deductively from legal rules, hence the judge makes no reference to prior cases and simply applies the governing legal rule in the case at hand.[257]

Starting from this first legal reasoning differentiation, currently developed algorithmic decision predictors can be classified in three types: (i) predictors on the basis of legally relevant factors (case-oriented approaches), where through the use of ML or symbolic model of legal reasoning, starting from the facts description of a case, the factors are assumed to be legally relevant for the case decision and they are used for generating informative explanations of a prediction; (ii) predictors on the basis of features unrelated to the merits of a case (document-oriented

253 Kaplan, J., Decision Theory and the Factfinding Process, *Stanford Law Review*, Vol. 20(6), 1968, pp. 1065–1066.

254 Klingler, N., Deep Learning—What Is an AI Model? Here's What You Need to Know, *Blog*, available at https://viso.ai/deep-learning/ml-ai-models/ (accessed 30 September 2023).

255 Socha, G., What Is an AI Model?, *Revealdata, Blog*, available at https://www.revealdata.com/blog/what-is-an-ai-model (accessed 30 September 2022).

256 Atkinson, K., et al., Toward Artificial Argumentation, *AI Magazine*, Vol. 38(3), 2017, pp. 25–26.

257 Teitelbaum, J. C., Analogical Legal Reasoning: Theory and Evidence, *American Law and Economics Review*, Vol. 17(1), 2015, p. 160 and Rigoni, A., An Improved Factor-Based Approach to Precedential Constraint, *AI and Law*, Vol. 25(2), 2015, pp. 133–160.

approaches), where some features/elements are the data at the base of the system; and (iii) predictors on the basis of the textual description of a case (corpus-oriented approaches), where according to statistical correlation between some elements extracted from the legal text case (e.g., words) an analysis is performed to predict the decisions.[258]

Based on the preceding, we can start the analysis of the different models from the question about the system aim: What is it expected to achieve? For instance, the minimization of prediction errors? The elucidation of human understanding?[259] Different types of models have been built over the years trying to initially compare the facts and substantive features of a prior case to those of a new case and later also trying to break away from the pure empirical approach and trying to predict the outcome of cases according to legal arguments or legal reasoning.

Moreover, for a better understanding of the results of these models, the conventional way of reporting the performance of a classification system is by using accuracy, that is, how many of the labels (outcomes) were correctly classified (i.e., identified, categorized, or forecasted), or by other classification metrics that try to balance errors of Type I and Type II and emphasize models with the most stable and reliable performance regardless of potential class imbalance.[260]

The first models started, by the application of statistical or symbolic ML techniques, the classification of new cases. However, due to the lack of legal reasoning techniques, prediction(s) based on old cases were generated on the basis of quantitative feature weights, thus missing the nexus with a specific case context or legal explanation behind decisions.[261]

In the early 1970s, MacKaay and Robillard developed a program to predict outcomes of Canadian tax cases using a k-nearest neighbour algorithm. This algorithm calculates

> a measure of similarity or dissimilarity between the fact patterns of cases and [predicts] the decision in a new case to be the same as that of its [k] closest neighbor [s] in terms of . . . dissimilarity measure.[262]

258 Bex, F., and Prakken, H., On the Relevance of Algorithm Decision Predictors for Judicial Decision Making, *Proceedings of the Eighteenth International Conference on AI and Law*, ACM Press, 2021, pp. 175–179 and Branting, K., Data-Centric and Logic-Based Models for Automated Legal Problem Solving, *Artificial Intelligence Law*, Vol. 25, 2017, pp. 13–18.

259 Mackaay, E., and Robillard, P., Predicting Judicial Decisions: The Nearest Neighbour Rule and Visual Representation of Case Patterns, *Band 3*, Heft 3/4 November, 1974, Berlin and Boston: De Gruyter, 2020, pp. 302–331.

260 Medvedeva, M., et al., Rethinking the Field of Automatic Prediction of Court Decisions, *AI and Law*, Vol. 30(3), 2022, pp. 1–18.

261 Bruninghaus, S., and Ashley, K. D., Predicting Outcomes of Case Based Legal Arguments, *ICAIL '03: Proceedings of the 9th International Conference on AI and Law*, 2003, pp. 233–242, https://doi.org/10.1145/1047788.1047838.

262 Mackaay, E., and Robillard, P., Predicting Judicial Decisions: The Nearest Neighbor Rule and Visual Representation of Case Patterns, *Band 3*, Heft 3/4 November, 1974, Berlin and Boston: De Gruyter, 2020, pp. 302–331.

Following this approach, around the 1980s and 1990s, the prominent paradigm was the induction approach, in which computers created rules based on data collections and by using algorithms such as decision trees.[263]

Based on the preceding, several systems that try to reason with precedents according to the rule of induction or feature comparison have been developed. These "case-based reasoning (CBR)" systems are described as systems that

> are based on the use of previous experience to analyze or solve new legal problems, explain why previous experiences are or not similar to the present issue and adapting past solutions to meet the requirements of the present problem. The model-based approach assumes that there is a strong causal model of the domain task. It generally involves selecting among partially matched cases, in which symbolic reasoning is used to determine the difference between the given problem and the retrieved cases.[264]

In this sense, some examples can be found in TAXMAN, HYPO, CABRET, CATO, IBP and VJAP.[265] TAXMAN is a system capable of performing a rudimentary form of "legal reasoning" according to a given description of the facts. Considering the corporate reorganization case *Eisner v Macomber*, it can develop an analysis of the facts in terms of several conclusory legal concepts through a technique called "semantic information processing".[266] In other words, it tried to computationally model the majority and minority arguments in the aforementioned leading case.[267]

HYPO is a case-based reasoning system that generates legal arguments, citing past cases as justifications for legal conclusions about who should win in problem disputes involving trade secret law. HYPO arguments present competing adversarial views of the problem, and pose hypothesis to alter the balance of the

263 Ashley, K. D., A Brief History of the Changing Roles of Case Prediction in AI and Law, *Law in Context*, Vol. 36(1), 2019, pp. 97–98.

264 Stranieri, A., and Zeleznikow, J., Knowledge Discovery from Legal Databases, *Springer Law and Philosophy Library*, 69, Springer Dodrecht, 2005, pp. 1–228.

265 Berman, D., and Hafner, C. D., Incorporating Procedural Context into a Model of Case-Based Legal Reasoning, *ICAIL '91: Proceedings of the 3rd International Conference on AI and Law*, May 1991, pp. 12–20, https://doi.org/10.1145/112646.112648 and Berman, D. and Hafner, C. D., Representing Teleological Structure in Case-Based Legal Reasoning: The Missing Link, *ICAIL '93: Proceedings of the 4th International Conference on AI and Law*, August 1993, pp. 50–59, https://doi.org/10.1145/158976.158982 and Berman, D., and Hafner, C. D., Understanding Precedents in a Temporal Context of Evolving Legal Doctrine, *ICAIL '95: Proceedings of the 5th International Conference on AI and Law*, May 1995, pp. 42–51, https://doi.org/10.1145/222092.222116.

266 McCarty, L. T., Reflections on TAXMAN: An Experiment in AI and Legal Reasoning, *Harvard Law Review*, Vol. 90(5), 1977, pp. 837–893 and McCarty, L. T., An Implementation of Eisner v. Macomber, in *ICAIL '95: Proceedings of the 5th International Conference on AI and Law*, New York: ACM, 1995, pp. 276–286.

267 Bench-Capon, T. J. M., Eveline T. Feteris: Fundamental of Legal Argumentation, *AI Law*, 26, 2018, pp. 307–314.

evaluation.[268] While in the pure case-based system the core idea is to reason from cases similar to the current case in order to argue for a particular interpretation; in the current case, having the justification in past cases, Rissland and Skalak developed a system called CABARET (Case-Based Reasoning Tool), which is a hybrid architecture with the ability to combine reasoning with cases and reasoning with rules in order to apply rules containing defined terms.[269]

After that, some other systems were developed based more on hypothesis testing like, for example, CATO. CATO uses its background knowledge to characterize and re-characterize cases to argue that two cases are similar or different. It uses abstract knowledge effectively to reason symbolically about partially matched cases, generating alternative interpretations of similarities and differences.[270] The base was to describe cases in term of factors, legally significant abstractions of patterns in facts found in different cases and then build base-level factors into a hierarchy of increasing abstraction with the final outcome to discover and present arguments.[271]

Following CATO, IBP (issue-based prediction) was created with the aim to reason with legal cases. IBP, using case-based AI models of legal reasoning techniques, has the purpose to generate reasonable precedential arguments and counterarguments, regardless of empirical likelihood to predict the outcomes of the cases (given a problem, represented by a set of factors, IBP identifies the issues raised and, for each one, retrieves cases that share the issues and issue-related factors with the problem).[272] Indeed, the system reasons by analogy to previous cases the same way a lawyer would do, and it needs to know certain things about the law: (i) the factors; (ii) the issues or, in other words, the legal issues and sub-issues and

268 Ashley, K. D., Reasoning with Cases and Hypotheticals in HYPO, *International Journal of Man-Machine Studies*, Vol. 34(6), 1991, pp. 753–796 and Feteris, E., and Prakken, H., Introduction: Dialectical Legal Argument: Formal and Informal Models, *AI and Law*, Vol. 8(2–3), 2000, pp. 107–113.

269 Rissland E. L., and Skalak, B. D., Cabaret: Rule Interpretation in a Hybrid Architecture, *International Journal Man-Machine Studies*, Vol. 34(6), 1991, pp. 839–888.

270 Aleven, V., *Teaching Case-Based Argumentation Through a Model and Examples*, Ph.D. Dissertation, University of Pittsburgh, 1997, p. 8., l-Abdulkarim, L., et al., A Methodology for Designing Systems to Reason with Legal Cases Using Abstract Dialectical Frameworks, *AI Law*, Vol. 24, 2016, p. 7 and Komamizu, T., et al., Exploring Relevant Parts Between Legal Documents Using Substructure Matching, in *New Frontiers in AI, JSAI-isAI International Workshops, JURISIN, AI-Biz, LENLS, Kansei-AI Yokohama, Japan, November 10–12, 2019 Revised Selected Papers, Maki Sakamoto Naoaki Okazaki Koji MineshimaKen Satoh (Eds.)*, Springer, 2020, pp. 5–19.

271 Al-Abdulkarim, L., et al., A Methodology for Designing Systems to Reason with Legal Cases Using Abstract Dialectical Frameworks, *AI and Law*, Vol. 24(1), 2016, pp. 1–49.

272 Dung, P. M., and Tang, P. M., Modular Argumentation for Modelling Legal Doctrines in Common Law of Contract, *AI Law*, Vol. 17(3), 2009, p. 168, Aleven, V., and Ashley, K. D., Doing Things with Factors, *ICAIL '95: Proceedings of the 5th International Conference on AI and Law*, Association for Computing Machinery, May 1995, pp. 31–41 and Ashley, K. D., and Brüninghaus, S., in predicting and explaining the outcomes of case scenarios input as texts. However, being still the initial stage adjustments need to be performed for accuracies.

how factors relate to them; and (iii) the cases, or the precedents, so what has happened before and how the cases were decided. (What factors existed in that case? And who won?) Then, when a description of a fact scenario (test case) has been provided, it can make a prediction about the answer to the legal question with a prediction on the winner/loser.[273]

Later, a value judgement formalism system (VJAP) was developed with the ability of arguing about and predicting outcomes of a set of trade secret misappropriation cases.[274] It starts from the point that judges assess the effects of values not in a hierarchy but according to the specific facts of the case to be decided, thus applying value judgements across cases, mapping them from one factual scenario to another, constructing arguments that a target set of facts relates to the source factual context in a manner that justifies a particular conclusion considering the applicable values.[275]

Again, in the tax field, Blue J. Legal and Thomson Reuters recently developed a software called Tax Foresight that, by using supervised ML algorithms, can analyse tax law and rules and accurately predict the treatment of new tax situations (it reached 90% of positive results in test environments).[276]

Applying ML for prediction based on metadata can be found in different works. A first example to mention is the case of tree-like algorithms used to predict the decisions of the US Supreme Court. This worked by using metadata such as: the kind of case, the decision date and the lower court that decided the original case.[277] According to the authors,

> In total, over the period from 1816–2015, our model exhibits accuracy of 71,9% at the Justice vote level. . . . Starting in 1816 and carrying through the conclusion of the October 2014 term, our model correctly predicts 70,2% of the Court's decisions.

273 Morris, J., Issue-Based Prediction Basics, *GitHub, Blog*, available at https://gauntlet173.github.io/docassemble-openlcbr/docs/ibp_basics.html (accessed 3 September 2022).

274 Grabmair, M., *Modeling Purposive Legal Argumentation and Case Outcome Prediction Using Argument Schemes in the Value Judgement Formalism*, PhD thesis, University of Pittsburgh, PA, 2016, p. iv.

275 Ashley, K. D., A Brief History of the Changing Roles of Case Prediction in AI and Law, *Law in Context*, Vol. 36(1), 2019, p. 98.

276 O'Grady, J., Blue J Legal Tax Foresight Predictive AI for Tax Lawyers, *Dewey B Strategic*, 2019, available at https://www.deweybstrategic.com/2019/10/blue-j-legal-tax-foresight-predictive-ai-for-tax-lawyers.html (accessed 15 September 2022) and Alarie, B., et al., *Using Machine Learning to Predict Outcomes in Tax Law*, SSRN, 2017, pp. 1–23, available at SSRN: https://papers.ssrn.com/sol3/papers.cfm?abstract_id=2855977 and also Alaire, B., The Rise of the Robotic Tax Analyst, *Tax Notes Federal*, Vol. 178(1), 2023, p. 60.

277 Katz, D., et al., General Approach for Predicting the Behaviour of the Supreme Court of the United States, *PLoS ONE*, Vol. 12(4), 2017, pp. 1–18, available at https://journals.plos.org/plosone/article?id=10.1371/journal.pone.0174698. See also Ashley, K. D., A Brief History of the Changing Roles of Case Prediction in AI and Law, *Law in Context*, Vol. 36(1), 2019, pp. 97–98 and Bex, F., and Prakken, H., On the Relevance of Algorithm Decision Predictors for Judicial Decision Making, *Proceedings of the Eighteenth International Conference on AI and Law*, ACM Press, 2021, pp. 175–179.

Most recently, other tentatives in developing ML systems have been performed. Some researchers developed a system that, by training an ML classifier, aimed at predicting the outcome of a restricted set of cases from the Germany jurisdiction, that is, based on a data set of German tax law cases, a set of cases that belong to an appeal decision have been selected and, with the help of an NLP algorithm, 11 features (the courts, courts chambers, decisive legal norms, guiding principles, petitioner, cited legal norms, duration of the case, keywords of statement of facts, keywords of the legal reasoning, year of dispute and heading) have been extracted and then used to train a Naive Bayes classifier to predict whether an appeal could be successful.[278]

In the continuous attempt to identify a model/system that could support an explainable legal decision prediction, L. Karl Branting et al., recently developed two approaches to explain legal decision prediction that operates on textual inputs. The experiments arose from the need to find a trade-off between explanation quality and representation effort, recognizing that, in purely machine learning–based systems, relatively little representation effort is required, but there is a total absence of explanatory capability. Instead, in systems in which case facts have been represented in manually engineered features and legal rules are represented in executable logic, explanations have a considerable match with human explanations, but require high levels of development efforts for application at scale.[279]

The first system, ANP (attention network-based prediction), used an attention network[280] for prediction and to highlight salient case text based on attention weights for decision support (i.e., identifying the portions of case text that are most predictive of the decision[281]). This first approach failed to improve the decision accuracy, as explanations and justifications are limited by being solely based on texts without any reference to legal-relevant values. An alternative approach has been developed with the semi-supervised case annotation for legal explanations (SCALE), which exploits structural and semantic regularities in case corpora to identify textual patterns that correspond to annotations in a subset of cases. However, also in this approach the effectiveness depends heavily on the consistency of the language used across different cases even if it reduces the manual representation efforts.[282]

278 Walt, B., et al., Predicting the Outcome of Appeal Decisions in Germany's Tax Law, *9th International Conference on Electronic Participation (ePart)*, St. Petersburg, Russia, 2017, pp. 88–99, https://doi.org/10.1007/978-3-319-64322-9_8.

279 Branting, L. K., et al., Scalable and Explainable Legal Prediction, *AI and Law*, Vol. 29, 2021, p. 214. See also Walton, D., et al., An Argumentation Framework for Contested Cases of Statutory Interpretation, *AI Law*, Vol. 24(1), 2016, pp. 51–91.

280 In deep learning, "attention" is a mechanism that determines the strength of relationship between pieces of data, and in this specific case, between the pieces of text of the decisions.

281 Branting, L. K., et al., Scalable and Explainable Legal Prediction, *AI and Law*, Vol. 29, 2021, p. 214. See also Walton, D., et al., An Argumentation Framework for Contested Cases of Statutory Interpretation, *AI Law*, Vol. 24(1), 2016, pp. 214 and 217.

282 Branting, L. K., et al., Scalable and Explainable Legal Prediction, *AI and Law*, Vol. 29, 2021, pp. 214–231.

Differently that the general attempt to deploy AI systems to the law field, in cases of MAP and arbitration process, no high digitalization has occurred and the use of technology has not yet been embraced with respect to international tax dispute resolution. Here note that tax administrations have very different levels of digitalization.[283] In recent years, also due to the COVID-19 pandemic, there has been a strong development of what can be called digital communication systems or electronic communication systems. These systems aim at exchange data among the participants of the dispute-resolution process (e.g., online filing, online notification, videoconferencing, etc. . . .).[284] Also, in the field of data exchange, an interesting role could be played by web portals. These can be defined as "an infrastructure providing secure, customizable, integrated access to dynamic content from a variety of sources, in a variety of sources formats, wherever it is needed".[285] More recently, OECD also provided a definition of smart portals, referring to them as

> a "web portal" that brings information together from diverse sources in a way that allows for a degree of tailoring by both the administration and the user. This configuration and customization allow information to be presented to the user either proactively or in response to service requests, in ways that reflect past use or preference. To deliver a service, a smart portal draws information from a variety of sources, particularly accessing Big Data.[286]

The utilization of smart portals within the MAP process can be intended as a project management tool that allows tax authorities to gain an overview of the overall workload, the case status, the individual workload of each officer and the essential information collection/storage. Essential features are (i) providing easy access to the portal for both taxpayers and tax authorities via a personalized and encrypted path (e.g., a code); (ii) providing the possibility of filing a MAP request by uploading it to the portal, together with the accompanying documentation; (iii) issuing an electronic protocol that would be directly linked with the taxpayer's electronic tax profile; (iv) enabling a classification of MAP requests and their grouping into electronic folders according to subject (e.g., based on the article of the applicable tax treaty, or, on a more basic level, into transfer pricing cases and "other" cases); (v) offering the possibility of software calculations of the deadlines for the MAP (e.g., the deadline for the request for information, the ideal timeframe suggested by the OECD for the transmission of the position paper) and the notification of the tax official in charge in due time before the respective deadline,

283 EY, *Tax Administration Goes Digital*, 2017, p. 1, available at https://assets.ey.com/content/dam/ey-sites/ey-com/en_gl/topics/tax/tax-pdfs/ey-tax-administration-goes-digital.pdf#:~:text=Tax%20administration%20goes%20digital%20As%20more%20tax%20administrations,the%20IRS%E2%80%99%20information%20exchange%20program%2C%20told%20EY%20recently%2C.

284 Cai, Q., and Malamis, S. E., Digitalizations of International Tax Disputes Resolution: Reflecting in Light of the Covid-19 Pandemic, *Intertax*, Vol. 49(8&9), 2021, p. 662.

285 Westholm, H., Models of Improving e-Governance by Back Office Re-Organisation and Integration, *Journal of Public Policy*, Vol. 25(1), 2005, pp. 99–132.

286 OECD, *Technologies for Better Tax Administration: A Practical Guide for Revenue Bodies*, 2016, pp. 77–78.

especially the deadline for MAP resolution in cases where an arbitration clause is applicable, expires; (vi) allowing the taxpayer to track the general status of the case by sending predesigned notices once the case reaches a certain stage (e.g., "assessment of the request", "waiting for additional information", "preparation of position paper", "consultation between competent authorities", "finalization") and informing about important developments, such as when the request is approved or when agreement is reached between the competent authorities; and (vii) offering the possibility of secure electronic communication through the portal between tax authorities, as well as between tax authorities and taxpayers, although with different levels of access to certain information for each category of user.

For these purposes, taxpayers would have restricted access, that is, they would only be able to view the documentation they submitted and upload new documents, whereas tax authorities would receive full access to the taxpayer documents, as well as their own and read-only access to the documents (e.g., position paper) produced by the other tax administration. Potentially, there would also be different levels of access depending on the seniority of the individual staff members within their own administration (i.e., a higher-ranking tax official would have broader access and may be the only person authorized to approve a position paper for transmission to the other tax administration).[287]

The web service could be implemented with cloud computing, which could allow gathering a large amount of taxpayer's data with the possibility to share such data.[288] Indeed, cloud computing is described as "a model for enabling ubiquitous, convenient, on-demand network access to a shared pool of configurable computing resources (e.g., networks, servers, storage, applications, and services) that can be rapidly provisioned and released with minimal management effort or service provider interaction".[289] Moreover, there has been an evolution of the automated registers due to the development of the case management systems (CMS), aiming at managing and monitoring cases from the time they are initially filed to their settlements.[290] To settle transfer pricing disputes, AI/robot-mediated processes can be considered and, since the transfer pricing disputes are also numerical, systems such Smart settle ONE[291] may be used to expedite the process and overcome the problem of lacking expertise or human resources.[292]

287 Dimitropoulou, C., et al., Applying Modern, Disruptive Technologies to Improve the Effectiveness of Tax Treaty Dispute Resolution, *Intertax*, Vol. 46(12), 2018, p. 961.

288 Dimitropoulou, C, et al., Applying Modern, Disruptive Technologies to Improve the Effectiveness of Tax Treaty Dispute Resolution, *Intertax*, Vol. 46(12), 2018, pp. 962–963.

289 US: Dept. of Commerce, *National Institute of Standards and Technology (NIST)*, The NIST Definition of Cloud Computing, 2011, available at https://csrc.nist.gov/pubs/sp/800/145/final (accessed 30 June 2022).

290 Velicogna, M., Justice Systems and ICT-What Can Be Learned from Europe, *Utrecht Law Review*, Vol. 3(1), 2007, p. 135 and see also Katsh, M. E., and Rabinovich-Einy, O., *Digital Justice: Technology and the Internet of Disputes*, Oxford University Press, 2017, pp. 3–21.

291 Smartsettle ONE is a negotiation app for two-party formal negotiations that can easily be reduced to a single numerical issue. See Smartsettle ONE | Smartsettle | Simple Cases.

292 Jinyan, L., et al., *Digitalization and International Tax Dispute Resolution: A Window of Opportunity for BRITACOM*, Osgoode Legal Studies Research Paper, 2020, pp. 13–14, available at https://papers.ssrn.com/sol3/papers.cfm?abstract_id=3664039.

The use of AI systems and ML models to MAPs can be theoretically implemented as has been described earlier, that is, predictive models can be developed to allow MAP decisions to be issued based on support provided by such models, which would refer to previous cases and the following criteria: (i) the factual background of the MAP case, which should be identical to cases examined in the past; (ii) the tax treaty provisions relied upon, which should also be identical (in substance) to the provisions applicable in the cases matching the pattern; (iii) the competent authorities involved, which should ideally be identical to those involved in the cases setting the precedent; and (iv) communications exchanged with other competent authorities on the subject matter and confirmation of the results.[293]

However, in the specific field of MAPs, missing a shared and available set of data, due to the secrecy of the information, the application of big data and ML models seems to remain, currently only theoretical.[294]

According to the analysis performed until now, there are some aspects that are worth mentioning to define the current status of the interaction between AI and law/disputes. As Prakken and Sartor pointed out, the work on the combination between AI and law is mainly based on systems that work on the interpretation of legal concepts around factors in a way that

> only capture part of legal interpretation, going from the step from middle-level concepts expressed by factors to the high-level legal concepts occurring in the conditions of legal rules. The logical accounts of factor-based reasoning study how precedents give rise to rules linking factors to legal predicates and how these rules can be used to decide new cases. One key idea here is that the rules involved in factor-based reasoning are defeasible in that new factors can motivate deviations from earlier decisions. Another important insight has been that cases are not just sources of rules but also of rule preferences.[295]

In this sense, these systems are not intended to carry out any retrieval process that is not transparent to the judge.[296]

From these experiments and experiences, it could be inferred that the performance of the decision-predicting model is still very unstable and that these predictive models are still lacking accuracy, thus judges or other decision bodies

293 Dimitropoulou, C., et al., Applying Modern, Disruptive Technologies to Improve the Effectiveness of Tax Treaty Dispute Resolution, *Intertax*, Vol. 46(12), 2018, pp. 966–967.

294 Dorigo, S., Intelligenza artificiale e norme antiabuso: il ruolo dei sistemi "intelligenti" tra funzione amministrativa e attività giurisdizionale, *Rassegna Tributaria*, no. 4, 2019, p. 733.

295 Prakken, H., and Sartor, G., Law and Logic: A Review from an Argumentation Perspective, *AI*, Vol. 227, 2015, pp. 214–245.

296 Tata, C., The Application of Judicial Intelligence and 'Rules' to Systems Supporting Discretionary Judicial Decision-Making, *AI and Law*, Vol. 6(2), 1998, pp. 207–208. See also McGinnis, J. O., and Pearce, R. G., The Great Disruption: How Machine Intelligence Will Transform the Role of Lawyers in the Delivery of Legal Services, *Fordham Law Review / edited by Fordham Law Students*, Vol. 82(6), 2014, p. 3052.

should use them cautiously. And it seems that the step of legal reasoning could not be avoided in favour of simply relying on model outcomes. Indeed, it should be kept in mind that the purpose of an algorithm decision predictor is different to the judge's purpose, as the former predicts the decision a judge would take, while the latter decides the case. Since not all the decisions are correct, one thing is to correctly predict a decision according to an *ad hoc* model and another is to predict a correct decision considering that even a correct prediction of a legally incorrect decision would count as a success for the predictive algorithm.[297]

It has been argued that ML is retrospective (trained on past decisions), whereas case law is prospective (intended to influence future decisions). When deciding a case, judges are not discovering something common in previous cases, but creating a rule to decide a particular case, which is moreover intended to constrain future cases. Hence, the new rule should be consistent with previous cases, but the new case may lead to a new theory and a reinterpretation of existing cases.[298] In fact, it is not wrong to say that the algorithms are "intelligent", but they are still only algorithms[299] that are to be adjusted, and the way they are adjusted and the data used for that adjustmnt will generate different results not always constant and aligned.

The examples that are shown by the current status of the AI application to law/dispute resolution clearly show that AI systems are definitely able to generate synthetic computer cognition that matches or surpasses human-level skills and can produce useful results, but they are not intelligent enough to interpret such results, which are generated by the detection of patterns in data through the use of knowledge, rules and information that have been specifically encoded by people into forms that can be processed by a computer.[300] The value of the use of AI in law can be seen especially in cases where, through a specific application of an AI system and algorithms, a special connection of a fact with a legal result is

297 Bex, F., and Prakken, H., On the Relevance of Algorithm Decision Predictors for Judicial Decision Making, *Proceedings of the Eighteenth International Conference on AI and Law*, ACM Press, 2021, pp. 175–179.

298 Bench-Capon, T., The Need for Good-Old Fashioned AI and Law. In *International Trends in Legal Informatics: Festschrift for Erich Schweighofer* (eds. W. Hötzendorfer, C. Tschol and F. Kummer), Editions Weblaw, Bern, 2020, pp. 23–36. See also Burri, T., *International Law and Artificial Intelligence (October 27, 2017), German Yearbook of International Law 2017* (Vol. 60), Berlin: Duncker & Humblot, 2019, pp. 91–108, available at https://papers.ssrn.com/sol3/papers.cfm?abstract_id=3060191.

299 Pfeifer, R., Das ist immer noch ein Hype, *Tages-Anzeiger—Wissen*, 2018, available at "Das ist immer noch ein Hype" | Tages-Anzeiger (tagesanzeiger.ch).

300 Surden, H., ML and Law, *Washington Law Review*, Vol. 89(87), 2014, pp. 87–115 and also Hildebrandt, M., Law as Computation in the Era of Artificial Legal Intelligence Speaking Law to the Power of Statistics, *University of Toronto Law Journal*, Vol. 68(1), 2018, pp. 12–35, and Cohen, J. E., Affording Fundamental Rights: A Provocation Inspired by Mireille Hildebrandt, *Critical Analysis of Law*, Vol. 4(1), 2017, pp. 78–90, available at https://papers.ssrn.com/sol3/papers.cfm?abstract_id=3060191. Interesting in this sense is the article written by Fungwacharakorn, W., et al., Resolving Counterintuitive Consequences in Law Using Legal Debugging, *AI and Law*, Vol. 29(1–2), 2021, pp. 1–17.

found, a connection hardly possible to discover if only based on human efforts.[301] It seems, therefore, that computer-automated decisions are only possible for the simplest cases[302] and, even then, human contribution and supervision are still required.[303]

Indeed, considering that humans are naturally limited in their observations, and when it comes to processing and deriving insights from large-scale data or document sets, the current quantitative legal prediction (QLP) technologies are designed to remedy or supplement the shortcomings of human analysis,[304] but not to replace the reasoning that follows the documents or contents research. In fact, the data-centric systems are better suited for tasks that involve exploitation of knowledge latent in legal documents and corpora or that require empirical or statistical characterization of a case than tasks that depend on generation or analysis of highly rule-governed discourse or documents.[305]

9 AI systems and tax law

AI systems, as stated at the beginning of this chapter, with specific attention to ML, have a multitude of possible applications and, if their application to the *jus dicere* function should be done *cum grano salis*—that is, considering their current supportive nature—, their application to the daily operational tax activities could play an important role. Especially in these challenging times where there is an increased scrutiny from public organizations and governments, higher pressure on closing periods, and a rising demand for transparency and disclosure,[306] both tax administrations and taxpayers are forced to speed up a digitalization process, particularly through the use and development of AI-related systems.

301 Mace, J., and Mitts, J., Finding Order in the Morass: The Three Real Justifications for Piercing the Corporate Veil, *Cornell Law Review*, Vol. 100(1), 2014, pp. 135–149 where the authors were able through a technique called text analysis to review 9.380 judicial opinions and systematically predict the veil-piercing outcome.

302 Van den Hoogen, R., *E-Justice, Beginselen van Behoorlijke Elektronische Rechtspraak*, 2007, p. 153. available at https://dspace.library.uu.nl/bitstream/handle/1874/20801/index.htm?sequence=8.

303 G. Lanzara, et al., 'Gli e-services per gli uffici giudiziari', *Tecnologie della informazione e della comunicazione per la giustizia, Conference*, Rome, 23 March 2007, available at https://dspace.library.uu.nl/bitstream/handle/1874/20801/index.htm?sequence=8.

304 Katz, D. M., Quantitative Legal Prediction-or-How I Learned to Stop Worrying and Start Preparing for the Data-Driven Future of the Legal Services Industry, *Emory Law Journal*, Vol. 62, 2013, pp. 928–929.

305 Branting, K., Data-Centric and Logic-Based Models for Automated Legal Problem Solving, *AI Law*, Vol. 25, 2017, p. 12.

306 Van den Brink, M., and Bakker, A. J., Technology: A Key Enabler for Tax Transformation, *Bulletin for International Taxation*, Vol. 74(10), 2020, p. 561 and Matthews, J., Patterns and Antipatterns, Principles, and Pitfalls: Accountability and Transparency in Artificial Intelligence, *AI Magazine*, Vol. 41(1), 2020, pp. 82–89.

9.1 Tax administrations and AI systems

The mitigation of loss in tax collection is one of the main goals of tax administrations, and, to achieve it, tax authorities need to accelerate the implementation of new technologies that allow digitalization of internal operations.[307] It is a matter of fact that the digital transformation affects the way tax administrations perform their functions with the need to adapt their processes to the new digital era.[308] Indeed, the introduction of AI systems will affect the ability of tax administrations to deal with a great amount of data.[309]

Data is the basis for performing a tax analysis. The increase of documentation and reporting requirements, as well as exchange of information, for tax purposes make a massive amount of data available for tax authorities.[310] The introduction of a big data analytics system allows the analysis and output of constantly growing data volumes in seconds, and data can be grouped with the possibility to search a certain item based on a single word in all related documents.[311]

For example, by means of clustering, the behaviour of taxpayers is recognized, such as:

- Companies that tend to have comparable tax characteristics;
- Expense-generating behaviour of employees or business units; and
- Grouping of tax implications in transactional data (such as research and development credits, sales tax, capital gains, indirect taxes, foreign tax credits and

307 Quiroga, A. F. P., Innovation of the Means of Tax Payment, a Tax Administration Challenge, *CIAT—Inter-American Center of Tax Administrations*, 25 May 2021, available at https://www.ciat.org/innovation-of-the-means-of-tax-payment-a-tax-administration-challenge/?lang=en and García-Herrera-Blanco, C., The Use of Artificial Intelligence by Tax Administrations, a Matter of Principles, *CIAT—Inter-American Center of Tax Administrations*, 2 March 2020, available at https://www.ciat.org/the-use-of-artificial-intelligence-by-tax-administrations-a-matter-of-principles/?lang=en.

308 Tostes Neto, J. B., and Ferreira de Almeida, A. F., *The Dilemmas of Digitalization*, CIAT, 2022, available at https://ciat.org/ciatblog-los-dilemas-de-la-digitalizacion/?lang=en#:~:text=The%20dilemmas%20of%20digitalization%201%20Dilemma%201%20%E2%80%93,policies%20should%20Tax%20Administrations%20adopt%3F%20 . . . %20Weitere%20Elemente.

309 Martín López, J., and Pérez Bernabeu, B., Inteligencia artificial, compliance risk management y conflictividad tributaria, en *Cumplimiento cooperativo y reducción de la conflictividad: hacia un nuevo modelo de relación entre la Administración tributaria y los contribuyentes* / coord. por José Angel Gómez Requena; Saturnina Moreno González (dir.), Pedro José Carrasco Parrilla (dir.), Miguel Ángel Collado Yurrita (pr.), 2021, pp. 577–592.

310 Zackrisson, M., et al., AI and Tax Administrations: A Good Match, *Bulletin for International Taxation*, Vol. 74(10), IBFD, 2020, p. 619 and Cockfield, A. J., Tax Law and Technological Change, in *The Oxford Handbook of Law, Regulation and Technology* (eds. Roger Brownsword, et al.), EogerBrwonsword, 2016, pp. 546–569 where the author recognizes that governments exchange bulk taxpayer information to discern whether resident taxpayers are disclosing and paying tax on international investments.

311 Sakanyan, M., Big Data Analysis Towards the Future, (IOTA 2020), in *Intra-European Organisation of Tax Administrations, in Applying New Technologies and Digital Solutions in Tax Compliance*, p. 15, available at https://www.iota-tax.org/sites/default/files/documents/publications/Books/iota_book_2020_may_applying_new_technologies_and_digital_solutions_in_tax_compliance-online.pdf.

export and import taxes, detection of unusual behaviour in expenses and purchasing, examination of legal entity structures and analysis of the transfer pricing impact on taxable events).[312]

Tax administrations have already started to shift to e-administration with the purpose to improve services and enhance compliance.[313] However, it should also be recognized that the need of tax administrations for data make them require new reporting obligations.[314] Governments across the world are leveraging digital platforms to assess taxpayer data, including cross-referencing information at the source, running it through increasingly sophisticated analytics and sharing it among other agencies. In fact, tax authorities are increasingly gaining access to the vast amount of information held by the private sector—such as data on bank transactions and interest income—using digital systems, standardized reporting formats and electronic interfaces.[315]

Through advanced analytics, tax administrations can perform (i) a predictive analysis with an aim to anticipate problems (e.g., with the tax return accuracy or the timeliness of a payment) and be able to determine what and when to take action, and (ii) prescriptive analytics, where tax administration can draw inferences about cause and effect on their actions on taxpayers and then decide which action suits more a taxpayer or a group of taxpayers.[316]

312 Stevens, S., Tax Transparency—Part II: Instruments of Transparency Towards the Tax Administration—Chapter 5, in *Thematic Report—Cutting-Edge Techniques to Collect Information from Taxpayers* (eds. Funda Başaran Yavaşlar and Johanna Hey), EATLP International Tax Series, IBFD, 2019, p. 150.

313 OECD, *Tax Administration 2019: Comparative Information on OECD and other Advanced and Emerging Economies*, 2019, p. 22.

314 Largeanu, C., The Data Journey: From Reporting Obligations to Advanced Analytics, in *Intra-European Organisation of Tax Administrations, in Applying New Technologies and Digital Solutions in Tax Compliance*, IOTA, 2020, p. 9, available at https://www.iota-tax.org/sites/default/files/documents/publications/Books/iota_book_2020_may_applying_new_technologies_and_digital_solutions_in_tax_compliance-online.pdf. See also Pinto Nogueira, J. F., Tax Administration and Technology: From Enhanced to No-Cooperation?, *Digital Transformation of Tax Administrations*, SSRN, 2022, p. 14, available at https://papers.ssrn.com/sol3/papers.cfm?abstract_id=4125999 and EY, Tax Technology and Transformation, *Tax Functions Go Digital*, 2017, p. 5. According to the OECD, *Tax Administration 2019: Comparative Information on OECD and other Advanced and Emerging Economies*, 2019, pp. 47–48.

315 Gupta, S., et al., Reshaping Public Finance: Digital Revolutions in Public Finance, *International Monetary Fund*, 2017, p. 2, available at https://www.elibrary.imf.org/display/book/9781484315224/9781484315224.xml.

316 OECD, *Advanced Analytics for Better Tax Administration*, Putting Data to Work, 2016, p. 11 and 17. See also Martín López, J., and Pérez Bernabeu, B., Inteligencia artificial, compliance risk management y conflictividad tributaria, en *Cumplimiento cooperativo y reducción de la conflictividad: hacia un nuevo modelo de relación entre la Administración tributaria y los contribuyentes* / coord. por José Angel Gómez Requena; Saturnina Moreno González (dir.), Pedro José Carrasco Parrilla (dir.), Miguel Ángel Collado Yurrita (pr.), 2021, pp. 577–592.

The benefits of these new systems could be seen in the following areas where tax administrations operate: (i) audit selection, (ii) supporting the taxpayers in the information and data provision and (iii) improvement of internal efficiencies.[317]

Digital technology in tax administration allows innovation in tax policy.[318] The support of taxpayers goes through secure and reliable business systems, where tax administrations with the provisions of tax rules, regulations and policy interpretations can constantly support the taxpayers' business systems with the outcome that businesses can provide right and reliable data.[319] AI can be used to provide automated responses and support through chat bots and tailor-made guidance through applications and online reporting systems.[320] A model example of creation of tax policy has been proposed considering the expected tax evasion behaviour and the risk aversion degree of an entity using a combination of Q-learning and deep reinforcement learning techniques.[321]

Lastly, the constant implementation of automated and AI systems could grant the possibility to tax authorities to concentrate their efforts and resources on activities that are other than compliance related. Tax administrations could focus on what is outside of the secure systems, which should be intended as the ability to avoid fraud and tax evasion engaging with individual taxpayers on a transaction level,[322] therefore leaving tasks such taxpayer identification, documentation, self-assessment, reporting and payment processes to machines.[323]

The use of neural networks in the field of taxation would involve analysing patterns of tax fraud, the circumstances that determine the failure to pay tax debts or the decisions issued by a tax administration department.[324] Indeed, the delay of

317 Zackrisson, M., et al., AI and Tax Administrations: A Good Match, *Bulletin for International Taxation*, Vol. 74(10), 2020, pp. 619–620.

318 Gupta, S., et al., Reshaping Public Finance: Digital Revolutions in Public Finance, *International Monetary Fund*, 2017, p. 114, available at https://www.imf.org/en/Publications/fandd/issues/2018/03/gupta.

319 Thorén, E., Compliance by Design—Easy, Secure and Safe Business Systems, in *Intra-European Organisation of Tax Administrations, in Applying New Technologies and Digital Solutions in Tax Compliance*, IOTA, 2020, p. 51, available at https://www.iota-tax.org/sites/default/files/documents/publications/Books/iota_book_2020_may_applying_new_technologies_and_digital_solutions_in_tax_compliance-online.pdf.

320 Zackrisson, M., et al., AI and Tax Administrations: A Good Match, *Bulletin for International Taxation*, Vol. 74(10), 2020, pp. 619–622.

321 Goumagias, N. D., et al., Using Deep Q-Learning to Understand the Tax Evasion Behavior of Risk-Averse Firms, *Expert Systems with Applications*, Vol. 101, 2018, pp. 258–270.

322 Thorén, E., Compliance by Design—Easy, Secure and Safe Business Systems, in *Intra-European Organisation of Tax Administrations, in Applying New Technologies and Digital Solutions in Tax Compliance*, IOTA, 2020, p. 51, available at https://www.iota-tax.org/sites/default/files/documents/publications/Books/iota_book_2020_may_applying_new_technologies_and_digital_solutions_in_tax_compliance-online.pdf.

323 Zackrisson, M., et al., AI and Tax Administrations: A Good Match, *Bulletin for International Taxation*, Vol. 74(10), 2020, pp. 619–622.

324 Serrano Antón, F., Artificial Intelligence and Tax Administration: Strategy, Applications and Implications, with Special Reference to the Tax Inspection Procedure, *World Tax Journal*, Vol. 13(4), 2021, p. 578.

the tax declaration filing could be a form of tax evasion, and through ML models it could be possible to predict potential return defaulters.[325] Considering the need for a constant interaction between tax agencies and taxpayers, especially to influence compliance behaviour, another example would be the identity resolution technology, which uses data to define and create a unique customer identity and reduces fraud by enabling faster, more accurate identification, while also making processing more accurate.[326]

In achieving that scope, however, tax administrations should be able to properly derive the correct information from the initial raw data to avoid mistakes that could affect taxpayers' positions.[327] In fact, when public administrations decide, according to a machine outcome, that is, an automated decision[328] nearly derived by an autonomous machine decision (i.e., with less or no human intervention), this could generate inconsistencies in the decision with the need of a proper human control.[329]

325 Mehta, P., et al., DeepCatch: Predicting Return Defaulters in Taxation System using Example-Dependent Cost-Sensitive Deep Neural Networks, *2020 IEEE International Conference on Big Data (Big Data)*, 2020, p. 4412, available at https://ieeexplore.ieee.org/abstract/document/9377805. The model is based on given historical data; such potential return defaulters can be predicted based on binary classification algorithms like logistic regression, SVM and neural networks.

326 Bellenger, G., Entering the Era of the Digital Tax Agency, in *Intra-European Organisation of Tax Administrations, in Applying New Technologies and Digital Solutions in Tax Compliance*, IOTA, 2020, pp. 11–12, available at https://www.iota-tax.org/sites/default/files/documents/publications/Books/iota_book_2020_may_applying_new_technologies_and_digital_solutions_in_tax_compliance-online.pdf. See also Parker, P., What Is Identity Resolution and How Are Platforms Adapting to Privacy Changes?, *MarTech*, 2021, available at https://martech.org/what-is-identity-resolution-and-how-are-platforms-adapting-to-privacy-changes/.

327 Virgillito, A., Emerging Risks in Massive Data Analytics—A Data Scientist's Perspective, in *Intra-European Organisation of Tax Administrations, in Applying New Technologies and Digital Solutions in Tax Compliance*, IOTA, 2020, pp. 54–56, available at https://www.iota-tax.org/sites/default/files/documents/publications/Books/iota_book_2020_may_applying_new_technologies_and_digital_solutions_in_tax_compliance-online.pdf.

328 Pérez Bernabeu, B., *Los contribuyentes ante las decisiones automatizadas de la administración tributaria, La digitalización en los procedimientos tributarios y el intercambio automático de información*/Ana María Pita Grandal (dir.), Luis Alberto Malvárez Pascual (dir.), Carmen Ruiz Hidalgo (dir.), Ernesto Eseverri Martínez (col.), Aranzadi, 2023, pp. 235–254.

329 Martín López, J., Inteligencia artificial, sesgos y no discriminación en el ámbito de la inspección tributaria, *Crónica Tributaria*, no. 182, 2022, p. 57 and Serrano Antón, F., Artificial Intelligence and Tax Administration: Strategy, Applications and Implications, with Special Reference to the Tax Inspection Procedure, *Word Tax Journal*, Vol. 13(4), 2021, p. 603. See also Iriarte Yanicelli, A. A., *Derechos y garantías de los contribuyentes en la cuarta revolución industrial: aproximación desde las transformaciones de la relación jurídica tributaria en la era de la inteligencia artificial, Fiscalidad e inteligencia artificial: Administración tributaria y contribuyentes en la era digital* / Fernando Serrano Antón (dir.), Aranzadi, 2020, pp. 221–296, Barmentlo, D., and Kraan, P., Safeguarding Taxpayer Rights, in *CFE Tax Advisers Europe 60th Anniversary—Liber Amicorum—Part II: Limits to Tax Jurisdiction and Taxpayer Rights* (eds. Servaas van Thiel, Piergiorgio Valente and Stella Raventós-Calvo), IBFD, 2019, pp. 169–178 and Hadwick, D., and Lan, S., Lessons to Be Learned from the Dutch Childcare Allowance Scandal: A Comparative Review of Algorithmic Governance by Tax Administrations in the Netherlands, France and Germany, *World Tax Journal*, Vol. 13(4), 2021, pp. 609–645.

Such risks (i.e., misusing and misinterpreting the data) will be further discuss in Section 10.

9.2 The evolution of the tax function in the AI era

As pointed out in the previous section, following the recent and continuing evolution of the tax world, the current trend moves toward more reporting requirements and increased transparency. This means that tax departments are confronted with masses of data that they need to manage.[330] Therefore, to counteract the governments' digital evolution, the tax function should implement the potentials derived from AI systems. Note that there is a huge potential for automation, especially because a lot of tax activities are rule-based and they can be, for example, downsized to a decision tree understandable for a computer.[331]

The basic idea of predictive process monitoring is to train an appropriate predictor, which allows predictions about a process. For this purpose, process sequences and data are extracted from historical processes, coded accordingly and clustered appropriately.[332] An example in this respect can be found in the ability to use clustering to identify and separate different rules concerning the different taxes, such as VAT, customs and duties, corporate tax and transfer pricing.

Therefore, tax departments, to fully benefit from new technologies, could implement a platform technology that serves as a single source of the truth for applications and processes, where to store, and master data elements like legal entities and user administration, and this will be the central place for managing business data enriched for different tax processes.[333]

The tax function, as just identified, can definitively benefit from modern AI systems, which would be used to identify the cause of some variables or to drive predictive insights for tax based on historical and actual time series information, thus reducing routine tasks to a minimum, with the result that internal tax departments would have more time for tasks that are truly important.[334]

10 Discussion and ethical implications of artificial intelligence

The issue of AI, which is part of the broader context of the digital revolution, affects not only the economic sphere of our society but also has extended to the

330 Baumann-Larsen, S., and Giannelli, A., The Latest Generation of Tax Functions and the Role of Technology, *Bulletin for International Taxation*, Vol. 74(10), 2020, p. 562.

331 Risse, R., Digitalization and the Tax Function in Multilateral Enterprises, *Transfer Pricing International, Linde*, Vol. 6, 2018, p. 308.

332 Fettke, P., et al., *Anwendungspotenziale von Deep Learning im Process Mining—Prozessoptimierung in der Steuerabteilung am Beispiel von Henkel*, IM+io, 4/2017, pp. 85, 86.

333 Kuijper, B., Technology-Enabled Tax Compliance, *Bulletin for International Taxation*, Vol. 74(10), 2020, pp. 584–585 and 595 and Dickler, A. M., et al., Cross-Functional Collaboration and Change Management: The Key Ingredients for Tax Technology Transformation, *Bulletin for International Taxation*, Vol. 74(10), 2020, p. 629.

334 Baumann-Larsen, S., and Giannelli, A., The Latest Generation of Tax Functions and the Role of Technology, *Bulletin for International Taxation*, Vol. 74(10), 2020, p. 567.

entire political and social spheres. The digital revolution, which has developed with alternating phases since the 1940s, has recently found a boost due to the enormous volume of data available on the web, which offers a possibility for developing and inplementing algorithms that cannot only reproduce the results obtained by humans but can also evolve into autonomous learning. Indeed, society perceives such trends in way that could be intended as Andreessen explained, "software is eating the world".[335] The major threats from AI concern the disputed sets of values adopted by AI developers and users, as there is an emerging tendency towards a technocratic and market-driven society, which pushes for personal data monetization, forms of social control and "cheap and fast" decision-making solutions on a large (e.g., smart cities) and small (e.g., precision medicine) scale.[336]

If we consider this phenomenon in the context of Western countries which are mainly based on liberal constitutions, we then need to understand how AI systems can be shaped according to the three main elements that constitute the base of such constitutional framework, that is, human rights, democracy and the rule of law (or said another way, the trinitarian formula of the constitutional faith).[337] These principles are necessary when designing in AI systems because the capabilities of AI, which are based on big data and sensors of IoT, will potentially govern core functions of society, from education, health, law, security, and defence and political spheres.[338]

The help that these technologies can offer to the development of today's society is certainly many and of great value,[339] but it is essential that in this hyperconnected era, fundamental human rights are not forgotten, allowing the power of these advanced systems and technologies, and of the people who implement

335 Andreessen, M., Why Software Is Eating the World, *Wall Street Journal*, 2011, available at https://www.wsj.com/articles/SB10001424053111903480904576512250915629460.

336 Council of Europe, Consultative Committee of the Convention of the Protection of Individuals with regard to Automatic Processing of Personal Data—(Convention 108), *Report on Artificial Intelligence, T-PD(2018)09Rev*, Strasbourg, 25 January 2019, p. 5 and Martínez, R., Cuestiones de ética jurídica al abordar proyectos de Big Data. El contexto del Reglamento general de protección de datos, *Dilemata*, Vol. 9(24), 2017, pp. 151–164. See also Günther, M., and Kasirzadeh, A., Algorithmic and Human Decision Making: For a Double Standard of Transparency, *AI & Society*, Vol. 37(4), 2022, pp. 375–381.

337 Kumm, M., The Cosmopolitan Turn in Constitutionalism: An Integrated Conception of Public Law, *Indiana Journal of Global Legal Studies*, Vol. 20(2), Article 4, 2013, pp. 605–628, available at https://www.repository.law.indiana.edu/cgi/viewcontent.cgi?article=1516&context=ijgls and Sun, H., The Fundamental Right to Technology, *Hofstra Law Review*, Vol. 48(2), 2020, pp. 445–481.

338 Nemitz, P., Constitutional Democracy and Technology in the Age of Artificial Intelligence, *Royal Society Philosophical Transactions A*, Vol. 376(2133), 2018, pp. 1–14, available at https://royalsocietypublishing.org/doi/epdf/10.1098/rsta.2018.0089.

339 Federal Trade Commission—Uniate States of America, Big Data—A Tool for Inclusion or Exclusions?, *FTC Report*, January 2016, pp. 1–33 and Stahl, B. C., *Artificial Intelligence for a Better Future an Ecosystem Perspective on the Ethics of AI and Emerging Digital Technologies*, Springer, 2021, p. 23.

and develop them, to accrue and be exercised without responsibility.[340] This new reality escapes traditional classifications and will impose itself on both institutions and members of society without them being able to fully understand the potentials and outcomes that can be realized.[341] Constitutional values and principles should be the basis for building up the new AI systems, functioning as to avoid and not repeat situations like what happened, for example, with the Facebook Cambridge Analytics scandal where one company overcame all the existing rules and seriously put at risk many of the recognized human rights.[342]

It is a matter of fact that algorithms, even if they do not try to imitate human consciousness, have become able to act as competent communications partners, responding appropriately to our questions/requests and providing information that no human mind has ever developed and that no human mind could reconstruct,[343] with the consequences that practitioners and doctrine identify the limit of algorithms underlying the fact that they are not self-explanatory. Some designers said, "We don't try and copy intelligence. They are not made to be intelligent, but to have the possibility of displaying new emergent behaviour that can develop into something that looks like and behaves like life".[344] To better understand that, Boellstorff identified that "contemporary computational language translation, for instance, does not work by trying to get a computer to intelligently understand language: systems like Google Translate work by matching texts from a vast corpus, without

340 Council of Europe, Committee of experts on human rights dimensions of automated data processing and different forms of artificial intelligence, Rapporteur: Yeung, Karen, *A Study of Advanced Digital Technologies (Including AI Systems) for the Concept of Responsibility Within a Human Rights Framework*, DGI(2019)05, 2019, p. 13 available at https://rm.coe.int/responsability-and-ai-en/168097d9c5. See also Mosakas, K., Smart Technologies and Fundamental Rights: Brill's Interview with John-Stewart Gordon, *AI & Society*, Vol. 36(2), 2020, pp. 1–4 and Gordon, J. S., AI and Law: Ethical, Legal, and Socio-Political Implications, *AI & Society*, Vol. 36(2), 2021, pp. 403–404.

341 Dorigo, S., *Il ragionamento giuridico nell'era dell'intelligenza artificiale*, Pacini EditoreSrl, 2020, Prefazione and Council of Europe, High-Level Conference Governing the Game Changer—Impacts of artificial intelligence development on human rights, democracy and the rule of law, Conference co-organised by the Finnish Presidency of the Council of Europe Committee of Ministers and the Council of Europe 26–27 February 2019, Helsinki, Finland—Finlandia Hall, pp. 1–17, available at https://rm.coe.int/conference-report-28march-final-1-/168093bc52.

342 UK House of Commons—Digital, *Culture, Media and Sport Committee, Disinformation and 'Fake News': Interim Report*, Fifth Report of Session 2017–19, 2018, pp. 3–87, available at https://publications.parliament.uk/pa/cm201719/cmselect/cmcumeds/363/363.pdf and Crawford, K., and Schultz, J., Big Data and Due Process: Toward a Framework to Redress Predictive Privacy Harms, *Boston College Law Review*, Vol. 55(1), 2014, pp. 93–128. See also Rodríguez Peña, N. L., Big data e inteligencia artificial: una aproximación a los desafíos éticos y jurídicos de su implementación en las administraciones tributarias, *IUS ET SCIENTIA: Revista electrónica de Derecho y Ciencia*, Vol. 7(1), 2021, pp. 62–84.

343 Esposito, E., Artificial Communication? The Production of Contingency by Algorithms, *Zeitschrift für Soziologie*, Vol. 46(4), 2017, p. 253

344 Solon, O., *Weavrs: The Autonomous, Tweeting Blog-Bots That Feed on Social Content*, WIRED, 28 March2012,availableathttps://www.wired.com/story/weavrs-spambots-or-discoverability-agents/.

the computer ever 'knowing' what is said",[345] while Grossman and Kitchin pointed out that recommendation programs that currently drive many of our choices and constantly provide different suggestions, using collaborative filtering, have no idea about the products (e.g., books, movies, etc.) that they are suggesting.[346]

Considering the lack of human consciousness in the algorithms and the fact that their outcomes are not immediately explainable, the central issue to be discussed here is the question of how learning and justification of results go hand in hand; to use a contemporary term, how to arrive at an explainable AI, explainable machine learning.[347] In fact, the algorithms themselves cannot be blamed and the technological evolution is already happening, therefore it is the social construct and the specific norms and values embedded in algorithms that need to be questioned, critiqued and challenged, with the decision-making processes around algorithms that must be scrutinized in terms of how they affect human rights.[348]

This brings us to the fact that AI systems should be used for the common good, should not be used to harm people or undermine their rights, and should respect some of our widely held values such as fairness, privacy and autonomy,[349] or otherwise said, "In order for AI to benefit the common good, at the very least its design and deployment should avoid harms to fundamental human values. International human rights provide a robust and global formulation of those values".[350] It is, therefore, important to use AI systems for good, respecting the human.[351]

345 Boellstorff, T., Making Big Data, in Theory, *First Monday*, Vol. 18(10), 2013, pp. 1–17, available at https://mediarep.org/server/api/core/bitstreams/2bf0cf7a-fe69-4567-b8ee-d2ebd6c9ca51/content.

346 Grossman, L., How Computers Know What We Want—Before We Do, *Time*, 27 May 2010, available at https://time.com/archive/6597117/how-computers-know-what-we-want-before-we-do/ and Kitchin, R., Big Data, New Epistemologies and Paradigm Shifts, *Big Data & Society*, April–June 2014, p. 4, https://doi.org/10.1177/2053951714528481.

347 Verheij, B., Presidential Address to the Seventeenth International Conference on Artificial Intelligence and Law, *Artificial Intelligence as Law*, Vol. 28(3), 2020, p. 195. In this sense see also Verma, S., Weapons of Math Destruction: How Big Data Increases Inequality and Threatens Democracy—Book Review, *Vikalpa*, Vol. 44(2), 2019, pp. 97–98, https://doi.org/10.1177/0256090919853933. See also Innerarity, D., Making the Black Box Society Transparent, *AI & Society*, Vol. 36(4), 2021, pp. 975–981.

348 Council of Europe, Algorithms and Human Rights, Study on the human rights dimensions of automated data processing techniques and possible regulatory implications, prepared by the Committee of experts on internet intermediaries (MSI-NET), DGI(2017)12, 2017, p. 8.

349 Whittlestone, J., et al., Ethical and Societal Implications of Algorithms, Data, and Artificial Intelligence: A Roadmap for Research, *Nuffield Foundation*, 2019, p. 11.

350 Latonero, M., *Governing Artificial Intelligence: Upholding Human Rights & Dignity*, Data&Society, 2018, p. 1 and OECD, *OECD Guidelines for Multinational Enterprises*, 2011, pp. 13–88, available at https://www.oecd.org/daf/inv/mne/48004323.pdf.

351 Whittlestone, J., et al., *Ethical and Societal Implications of Algorithms, Data, and Artificial Intelligence: A Roadmap for Research*, Nuffield Foundation, 2019, p. 11 and Stahl, B. C., *Artificial Intelligence for a Better Future an Ecosystem Perspective on the Ethics of AI and Emerging Digital Technologies*, Springer, 2021, p. 25.

Already starting from 2016, the US,[352] EU[353] and UK[354] each issued a report where they provided their visions on how to prepare society for the advent and use of AI.[355] The US Report started with the premise that the implementation of new technology can be in support of human functions, that is, go together with humans.[356]

The application of AI has been seen in the interest of public good in a way that it could improve people's lives by helping to solve some of the world's greatest challenges and inefficiencies,[357] and this can be achieved especially through proper cooperation between public and private institutions.[358] With the purpose that AI development should be fostered, the regulation in the already existing products, such as automotive or aviation industry, should occur in a light way, therefore the government should aim to fit AI into already existing regulatory schemes.[359] However, not only benefits are foreseen, but also concerns in relation to justice, fairness and accountability have been addressed and an enhanced transparency could be the solution to tackle such issues.[360] To achieve this, the report emphasizes

352 White House Office of Science and Technology Policy (OSTP), *Preparing for the Future of Artificial Intelligence*, Report, 2016, pp. 1–45, available at https://obamawhitehouse.archives.gov/sites/default/files/whitehouse_files/microsites/ostp/NSTC/preparing_for_the_future_of_ai.pdf.

353 European Parliament, Civil Law Rules on Robotics—European Parliament resolution of 16 February 2017 with recommendations to the Commission on Civil Law Rules on Robotics (2015/2103(INL), available at TA (europa.eu). The initial draft Report was published in 2016 by the European Parliament's Committee on Legal Affairs (JURI). See also Smuha, N. A., The EU Approach to Ethics Guidelines for Trustworthy Artificial Intelligence, *Computer Law Review International*, Vol. 20(4), 2019, pp. 97–106.

354 House of Commons—Science and Technology Committee, *Robotics and Artificial Intelligence—Fifth Report of Session 2016–17*, 13 September 2016, available at Science and Technology Committee Report (parliament.uk).

355 Scipione, J., Artificial Intelligence and Europe: Risks, Developments and Implications, *SSRN*, 2020, pp. 1–22, available at https://papers.ssrn.com/sol3/papers.cfm?abstract_id=3598543 and Access Now, *Mapping Regulatory Proposal for Artificial Intelligence in Europe*, 2018, pp. 6–10, available at https://www.icnl.org/wp-content/uploads/mapping_regulatory_proposals_for_AI_in_EU.pdf.

356 The OSTP report states that: "Developing and studying machine intelligence can help us better understand and appreciate our human intelligence. Used thoughtfully, AI can augment our intelligence, helping us chart a better and wiser path forward", White House Office of Science and Technology Policy (OSTP), *Preparing for the Future of Artificial Intelligence*, Report, 2016, pp. 4, 39, available at preparing_for_the_future_of_ai.pdf (archives.gov).

357 OSTP Report, 2016, p. 13.

358 The OSTP report states that: "Private and public institutions are encouraged to examine whether and how they can responsibly leverage AI and machine learning in ways that will benefit society", 2016, p. 14.

359 White House Office of Science and Technology Policy (OSTP), Preparing for the Future of Artificial Intelligence, Report, 2016, p. 17.

360 White House Office of Science and Technology Policy (OSTP), Preparing for the Future of Artificial Intelligence, Report, 2016, p. 2. See also Cheng, L., Socially Responsible AI Algorithms: Issues, Purposes, and Challenges, *Journal of Artificial Intelligence Research*, Vol. 71, 2021, pp. 1137–1181.

the need to provide ethical training to practitioners and students and to create technical precautions when building the systems and during the testing phase.[361]

The EU Report, even if it focuses more on robotics than AI systems, recognizes that the envisaged development and the ever-increasing use of automated and algorithmic decision-making definitively impacts on the choices that a private person (such as a business or an internet user) and an administrative, judicial or other public authority take in rendering their final decisions of a consumer, business or authoritative nature with the consequence that safeguards and the possibility of human control and verification need to be built into the process of automated and algorithmic decision-making.[362] The EU as well as the US Report identified the need for a series of rules, aiming at governing in particular liability, transparency and accountability, principles that reflects the European and universal humanistic values but having in mind that those rules must not affect the processes of research and innovation and the development of robotics.[363]

The EU Report claims the need to have EU provisions that are recognized by the EU member states as to grant an efficient, coherent and transparent approach to the issues created by the AI systems.[364] These rules, which focus on the prominent roles of the governments and policymakers, define a long-term strategy for AI systems being part of society, instead of leaving them to industry and the research sector. They should start for the risk assessment from the point of view of human safety, health and security; freedom, privacy, integrity and dignity; self-determination and non-discrimination; and personal data protection.[365] Transparency is recognized as the base for each AI system in the sense that it should always be possible to supply the rationale behind any decision taken with the aid of AI that can have a substantive impact on one or more persons' lives with the possibility to reduce the AI system's computations to a form comprehensible by humans, including the logic that contributed to its decisions.[366]

At the EU level, following this first report, to address these challenges and make the most of the opportunities offered by AI, the Commission published a European

361 OSTP, *Report 2016*, p. 32.

362 European Parliament, Civil Law Rules on Robotics—European Parliament resolution of 16 February 2017 with recommendations to the Commission on Civil Law Rules on Robotics (2015/2103(INL), Introduction, lett. Q, available at TA (europa.eu).

363 European Parliament, Civil Law Rules on Robotics—European Parliament Resolution of 16 February 2017 with Recommendations to the Commission on Civil Law Rules on Robotics (2015/2103(INL), Introduction, lett. U, available at TA (europa.eu),

364 European Parliament, Civil Law Rules on Robotics—European Parliament Resolution of 16 February 2017 with recommendations to the Commission on Civil Law Rules on Robotics (2015/2103(INL), Introduction, lett. S. available at TA (europa.eu),

365 EU Report, 2017, General Principles Concerning the Development of Robotics and Artificial Intelligence for Civil Use, n. 11 and 13.

366 EU Report, 2017, General Principles Concerning the Development of Robotics and Artificial Intelligence for Civil Use, n. 12 and Walmsley, J., Artificial Intelligence and the Value of Transparency, *AI & Society*, Vol. 36(2), 2021, pp. 585–595.

strategy in April 2018[367] based on three pillars: (i) boosting the EU's technological and industrial capacity and AI uptake across the economy, both by the private and public sectors; (ii) preparing for socio-economic changes brought about by AI; and (iii) encouraging the modernization of education and training systems, nurturing talent, anticipating changes in the labour market, supporting labour market transitions and adaptation of social protection systems and ensure an appropriate ethical and legal framework, based on the EU's values and in line with the Charter of Fundamental Rights of the EU with the vision of joining forces among EU member states.[368]

The joint work among the member states led to the creation of a coordinated plan that identified actions to be undertaken starting from 2019–2020 and that prepared the ground for the incoming years,[369] and on a yearly basis the goals set in the previous year will be monitored and checked to evaluate the development on the common EU designated path.[370] Together with the coordinated plan, the Commission established a High-Level Expert Group that published Guidelines on trustworthy AI in April 2019.[371] The seven key requirements identified in the Guidelines of the High-Level Expert Group, as better further explained, are (i) human agency and oversight; (ii) technical robustness and safety; (iii) privacy and data governance; (iv) transparency; (v) diversity, non-discrimination and fairness; (vi) societal and environmental well-being; and (vii) accountability.[372]

Always at the European level, The European Commission for the Efficiency of Justice (CEPEJ)[373] established an AI governance framework by adopting, on

367 European Commission, Communication from the Commission to the European Parliament, the European Council, the Council, the European Economic and Social Committee and the Committee of the Regions on Artificial Intelligence for Europe, Brussels, COM(2018) 237 final. See also Castellano, P. S., Inteligencia artificial y valoración de la prueba: las garantías jurídico-constitucionales del órgano de control, *THĒMIS-Revista de Derecho 79*, enero–junio 2021, pp. 283–297.

368 European Commission, Communication from the Commission to the European Parliament, the European Council, the Council, the European Economic and Social Committee and the Committee of the Regions on Artificial Intelligence for Europe, Brussels, COM(2018) 237 final, p. 3.

369 European Commission, Communication from the Commission to the European Parliament, the European Economic and Social Committee and the Committee of the Regions—Coordinated Plan on Artificial Intelligence, Brussels, COM(2018) 795 final, p. 2, available at resource.html (europa.eu).

370 European Commission, ANNEXES to the Communication from the Commission to the European Parliament, the European Council, the Council, the European Economic and Social Committee and the Committee of the Regions Fostering a European approach to Artificial Intelligence Brussels, 2021, COM(2021) 205 final, available at https://digital-strategy.ec.europa.eu/en/library/coordinated-plan-artificial-intelligence-2021-review.

371 European Commission, *Ethics Guidelines for Trustworthy AI*, 2019, pp. 2–45, available at https://digital-strategy.ec.europa.eu/en/library/ethics-guidelines-trustworthy-ai. See also Hofmann, C. H., and Hahn, B., Decentred Ethics in the Machine Era and Guidance for AI Regulation, *AI & Society*, Vol. 35(3), 2020, pp. 635–644.

372 European Commission, White Paper on Artificial Intelligence—A European Approach to Excellence and Trust, COM(2020) 65 final, p. 9.

373 It is the intergovernmental body responsible for promoting the efficiency and proper functioning of justice in the 47 member states of the Council of Europe.

December 3–4, 2018, the Ethical Charter for the use of AI in judicial systems and their environment.[374] This is the first text at European and global levels, setting out five substantive and methodological principles that should guide the integration of AI tools and services into national judicial systems.[375] It is aimed at private companies; public actors in charge of designing and deploying AI tools and services in this field; public decision-makers in charge of the legislative or regulatory framework, and the development, audit or use of such tools and services; as well as legal professionals in order to improve the efficiency and quality of justice when it comes to the use of AI tools and services in judicial systems according to the respect of the fundamental rights of individuals as set out in the European Convention on Human Rights (ECHR) and Council of Europe Convention n. 108 on the Protection of Personal Data, as well as the other fundamental principles set out in the Charter.[376]

The five principles identified in the Ethical Charter are (i) principle of respect for fundamental rights: ensure that the design and implementation of artificial intelligence tools and services are compatible with fundamental rights; (ii) principle of non-discrimination: specifically prevent the development or intensification of any discrimination between individuals or groups of individuals; (iii) principle of quality and security: with regard to the processing of judicial decisions and data, use certified sources and intangible data with models elaborated in a multidisciplinary manner, in a secure technological environment; (iv) principle of transparency, impartiality and fairness: make data processing methods accessible and understandable, authorize external audits; and (v) principle "under user control": preclude a prescriptive approach and ensure that users are informed actors and in control of the choices made.[377]

Lastly, the UK Report aimed to identify "the [AI and robotics] potential value and capabilities, as well as examining prospective problems, and adverse consequences, that may require prevention, mitigation, and governance".[378] The

374 Council of Europe, European Commission for the Efficiency of Justice (CEPEJ), European Ethical Charter on the Use of Artificial Intelligence in Judicial Systems and Their Environment, Adopted at the 31st Plenary Meeting of the CEPEJ (Strasbourg, 3–4 December 2018), available at https://rm.coe.int/ethical-charter-en-for-publication-4-december-2018/16808f699c.

375 Barbaro, C., *The European Ethical Charter of the CEPEJ on the Use of Artificial Intelligence (AI) in Judicial Systems and Their Environment*, European Expertise & Expert Institute (EEEI), 2019, available at https://experts-institute.eu/en/europe-of-justice/cepej-en/the-european-ethical-charter-of-the-cepej/.

376 European Commission, Directorate of the Human Rights, The CEPEJ European Ethical Charter on the Use of Artificial Intelligence (AI) in Judicial Systems and Their Environment, *Presentation Note*, 4 December 2018, available at https://rm.coe.int/presentation-note-en-for-publication-4-december-2018/16808f699d.

377 Council of Europe, European ethical Charter on the Use of Artificial Intelligence in Judicial Systems and Their Environment, 2018, p. 7. See also Bench-Capon, T. J. M. and Modgil, S., Norms and Value Based Reasoning: Justifying Compliance and Violation, *Artificial Intelligence and Law*, Vol. 25(1), 2017, pp. 29–64 and Scheutz, M., The Case for Explicit Ethical Agents, *AI Magazine*, Vol. 38(4), 2017, pp. 57–64 where the author where the author pushes for the need to instill moral and ethical competence in all cognitive system intended to be employed in human social context.

378 UK Report, 2016, p. 7.

report recognized that it is the moment to scrutinize the ethical, legal and societal dimensions of artificially intelligent systems.[379] In achieving that, it is important to ensure that AI technology is operating as intended and that unwanted, or unpredictable, behaviours are not produced, either by accident or maliciously, with the strong need that methods are required to verify that the system is functioning correctly.[380] Moreover, in recognizing the importance of clarifying the transparency and accountability issues generated by the AI systems, the Report pointed out that

> Appropriate legal and regulatory frameworks will have to be developed to support the more widespread deployment of robots and autonomous systems. Frameworks need to be created to establish where responsibilities lie, to ensure the safe and effective functioning of autonomous systems, and how to handle disputes in areas where no legal precedence has been set.[381]

Also, some non-governmental organizations, following this need to develop principles that could be of guidance in the implementation of AI systems in society, tried to implement such guiding principles. In this path, governments, researchers, business representatives and companies reunited at the Asilomar Conference on Beneficial AI in 2017 in Pacific Grove, California, organized by the Future of Life Institute,[382] where the 23 Asilomar AI principles were created as guidelines for the research and development of AI. The Asilomar principles outline AI developmental issues, ethics and guidelines for the development of beneficial AI and to make beneficial AI development easier.

Furthermore, the Declaration for a Responsible Development of Artificial Intelligence (Montréal Declaration) is of interest.[383] On November 3, 2017, the Université de Montréal, in collaboration with the Fonds de recherche du Québec, launched a co-construction process, based on the Montréal Declaration for a Responsible Development of Artificial Intelligence, that was the outcome of dozens of events organized to stimulate discussion on social issues that arise with AI. There were 15 deliberation workshops held over three months, involving over 500 citizens, experts and stakeholders from all backgrounds with the aim to set a series of rules in order to help the development of an artificial intelligence that is socially

379 UK Report, 2016, p. 25, where it is stated that "While it is too soon to set down sector-wide regulations for this nascent field, it is vital that careful scrutiny of the ethical, legal and societal dimensions of artificially intelligent systems begins now".

380 UK Report, 2016, p. 16.

381 UK Report, 2016, p. 22.

382 Future of Life, *A Principled AI Discussion in Asilomar*, 18 January 2017, available at https://futureoflife.org/principles/principled-ai-discussion-asilomar/ (accessed 20 December 2020).

383 Montréal Declaration Responsible AI, *Montréal Declaration for a Responsible Development of Artificial Intelligence*, 2018, available at https://www.montrealdeclaration-responsibleai.com/_files/ugd/ebc3a3_506ea08298cd4f8196635545a16b071d.pdf.

responsible and morally acceptable.[384] The Montréal Declaration for Responsible AI Development has three main objectives: (i) develop an ethical framework for the development and deployment of AI; (ii) guide the digital transition so everyone benefits from this technological revolution; and (iii) open a national and international forum for discussion to collectively achieve equitable, inclusive and ecologically sustainable AI development.[385]

To summarize, the ethical risks faced with the advent of AI can be identified as follows: (i) privacy and data protection: lack of privacy, misuse of personal data and security problems; (ii) reliability: lack of quality data, lack of accuracy of data, problems of integrity; (iii) lack of accountability and liability, lack of transparency, bias and discrimination, lack of accuracy of predictive recommendations and lack of accuracy of non-individual recommendations; and (iv) safety: harm to physical integrity.[386] These will be described in the next sections.

Therefore, if machines engage in human communities as partially or fully autonomous agents, then it will be expected they follow the community's social and moral norms, which should be set up considering the kinds of tasks the machines are designed to perform with the recognition that machines should serve humans and not the other way around but without jeopardizing the importance that these systems have, if properly developed, in increasing economic value for society.[387]

10.1 Lack of transparency and interpretation of the AI answers

The issue of the lack of transparency in the decisions of algorithms is a problem that significantly affects the protection of the rights of citizens and, with reference to taxation, of taxpayers.[388] Therefore, explainability[389] and transparency

384 Montréal Declaration Responsible AI, *Montréal Declaration for a Responsible Development of Artificial Intelligence*, 2018, available at https://www.montrealdeclaration-responsibleai.com/_files/ugd/ebc3a3_5c89e007e0de440097cef36dcd69c7b0.pdf and Anderson, M., and Leigh Anderson, S., Machine Ethics: Creating an Ethical Intelligent Agent, *AI Magazine*, Vol. 28(4), 2007, pp. 15–26.

385 Montréal Declaration Responsible AI, *Montréal Declaration for a Responsible Development of Artificial Intelligence*, 2018, p. 5, available at https://www.montrealdeclaration-responsibleai.com/_files/ugd/ebc3a3_506ea08298cd4f8196635545a16b071d.pdf.

386 Stahl, B. C., *Artificial Intelligence for a Better Future An Ecosystem Perspective on the Ethics of AI and Emerging Digital Technologies*, Springer, 2021, p. 49.

387 IEEE Global Initiative on Ethics of and Autonomous and Intelligent Systems, *Ethically Aligned Design: A Vision for Prioritizing Human Well-Being with Autonomous and Intelligent Systems*, IEEE, 2017, p. 8, available at https://standards.ieee.org/wp-content/uploads/import/documents/other/ead_v2.pdf and Nurock, V., et al., What Does "Ethical by Design" Mean?, in *Reflections on Artificial Intelligence for Humanity* (ed. Bertrand Braunschweig Malik Ghallab), Springer, 2021, pp. 171–190. See also Tsamados, A., et al., The Ethics of Algorithms: Key Problems and Solutions, *AI & Society*, Vol. 37(3), 2022, pp. 215–230.

388 Pérez Bernabeu, B., El principio de explicabilidad algorítmica en la normativa tributaria española hacia un derecho a la explicación individual, *Civitas. Revista española de derecho financiero*, no. 192, 2021, pp. 143–178.

389 Pérez Bernabeu, B., El principio de explicabilidad algorítmica en la normativa tributaria española hacia un derecho a la explicación individual, *Civitas. Revista española de derecho financiero*, no. 192, 2021, pp. 143–178, where the author provides that "*el 'principio de explicabilidad' exige que los procesos sean transparentes y que las decisiones puedan explicarse a las partes que se vean afectadas por ellas*".

when dealing with AI systems are focal points, especially in relation to their outcomes.[390] Indeed, it has been identified that, if from one side AI has the potential to improve the welfare and well-being of people, to contribute to positive sustainable global economic activity, to increase innovation and productivity, and to help respond to key global challenges, on the other side it also raises challenges for societies and economies, notably regarding economic shifts and inequalities, competition, transitions in the labour market, and implications for democracy and human rights.[391]

The possibility of big multinationals as well as governments obtaining and storing enormous quantities of data (considering the great power hidden and embedded in such data) and the possibility of that data being used without the knowledge of the citizens[392] is an element that should be considered for the human rights preservation. Some authors recognized this: "GAFA—an acronym combining the names of some of the largest consumer tech companies, Google, Apple, Facebook and Amazon—have become what I call the iLeviathan, the ruler of a new commonwealth where people trade freedom for utility".[393]

The accumulation of digital power, which shapes the development and deployment of AI, is based on fours source of power: (i) due to the large amount of money the big tech players can invest in political and social influence or invest in any ideas and start-ups in the AI area; (ii) the big tech companies control of the infrastructures of public discourse and the digital environment, which is decisive for elections because internet services become the main source citizens to access political information; (iii) being able to collect personal data and profit from the behaviour of any of us, both when online and offline (it seems that we can say that they know us better than our families); and (iv) they dominate development and systems integration into usable AI services.[394] Furthermore, not only is data storage an issue, but also the mistakes derived using such data can jeopardize human rights. There may be cases where ML-based systems make mistakes, for example it is wrong for Google Photos to identify men of colour as gorillas, or for the recommendation

390 Federal Trade Commission—United States of America, Big Data—A Tool for Inclusion or Exclusions?, *FTC Report*, January 2016, pp. 1–33 and Burkart, N., and Huber, M., A Survey on the Explainability of Supervised Machine Learning, *Journal of Artificial Intelligence Research*, Vol. 70, 2021, pp. 245–317, available at jair.1.12228 (acm.org). See also Bruneault, F., and Sabourin Lafamme, A., AI Ethics: How Can Information Ethics Provide a Framework to Avoid Usual Conceptual Pitfalls? An Overview, *AI & Society*, Vol. 36(3), 2021, pp. 757–766.

391 OECD, *Recommendation of the Council on OECD Legal Instruments Artificial Intelligence*, 2022, p. 3, available at https://oecd.ai/en/assets/files/OECD-LEGAL-0449-en.pdf and Aghemo, R., Algoritmi e discriminazione: non veridicità della neutralità tecnologica, *Medium Blog*, 7 January 2021, available at https://oecd.ai/en/assets/files/OECD-LEGAL-0449-en.pdf.

392 Amnesty International, Artificial Intelligence for Good, 2017, available at https://www.amnesty.org/en/latest/news/2017/06/artificial-intelligence-for-good/ y Angwin, J., et al., *Machine Bias*, ProPublica, 2016, available at https://www.amnesty.org/en/latest/news/2017/06/artificial-intelligence-for-good/.

393 Prainsack, B., Logged Out: Ownership, Exclusion and Public Value in the Digital Data and Information Commons, *Big Data & Society*, Vol. 6(1), 2019, pp. 1–2.

394 Nemitz, P., Constitutional Democracy and Technology in the Age of Artificial Intelligence, Vol. 376(2133), 2018, p. 4, available at https://royalsocietypublishing.org/doi/10.1098/rsta.2018.0089 and Walsh, T., Experiments in Social Media, *AI Magazine*, Vol. 40(4), 2019, pp. 74–77.

system to choose that men of colour have to go to jail while white men do not based on race alone, or that military weapons identify targets based on race.[395]

The facts, as just described, are derived mainly from the fact that AI systems, both those exclusively based on human instructions and those that operate without the direct oversight and control of humans, can encompass a series of characteristics that can have a direct implication on the guarantee of human rights. In this regard, the current most important characteristics can be summarized as follows: (i) inscrutability and opacity; (ii) complexity and dynamism; (iii) human input, interaction and discretion; (iv) a general purpose technology; (v) global interconnectivity, ubiquity and scalability; (vi) real-time automated and continuous operation; (vii) reliance on large data sets; (viii) capacity to generate insight from merging data sets; (ix) capacity to imitate human traits; (x) greater software complexity; (xi) capacity to "personalize" and configure individual choice environments; (xii) capacity to redistribute risks, benefits and burdens among and between individuals and groups via the use of AI-driven optimization systems which reconfigure social environments and choice architectures; and (xiii) the capacity to generate problems of collective action.[396]

Following is an overview of these elements and how they can affect society:

1. Inscrutability and opacity

This characteristic is one of great concern among technology experts and policymakers. When dealing with algorithms' outputs, the recipient rarely has any concrete sense of how or why a particular classification has been arrived at from inputs.[397] Even if there are algorithms that are understandable and their reasoning can be traced, for example, decision-trees algorithms, others such as neural networks leave their underlying logic shrouded in mystery.[398] Furthermore, intellectual property and expert knowledge are elements that should be considered when dealing with the opacity of an algorithm, as they somehow can create a barrier between the inputs and outputs of a system. In fact, intellectual property rights can

395 Weinberger, D., *Optimization Over Explanation—Maximizing the Benefits of Machine Learning Without Sacrificing Its Intelligence*, Berkman Klein Center Collection, 28 January 2018, available at https://medium.com/berkman-klein-center/optimization-over-explanation-41ecb135763d. See also Milano, S., et al., Recommender Systems and Their Ethical Challenges, *AI & Society*, Vol. 35(4), 2020, pp. 957–967.

396 Council of Europe, Committee of experts on human rights dimensions of automated data processing and different forms of artificial intelligence, Rapporteur: Yeung, Karen, A study of advanced digital technologies (including AI systems) for the concept of responsibility within a human rights framework, DGI(2019)05, 2019, p. 21–25 available at https://rm.coe.int/responsability-and-ai-en/168097d9c5.

397 Burrell, J., How the Machine "Thinks": Understanding Opacity in Machine Learning Algorithms, *Big Data & Society*, Vol. 3(1), 2016, p. 1.

398 Zalnieriute, M., and Bennett Moses, L., The Rule of Law and Automation of Government Decision-Making, *Modern Law Review*, Vol. 82(3), 2019, pp. 397–424.

limit, even not completely block, the availability of the systems for scrutiny,[399] and in cases where the algorithms can be considered as understandable, only experts can derive information from and get the inside process while most of the people remain unaware.[400]

2. Complexity and dynamism

In this respect, consider that data can be either static or dynamic. Static data does not change after it has been collected, whereas for dynamic data a differentiation can be made between (i) dynamic data updated from time-to-time, where the initially provided data is changed in order to grant the system integrity but it is not necessarily real-time data and (ii) dynamic real-time data that is delivered immediately after collection with no delay.[401] The degree to which data is static or dynamic is relevant for AI systems, which can iterate and evolve over time and may change their behaviour in unforeseen ways; hence the outcome may not fit the reality.[402] Therefore, considering dynamism, the rate of change of the environment, independent of the activities of the agent; accessibility, the extent to which an agent has access to the state of the environment; and determinism, the degree of predictability of the system behaviour for identical system inputs, it is quite challenging to predict the outcomes when the environment is changing quite fast.[403]

3. Human input, interaction and discretion

Machines and humans are currently interacting, and it is of fundamental importance to maintain human-centric AI for society's long-term stability through the

399 Noto La Diega, G., Against the Dehumanisation of Decision-Making—Algorithmic Decisions at the Crossroads of Intellectual Property, Data Protection, and Freedom of Information, *JIPITEC—Journal of Intellectual Property, Information Technology and E-Commerce Law*, Vol. 9(1), 2018, pp. 3–34.

400 Burrell, J., How the Machine "Thinks": Understanding Opacity in Machine Learning Algorithms, *Big Data & Society*, Vol. 3(1), p. 4 and Zalnieriute, M., and Bennett Moses, L., The Rule of Law and Automation of Government Decision-Making, *Modern Law Review*, Vol. 82(3), pp. 397–424 according to which there are systems that are so complex that make possible to be recognized a human limitation in fully comprehending or explaining the operation of such complex systems, especially due to the different way humans and machines reasons. Hence, in this respect also the experts are hardly able to extract useful information from the systems.

401 OECD, *OECD Framework for the Classification of AI Systems—OECD Digital Economy Papers No. 323*, 2022, p. 35, available at https://www.oecd-ilibrary.org/science-and-technology/oecd-framework-for-the-classification-of-ai-systems_cb6d9eca-en;jsessionid=Sd0YsL3sGhG9v_yZbKRbIGlb-bjD4C3ckRB2nM8w.ip-10-240-5-82.

402 OECD, *OECD Framework for the Classification of AI Systems—OECD Digital Economy Papers No. 323*, 2022, p. 36, available at https://www.oecd-ilibrary.org/science-and-technology/oecd-framework-for-the-classification-of-ai-systems_cb6d9eca-en.

403 Schut, M., and Wooldridge, M., Intention Reconsideration in Complex Environments, *Proceedings of the Fourth International Conference on Autonomous Agents*, 2000, pp. 209–216, https://doi.org/10.1145/336595.337377.

involvement of humans in idea and proposal phases for the build-up of the models, data collection and data analysis, as well as testing, implementation, validation.[404] In fact, as we defined in this chapter, the machines have a large impact on the choices that humans are making. In this sense we can refer to the recommendations that different systems provide when it comes to buying any type of product, and this is even more troublesome when a decision has to be made when dealing with the personal sphere of individuals (e.g., court decisions). In all these cases, but especially the last, important intervention of humans is still required.

4. A general purpose technology

Objects that are common in our daily lives can have a dual use, that is, they can provide benefits to the society or they can be harmful. AI systems are no different. Thus, it is of fundamental importance that policymakers collaborate closely with technical researchers to investigate, prevent and mitigate potential malicious uses of AI.[405]

5. Global interconnectivity, ubiquity and scalability

Human beings have learned how to live with technology but, especially in these last years, technology has invaded our lives, with the consequence that it seems impossible to foresee a life without a technological device.[406] We are facing an era that has been named "surveillance capitalism" when data accumulation is used to predict and modify human behaviours as a mean to produce revenue and market control.[407] However, it does not mean that all the people living on earth have access to such technology and this imbalance can even create more inequality in the long term.[408] In this last respect, not only poor people risk being permanently left out

404 Bryson, J. J., and Theodorou, A., How Society Can Maintain Human-Centric Artificial Intelligence, in *Human-Centered Digitalization and Services 2019* (eds. Marja Toivonen and Eveliina Saari), Springer, pp. 305–323 and Kritikos, M., What If Technologies Had Their Own Ethical Standards?, *At Glance—Scientific Foresight: What If?*, European Parliament (Panel for the Future of Science and Technology (STOA), 2018, available at https://www.europarl.europa.eu/stoa/en/document/EPRS_ATA(2018)624247.

405 Brundage, M., et al., *The Malicious Use of Artificial Intelligence: Forecasting, Prevention, and Mitigation*, Report of the workshop entitled "Bad Actor Risks in Artificial Intelligence" in Oxford, 2018, p. 4.

406 Zuboff, S., Big Other: Surveillance Capitalism and the Prospects of an Information Civilization, *Journal of Information Technology*, Vol. 30, 2015, pp. 75–89.

407 Zuboff, S., Big Other: Surveillance Capitalism and the Prospects of an Information Civilization, *Journal of Information Technology*, Vol. 30, 2015, pp. 75–89. See also Council of Europe, Declaration by the Committee of Ministers *on the manipulative capabilities of algorithmic processes, (Adopted by the Committee of Ministers on 13 February 2019 at the 1337th meeting of the Ministers' Deputies), Decl(13/02/2019)1*, available at https://search.coe.int/cm#{%22CoEIdentifier%22:[%22090000168092dd4b%22],%22sort%22:[%22CoEValidationDate%20Descending%22]}.

408 The Royal Society, *Machine Learning: The Power and Promise of Computers That Learn by Example*, 2017, pp. 5–124, available at https://royalsociety.org/~/media/policy/projects/machine-learning/publications/machine-learning-report.pdf. See also Lanzing, M., Strongly Recommended Revisiting Decisional Privacy to Judge Hypernudging in Self-Tracking Technologies, *Philosophy & Technology*, Vol. 32(4), 2019, pp. 549–568.

from the use of technologies, but they, on the other side, are the highest monitored. Recently it has been stated: "For many poor people in the U.S., the data that's gathered about them at every turn can obstruct attempts to escape poverty. . . . Low-income communities are among the most surveilled communities in America".[409]

6. Real-time automated and continuous operation

When a person needs to reach a certain place, whether on foot or by car, or find out information on the internet, a large amount of data is moving and automatically stored. That means that being part of a connected world—continuously internet-connected, generating and transmitting data—could be, on the one hand, very helpful but also raises security and privacy concerns.[410]

7. Reliance on large data sets

Data is best understood narrowly as a raw material for generating new knowledge and due to the "data-ization" of our lives should properly follow a data set's life cycle, which can roughly be summarized in the following order: collection → cleaning → processing → analysis → modeling → visualization → policy relevance.[411] Embedding the data in this evaluation and validation process is fundamental to avoid that algorithm, whose base is the large amount of data, will provide outputs that can affect human rights.[412]

8. Capacity to generate insight from merging data sets

Currently, human behaviours are digitally mediated in a way that they are recorded and analysed to implement the systems and models that are then used to predict these same behaviours.[413] Therefore, from this little basic information record, behaviours as well as personality can be the object of prediction, thus generating an indirect disclosure of personal information that individuals would have liked to

409 Waddell, K., How Big Data Harms Poor Communities, *The Atlantic*, 2016, available at https://www.theatlantic.com/technology/archive/2016/04/how-big-data-harms-poor-communities/477423/ (accessed 15 October 2022).

410 Swan, M., Connected Car: Quantified Self Becomes Quantified Car, *Journal of Sensor and Actuator Networks*, Vol. 4(1), 2015, pp. 2–29.

411 Lovelace, R., Review of "The Data Revolution: Big Data, Open Data, Data Infrastructures & their Consequences", *Rob Kitchin Journal of Regional Science*, Vol. 56(4), 2016, pp. 722–723.

412 Prainsack, B., Logged Out: Ownership, Exclusion and Public Value in the Digital Data and Information Commons, *Big Data & Society*, Vol. 6(1), 2019, pp. 1–15 and Council of Europe, Committee of experts on human rights dimensions of automated data processing and different forms of artificial intelligence, Rapporteur: Yeung, Karen, A study of advanced digital technologies (including AI systems) for the concept of responsibility within a human rights framework, DGI(2019)05, 2019, p. 23, available at https://rm.coe.int/responsability-and-ai-en/168097d9c5. See also Lyons, J. B., et al., Certifiable Trust in Autonomous Systems: Making the Intractable Tangible, *AI Magazine*, Vol. 38(3), 2017, pp. 37–49.

413 Kosinski, M., et al., Private Traits and Attributes Are Predictable from Digital Records of Human Behavior, *Proceedings of the National Accademy of Science*, Vol. 110(15), 2013, pp. 5802–5805.

have kept secret, thus generating a privacy issue that should then be mitigated by correctly governing the data collection and data processing.[414]

9. Capacity to imitate human traits

Humans are threatened by the ability of machines to replicate what characterizes humans, such as, for example, voice, behaviours and creating what is known as "fake news", which is misleading for the society.[415] In this sense, deep fake technology has been defined by Chesney and Citron[416] as "leverages machine-learning algorithms to insert faces and voices into video and audio recordings of actual people and enables the creation of realistic impersonations" or put another way "makes it possible to create audio and video of real people saying and doing things they never said or did".

10. Greater software complexity

Binary classification, which makes it possible to allocate an input to a given class began in 1957 with the perceptron invention, and since then AI systems and models have reached a quite high level of complexity, generating three types of vulnerability: (i) propensity to generate stochastic components, that is, make mistakes; (ii) adversarial attacks; and (iii) unpredictability of their outputs that can generate adverse third-party effects.[417]

11. Capacity to personalize and configure individual choice environments

Recommendation systems are part of our daily lives in a way that many of the choices we make are guided; even our decisional power is indirectly replaced by what the algorithms suggest. The well-known big tech companies, such as Google,

414 See among others, Fast, A. F., and Funder, D. C., Personality as Manifest in Word Use: Correlations with Self-Report, Acquaintance Report, and Behavior, *Journal of Personality and Social Psychology*, Vol. 94(2), 2008, pp. 334–346, De Bock K., and Van Den Poel, D., Predicting Website Audience Demographics for Webadvertising Targeting Using Multi-Website Clickstream Data, *FundamentaInformaticae*, Vol. 98(1), 2010, pp. 49–70, Rentfrow, P. J., and Gosling, S. D., The Do re mi's of Everyday Life: The Structure and Personality Correlates of Music Preferences, *Journal of Personality and Social Psychology*, Vol. 84(6), 2003, pp. 1236–1256.

415 Siekiersky, B. J., *Deep Fake: What Can Be Done About Synthetic Audio and Video?*, Library of Parliament, Ottawa, Canada 2019, Publication No. 2019-11-E, pp. 1–6.

416 Chesney, B., and Citron, D., Deep Fakes: A Looming Challenge for Privacy, Democracy, and National Security, *California Law Review*, Vol. 107(1753), 2019, pp. 1755–1786.

417 Council of Europe, Committee of experts on human rights dimensions of automated data processing and different forms of artificial intelligence, Rapporteur: Yeung, Karen, A study of advanced digital technologies (including AI systems) for the concept of responsibility within a human rights framework, DGI(2019)05, 2019, pp. 21–25. available at https://rm.coe.int/responsability-and-ai-en/168097d9c5, Yao, M., Chihuahua or Muffin? My Search for the Best Computer Vision API, *Blog*, 12 October 2017, available at https://www.freecodecamp.org/news/chihuahua-or-muffin-my-search-for-the-best-computer-vision-api-cbda4d6b425d/ and Polyakov, A., Seven Ways Cybercriminals Can Use Machine Learning, *Forbes*, 11 January 2018, available at https://www.forbes.com/sites/forbestechcouncil/2018/01/11/seven-ways-cybercriminals-can-use-machine-learning/?sh=29f6f68c1447.

Facebook, Amazon and Netflix, are mainly based on the use of such algorithms, which they use to direct their customers' choices. Indeed, as it is pointed out by some researchers, these algorithms operate

> By highlighting correlations between data items that would not otherwise be observable, these techniques are being used to shape the informational choice context in which individual decision-making occurs, with the aim of channelling attention and decision-making in directions preferred by the "choice architect"

with the need to create a way to make that the choice architect's purpose is duly notified.[418]

12. Capacity to redistribute risks, benefits and burdens among and between individuals and groups via the use of AI-driven optimization systems which reconfigure social environments and choice architectures

When dealing with AI systems and specifically with recommendation systems it should be considered that "Big Data's value comes from patterns that can be derived from making connections about pieces of data, about an individual, about individuals in relation to others, about groups of people, or simply about the structure of information itself".[419] Hence, these systems should be able to operate not only in real time but also at scale via the internet's global networked architecture with the risk that operating at scale they can influence not only the behaviour of one individual user but of a larger society.[420]

13. The capacity to generate problems of collective action

The large-scale impact of AI systems can be detrimental to the entire community and at the same time can also affect individuals in a marginal way. According to the Olson theory on collective action, just this scale dimension could create an issue in the capability of individuals to recognize the negative impact that such a system can have on their spheres and avoid acting against the infringement of their rights.[421]

418 Yeung, K., 'Hypernudge': Big Data as a Mode of Regulation by Design, *Information, Communication & Society*, Vol. 20(1), 2017, pp. 118–136 and Sandvig, C., et al., Uncovering Algorithms: Looking inside the Facebook News Feed, Cyber Harvard Edu, *Blog*, 2014, available at https://cyber.harvard.edu/events/luncheon/2014/07/sandvigkarahalios.

419 Yeung, K., 'Hypernudge': Big Data as a Mode of Regulation by Design, *Information, Communication & Society*, Vol. 20(1), 2017, pp. 118–136.

420 Council of Europe, Committee of experts on human rights dimensions of automated data processing and different forms of artificial intelligence, Rapporteur: Yeung, Karen, A study of advanced digital technologies (including AI systems) for the concept of responsibility within a human rights framework, DGI(2019)05, 2019, pp. 21–25, available at https://rm.coe.int/responsability-and-ai-en/168097d9c5.

421 Olson, M., *The Logic of Collective Action—Public Goods and the Theory of Groups*, Cambridge, MA: Harvard University Press, 1965, pp. 33–34.

Therefore, it is important to ensure that AI technology is operating as intended and that unwanted or unpredictable behaviours are not produced, either by accident or maliciously.[422] In this respect, the Association for the Advancement of Artificial Intelligence (AAAI) recognized that "it is critical that one should be able to prove, test, measure and validate the reliability, performance, safety, and ethical compliance—both logically and statistically/probabilistically—of such robotics and artificial intelligence systems before they are deployed".[423]

Given the implications to transparency, explainability and accountability of the systems, some authors tried to propose tackling the issue with a "thick" approach to technologies. According to this approach, the following criteria should be met when creating a system: (i) external participation: early and regular engagement with all relevant stakeholders; (ii) provide a mechanism for external independent (not necessarily public) oversight; (iii) ensure transparent decision-making procedures on why decisions were taken; (iv) develop a stable list of non-arbitrary standards where the selection of certain values, ethics and rights over others can be plausibly justified; (v) ensure that ethics do not substitute fundamental rights or human rights; (vi) provide a clear statement on the relationship between the commitments made and existing legal or regulatory frameworks, in particular on what happens when the two are in conflict.[424]

Following the aforementioned criteria, an examination is made of the fundamental rights that may be jeopardized by improper use of AI as well as the principles and guarantees set up to try to avoid jeopardizing such rights.

10.1.1 Fundamental rights: biases of AI implementation

Algorithms may be used to prepare humans to make decisions or to take decisions immediately through automated means. In fact, boundaries between human and automated decision-making are often blurred, resulting in the notion of quasi or semi-automated decision-making.[425] Human rights in the law/tax field can be affected by the automated data processing techniques, and the development of decision-making systems may violate or threaten the fundamental rights,[426] which

422 House of Commons—Science and Technology Committee, *Robotics and Artificial Intelligence—Fifth Report of Session 2016–17*, 13 September 2017, p. 16, available at https://publications.parliament.uk/pa/cm201617/cmselect/cmsctech/145/145.pdf.

423 The Association for the Advancement of Artificial Intelligence and the UK Computing Research Committee, Joint written evidence submitted by AAAI and UKCRC, April 2016, available at https://data.parliament.uk/writtenevidence/committeeevidence.svc/evidencedocument/science-and-technology-committee/robotics-and-artificial-intelligence/written/32533.html.

424 Wagner, B., Ethics as an Escape from Regulation: From Ehics-Washing to Ethics-Shopping?, in *Being Profiling: Cogitas Ergo Sum* (eds. M. Hildebrandt). Amsterdam University Press, 2018, pp. 36–37.

425 Council of Europe, Algorithms and Human Rights, Study on the Human Rights Dimensions of Automated Data Processing Techniques and Possible Regulatory Implications, Prepared by the Committee of Experts on Internet Intermediaries (MSI-NET), DGI(2017)12, 2017, p. 3.

426 Sartor, G., *Human Rights and Information Technologies*, Ed. Roger Brownsword et al., Oxford University Press, 2017, pp. 424–450.

can be identified as follows according to the Universal Declaration of Human Rights (UDHR)[427] and the European Convention of Human Rights (ECHR).[428]

- A fair trial and due process (Article 11 UDHR and 6 ECHR)

Application of algorithms can have a significant impact when dealing with the fair trial standards. In fact, an improper use of AI systems can affect the presumption of innocence, the right to be informed promptly of the cause and nature of an accusation, the right to a fair hearing and the right to defend oneself in person.[429] In this sense, the use of such systems in criminal law and related decisions for the biases that can be created are of high concern.[430] Concerns are also present when dealing with other law fields such as civil or tax law. Indeed, replacing the decision-making by human judges could especially jeopardize the ability of individuals to understand the nature of the accusation with the consequence of having a lack of defence.[431] In this sense, it has been pointed out that based on the way ML works it is hard to avoid status quo bias in decision-making, and explainable AI is vulnerable to reverse-engineering (i.e., determine the rules which determine the judgements), with the consequences that if one knows that the machine will judge systematically, given enough data, one may be able to predict the outcome of a case in all cases.[432]

These aspects are supported by the provision of Article 42 of the ECHR "Right to a Good Administration". The provision states that when the public administration provides a decision that may affect a person, the public administration is obliged to

427 United Nations, Universal Declaration of Human Rights, General Assembly resolution 217 A, Paris on 10 December 1948, available at Universal Declaration of Human Rights | United Nations.

428 Council of Europe, European Convention on Human Rights, Rome, 4.XI.1950, available at European Convention on Human Rights (coe.int). See also Raso, F. A., et al., *Artificial Intelligence & Human Rights: Opportunities & Risks*, Berkman Klein Center for Internet & Society at Harvard University Research Publication No. 2018-6, 2018, p. 4.

429 Council of Europe, Algorithms and Human Rights, Study on the Human Rights Dimensions of Automated Data Processing Techniques and Possible Regulatory Implications, Prepared by the Committee of Experts on Internet Intermediaries (MSI-NET), DGI(2017)12, 2017, p. 10.

430 Angwin, J., et al., *Machine Bias: There's Software Used Across the Country to Predict Future Criminals. And It's Biased Against Blacks*, ProPublica, 2016, available at https://www.propublica.org/article/machine-bias-risk-assessments-in-criminal-sentencing, and Ferguson, A. G., Policing Predictive Policing, *Washington University Law Review*, Vol. 94(5), 2017, pp. 1109–1189. See also Marks, A., Automatic Justice? Technology, Crime, and Social Control, in *The Oxford Handbook of Law, Regulation and Technology* (eds. Roger Brownsword et al.), Oxford University Press, 2017, pp. 705–730. See also Miron, M., Evaluating Causes of Algorithmic Bias in Juvenile Criminal Recidivism, *Artificial Intelligence and Law*, Vol. 29(1), 2021, pp. 111–147.

431 Aletras, N., et al, Predicting Judicial Decisions of the European Court of Human Rights: A Natural Language Processing Perspective, *PeerJ Computer Science Open Access*, 2016, p. 2, available at https://peerj.com/articles/cs-93.pdf and see also Fouzder, M., Artificial Intelligence Mimics Judicial Reasoning, *The Law Society Gazette*, 2016, available at Artificial intelligence mimics judicial reasoning | News | Law Gazette.

432 Medvedeva, M., et al., The Danger of Reverse-Engineering of Automated Judicial Decision-Making Systems, *ArXiv*, vol. abs/2012.10301, 2020, pp. 1–6, available at https://www.lawgazette.co.uk/law/artificial-intelligence-mimics-judicial-reasoning/5056017.article.

hear the person, grant this person the access to its documents and archive, and provide the reasons behind its decision. In this context, it is easy to recognize the two principles of cognitive capacity and comprehensibility that require algorithms to have a logic, that is, that there is a traceable and verifiable argumentative sequence based on inductions and deductions that are founded on the principle of causality.[433]

- Privacy and data protection (Article 12 UDHR and 8 ECHR)

In our society there is an intermingling or even a hole between data and individuals. In fact, individuals' data is constantly provided to companies that in exchange for offers or any other commercial benefits are gaining such precious information.[434] In this respect, we can say that there is a *double face* of the use of such machines, as from one side customers/individuals gets the information needed from the systems, but on the other hand machines use the information to target the users.[435] In this respect, cookies, fingerprints and online tracking are ways users are tracked and information is gained,[436] and all the information so obtained can be merged in such a way that new data is created based on the initial data, generating unpredictability for the users as well as avoiding their consent, the data transparency.[437] At the EU level it has been recognized that the consent is not the only legitimate basis for the data treatment, as even if it has been provided, it is the responsibility of the person using the data to not use such data in a more extensive way than the consent provides.[438]

- Freedom of expression (Article 19 UDHR and 10 ECHR)

AI systems can potentially harm the freedom of information and freedom of expression of individuals and groups,[439] as these systems can act as gatekeepers for human beings who wish to seek, receive or impart information, as the content that is not

433 Simoncini, A., *Diritto Costituzionale e decisioni algoritmiche, in Il ragionamento giuridico nell'era dell'intelligenza artificiale, a cura di Stefano Dorigo*, Pacini Giuridica, 2020, p. 53.

434 Mayer-Schonberger, C., *Big Data. Una rivoluzione chet rasformerà il nostro modo di vivere e già minaccia la nostra libertà*, Garzanti, 2013, p. 139 ff.

435 Duhigg, C., How Companies Learn Your Secrets, *The New York Times*, 2012, available at https://www.nytimes.com/2012/02/19/magazine/shopping-habits.html?pagewanted=all&_r=1&.

436 Hoofnagle, C. J., Behavioural Advertising: The Offer You Cannot Refuse, *Harvard Policy & Law Review*, Vol. 6(2), 2012, pp. 273–296.

437 Stanford News, *New Stanford Research Finds Computers Are Better Judges of Personality Than Friends and Family*, 2015, available at https://www.nytimes.com/2012/02/19/magazine/shopping-habits.html?pagewanted=all&_r=1&.

438 European Data Protection Supervisor (EDPS), *Hacia una nueva ética digital*, Dictamen 4/2015, 2015, pp. 1–24.

439 United Nations, General Assembly, 2016 Report of the UN Special Rapporteur on the promotion and protection of the right to freedom of opinion and expression, David Kaye, to the Thirty-second session of the Human Rights Council (A/HRC/32/ 38), available at 1607644 (un.org), where it is stated that "search engine algorithms dictate what users see and in what priority, and they may be manipulated to restrict or prioritise content".

indexed or ranked highly by an internet search engine is less likely to reach a large audience or to be seen at all.[440] Indeed, algorithm systems are set in a way that can target directly the advertisement to certain individuals or groups of individuals and provide news that is arranged and channelled according to pre-organized schemes that leave aside what is considered not in line with certain thoughts or ways of thinking. This could create a "filter bubble", as online personalization effectively isolates people from a diversity of viewpoints or content.[441] As these systems are currently in use in the fields of taxation, social security, healthcare and the justice system, questions about transparency and accountability for the correct provision of public service are constantly under analysis.[442]

- Freedom of association (Article 17 UDHR and 11 ECHR)

Social networking is important in the development and growth of today's community, and identified as a

> tool for expression and communication between individuals, and for direct mass communication or mass communication in aggregate. This complexity gives operators of social networking services or platforms a great potential to promote the exercise and enjoyment of human rights and fundamental freedoms, in particular the freedom to express, to create and to exchange content and ideas, and the freedom of assembly.[443]

An example of how social networking is connected with freedom of association is the fact that social media can be seen as a sort of facilitator to organize protests and demonstrations, as it "gives protestors a loud voice internationally, independent of

440 Council of Europe, Algorithms and Human Rights, Study on the Human Rights Dimensions of Automated Data Processing techniques and Possible Regulatory Implications, Prepared by the Committee of Experts on Internet Intermediaries (MSI-NET), DGI(2017)12, 2017, p. 17.

441 Nguyen, T., et al., Exploring the Filter Bubble: The Effect of Using Recommender Systems on Content Diversity, in *Proceedings of the 23rd International Conference on World Wide Web*, WWW '14. New York, NY: ACM, 2014, pp. 677–686, available at https://www.nytimes.com/2012/02/19/magazine/shopping-habits.html?pagewanted=all&_r=1& and Zuiderveen Borgesius, F., et al., Should We Worry About Filter Bubbles?, *Internet Policy Review Journal on Internet Regulation*, Vol. 5(1), 2016, available at https://papers.ssrn.com/sol3/papers.cfm?abstract_id=2758126.

442 van Haastert, H., Government as a Platform: Public Values in the Age of Big Data, *Policy&Internet*, Vol. 11(2), 2019, pp. 128–148 available at Public Values in the Age of Big Data: A Public Information Perspective (wiley.com).

443 Council of Europe, Recommendation CM/Rec(2012)4 of the Committee of Ministers to member States on the protection of human rights with regard to social networking services, Adopted by the Committee of Ministers on 4 April2012 at the 1139th meeting of the Ministers' Deputies, available at https://www.coe.int/en/web/freedom-expression/committee-of-ministers-adopted-texts/-/asset_publisher/aDXmrol0vvsU/content/recommendation-cm-rec-2012–4-of-the-committee-of-ministers-to-member-states-on-the-protection-of-human-rights-with-regard-to-social-networking-service?_101_INSTANCE_aDXmrol0vvsU_viewMode=view/.

traditional media structures and of the government".[444] However, it is also possible that the information gained from an individual's participation in demonstrations is used to track the person or is stored for future purposes. Therefore, there is a need to properly counteract a misuse of individual information.

- An effective remedy (Article 8 UDHR and 13 ECHR)

This right should grant everyone whose rights have been violated to have an effective remedy before a national authority and to be able to seek remedy against any violation of right. However, when dealing with automated decision-making processes, the possibility of obtaining an effective remedy, that is, receiving a reasoned and individual decision, could be threated due to the characteristics of such systems, as they are opaque and many times it is not even possible to identify when and how individuals provided the consent for the usage of their data. And, as the decision is taken automatically, it is difficult to identify who is responsible for the decision itself, that is, to whom to address the decision.[445]

- The prohibition on discrimination (Article 7 UDHR and 14 ECHR)

Everyone has the right to enjoy fundamental rights without discrimination, however, when approaching the use of computational systems there is a risk that discrimination could occur. In fact, computer algorithms organize and select information across a wide range of applications and industries, from search results to social media, and abuses of power by internet platforms have led to calls for algorithm transparency and regulation.[446] These systems, for example, determine how our questions are answered, decide what is relevant for us, or suggest who we should date and what we should watch.[447] Consequently, it can be argued that a biased algorithm that systematically discriminates one group in society, for exam-

444 Barberá, P., Tweeting the Revolution: Social Media Use and the #Euromaidan Protests, *Huffpost*, 2014, available at http://www.huffingtonpost.com/pablo-barbera/tweeting-the-revolution-s_b_4831104.html.

445 Council of Europe, Algorithms and Human Rights, Study on the Human Rights Dimensions of Automated Data Processing Techniques and Possible Regulatory Implications, Prepared by the Committee of Experts on Internet Intermediaries (MSI-NET), DGI(2017)12, 2017, pp. 24–25 and Citron, D. K., Technological Due Process, *Washington University Law Review*, Vol. 85(6), 2008, pp. 1249–1313.

446 Sandvig, C., et al., When the Algorithm Itself Is a Racist: Diagnosing Ethical Harm in the Basic Components of Software, *International Journal of Communication*, 2016, Vol. 10, pp. 4972–4990, available at https://www.researchgate.net/publication/321371928_When_the_Algorithm_Itself_Is_a_Racist_Diagnosing_Ethical_Harm_in_the_Basic_Components_of_Software.

447 See in this sense Introna, L. D., & Nissenbaum, H., Shaping the Web: Why the Politics of Search Engines Matters, *Information Society*, Vol. 16(3), 2000, pp. 169–185 and Gillespie, T., Can an Algorithm Be Wrong?, *Limn*, 2012, available at Limn Can an Algorithm be Wrong?

ple based on their age, sexual orientation, race, gender, or socio-economic standing, may raise considerable concerns, not just in terms of the access to rights of the individual end-users or customers affected by these decisions but also for society as a whole.[448]

The way AI systems could affect human rights can be summarized in three different sources, out of which two can be considered by conducting a human rights impact assessment before a particular system is deployed, while the third one, is related to the phase after the implementation of the system itself and derives from the complexity of the systems: (i) quality of training data, (ii) system design, and (iii) complex interactions.[449]

10.1.2 Principles for a trustworthy and responsible implementation/use of AI

The need to maximize the benefits of AI systems together with prevention and minimization of the risks was initially tackled at the EU level with the Ethics Guidelines for Trustworthy AI (also called the Guidelines).[450] The Guidelines identify three main components for trustworthy AI, which should be met throughout a system's entire life cycle: (i) it should be lawful, that is, complying with all applicable laws and regulations; (ii) it should be ethical, so to ensure adherence to ethical principles and values; and (iii) it should be robust, both from a technical and social perspective, since, even with good intentions, AI systems can cause unintentional harm.[451] AI ethics should be based on the fundamental rights enshrined in the EU Treaties, the EU Charter and international human rights law, and AI trustworthiness can be achieved according to steps identified in Figure 2.6.[452]

448 Council of Europe, Algorithms and Human Rights, Study on the Human Rights Dimensions of Automated Data Processing Techniques and Possible Regulatory Implications, Prepared by the Committee of Experts on Internet Intermediaries (MSI-NET), DGI(2017)12, 2017, p. 27 and Palmatier, R. W., and Martin, K. D., *The Intelligent Marketer's Guide to Data Privacy, The Impact of Big Data on Customer Trust*, Palgrave Macmillan, 2019, pp. 1–192.

449 Raso, F. A., et al., *Artificial Intelligence & Human Rights: Opportunities & Risks, Research Publication No. 2018-6 September 25, 2018*, Berkman Klein Center for Internet & Society at Harvard University, p. 15 and Zliobaite, I., and Custers, B., Using Sensitive Personal Data May Be Necessary for Avoiding Discrimination in Data-Driven Decision Models, *Artificial Intelligence and Law*, Vol. 24(2), 2016, pp. 183–201.

450 European Commission, *Ethics Guidelines for Trustworthy AI*, 8 April 2019, available at https://digital-strategy.ec.europa.eu/en/library/ethics-guidelines-trustworthy-ai and by Donahoe, E., So Software Has Eaten the World: What Does It Mean for Human Rights, Security & Governance?, *Just Security*, 18 March 2016, available at https://www.justsecurity.org/30046/software-eaten-world-human-rights-security-governance/. See also Gonzalez Fabre, R., et al., Moral Control and Ownership in AI Systems, *AI & Society*, Vol. 36(2), 2021, pp. 289–303.

451 European Commission, *Ethics Guidelines for Trustworthy AI*, 8 April 2019, p. 2, available at https://digital-strategy.ec.europa.eu/en/library/ethics-guidelines-trustworthy-ai.

452 European Commission, *Ethics Guidelines for Trustworthy AI*, 8 April 2019, p. 8, available at https://digital-strategy.ec.europa.eu/en/library/ethics-guidelines-trustworthy-ai.

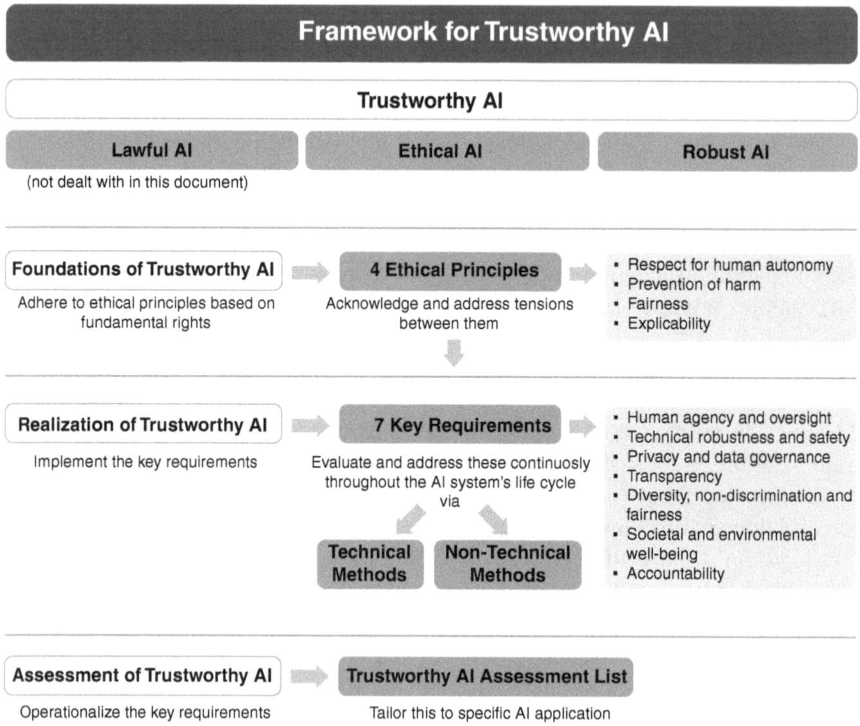

Figure 2.6 The Guidelines as a framework for trustworthy AI.

Four ethical imperatives create the foundation of trustworthy AI and should be at the base when it comes to building AI systems:[453]

- Respect for human autonomy

Humans interacting with AI systems must be able to keep full and effective self-determination in a way where AI systems should not unjustifiably subordinate, coerce, deceive, manipulate, condition or herd humans. Allocation of functions between humans and AI systems should follow human-centric design principles and leave meaningful opportunity for human choice. AI systems should be

453 European Commission, *Ethics Guidelines for Trustworthy AI*, 8 April 2019, p. 12, available at https://digital-strategy.ec.europa.eu/en/library/ethics-guidelines-trustworthy-ai. See also Chatila, R., et al., Trustworthy AI, in *Reflections on Artificial Intelligence for Humanity* (ed. Bertrand Braunschweig Malik Ghallab), Springer, 2021, pp. 13–39.

Values-based principles for all AI actors	Recommendations to policymakers for AI policies
Principle 1.1. People and planet	*Principle 2.1.* Investment in R&D
Principle 1.2. Human rights, privacy, fairness	*Principle 2.2.* Data, compute, technologies
Principle 1.3. Transparency, explainability	*Principle 2.3.* Enabling policy and regulatory environment
Principle 1.4. Robustness, security, safety	*Principle 2.4.* Jobs, automation, skills
Principle 1.5. Accountability	*Principle 2.5.* International cooperation

Figure 2.7 The OECD AI principles.

designed to augment, complement and empower human cognitive, social and cultural skills.

- Prevention of harm

AI systems and the environments in which they operate must be safe and secure. AI systems must be technically robust, and it should be ensured that they are not open to malicious use.

- Fairness

The development, deployment and use of AI systems must be fair and that means ensuring equal and just distribution of both benefits and costs and ensuring that individuals and groups are free from unfair bias, discrimination and stigmatization.

- Explicability

Processes need to be transparent, the capabilities and purpose of AI systems openly communicated, and decisions explainable to those directly and indirectly affected. The AI system functioning should be commensurate on the context and the severity of the consequences deriving from an erroneous or inaccurate output.

Following the EU approach, at the international level, the first intergovernmental standard concerning AI was the OECD Recommendation on Artificial Intelligence, which was reached in Osaka in 2019 by the G20 leaders.[454] The Recommendation identifies five complementary values-based principles for the responsible stewardship of trustworthy AI and five national policies and international cooperation for trustworthy AI, as described in Figure 2.7.[455]

454 OECD, *Recommendation of the Council on OECD Legal Instruments Artificial Intelligence*, 2022, pp. 3–10, available at OECD-LEGAL-0449-en.pdf.

455 OECD, *OECD Framework for the Classification of AI Systems—OECD Digital Economy Papers No. 323*, 2022, p. 16, available at https://www.oecd-ilibrary.org/science-and-technology/oecd-framework-for-the-classification-of-ai-systems_cb6d9eca-en.

The principles for responsible stewardship of trustworthy AI are (i) inclusive growth, sustainable development and well-being; (ii) human-centred values and fairness; (iii) transparency and explainability; (iv) robustness, security and safety; and (v) accountability. For points (iii) to (v), which are of most interest here, the Recommendation provides the following.

- Transparency and explainability

AI actors should commit to transparency and responsible disclosure regarding AI systems. To this end, they should provide meaningful information, appropriate to the context and consistent with the state of art (i) to foster a general understanding of AI systems; (ii) to make stakeholders aware of their interactions with AI systems, including in the workplace; (iii) to enable those affected by an AI system to understand the outcome; and (iv) to enable those adversely affected by an AI system to challenge its outcome based on plain and easy-to-understand information on the factors and on the logic that served as the basis for the prediction, recommendation or decision. Indeed, transparency is important for two reasons: (i) to enable those affected by a decision or action to know the reasons for the action or decision, and (ii) to enable the affected party to evaluate the quality of those reasons.[456]

Machine learning algorithms are encapsulated in computer programs, and it could be inferred that when publishing the program the algorithm is automatically explained, but the problem is that application of the algorithm will usually occur only after it has interacted with training data and due to the fact that the algorithm learns from the training data, simply knowing the underlying program is different from knowing which features of the data the algorithm puts weight on in general, or in a particular instance.[457] As a matter of fact, the issues related to transparency and interpretability cannot be resolved simply by making computer code available, but there is the need to examine the algorithm, consider the outcome and involve different methods of model validation such as (i) machines could be certified, demonstrating confidence that they achieve a certain level of competence, or (ii) more advanced algorithms could create "input-output" mappings of data, showing how different inputs influenced the output.[458]

- Robustness, security and safety

    1. AI systems should be robust, secure and safe throughout their entire life cycle.

456 Yeung, K., and Weller, A., How Is "Transparency" Understood by Legal Scholars and the Machine Learning Community?, *Being Profiling. Cogitas Ergo Sum*, E. Bayamlioglu, I. Baraluic, 2018, pp. 36–41.

457 The Royal Society, *Machine Learning: The Power and Promise of Computers That Learn by Example*, 2017, pp. 5–124, available at https://royalsociety.org/~/media/policy/projects/machine-learning/publications/machine-learning-report.pdf.

458 The Royal Society, *Machine Learning: The Power and Promise of Computers That Learn by Example*, 2017, pp. 5–124, available at https://www.tandfonline.com/doi/abs/10.1080/713768525.

2. To this end, AI actors should ensure traceability, including in relation to data sets, processes and decisions made during the AI system life cycle, to enable analysis of the AI system's outcomes and responses to inquiry, appropriate to the context and consistent with the state of art.
3. AI actors should, based on their roles, the context and their ability to act, apply a systematic risk management approach to each phase of the AI system life cycle on a continuous basis to address risks related to AI systems, including privacy, digital security, safety and bias.

- Accountability

AI actors should be accountable for the proper functioning of AI systems and for the respect of the aforementioned principles, based on their roles, the context. The problem of accountability is an older one and can be summarized in the Latin maxim *quis custodiet custodes* (who shall guard the guardians),[459] as usually there are many agents involved in a function or operation, and it is important to define their roles also regarding the final outcomes. Furthermore, when dealing with accountability, and especially when AI systems are involved, we are obliged to start from an important analysis in relation to quantify our values,[460] as to define how and to which extent these systems can operate and enter in the human's sphere and where lays the responsibility when it comes to harmful behaviours.

The overall accountability topic is of vital importance because the identification of those responsible ensures that, within a constitutional democratic order, individuals and organizations are held to account for the adverse effects emanating from their actions, that is, basic responsibility is essential not only for self-understanding as individuals but also as members of a community of moral agents with the capacity and freedom to make choices that can be wrong or cause harm.[461] Indeed, accountability "is about requiring a person to explain and justify—against criteria of some kind—their decisions or acts, and then to make amends for any fault or error",[462] and further "a relationship between an actor and a forum, in which the actor has an obligation to explain and to justify his or her

459 Six, P., Ethics, Regulation and the New Artificial Intelligence, Part I: Accountability and Power, *Information Communication and Society*, Vol. 4(2), 2001, pp. 199–229, available at https://www.tandfonline.com/doi/abs/10.1080/713768525.

460 Been, K., and Finale, D. V., Machine Learning Techniques for Accountability, *AI Magazine*, Vol. 42(1), 2021, pp. 47–52.

461 Council of Europe, Committee of experts on human rights dimensions of automated data processing and different forms of artificial intelligence, Rapporteur: Yeung, Karen, A study of advanced digital technologies (including AI systems) for the concept of responsibility within a human rights framework, DGI(2019)05, 2019, p. 45–47 available at https://rm.coe.int/responsability-and-ai-en/168097d9c5. See also Nissenbaum, H., Accountability in a Computized Society, *Science and Engineering Ethics*, Vol. 2(1), 1996, p. 26 and Hooker, J., and Tae Wan, K., Truly Autonomous Machines Are Ethical, *AI Magazine*, Vol. 40(4), 2019, pp. 66–73.

462 Oliver, D., *Law, Politics and Public Accountability. The Search for a New Equilibrium*, Public Law, 1994, p. 238.

conduct, the forum can pose questions and pass judgment, and the actor may face consequences".[463]

Considering accountability as a mechanism that is defined by mapping out the answers to a series of questions such as: Who is to be accountable to whom, about what, how and why?,[464] and that algorithms, better said, the outputs that these provide, can have the power to affect others, being their character opaque, inscrutable "black boxes", owing to the sophisticated computational processes upon which they rely and their protection from disclosure as trade secrets, yet capable of exercising or informing decision-making power with highly consequential effects, is fuelling demands to secure algorithmic accountability.[465]

Indeed, robotic systems are increasingly expected to achieve human-level performance, including the capacities associated with responsibility and other criteria which are necessary to act responsibly, especially considering that while human agents are perceived to control robotic patients, the prospect for this to become reversed is beginning.[466] The EU Group on Ethics has observed that AI technologies raise

> questions about human moral responsibility. Where is the morally relevant agency located in dynamic and complex socio-technical systems with advanced AI and robotic components? How should moral responsibility be attributed and apportioned and who is responsible (and in what sense) for untoward outcomes?[467]

Hence, being these complex systems, AI technology can operate in ways that are completely unexpected, with the consequence to harm or violate human rights

463 Bovens, M., Analysing and Assessing Accountability: A Conceptual Framework, *European Law Journal*, Vol. 13(4), 2007, pp. 447–448.

464 Rock, E., Accountability: A Core Public Law Value?, *Administrative Law Journal*, Vol. 24(3), 2017, p. 6 available at https://www.researchgate.net/.

465 Yeung, K., Algorithmic Regulation: A Critical Interrogation, *Regulation & Governance*, Vol. 12(6), 2017, p. 26. See also Datta, A., Algorithmic Transparency via Quantitative Input Influence: Theory and Experiments with Learning Systems, *Conference: 2016 IEEE Symposium on Security and Privacy (SP)*, 2016, pp. 598–617 and Wojciech, S., Müller, K.-R., Towards Explainable Artificial Intelligence, in *Explainable AI: Interpreting, Explaining and Visualizing Deep Learning* (eds. Wojciech Samek, Grégoire Montavon, Andrea Vedaldi, Lars Kai Hansen and Klaus-Robert Müller (Springer, 2019), pp. 5–7. See also Carabantes, M., Black-Box Artificial Intelligence: An Epistemological and Critical Analysis, *AI & Society*, Vol. 35(7), 2020, pp. 309–317.

466 Liu, H. Y., and Zawieska, K., From Responsible Robotics Towards a Human Rights Regime Oriented to the Challenges of Robotics and Artificial Intelligence, *Ethics and Information Technology*, Vol. 22, 2020, pp. 321–333.

467 European Commission, European Group on Ethics in Science and New Technologies, Statement on Artificial Intelligence, Robotics and 'Autonomous' Systems, 2018, p. 8, available at https://op.europa.eu/en/publication-detail/-/publication/dfebe62e-4ce9-11e8-be1d-01aa75ed71a1/language-en. See also Stanford Encyclopedia of Philosophy, *Moral Responsibility*, 16 October 2019, available at https://plato.stanford.edu/entries/moral-responsibility/#AttrVersAcco and Andrade, F., et al., Contracting Agents: Legal Personality and Representation, *Artificial Intelligence and Law*, Vol. 15(4), 2007, pp. 357–373.

or create tangible harm—let's think about a self-driving car that crashes against a public or private building.[468] The problem of accountability can be differentiated between an automated system and an autonomous system, as there is a range of levels of control or involvement that human operators can have in a system: (i) controlled systems, where humans have full or partial control, such as an ordinary car; (ii) supervised systems, which do what an operator has instructed, such other industrial machinery; (iii) automatic systems, which carry out fixed functions without the intervention of an operator, such as an elevator; and (iv) autonomous systems, which are adaptive, learn and can make "decisions".[469]

Due to the existence of a mixture between humans and machines, the idea could be to diversify the relationship of responsibilities considering it as twofold: (i) the prospective responsibility, which aims to identify and allocate the responsibility considering those involved in each stage of the design, development and deployment of the technologies, that is, role responsibility involves the fulfilment of specific obligations attached to a role, function, or office;[470] and (ii) the alleged control, where the machine should be held responsible in cases where it operates in an autonomous way without direct human intervention, and control from outside is barely impossible. Furthermore, it has been recognized that the allocation of accountability for algorithmic decision-making is complicated by the fact that it is not clear who has the necessary degree of control to be imputed with legal or political accountability.[471]

It is a matter of fact that the current systems are created with the cooperation of many different actors with different skills and expertise, including designers, engineers, programmers, writers, psychologists, graphic artists and salespeople. As a result, a malfunctioning system, with the consequence of creating harm, generates difficulties in defining who among all the actors is really accountable or the degree of accountability that is attributable to the people involved in the system creation.[472] Moreover, considering that once built up a system is in a constant evo-

468 Council of Europe, Committee of experts on human rights dimensions of automated data processing and different forms of artificial intelligence, Rapporteur: Yeung, Karen, A Study of Advanced Digital Technologies (Including AI Systems) for the Concept of Responsibility within a Human Rights Framework, DGI(2019)05, 2019, pp. 51–52, available at https://rm.coe.int/responsability-and-ai-en/168097d9c5.

469 The Royal Academy of Engineering, *Autonomous Systems: Social Legal and Ethical Issues*, 2009, p. 2, available at https://www.raeng.org.uk/publications/reports/autonomous-systems-report.

470 Liu, H. Y., and Zawieska, K., From Responsible Robotics Towards a Human Rights Regime Oriented to the Challenges of Robotics and Artificial Intelligence, *Ethics and Information Technology*, Vol. 22, 2020, pp. 321–333.

471 Council of Europe, Algorithms and Human Rights, Study on the Human Rights Dimensions of Automated Data Processing Techniques and Possible Regulatory Implications, Prepared by the Committee of Experts on Internet Intermediaries (MSI-NET), DGI(2017)12, 2017, p. 39.

472 Nissenbaum, H., Accountability in a Computized Society, *Science and Engineering Ethics*, Vol. 2(1), 1996, p. 29 and also Johnson, D. G. and Powers, T. M., Computer Systems and Responsibility: A Normative Look at Technological Complexity, *Ethics and Information Technology*, Vol. 7(2), 2005, pp. 99–107. See also Díaz Calvarro, J. M., Garantías de los derechos de los obligados tributarios. Los principios de seguridad y transparencia ante el uso de la informática decisional en la Administración tributaria, *Anuario de la Facultad de Derecho. Universidad de Extremadura*, no. 36, 2020, pp. 219–248.

lution, its modules and codes can be subject to continuing changes elaborated from sub-teams of the initial team that developed it, and the problem of accountability becomes even bigger as a bunch of agents participate in different stages to the creation and evolution of the system, and a single group who is able to catch the full system is not identifiable anymore.[473]

All these elements brought researchers to provide and develop different theories on the accountability and responsibilities of machines. Some authors argued that

> the agent can be considered responsible only if he knows the particular facts surrounding his action, and if he is able to freely form a decision to act, and to select of a suitable set of available alternative actions based on these facts.[474]

Therefore, the experts who programmed the machines no longer have control over the machine agent's behaviour and it would not be correct to still hold humans responsible for actions perpetrated by a machine lacking control over them.[475]

On the contrary, other authors have disregarded the possibility that machines are held responsible while humans are not. In fact, the identification of humans as the unique subject starts from the consideration that the former are able to maintain their identity and integrity over time and to enter into deep and complex relationships with nonbiological constructs,[476] while computers do not create any configurations themselves, accidentally or spontaneously, but have structuring applied from outside; hence they could be seen as no more than objects that people encounter and manipulate in the course of their actions.[477] Therefore, every action is ultimately attributable to human individuals, and whatever role computers, robots, dogs, lawnmowers or hammers may play is ancillary.[478] New AI technologies should be intended as tools employed by humans according to the fact that "computer systems do not have mental states, and even if they could be construed

473 Weizenbaum, J., On the Impact of the Computer on Society, *Science*, Vol. 176(4035), 1972, pp. 609–614, available at https://www.jstor.org/stable/1734465.

474 Matthias, A., The Responsibility Gap: Ascribing Responsibility for the Actions of Learning Automata, *Ethics and Information Technology*, Vol. 6, 2004, pp. 175–183.

475 Matthias, A., The Responsibility Gap: Ascribing Responsibility for the Actions of Learning Automata, *Ethics and Information Technology*, Vol. 6, 2004, pp. 175–183.

476 Clark, A., *Natural-born Cyborgs: Minds, Technologies, and the Future of Human Intelligence*, New York: Oxford University Press, 2003, p. 5, available at https://dl.acm.org/doi/10.5555/861694. See also Brożek, B., and Jakubiec, M., On the Legal Responsibility of Autonomous Machines, *Artificial Intelligence and Law*, Vol. 25(1451), 2017, pp. 1–12.

477 Jones, R. H., *Reductionism: Analysis and the Fullness of Reality*, Lewisburg, PA: Bucknell University Press, 2000, p. 160 and Allan Hanson, F., Beyond the Skin Bag: On the Moral Responsibility of Extended Agencies, *Ethics and Information Technology*, Vol. 11(1), 2009, p. 92.

478 Allan Hanson, F., Beyond the Skin Bag: On the Moral Responsibility of Extended Agencies, *Ethics and Information Technology*, Vol. 11(1), 2009, p. 92 and Hage, J., Theoretical Foundations for the Responsibility of Autonomous Agents, *Artificial Intelligence and Law*, Vol. 25(3), 2017, pp. 1–17.

as having mental states, they do not have intendings to act, which arise from an agent's freedom"[479] or said another way, "Robots should rather be viewed as tools we use to extend our own abilities and to accelerate progress on our own goals"[480] so the responsibility of any action stays with the humans.

Considering that the relationship between humans and computers becomes more and more stringent, according to who writes, the aforementioned theories cannot be read in isolation from each other. In this respect, the causal condition and the fault condition should be recognized when blaming an agent for accountability. Nowadays, computer systems mediate the interaction between machines and humans with the consequence that humans are somehow distanced from their causal impacts and the computer can be identified as closer to the causal antecedent.[481] However, it should also be considered the fault element in a way that even if it was the computer creating the (harmful) event, the system outcomes are derived from an initial setting defined by humans.[482]

Nevertheless, if humans must be held responsible because they are always part of the chain, it is unclear, in case of injury, which human in the chain should be held responsible, that is, the designer, manufacturer, programmer or user.[483] In general terms, even if there is evolution where machines can develop further with respect to the initial inputs that humans provided, it is also true that AI technologies are for the majority intended to operate considering the constant involvement of humans, as human oversight helps ensure that an AI system does not undermine human autonomy or cause other adverse effects.[484] However, the doggedness in always recognizing a role of responsibility for human beings' risks placing humans in what Elish called a "moral crumple zone" where humans' role became that of soaking up fault independently of the degree of their involvement, with the consequence that

479 Johnson, D. G., Computer Systems: Moral Entities But Not Moral Agents, *Ethics and Information Technology*, Vol. 8(4), 2006, p. 195.

480 Bryson, J. J., Robots Should Be Slaves, in *Close Engagements with Artificial Companions: Key Social, Psychological, Ethical and Design Issues* (eds. Yorick Wilks), Amsterdam: John Benjamins Publishing Company, 2010, pp. 63–74.

481 Nissenbaum, H., Accountability in a Computized Society, *Science and Engineering Ethics*, Vol. 2(1), 1996, p. 34 and Mani, G., et al., Artificial Intelligence's Grand Challenges: Past, Present, and Future, *AI Magazine*, Vol. 42(1), 2021, pp. 61–75.

482 Nissenbaum, H., Accountability in a Computized Society, *Science and Engineering Ethics*, Vol. 2(1), 1996, p. 34. See also Johnson, D. G., and Powers, T. M., Computer Systems and Responsibility: A Normative Look at Technological Complexity, *Ethics and Information Technology*, Vol. 7(2), 2005, pp. 99–107.

483 The Royal Academy of Engineering, *Autonomous Systems: Social Legal and Ethical Issues*, 2009, p. 2, available at https://raeng.org.uk/media/tommwqvv/autonomous_systems_report.pdf and Brożek, B., et al., Introduction to the Special Issue on Machine Law, *Artificial Intelligence and Law*, Vol. 25(3), 2017, pp. 251–253.

484 European Commission, *High Level Expert Group on AI*, Ethics Guidelines for Trustworthy AI, 2019, p. 16, available at https://digital-strategy.ec.europa.eu/en/library/ethics-guidelines-trustworthy-ai.

they could become scapegoats by tech companies that will avoid responsibilities for unintended adverse consequences.[485]

The analysis of the interaction between humans and machines can be better understood considering the concept of "meaningful human control" (MHC), which is used to describe a threshold of human control and develops from two premises: (i) that a machine applying force and operating without any human control whatsoever is broadly considered unacceptable, and (ii) that a human simply pressing a "fire" button in response to indications from a computer, without cognitive clarity or awareness, is not sufficient to be considered "human control" in a substantive sense.[486]

It seems possible to deduce that the difference in this level of control could define that, where human efforts and involvement are strong, the human agent is responsible for the problem generated by the system, but in the case of autonomous systems, the matter might not be so simple, since humans are still part (at least initially) of the chain, but then it is the machine that creates its own development.[487]

In addition to these issues, there are also cases where although human intervention is required, this may be more harmful than letting the machine act autonomously. In this sense, the Royal Academy of Engineering pointed out that

> it might be thought that there is always need for human intervention, but sometimes autonomous systems are needed where humans might make bad choices as a result of panic—especially in stressful situations—and therefore the human override would be problematic. Human operators are not always right not do they always have the best intentions. Could autonomous systems be trusted more that human operators in some situations?[488]

In this latter example then should we still blame humans for not intervening or in case of mistakes when intervening or should the machines only be responsible for whatever results.

485 Elish, M. C., Letting Autopilot Off the Hook, Why Do We Blame Humans When Automation Fails?, *Slate*, 2016, available at https://slate.com/technology/2016/06/why-do-blame-humans-when-automation-fails.html.

486 Roff, H., *Meaningful Human Control, Artificial Intelligence and Autonomous Weapons*, Briefing Paper for Delegates at the Convention on Certain Conventional Weapons (CCW) Meeting of Experts on Lethal Autonomous Weapons Systems (LAWS), 2016, pp. 1–6, available at www.article36.org/wp-content/ uploads/2016/04/MHC-AI-and-AWS-FINAL.pdf.

487 The Royal Academy of Engineering, *Autonomous Systems: Social Legal and Ethical Issues*, 2009, p. 2, available at https://www.raeng.org.uk/publications/reports/autonomous-systems-report.

488 The Royal Academy of Engineering, *Autonomous Systems: Social Legal and Ethical Issues*, 2009, p. 3, available at https://raeng.org.uk/media/tommwqvv/autonomous_systems_report.pdf.

The answer is not and could not be easy, as the evolution of the machines create difficulties to identify, anticipate and prevent adverse events when complex, algorithm-driven socio-technical systems interact at a speed and scale that was not possible before with the consequence that we face risks that go further than what we have until now identified as a risky event.[489] Examples in this sense could be found in the "flash crash" that occurred in 2010, during which the market went into freefall for five traumatic minutes, then righted itself over another five—for no apparent reason. Or when an Uber Volvo XC90 self-driving vehicle drives autonomously, with no input from its human backup driver for 19 minutes, but when faced with an obstacle that it was able to detect only at the last moment, and barred from taking evasive action on its own, gave the control to the human driver, who did not react promptly enough to avoid running over a lady and killing her.[490]

Given the interaction of humans and machines that makes it hard to properly identify responsibility in case of any damage and, as already mentioned, having the big tech firms a relevant power that could jeopardize the human rights system if leaving in their hands the possibility to identify codes that most probably will holds them harmless from any liability and discharging the responsibility on the individuals, it is fundamental that the states take actions to develop provisions that act as a shield for human rights protection.[491] The ECHR Article 1 provides that the contracting parties shall secure to everyone within their jurisdiction the rights and freedoms set by the Convention and that read together with Article 13 that provides for an effective remedy grants the basis to impose mechanisms that will be able to ensure accountability in case of human rights violations.

10.1.3 Guarantees: mechanisms to possibly protect human rights

Hence, to obtain the proper protection of human rights, research has started to develop mechanisms that could counteract ethical and legal concerns generated by AI systems. On this subject, the technical response is to use mechanisms with an aim to "hard-wire" particular values when designing algorithms that are incorporated in the AI systems, that is, human rights are protected by design, thus in real

489 Council of Europe, Committee of Experts on Human Rights Dimensions of Automated Data Processing and Different Forms of Artificial Intelligence, Rapporteur: Yeung, Karen, A Study of Advanced Digital Technologies (Including AI Systems) for the Concept of Responsibility Within a Human Rights Framework, DGI(2019)05, 2019, p. 67 available at https://rm.coe.int/responsability-and-ai-en/168097d9c5.

490 See Akansu, A. N., The Flash Crash: A Review, *Journal of Capital Markets Studies*, Vol. 1(1), 2017, pp. 89–100 and Smith, A., Franken-Algorithms: The Deadly Consequences of Unpredictable Code, *The Guardian*, 30 August 2018, available at https://www.theguardian.com/technology/2018/aug/29/coding-algorithms-frankenalgos-program-danger.

491 Rainey, B., et al., *Jacobs, White and Ovey: The European Convention on Human Rights* (Sixth Edition), Oxford: Oxford University Press, 2014, p. 102.

time and not on an *ex-post* or *ex-ante* basis.[492] With the idea to secure human rights at the moment of creating an algorithm the research goes in the direction to:

1. Explainable AI (XAI),[493] where there is a need to make the AI systems intelligible to the users, thus these systems have to make their logic explainable.[494]
2. Fairness, accountability and transparency in machine learning (FATML). In the past few years we have seen growing recognition that machine learning raises novel challenges for ensuring non-discrimination, due process and understandability in decision-making.[495] Policymakers, regulators and advocates have expressed fears about the potentially discriminatory impact of machine learning, with many calling for further technical research into the dangers of inadvertently encoding bias into automated decisions, and ML researchers have start to develop mechanisms that try to avoid bias and discrimination coming from the use of big data and machine learning.[496]
3. Algorithmic/Human rights assessments that encompass risk-assessment models that can be applied by those seeking to procure or deploy algorithmic systems to identify human rights and ethical and social implications connected to their systems with the intention to improve them in order to comply with the human rights involved.[497]
4. Algorithmic auditing, aiming at testing and evaluate the system not ex-ante but during its functioning. In this case, in order to detect unwanted effects of the algorithms the idea is to review a software-driven action after the fact of the

492 Yeung, K., *Design for Regulation, in Handbook of Ethics, Values and Technological Design* (eds. M. J. Van Den Hoven, P. E. Varmaas and I. van de Poel), Dordecht: Springer, 2015, pp. 447–472.

493 Colaner, N., Is Explainable Artificial Intelligence Intrinsically Valuable?, *AI & Society*, Vol. 37(4), 2022, pp. 231–238.

494 Weller, A., Challenges for Transparency, *Paper Presented at 2017 ICML Workshop on Human Interpretability in Machine Learning*, WHI 2017, Sidney, NSW, Australia, pp. 55–62, available at https://www.researchgate.net/publication/318981705_Challenges_for_Transparency and Kuźniacki, B., How Constitutional Principles Pave the Way to eXplainable AI in Tax Law, *Kluwer International Tax Blog*, 11 February 2022.

495 de Fine Licht, K., and de Fine Licht, J., Artificial Intelligence, Transparency, and Public Decision-Making—Why Explanations Are Key When Trying to Produce Perceived Legitimacy, *AI & Society*, Vol. 35(4), 2020, pp. 917–926.

496 FAT/ML, FAT* '19: Conference on Fairness, Accountability, and Transparency in Machine Learning, FAT/ML, Association for Computing Machinery, New York, NY, United States, 2019, available at https://www.fatml.org/. See also Serrat, M., Equality and AI. Bias and Discrimination, in *Artificial Intelligence and the Law* (eds. P. García-Mexía and F. Pérez Bes), Wolters Kluwer Legal & Regulatory Spain, S.A., 2021, pp. 149–182, and Kritikos, M., European Parliament (Panel for the Future of Science and Technology (STOA)), What If Technologies Could Abide by Ethical Principles?, At Glance—Scientific Foresight: What If?, 2018, available at https://www.fatml.org/.

497 Council of Europe, Committee of experts on human rights dimensions of automated data processing and different forms of artificial intelligence, Rapporteur: Yeung, Karen, A study of advanced digital technologies (including AI systems) for the concept of responsibility within a human rights framework, DGI(2019)05, 2019, p. 70 available at https://rm.coe.int/responsability-and-ai-en/168097d9c5.

action.[498] This activity can be done by an external set of experts that will check the running algorithms with the development of an external algorithm as a sort of external review.[499] In this sense, where a machine cannot fully align with the human way of reasoning, it is then important to constantly perform a sort of risk assessment[500] and management of the AI system life cycle to help to determine its transparency and explainability.

The elements of predictability, reliability and transparency of technology, as just described, must be at the base of any algorithm system. This is even more true when considering decision-making systems (e.g., the ones that have been development in the field of law). According to Dave Coplin,

> The building blocks . . . the way in which we create the algorithms. They must be transparent. I must be able to see the patterns or rules that have been used to create the outcome. As a human I need to be able to inspect that, as much as the algorithms need to understand what the humans may choose to do with that information.[501]

Machine learning algorithms are rarely set up to give a reason for a particular decision or output, hence it is important to have clear justifications for a decision, as it is not good enough to rely on the supposed quality of the algorithm. This is particularly important when systems may be prone to errors or the decisions behind the choice of model is not known.[502] The lack of reasoning makes us perceive these systems as an opaque decision-making tool with a consequent level of mistrust in their outputs[503] and a possible erosion of human rights.

In the field of tax law, it is interesting to analyse a recent French Constitutional Council decision[504] that evaluated the constitutionality of a new legal instrument, introduced by the 2020 Budget Bill, that is based on the use of artificial

498 Desai, D. R., and Kroll, J., Trust But Verify: A Guide to Algorithms and the Law, *Harvard Journal of Law & Technology*, Vol. 31(1), 2017, pp. 1–64, available at https://jolt.law.harvard.edu/assets/articlePDFs/v31/31HarvJLTech1.pdf.

499 Dunham, I. M., Big Data: A Revolution that Will Transform How We Live, Work, and Think, *The AAG Review of Books*, Vol. 3(1), 2015, pp. 19–21.

500 Reisman, D., et al., *Algorithmic Impact Assessments: A Practical Framework for Public Agency Accountability*, AINOW Institute, 2018, pp. 3–22. See also Mantelero, A., AI and Big Data: A Blueprint for a Human Right, Social and Ethical Impact Assessment, *Computer Law & Security Review*, Vol. 34(4), 2018, pp. 754–772.

501 House of Commons—Science and Technology Committee, Robotics and Artificial Intelligence—Fifth Report of Session 2016–17, 13 September 2017, p. 17, available at https://publications.parliament.uk/pa/cm201617/cmselect/cmsctech/145/145.pdf.

502 Armstrong, H., Machines That Learn in the Wild, *Nesta*, 2015, p. 14, available at https://media.nesta.org.uk/documents/machines_that_learn_in_the_wild.pdf.

503 Armstrong, H., Machines That Learn in the Wild, *Nesta*, 2015, p. 14, available at https://media.nesta.org.uk/documents/machines_that_learn_in_the_wild.pdf.

504 Conseil Constitutionnel, Décision n° 2019–796 DC du 27 décembre 2019, Loi de finances pour 2020, available at https://www.conseil-constitutionnel.fr/decision/2019/2019796DC.htm.

intelligence to fight tax fraud. Article 154 of the Budget Bill authorizes, on an experimental basis and for a period of three years, the tax and customs administrations to collect and use in an automated manner the publicly accessible content on the websites of certain platform operators for the purpose of investigating tax and customs offences.[505] The French Constitutional Council provided its opinion in favour of the new mechanism, recognizing that the limits imposed by legislators[506] in drafting the way this new mechanism could be applied, will not restrict fundamental rights, such as freedom of thought and speech, freedom of belief, freedom of association, the right to privacy and data protection, in a way that could be considered disproportionate.[507] The proportionality and balance are identified by the Council as follows, and by the fact that, after the probation period the tool will be checked: (i) the AI tool can only gather public data displayed on social network sites and electronic commerce platforms, that is, information that the users provide voluntarily; (ii) collection of data on political, religious and philosophical opinions, ethnicity or race, sexual orientation, genetics and biometrics are excluded; (iii) the information are used only for tax purposes, that is, to combat tax fraud; (iv) data not tax relevant should be deleted; (v) confidentiality and professional secrecy should be the base for tax officers when operating the data; (vi) the data so collected could be the basis and further non-automated checks should be operated before performing any further action; and

505 Conseil Constitutionnel, CommentaireDécisionn° 2019–796 DC du 27 décembre 2019, Loi de financespour 2020, available at https://www.conseil-constitutionnel.fr/sites/default/files/as/root/bank_mm/decisions/2019796dc/2019796dc_ccc.pdf and Calderón Carrero, El encuadramiento legal y límites del uso de herramientas de inteligencia artificial con fines de control fiscal, Estudios financieros. Revista de contabilidad y tributación: Comentarios, casos prácticos, ISSN 1138-9540, n. 444, 2020, pp. 119–128.

506 Conseil Constitutionnel, Décisionn° 2019–796 DC du 27 décembre 2019, Loi de financespour 2020, paragraphs 89 and 90, available at https://www.conseil-constitutionnel.fr/sites/default/files/as/root/bank_mm/decisions/2019796dc/2019796dc_ccc.pdf. This decision should be read together with the discussion related to the implementation of the "programming law for the judicial system" adopted on March 23, 2019 (LOI n° 2019–222 du 23 mars 2019 de programmation 2018–2022 et de réforme pour la justice, available at https://www.legifrance.gouv.fr/loda/id/JORFTEXT000038261631/. See also Livermore, M., and Rockmore, D., France Kicks Data Scientists Out of Its Courts, Slate, *Slate*, 21 June 2019, available at https://slate.com/technology/2019/06/france-has-banned-judicial-analytics-to-analyze-the-courts.html, and Tashea, J., France Bans Publishing of Judicial Analytics and Prompts Criminal Penalty, *ABAJOURNAL*, 7 June 2019, available at https://www.abajournal.com/news/article/france-bans-and-creates-criminal-penalty-for-judicial-analytics. According to others this is not a ban but should be read according to two basic safeguards in the French law. See in this sense G'sell, F., Predicting Courts' Decisions Is Lawful in France and Will Remain So, *Blog de Florence G'sell*, 24 June 2019, available at https://gsell.tech/predicting-courts-decisions-is-lawful-in-france-and-will-remain-so/.

507 Conseil Constitutionnel, Décisionn° 2019–796 DC du 27 décembre 2019, Loi de financespour 2020, paragraphs 89 and 90, available at Décisionn° 2019–796 DC du 27 décembre 2019 | Conseilconstitutionnel (conseil-constitutionnel.fr), para. 93.

(vii) if the data does not reveal any tax fraud it should be deleted after 30 days, and if the data identifies a tax fraud it can be kept for one year or until criminal, tax or customs proceedings are started.[508]

This approach followed by the French Council can be seen as a good omen, as it restricts the application of AI systems within certain limits that grant human rights protection. However, the fact that human control is required not only on the functioning of the algorithm but also on its results when needed to proceed further on the investigation, it seems a very naive approach, and a Pandora's box has been opened, as it leaves the door open to more arbitrariness in administrative decisions: How can the result of an algorithm that cannot be explained and reproduced be controlled?[509] Tax authorities, and in general the use of AI systems from whatever public office and even in the private sector, should be governed by monitoring mechanisms and where possible third-party experts' checks that could try to avoid any arbitrary functioning of the underlying algorithms.

This approach, of a reinforced extra control on the AI systems, is also supported, as better explained in the next paragraph, by the GDPR Regulation at Article 22 in a way that excludes administrative decisions merely based on algorithms' outcomes and Articles 13, 14 and 15 where it requires the explainability of the decision taken. This view has also been supported by the European Court of Justice where in its decision (C-73/16) it pointed out that tax authorities are not precluded by processing personal data for the purpose of collecting tax and combating tax fraud, but they have to respect the provisions set up in the GDPR and to grant the possibility of the right of defence to the taxpayer.[510] On another occasion the European Court of Justice intervened to support the fact that the taxpayer should not be deprived of the right to effectively challenge the findings of fact and legal classifications during a procedure brought against him with the consequence being the right to have access to data, information that is the base of the act of tax administrations.[511]

508 Calderón Carrero, J. M., and Ribeiro, J. S., Fighting Tax Fraud through Artificial Intelligence Tools: Will the Fundamental Rights of Taxpayers Survive the Digital Transformation of Tax Administrations?, *European Taxation*, Vol. 60(6), 2020, pp. 235–236.

509 La Quadrature du Net, Le Conseil Constitutionnel Autorise Le Fisc À La Surveillance De Masse, *Blog*, 2019, available at https://gsell.tech/predicting-courts-decisions-is-lawful-in-france-and-will-remain-so/.

510 European Court of Justice, Case C-73/16, Peter Puškár v Finančnériaditeľstvo Slovenskejrepubliky and Kriminálnyúradfinančnejsprávy, Judgment of the Court of 27 September 2017, para. 125.

511 European Court of Justice, Case C-189/18, Glencore Agriculture Hungary Kft. v NemzetiAdó-ésVámhivatalFellebbviteliIgazgatósága, Judgment of the Court of 16 October 2019, para. 70. See also Deotto, D. and Dorigo, S., I Sistemi Utilizzati per Motivare un Atto Vanno Resi Conoscibili al Cittadino, IlSole24Ore, 26 Aprile 2021, Clarizia, P., La nozione di algoritmo "tecnologico" secondo una recente decisione del Consiglio di Stato, IRPA (Instituto di Ricercche sulla Pubblica Amministrazione), 2022.

Slightly different but related to the use of internet sources based on an algorithm, is the possibility, recognized in Italy, at the administrative level, to use internet sources to support tax investigations. In 2016, with a Circular Letter of the local tax administration, with operational guidelines from preventive and combating evasion, it has been provided that information can be retrieved not only by the database but also by other sources, including the one derived by open sources.[512] To support this view, in 2018, the Italian Tax Police issued a Circular Letter where it recognized the possibility to obtain information also from "open sources", which includes "media, websites of local authorities or local bodies, websites of companies present in territory".[513]

According to the preceding, for the proper use of an AI system, answering the following questions could be of help in defining if the system is working and respecting fundamental human rights: (i) Is it clear what the objectives of the AI system are, that is, is it possible to formalize the problem that the system is being asked to solve? (ii) Does the AI system provide useful and meaningful information for understanding its performance and output/decisions? (iii) Can all of the AI system's outputs—both intermediary and final—for achieving a given goal be explained? (iv) Can the determinant data or knowledge that an AI system uses to make decisions be identified? (v) Do two similar-looking cases verifiably result in similar outcomes, that is, can the consistency and integrity of AI system outcomes be verified?[514]

10.2 Privacy and data protection

A 2014 White House report on big data concluded that "The technological trajectory, however, is clear: more and more data will be generated about

512 Agenzia delle Entrate, Circolare N. 16/E del 28/04/2016—Prevenzione e contrasto all'evasione—Indirizzi operativi, 2016, para. 1, p. 9, available at https://www.agenziaentrate.gov.it/portale/documents/20143/298247/Circolare+16E+del+28+aprile+2016_Cir16e+del+28.04.16.pdf/bab7d377-1561-fbb2-c17f-e99062b0fde3. See also Jattoni Dall'Asèen, Evasione fiscale, ora in Francia un algoritmo andrà a caccia dei "furnetti" sui social network, Corriere della Sera-Economia, 19 February 2021.

513 Guardia di Finanza, Circolare N. 1/2018, 27 November 2017, Volume 1, Chapter 6, p. 80, available at https://www.gdf.gov.it/documenti-e-pubblicazioni/circolari/circolare-1-2018-manuale-operativo-in-materia-di-contrasto-allevasione-e-alle-frodi-fisca/circolare-n-1-2018-volume-i.pdf.

514 OECD, OECD Framework for the Classification of AI Systems—OECD Digital Economy Papers No. 323, 2022, p. 43, available at https://www.oecd-ilibrary.org/science-and-technology/oecd-framework-for-the-classification-of-ai-systems_cb6d9eca-en. See also European Union Agency for Fundamental Rights (FRA), #BigData: Discrimination in data-supported decision making, 2018, pp. 2–13, available at https://www.oecd-ilibrary.org/science-and-technology/oecd-framework-for-the-classification-of-ai-systems_cb6d9eca-en.

individuals and will persist under the control of others".[515] Looking at our society today, it is difficult to imagine it without any access to the internet or to any electronic-based system, as they have become necessary to participate in the daily life.[516] However, the use of these instruments should be according to our common society rights, that is, it must be carried out with respect for fundamental human rights.[517] An AI system can be based either on expert input or on data, both of which can be generated by humans or automated tools such as ML algorithms, and the awareness and consent for the provision of personal data about individuals is a critical focus area for privacy protection and consumer protection.[518]

The problem related to data privacy has particular significance in the relationship between tax authorities and taxpayers. Indeed, when formulating tax rules, the legislator enters directly into the personal sphere of individuals, that is, tax legislation constitutes the competence of tax authorities to exercise a special type of power over an individual, especially when it enters in its property and privacy sphere, to enforce the tax benefit due from them.[519] This is especially the case when dealing with the automatic exchange of information (AEoI), which has gained great importance in recent years. Just think of, among others, the Foreign Accountant Tax Compliance Act (FATCA), Common Reporting Standard (CRS) and BEPS Action 13 with the Country-by-Country Reporting (CbCR). With all these initiatives, data is required to be transferred periodically among the different tax authorities with all the consequences that are derived, such us, systems hankering, stolen information or profiling.[520] Therefore, we have a need to protect the taxpayers when their data is constantly moving around the globe.

515 White House, *Big Data: Seizing Opportunities, Preserving Values* (Report for the President), Washington, DC: Executive Office of the President, 2014, available at http://www.whitehouse.gov/sites/default/files/docs/big_data_privacy_report_may_1_2014.pdf and Greene, D., et al., Better, Nicer, Clearer, Fairer: A Critical Assessment of the Movement for Ethical Artificial Intelligence and Machine Learning, Proceedings of the 52nd Hawaii International Conference on System Sciences, Critical and Ethical Studies of Digital and Social Media 2019, pp. 1–10, available at https://scholarspace.manoa.hawaii.edu/items/2c91a03d-caad-4c6f-9069-9bca4f393ce6.

516 Rothkopf, D., Unrestricted Internet Access a Modern Human Right?, *Foreign Policy Magazine*, 2 February 2015, available at https://foreignpolicy.com/2015/02/02/unrestricted-internet-access-human-rights-technology-constitution/.

517 Council of Europe, Consultative Committee of the Convention of the Protection of Individuals with regard to Automatic Processing of Personal Data—(Convention 108), Report on Artificial Intelligence, T-PD(2018)09Rev, Strasbourg, 25 January 2019, p. 5.

518 OECD, Recommendation of the Council on OECD Legal Instruments Artificial Intelligence, 2022, pp. 35–36, available at OECD-LEGAL-0449-en.pdf.

519 Drywa, A., Taxpayer's Right to Privacy?, *Intertax*, Vol. 50(1), 2022, pp. 40–55.

520 Liotti, B. F., Taxpayers' Data Protection: Do International, Regional, and Domestic Instruments Guarantee Adequate Rights in Tax (A)EoI?, *Intertax*, Vol. 50(2), 2022, pp. 138–158 and Debelva, F., and Mosquera, I., Privacy and Confidentiality in Exchange of Information Procedures: Some Uncertainties, Many Issues, But Few Solutions, *Intertax*, Vol. 45(5), 2017, pp. 362–381.

To sum up, AI systems can affect privacy in many ways[521] through data exploitation, identification, and tracking;[522] voice and facial recognition;[523] prediction;[524] and profiling.[525]

At the international level the right to privacy is recognized in the Universal Declaration of Human Rights at Article 12,[526] the International Covenant on Civil and Political Rights at Article 17,[527] the Convention of the Rights of the Child at Article 16[528] and the International Convention on the Protection of All Migrant Workers and Members of Their Families at Article 14.[529] The right to privacy is part of the 1950 European Convention on Human Rights, which states, "Everyone has the right to respect for his private and family life, his home and his correspondence".[530]

521 Jain, S. A., and Jain, S. A., Artificial Intelligence: A Threat to Privacy?, *Nirma University Law Journal*, Vol. 8(2), 2019, pp. 33–34.

522 The Royal Society, *Machine Learning: The Power and Promise of Computers That Learn by Example*, 2017, pp. 5–124, available at https://royalsociety.org/~/media/policy/projects/machine-learning/publications/machine-learning-report.pdf and also Martínez, R., Cuestiones de ética jurídica al abordar proyectos de Big Data. El contexto del Reglamento general de protección de datos, *Dilemata*, Vol. 9(24), 2017, pp. 151–164, available at https://royalsociety.org/~/media/policy/projects/machine-learning/publications/machine-learning-report.pdf, Kosinski, M., et al., Private Traits and Attributes Are Predictable from Digital Records of Human Behaviours. 2013, PNAS 110, pp. 5802–5805, available at Private traits and attributes are predictable from digital records of human behavior (pnas.org).

523 Garante per la Protezione dei dati Personali (GPDP), Riconoscimento facciale: il Garante privacy sanziona Clearview per 20 milioni di euro. Vietato l'uso dei dati biometrici e il monitoraggio degli italiani, *Press Release*, 9 March 2022, available at https://royalsociety.org/~/media/policy/projects/machine-learning/publications/machine-learning-report.pdf, where The Italian SA (Garante per la protezione dei dati personali) fined the US-based company Clearview AI EUR 20 million after finding it applied what amounted to biometric monitoring techniques also to individuals in the Italian territory.

524 The Royal Society, *Machine Learning: The Power and Promise of Computers That Learn by Example*, 2017, pp. 5–124, available at https://royalsociety.org/~/media/policy/projects/machine-learning/publications/machine-learning-report.pdf. For example, by merging overlapping records which are in the public domain, advanced analytics can draw personal insights from open data.

525 Ferraris, V., et al., The Impact of Profiling on Fundamental Rights, *SSRN*, 2013, available at SSRN: https://papers.ssrn.com/sol3/papers.cfm?abstract_id=2366753 and Janasik, N., Reframing Autonomy: My Data, Our Data, and the Question of Human Dignity, in *Human-Centered Digitalization and Services* (eds. Marja Toivonen and Eveliina Saari), Springer, 2019, pp. 245–258.

526 United Nations, *Universal Declaration of Human Rights*, General Assembly resolution 217 A, Paris on 10 December 1948, available at https://www.un.org/en/about-us/universal-declaration-of-human-rights.

527 United Nations, *International Covenant on Civil and Political Rights*, 16 December 1966, available at https://www.ohchr.org/en/instruments-mechanisms/instruments/international-covenant-civil-and-political-rights.

528 United Nations, *Convention on the Rights of the Child*, 20 November 1989, available at https://www.ohchr.org/en/instruments-mechanisms/instruments/convention-rights-child.

529 United Nations, *International Convention on the Protection of the Rights of All Migrant Workers and Members of Their Families*, 18 December 1990, available at International Convention on the Protection of the Rights of All Migrant Workers and Members of Their Families.

530 ECHR, Article 8.1.

From this basis, the European Union has sought to ensure the protection of this right through legislation. The rules on the protection of personal data processing finds its roots at the European level, as this environment is the most developed in this area, in the Council of Europe Convention No. 108 on data protection of 1981.[531] Later Directive 95/46/CE was introduced,[532] and this complex set of rules has been entirely replaced by the Regulation n. 2016/679 (GDPR) entered into force in 2016 after passing European Parliament, and as of May 25, 2018, all organizations were required to be compliant.[533] The current regulatory framework should be read together with the Guidelines on the Protection of Individuals with Regard to the Processing of Personal Data in a World of Big Data,[534] adopted in 2017, which provides a general framework to apply appropriate policies and measures to continue to make effective the data protection principles in the context of big data and with the European Parliament resolution of March 14, 2017, on fundamental rights implications of big data.[535]

One of the most important aspects of the GDPR is the recognition of privacy rights for data subjects, having the purpose to give individuals more control over the data they provide to different organizations. These rights can be summarized as follows: (i) the right to be informed, (ii) the right of access, (iii) the right to rectification, (iv) the right to erasure, (v) the right to restrict processing, (vi) the right to data portability, (vii) the right to object and (viii) rights in relation to automated

531 Convention for the protection of individuals with regard to automatic processing of personal data (ETS No. 108, 28.01.1981), available at https://www.coe.int/en/web/conventions/full-list?module=treaty-detail&treatynum=108.

532 European Parliament, Directive 95/46/EC of the European Parliament and of the Council of 24 October 1995 on the protection of individuals with regard to the processing of personal data and on the free movement of such data, available at eur-lex.europa.eu/legal-content/EN/TXT/PDF/?uri=CELEX:31995L0046&from=FR. See also EU—Article 29 Data Protection working party, Statement on Statement of the WP29 on the impact of the development of big data on the protection of individuals with regard to the processing of their personal data in the EU, 16 September 2014.

533 European Parliament and the European Council, Regulation (EU) 2016/679 of the European Parliament and of the Council of 27 April 2016 on the protection of natural persons with regard to the processing of personal data and on the free movement of such data, and repealing Directive 95/46/EC (General Data Protection Regulation), available at https://eur-lex.europa.eu/legal-content/EN/TXT/PDF/?uri=CELEX:32016R0679&from=EN and Goodman, B., and Flaxman, S., European Union Regulations on Algorithmic Decision Making and a "Right to Explanation", *AI Magazine*, Vol. 38(3), 2016, pp. 50–57.

534 Council of Europe, *Guidelines on the Protection of Individuals with Regard to the Processing of Personal Data in a World of Big Data*, 17 January 2017, available at https://rm.coe.int/CoERMPublicCommonSearchServices/DisplayDCTMContent?documentId=09000016806f06d0

535 European Parliament, Resolution of 14 March 2017 on Fundamental Rights Implications of Big Data: Privacy, Data Protection, Non-Discrimination, Security and Law-Enforcement (2016/2225(INI)) (OJ C, C/263, 25.07.2018), p. 82, CELEX, https://eur-lex.europa.eu/legal-content/EN/TXT/?uri=CELEX:52017IP0076 and Nielsen, K., *Big Data and Sensitive Data, in Big Data for the Greater Good* (eds. Ali Emrouznejad and Vincent Charles), Springer International Publishing AG, 2018, pp. 183–204.

decision-making and profiling. On top of this, consensus plays a fundamental role. Consensus should be "freely given, specific, informed and unambiguous".[536]

To support such principles, Article 6 of GDPR provides that it is not possible to collect, store or sell personal data to advertisers unless it can be justified, with some specific exceptions.[537] In fact, these requirements that could be summarized as transparency, right of information, access and deletion guarantee an active role of the human being, since they must be confirmed by the individuals to whom they refer, since inactivity or silence can no longer be considered as an automatic consent by individuals. Furthermore, the principle of accountability also consists of a proactive and dynamic behaviour so that all parties involved in the processing of personal data ensure that fundamental rights are maintained during the use of such data and that the same can also be guaranteed in future actions.[538]

Article 22 of GDPR[539] is also of great importance, as it concerns the protection of individuals regarding the processing of personal data and on the free movement of such data. Articles 13 and 14 of the same regulation are also of great importance in general and for the protection of taxpayers. Article 13 provides the obligation to disclose information, and at paragraph 2 it obliges the controller to provide the data subject with additional information when obtaining personal data in order to guarantee proper and transparent processing and at letter (b) of the same paragraph the person concerned has the right to demand access to his personal data.[540] Article 14 contains the rules for the provision of information when collecting data via third parties and although, in general, it provides for the provision of personal information, at paragraph 5(b) and (c) it provides restriction in the provision of such information if the obligation to disclose is likely to render impossible or seriously impair the achievement of the objective of the processing, or if the provision of data is explicitly required by the EU or member state law.[541]

Indeed, considering that data could be poorly selected, incomplete, incorrect or outdated,[542] basing the final decision on the outcome of an automated process could generate discrimination. In this sense, the combined reading of Article 11(3) of EU Directive 2016/680 together with recital 71 of the GDPR highlight the importance of a correct data processing that tries to minimize the risk of discrimination when dealing with data-supported decision making.[543]

536 GDPR, Article 7.

537 GDPR, Article 6.1, provides exceptions to data process where.

538 Cirone, E., *Big Data e Tutela dei Diritti Fondamentali, in Il ragionamento giuridico nell'era dell'intelligenza artificiale, a cura di Stefano Dorigo*, Pacini Giuridica, 2020, p. 150.

539 GDPR, Article 22.

540 See also Offermanns, R., Report on the Symposium, "Tax Digitization, Help or Obstacle to Legal Protection?", *European Taxation*, Vol. 60(6), 2020, pp. 261–268.

541 GDPR, Article 14.

542 The White House, *Big Data: A Report on Algorithmic Systems*, Opportunity and Civil Rights, 2016, pp. 4–22, available at https://obamawhitehouse.archives.gov/sites/default/files/microsites/ostp/2016_0504_data_discrimination.pdf.

543 Bibal, A., et al., Legal Requirements on Explainability in Machine Learning, *Artificial Intelligence and Law*, Vol. 29(2), 2021, pp. 149–169.

The 2017 Guidelines are organized on three main areas: (i) ethical common values, which are the base of the evaluation of big data to safeguard human rights and fundamental freedoms; (ii) the evaluation of personal data according to the social and ethical impact according to the context in which are used (i.e., personal data processing), (iii) provides the evaluation of the use of single specific data, where it is suggested the establishment of an *ad hoc* ethics committee, or rely on existing ones, to identify the specific ethical values to be safeguarded in the use of data through the provision of a guideline of the risk evaluation.[544]

Furthermore, the Guidelines identify the interaction between experts, as part of the committees and different stakeholders—that is, group of people, that should be part of the analysis, as they are directly affected by a certain use of the data.[545] In this sense, it is evident how the Guidelines see the importance of creating awareness on the part of interested persons about the potential negative impact of big data and how to behave in the future through an active role of the controllers. In this context, the informed consent of the interested party plays an important role and must be given freely and this occurs if there is no imbalance of power between the interested party and the data controller, which affects the decisions of the interested party regarding the processing.[546] To reach this objective, the Guidelines suggest the possibility that the consensus could be provided "by means of an interface which simulates the effects of the use of data and its potential impact on the data subject, in a learn-from-experience approach".[547]

The European Parliament with the aim to counteract these risks identifies the need to define and set up strong scientific and ethical standards to manage data collection to further judge the results of the analysis performed by the algorithms.[548] The Parliament recognizes not only the need to build the use of big data on ethical standards but also the importance of the role of humans in the assumption of

544 Council of Europe, Guidelines on the Protection of Individuals with Regard to the Processing of Personal Data in a World of Big Data, 17 January 2017, par. IV.2.6, available at: https://rm.coe.int/CoERMPublicCommonSearchServices/DisplayDCTMContent?documentId=09000016806f06d0 and Gutiérrez, D. M. E., Discutiendo la transparencia de las políticas de privacidad en la Era del Big Data. Hacia la "Norma Social" como nueva Regla de Derecho, *Dilemata, año 9*, n. 24, 2017, pp. 165–184.

545 Council of Europe, Guidelines on the Protection of Individuals with Regard to the Processing of Personal Data in a World of Big Data, 17 January 2017, par. IV.2.7, available at: https://rm.coe.int/CoERMPublicCommonSearchServices/DisplayDCTMContent?documentId=09000016806f06d0.

546 Council of Europe, Guidelines on the Protection of Individuals with Regard to the Processing of Personal Data in a World of Big Data, 17 January 2017, par. IV, 5.3, available at: https://rm.coe.int/t-pd-2017-1-bigdataguidelines-en/16806f06d0.

547 Council of Europe, Guidelines on the Protection of Individuals with Regard to the Processing of Personal Data in a World of Big Data, 17 January 2017, par. IV, 5.1, available at: Microsoft Word-T-D(2017)1_BigDataGuidelines_En.docx (coe.int).

548 European Parliament resolution of 14 March 2017 on fundamental rights implications of big data: privacy, data protection, non-discrimination, security and law-enforcement (2016/2225(INI)), general considerations n. 2 (OJ C, C/263, 25.07.2018), p. 82, CELEX: https://eur-lex.europa.eu/legal-content/EN/TXT/?uri=CELEX:52017IP0076.

responsibilities in the different decisional process phases, especially to evaluate the adequacy of the decision that should be taken according to the algorithms' inputs.[549]

10.3 Vulnerability, sabotage, hacking: adversarial machine learning

Additional concerns and threats also come from the malicious attacks that AI technologies can suffer. IoT can be the perfect way for any hacker, intelligence service or criminal organization to overcome the limits that separate the lawful surveillance from unlawful, so as to create the privacy erosion.[550] Consequently, AI systems should consider their need from a cybersecurity perspective, with a proper implementation of controls that grants the integrity of data and functionalities that include privacy protection and confidentiality and maintain at the same time availability.[551] It is a matter of fact, as pointed out by the Royal Academy of Engineering, that "all technologies are liable to failure, and autonomous systems will be no exception (which is pertinent to the issue of whether autonomous systems should ever be created without manual override)".[552] Therefore, in general terms, we can ask ourselves what if one of the components of the system fails, what are the consequences of the failure, hence there is the need to ensure the safety and security of such systems.[553] Attacks cannot be directed only at a specific system, but extend the scope of the attack to a range of systems through network effects that enable the ability to target and communicate with individuals on a large scale.[554] When a learning algorithm performs well in adversarial conditions, it is an algorithm for secure learning.[555] Therefore, there is the need to properly understand when an

549 European Parliament resolution of 14 March 2017 on fundamental rights implications of big data: privacy, data protection, non-discrimination, security and law-enforcement (2016/2225(INI)), general considerations n. 32, (OJ C, C/263, 25.07.2018, p. 82, CELEX: https://eur-lex.europa.eu/legal-content/EN/TXT/?uri=CELEX:52017IP0076. See also Pérez Bernabeu, B., *Los contribuyentes ante las decisiones automatizadas de la administración tributaria, La digitalización en los procedimientos tributarios y el intercambio automático de información*/Ana María Pita Grandal (dir.), Luis Alberto Malvárez Pascual (dir.), Carmen Ruiz Hidalgo (dir.), Ernesto Eseverri Martínez (col.), Aranzadi, 2023, pp. 235–254.

550 Astobiza Monasterio, A., Ética algorítmica: Implicaciones éticas de una sociedad cada vez más gobernada por algoritmos, *Dilemata*, Vol. 9(24), 2017, pp. 185–217.

551 White House Office of Science and Technology Policy (OSTP), *Preparing for the Future of Artificial Intelligence*, Report, 2016, p. 36, available at https://obamawhitehouse.archives.gov/sites/default/files/whitehouse_files/microsites/ostp/NSTC/preparing_for_the_future_of_ai.pdf.

552 The Royal Academy of Engineering, Autonomous Systems: Social Legal and Ethical Issues, 2009, p. 3, available at https://www.raeng.org.uk/publications/reports/autonomous-systems-report.

553 Thomas, M., *Safety Critical Systems*, Gresham Lectures: London, 2017, YouTube, available at https://www.gresham.ac.uk/watch-now/safety-critical-systems.

554 Council of Europe, Committee of experts on human rights dimensions of automated data processing and different forms of artificial intelligence, Rapporteur: Yeung, Karen, A study of advanced digital technologies (including AI systems) for the concept of responsibility within a human rights framework, DGI(2019)05, 2019, p. 38, available at https://rm.coe.int/responsability-and-ai-en/168097d9c5.

555 Barreno, M., et al., The Security of Machine Learning, *Machine Learning*, Vol. 81(2), 2010, pp. 121–148 available at https://link.springer.com/content/pdf/10.1007/s10994-010-5188-5.pdf.

algorithm is secure and not subject to vulnerabilities (such as inducing misclassification via adversarial attacks or via poisoning the training data[556]).

Software vulnerabilities can occur in different ways. Next to the common buffer overflows, which have been the most common form of security vulnerability for the last ten years and provide that an anonymous internet user seeks to gain partial or total control of a host by manipulating the coding error to carry out malicious actions and compromise the affected system,[557] other new forms of vulnerabilities are (i) poisoning attacks,[558] (ii) adversarial examples,[559] and (iii) the exploitation of flaws in design of the goals of autonomous systems.[560]

Considering that, like the human brain, AI is a dual-use area of technology, meaning that AI systems and the knowledge on how to design them can be out toward both civilian and military uses with beneficial or harmful ends,[561] in general terms, malicious use of AI could threaten (i) digital security and (ii) physical security.[562]

Of the vast categories of cybercrimes, the most popular include malicious scan, new malware, phishing, ransomware and records lost to hacking, and they are

556 See, Szegedy, C., et al., Intriguing Properties of Neural Networks, *2nd International Conference on Learning Representations, ICLR 2014—Banff*, Canada, 2014, pp. 1–10, available at https://www.researchgate.net/publication/259440613_Intriguing_properties_of_neural_networks.

557 Cowan, C., et al., Buffer Overflows: Attacks and Defences for the Vulnerability of the Decade, *Foundations of Intrusion Tolerant Systems*, 2003 [Organically Assured and Survivable Information Systems], 2003, pp. 227–237, https://doi.org/10.1109/FITS.2003.1264935 and Fortinet, Buffer Overflow, *Blog*, available at https://www.fortinet.com/resources/cyberglossary/buffer-overflow.

558 Biggio, B., et al, Poisoning Attacks Against Support Vector Machines, *International Conference on Machine Learning (ICML 2012)*, 2012, pp. 1467–1474, available at Poisoning Attacks against Support Vector Machines (arxiv.org). According to the authors "Central to the motivation for these attacks is the fact that most learning algorithms assume that their training data comes from a natural or well-behaved distribution".

559 Szegedy, C., et al., Intriguing Properties of Neural Networks, *2nd International Conference on Learning Representations, ICLR 2014—Banff*, Canada arXiv preprint server, 2013, pp. 1–10, available at https://www.researchgate.net/publication/259440613_Intriguing_properties_of_neural_networks and Venkatachalam, M., About Adversarial Examples, Towards Data Science, *Blog*, 2019, available at https://towardsdatascience.com/about-adversarial-examples-2a7a7b4d2670.

560 Amodei, D., et al., Concrete Problems in AI Safety, *arXiv*, 2016, p. 2, available at https://arxiv.org/pdf/1606.06565.

561 Scharre, P., Autonomous Weapons and Operational Risk, Center for a New American Security, 2016, pp. 3–53, available at https://www.files.ethz.ch/isn/196288/CNAS_Autonomous-weapons-operational-risk.pdf#:~:text=From%20an%20operational%20standpoint%2C%20autonomous%20weapons%20pose%20a,the%20environment%2C%20or%20simple%20malfunctions%20or%20software%20errors.

562 Brundage, M., et al., The Malicious Use of Artificial Intelligence: Forecasting, Prevention, and Mitigation, report on workshop entitled "Bad Actor Risks in Artificial Intelligence" in Oxford, United Kingdom, 2018, p. 10, available at 1802.07228.pdf (cam.ac.uk), The Royal Society, Machine Learning: The Power and Promise of Computers That Learn by Example, 2017, pp. 5–124, available at https://royalsociety.org/~/media/policy/projects/machine-learning/publications/machine-learning-report.pdf and Six, P., Ethics, Regulation and the New Artificial Intelligence, Part II: Autonomy and Liability, *Information, Communication & Society*, Vol. 4(3), 2001, 406–434, https://doi.org/10.1080/713768548.

perpetrated by highly skilled professionals and organizations.[563] As a matter of fact, all these harmful forms of cyberattack can be spread through AI systems, as skilled people can operate on a wider scale.

In the field of digital security, let's think about social engineering, which, as demonstrated by some scientists, can suffer attacks on larger scale.[564] As the scientists pointed out, phishing is one of the oldest yet still most effective weapons for exploitation. Early phishing attempts took a shotgun approach: only a few targets out of millions needed to bite for an attack to succeed. Instead, with spear phishing, specificity into this process has been introduced by narrowing the target base to fewer people, enabling attackers to focus efforts on high-value targets. It increased the likelihood of success by preventively gathering personal information and using it to gain the target's trust.

In the field of physical security, some of the ways AI will affect security practices include, among others, Video—Analyzing what we see, Drones & Robots—(Unmanned Aerial Vehicles (UAVs) and Unmanned Ground Vehicles (UGVs)), Natural Language Processing—Understanding what we say, Speech Translation—Translating what we say into other languages for better communication, Anomaly Detection—Detecting things/activities that are out of the ordinary and Activity Recognition—interpreting human movement.[565] AI systems are used to enable unmanned vehicles such as robots and drones to process visual and many other types of data as well as to learn from their experiences and teach other machines, thus ML technology can extend the scope of surveillance areas, increase efficiency and save lives when deployed in dangerous scenarios.[566] Safer workplaces, faster investigations, real-time detection and easier processes are all the result of improved security operations, and when solutions like video surveillance, access control and new devices such as robots and drones work together seamlessly in a digital environment, businesses are better able to manage security threats.[567]

563 Centre for Strategic and International Studies (CSIS) and McAfee, The Economic Impact of Cybercrime Report, written by James Lewis, 2018, pp. 3–27, available at https://csis-website-prod.s3.amazonaws.com/s3fs-public/publication/economic-impact-cybercrime.pdf and Nobles, C., The Cyber Talent Gap and Cybersecurity Professionalizing, *International Journal of Hyperconnectivity and the Internet of Things*, Vol. 2(1), 2018, pp. 42–51, available at https://www.researchgate.net/publication/326757330_The_Cyber_Talent_Gap_and_Cybersecurity_Professionalizing.

564 Seymour, J., and Tully, P., Weaponizing Data Science for Social Engineering: Automated E2E Spear Phishing on Twitter, *Black Hat Conference*, 2016, pp. 1–7, available at https://www.researchgate.net/publication/326757330_The_Cyber_Talent_Gap_and_Cybersecurity_Professionalizing.

565 Tyriver, C., Part 1: Artificial Intelligence in Physical Security, *Security 101*, *Blog*, available at https://www.security101.com/blog/artificial-intelligence-in-physical-security.

566 Julie, B., The Role of Artificial Intelligence in Physical Security, *Writeclick, Blog*, available at https://www.writeclick.co.il/the-role-of-artificial-intelligence-in-physical-security/.

567 Paripally, G., and Controls, J., Artificial Intelligence Will Revolutionize Physical Security: Intelligent, Autonomous Systems That Prevent Incidents Are Coming, *SIA—Security Industry Association*, 2021, available at https://www.securityindustry.org/2021/11/09/artificial-intelligence-will-revolutionize-physical-security-intelligent-autonomous-systems-that-prevent-incidents-are-coming/.

However, it is also true that AI systems can go against these purposes and harm the physical security if used in an improper way.[568] This could be the case of the deployment of unmanned aircraft[569] and autonomous weapons systems (AWS) where, as sensors, algorithms and munitions are increasingly interlinked, questions arise about the acceptability of autonomy in certain "critical functions", particularly around identification, selection and application of force to targets[570] (attacks with the use of these technologies have already been performed by terrorist groups such ISIS and Hamas[571]). The fact that computing is embedded into the hardware itself—as with the IoT—creates enormous risks and vulnerabilities, as all our devices are connected to the internet and hence there is a constant possibility that these are remotely manipulated.[572]

To counteract the side effects that threaten physical security, in the US, for example, there is an official Department of Defense directive defining policies for the development and autonomy in weapons[573] and also the International Committee of the Red Cross recognizes that

> States assess the type and degree of human control required in the use of autonomous weapon systems. . . . States will identify and build on common

568 Tegmark, M., Benefits & Risks of Artificial Intelligence, *Future of Life Institute*, 2015, available at https://futureoflife.org/ai/benefits-risks-of-artificial-intelligence/?cn-reloaded=1. See also Lawless, W. F., et al., Artificial Intelligence, Autonomy, and Human-Machine Teams: Interdependence, Context, and Explainable AI, *AI Magazine*, Vol. 40(3), 2019, pp. 5–13.

569 Singer, P., *Wired for War: The Robotics Revolution and Conflict in the 21st Century*, New York: Penguin, 2009, p. 512.

570 Roff, H., Meaningful Human Control, Artificial Intelligence and Autonomous Weapons, briefing paper for delegates at the Convention on Certain Conventional Weapons (CCW) Meeting of Experts on Lethal Autonomous Weapons Systems (LAWS), 2016, pp. 1–6, available at www.article36.org/wp-content/uploads/2016/04/MHC-AI-and-AWS-FINAL.pdf and IEEE Global Initiative on Ethics of and Autonomous and Intelligent Systems, *Ethically Aligned Design: A Vision for Prioritizing Human Well-Being with Autonomous and Intelligent Systems*, IEEE, 2017, p. 9, available at ead_v2.pdf (ieee.org) and also Hin-Yan, L., Refining Responsibility: Differentiating Two Types of Responsibilities Issues Raised by Autonomous Weapons Systems, in *Autonomous Weapons Systems: Law, Ethics, Policy* (eds. N. Butha, S. Beck, R. Geiß, H. Liu and C. Kreß), Cambridge: Cambridge University Press, 2016, pp. 325–344.

571 Solomon, B., Witnessing an ISIS Drone Attack, *New York Times*, 2017, available at https://www.nytimes.com/video/world/middleeast/100000005040770/isis-drone-attack-mosul.html and Cohen, G., *Israel Shoots Down Hamas Drone Over Gaza Strip*, Haaretz, 2017, available at https://www.haaretz.com/israel-news/2017-02-23/ty-article/israel-shoots-down-hamas-drone-over-gaza-strip/0000017f-e62a-dc7e-adff-f6af11670000 (accessed 10 November 2022).

572 Schneier, B., The Internet of Things Is Wildly Insecure—and Often Unpatchable, *Wired*, 2014, available at https://www.wired.com/2014/01/theres-no-good-way-to-patch-the-internet-of-things-and-thats-a-huge-problem/ and Schneier, B., Security and the Internet of Things, *Schneier on Security*, 2017, available at https://www.schneier.com/essays/archives/2014/01/the_internet_of_thin.html.

573 US Department of Defense, DoD Directive 3000.09: Autonomy in Weapon Systems, 2012, available at https://www.esd.whs.mil/portals/54/documents/dd/issuances/dodd/300009p.pdf. See also Hynek, N., and Solovyeva, A., Operations of Power in Autonomous Weapon Systems: Ethical Conditions and Socio-Political Prospects, *AI & Society*, Vol. 36(5), 2021, pp. 79–89.

ground, such as the broad agreement that human control must be retained over weapon systems and the use of force.[574]

Moreover, methods to properly provide a defence against the attacks coming from the machines can be found in global positioning systems, radio waves, infrared, and audible sound or ultrasound signals.[575]

Lastly, the possibility of threats that AI systems can lead in the political security area is described. Social media increasingly plays a role in conflict and contentious politics, and politicians, leaders, insurgents and protestors have all used it as a tool for communication.[576] The fact that AI systems operate on scale means a vast amount of people can be reached simultaneously, with the risk that in case of malicious attacks, distorted information can be spread out with no means of control.[577] "Computational propaganda" is a term and phenomenon that encompasses recent digital misinformation and manipulation efforts, and it is best defined as "the assemblage of social media platforms, autonomous agents, and big data tasked with the manipulation of public opinion".[578]

Also, in this case, there are measures and technologies that have been developed or are under study that help or will help as countermeasures for the rampant risks associated with the employment of AI systems that undermine the political security. The possibility to certify that a video was filmed live and not produced online could definitely reduce the risk of fakes,[579] and this is also possible for images, which can be the object of forgeries through, for example resampling, splicing and copy-move.[580] Another way to protect information, such as videos and images, is encryption, which is a way of encoding data so that only authorized parties can

574 International Committee of the Red Cross, *Expert Meeting on Lethal Autonomous Weapon Systems*, 2017, available at https:// www.icrc.org/en/document/expert-meeting-lethalautonomous-weapons-systems.

575 Aker, C., and Kalkan, S., *14th IEEE International Conference on Advanced Video and Signal Based Surveillance (AVSS)*, 2017, pp. 1–6, available at https://www.semanticscholar.org/paper/Using-deep-networks-for-drone-detection-Aker-Kalkan/64fcde870588026b026b16875fdad67df77d10f9 and Yin, T., Game of Drones: Defending Against Drone Terrorism, *Texas A&M University Law Review*, Vol. 2(4), 2015, pp. 635–673, available at https://papers.ssrn.com/sol3/papers.cfm?abstract_id=2944426.

576 Zeitzoff, T., How Social Media Is Changing Conflict, *Journal of Conflict Resolution*, Vol. 61(9), 2017, pp. 1970–1991.

577 Skilton, M., and Hovsepian, F., *The 4th Industrial Revolution—Responding to the Impact of Artificial Intelligence on Business*, Palgrave Macmillan, 2018, p. 218.

578 Woolley, S. C., and Howard, P. N., Political Communication, Computational Propaganda, and Autonomous Agents, *International Journal of Communication*, Vol. 10(2016), 2016, pp. 4882–4890, available at https://ijoc.org/index.php/ijoc/article/view/6298/1809.

579 Rahman, M., Video Liveness for Citizen Journalism: Attacks and Defenses, *IEEE Transactions on Mobile Computing*, Vol. 16(11), 2017, pp. 3250–3263.

580 Kashyap, A., et al., An Evaluation of Digital Image Forgery Detection Approaches, *International Journal of Applied Engineering Research*, Vol. 12(15), 2017, pp. 4747–4758.

understand the information.[581] However, it seems that currently the development in detecting fakes in videos and images, especially due to evolving technology in this field, is not a problem that could be intended as solved and much is still to be done.[582]

As we saw, there is a strong interpenetration among digital security, physical and political security, and artificial intelligence in a way that the possibilities to perform attacks is even increasing considering the velocity at which AI systems are developing, and measures that counteract new forms of attacks are not always following this development, with the risk that these holes will be increasingly used by hackers to generate new attacks. Artificial intelligence systems can be used to target different objectives,[583] with the consequence that damages are expanded on a vast scale, and it is worth reflecting on the scalability of such approaches and understanding what challenges remain to reduce accident risk in modern machine learning systems[584] with policymakers, politicians and experts aiming to mitigate this scale effects with proper solutions.[585] In other words, the role of policymakers is to restrain the "bad" effects of AI systems without unduly stifling innovation.[586] There is the need to see through the opacity of machine automation logic to be able to understand and trace back where errors caused by automation or deviancy and criminal activity caused directly or overtly by machine intelligence computation or rules built in by humans.[587]

11 Summary

Changes caused by new technologies are important for our society in order to help daily activities while granting, among other things, a high task efficiency. This means reducing, when possible, the amount of time that humans need to dedicate to their jobs or increasing the possibility to have better cures against a wider range of illnesses, preventing the onset of diseases, or the possibility of accessing a mass culture.

581 Cloudflare, What Is Encryption? | Types of Encryption, *Blog*, available at https://www.cloudflare.com/learning/ssl/what-is-encryption/.

582 Brundage, M., et al., The Malicious Use of Artificial Intelligence: Forecasting, Prevention, and Mitigation, report of the workshop entitled "Bad Actor Risks in Artificial Intelligence" in Oxford, 2018, p. 48.

583 Bostrom, N., *Superintelligence: Paths, Dangers, Strategies*, Oxford: Oxford University Press, 2014, p. 107 and Burton, E., Ethical Considerations in Artificial Intelligence Courses, *AI Magazine*, Vol. 38(2), 2017, pp. 22–34.

584 Amodei, D., et al, Concrete Problems in AI Safety, *arXiv*, 2016, pp. 1–29, available at preprint available at https://deepai.org/publication/concrete-problems-in-ai-safety.

585 An example in this sense could be found in Article 33 of GDPR (Regulation (EU) 2016/679) that outlines the procedure to follow in the event of a personal data breach. Under the terms of GDPR, companies are required to notify a personal data breach to the supervisory authority within 72 hours of becoming aware of the breach.

586 Ofili, F., How to Tame the Tech Titans, *The Economist*, 20 January 2018, available at How to tame the tech titans | The Economist.

587 Skilton, M., and Hovsepian, F., *The 4th Industrial Revolution—Responding to the Impact of Artificial Intelligence on Business*, Palgrave Macmillan, 2018, p. 224.

It is worth noticing, however, that when exploring the question of how much AI has really affected the practice of law, the answer would be "so far not much as the AI hype seems to foresee", yet the potential for adopting models exists.[588] Indeed, the motor of these new disruptive technologies is still the human being, meaning we need people who are able to make AI work in a proper way as well as to continue developing new systems. Indeed, computers are still considered to be plain machines, and AI, even if encompassing the term "intelligence", is a superficial approach of algorithms that are imagined and built by humans' minds.

Indeed, AI, despite the word "intelligence", is just based on algorithms and statistical processes that lack aspects of human intelligence, such as the ability to abstract concepts and infer emotional aspects, creativity and consciousness.[589] The digital culture does not narrate, as the digital human is limited to calculating and counting, that is, there is the tendency to transform all into something numerical under the aegis of performance and effectiveness.[590] A major problem with today's large language model is its inability to distinguish truth from falsehood and "we humans are prone to giving machines ambiguous or mistaken instructions, and we want them to do what we mean, not necessarily what we say" with the consequences that the outcomes can be unexpected and amusing.[591]

Moreover, and especially for unsupervised systems, the ongoing relationship between humans and machines shows that the functioning of these systems and models need to be analysed not only from a mere technical point of view but also according to the way these can be controlled and the responsibilities that derive both at social and ethic levels when the existing and the new technologies become part of our society (considering that the algorithms receive, at least at an initial stage, inputs from humans). In other words, they cannot be isolated and cut off from the society in which they operate, as they are not autonomous and detached from our world.[592] In fact, machines are not yet able to match high human abilities such reasoning, concept comprehension, flexible understanding or problem-solving skills.[593] Currently,

588 Nissan, E., Digital Technologies and AI's Present and Foreseeable Impact on Lawyering, *Judging, Policing and Law Enforcement*, Vol. 32(3), 2017, pp. 441–464.

589 Quintarelli, S., et al., *Intelligenza Artificiale—cos'è davvero, come funziona, che effetti avrà, A cura di Claudia Giulia Ferrauto*, Bollati Boringhieri, 2020, p. 58 and Andreotta, A. J., The Hard Problem of AI Rights, *AI and Society*, Vol. 36(1), 2021, pp. 19–32.

590 Galparsoro, J. I., *Big Data y Psicopolítica. Vía de escape: de la vida calculable a la vida como obra de arte*, Dilemata, año 9, n. 24, 2017, pp. 25–43 and Stephan, K. D., and Klima, G., Artificial Intelligence and Its Natural Limits, *AI and Society*, Vol. 36(1), 2021, pp. 9–18.

591 Mitchell, M., What Does It Mean to Align AI with Human Values?, *Quantamagazine*, December 13, 2023.

592 Europa Press Islas Canarias, Marchena ve "indispensable" la inteligencia artificial pero sostiene que no puede sustituir al juez, europapress, published on 07/06/2022, available at Marchena ve "indispensable" la inteligencia artificial pero sostiene que no puede sustituir al juez (europapress.es) y Comisionado de Transparencia de Canarias, Manuel Marchena en el Parlamento de Canarias: "Hay que lograr que la Justicia siga siendo humana", Youtube, 2022, available at https://www.youtube.com/watch?v=9OVzAny9R_0 (accessed 7 July 2022).

593 Krupasnky, J., Untangling the Definitions of AI, Machine Intelligence, and ML, *Medium*, June 13 2017, available at https://jackkrupansky.medium.com/untangling-the-definitions-of-artificial-intelligence-machine-intelligence-and-machine-learning-7244882f04c7 (accessed 1 February 2023).

the improvement of algorithms' performances derives from the examination of more data and patterns to make better automated decisions.[594] Indeed, "Intelligence is different from data processing. . . . The premise for intelligence is the understanding of what it takes to address a question leading to some action or to no action".[595]

This clarification of the scope of the law when placed in the context of the application of AI identifies that computation systems do perform certain functions and they can for sure have advantages in terms of memory or logic induction compared to humans, so much so that their decisions have a normative effect as they will induce, enforce, inhibit or rule out some human actions, but it has to be clear that no confusion should be generated between the performativity of positive law with the performance of artificial legal intelligence as the mere prediction is not the aim of the legal activity (being from the lawyer or judge/decisional body side).[596]

Therefore, due to the complex reasoning behind the application of law, current AI development could also bring benefits to the law field, but it works much better for fields and activities where patterns, rules, processes and structures can normally lead to a definitive right answer, whereas in areas permeated by abstraction, open-ended, intuition, social norms and behaviours, and judgements, the functioning is still severely limited,[597] and their deployment can be seen in assisting in the decision-making.[598]

If in the field of law, including tax law, when dealing with the decision functions that are performed by the courts and other decision bodies, such as arbitration courts or arbitration commissions, the implementation of AI systems has reached a supportive role, leaving the central functions for the final decision to humans. The role of AI

594 Surden, H., AI and Law: An Overview, *Georgia State University Law Review*, Vol. 35(4), 2019, p. 1312., therefore if the programmer set a specific algorithm, then the machine will use it to "learn" automatically based on the given algorithm.

595 Nadin, M., Machine Intelligence: A Chimera, *AI & Society*, Vol. 34(2), 2019, pp. 215–242.

596 Hildebrandt, M., Law as Computation in the Era of Artificial Legal Intelligence Speaking Law to the Power of Statistics, *University of Toronto Law Journal*, Vol. 68(1), 2018, pp. 12–35 and Hildebrandt, M., The Force of Law and the Force of Technology, in *The Routledge International Handbook of Technology, Crime and Justice* (eds. M. R. P. McGuire and Holt), Routledge, 2017, pp. 579–608 and Alarie, B., The Path of the Law: Towards Legal Singularity, *The University of Toronto Law Journal*, Vol. 66(4), 2016, pp. 443–455.

597 Vincent, J., The State of AI in 2019, *VERGE*, 28 January 2019, available at https://www.theverge.com/2019/1/28/18197520/ai-artificial-intelligence-machine-learning-computational-science (accessed 10 May 2022) and Chui, M., et al., What AI Can and Can't Do (Yet) for Your Business, *MCKINSEY Q.*, 10 May 2022, available at https://www.mckinsey.com/capabilities/quantumblack/our-insights/what-ai-can-and-cant-do-yet-for-your-business (accessed 10 May 2022); Pontin, J., et al., The Downsides to Deep Learning, *WIRED*, 2 February 2018, available at https://www.wired.com/story/greedy-brittle-opaque-and-shallow-the-downsides-to-deep-learning/ (accessed 10 May 2022); Waters, R., Why We Are in Danger of Overestimating AI, *Financial Times*, 5 February 2018, available at https://www.ft.com/content/4367e34e-db72-11e7-9504-59efdb70e12f (accessed 10 May 2022).

598 Stanford University, Gathering Strength, Gathering Storms: The One Hundred Year Study on AI (AI100), *2021 Study Panel Report*, p. 49, available at https://ai100.stanford.edu/gathering-strength-gathering-storms-one-hundred-year-study-artificial-intelligence-ai100-2021-study and Mocchegiani, M., Algoritmi e diritto: I nuovi orizzonti (più o meno rassicuranti) della decisione robotica, Cronache dal Convegno "Decisionerobotica" Accademia deiLincei, forumcostituzionale.it, *Roma 5 luglio 2018*, pp. 1–5, available at https://www.forumcostituzionale.it/wordpress/wp-content/uploads/2018/10/mocchegiani.pdf.

and ML systems can find a substantive place when dealing with operational tax activities, such as those performed by the tax administrations and the tax departments.

With reference to the possible implications and impacts that AI and ML could have on the tax dispute resolution, it is important to find a trade-off solution between available data and data protection. Indeed, the current tax dispute resolution procedure, as described in Chapter 3 of this work, provides a limit to the data availability due, mainly, to data protection/privacy reasons. The unavailability or restricted availability of data can limit or impede the proper functioning of system-based algorithms that could be useful to create a first line of support for future decisions.

However, the benefit of implementing and deploying such systems should not make us forget that big data and artificial intelligence can create some dangers, since data and algorithms are not always objective and can have significant biases, with the need to create safeguards to avoid any bias or discrimination.[599] It is important to bear in mind that AI systems and ML algorithms should perform in accord with respect for human rights. In this sense, there is a need from one side to create direct regulatory mechanisms to influence the code of algorithms and from the other side to regulate the production processes or the producers of algorithms and attempt to ensure their awareness of the legal challenges, ethical dilemmas and human rights concerns that arise from automated data-processing and decision-making techniques.[600]

Governments have an important role to play in creating effective mechanisms to remedy the adverse human rights impacts of AI, and their role is essential to addressing the distributive consequences of AI by means of the democratic process.[601] The increasing work on ethic must definitively be performed and should still go on, but it should be seen as an orientation and preparation for the content of

599 Hueso Cotino, L., Big Data e inteligencia artificial. Una aproximación a su tratamiento jurídico desde los derechos fundamentales, *Dilemata*, Vol. 9(24), 2017, pp. 131–150, Hueso Cotino, L., Ética en el diseño para el desarrollo de una inteligencia artificial, robótica y big data confiables y su utilidad desde el derecho, *Revista catalana de dretpúblic*, Vol. 58, 2019, pp. 29–48, http://revistes.eapc.gencat.cat/index.php/rcdp/article/view/10.2436-rcdp.i58.2019.3303 and Hueso Cotino, L., Algunas cuestiones clave de protección de datos en la nube. Hacia una "regulación nebulosa", *Revista catalana de dretpúblic*, Vol. 51, 2015, pp. 85–103, available at https://www.academia.edu/38738426/Derechos_fundamentales_y_control_e_investigaci%C3%B3n_de_las_comunicaciones_y_de_la_informaci%C3%B3n_que_est%C3%A1_en_la_nube_Especial_atenci%C3%B3n_a_las_m%C3%A1s_recientes_leyes_en_Europa#:~:text=Hacia%20una%20%E2%80%98regulaci%C3%B3n%20nebulosa%E2%80%99%20Resumen%20Se%20abordan%20algunas,de%20instituciones%20de%20protecci%C3%B3n%20de%20datos%20para%20corregirlas.

600 Council of Europe, Algorithms and Human Rights, Study on the Human Rights Dimensions of Automated Data Processing Techniques and Possible Regulatory Implications, Prepared by the Committee of Experts on Internet Intermediaries (MSI-NET), DGI(2017)12, 2017, p. 40.

601 Raso, F. A., et al., Artificial Intelligence & Human Rights: Opportunities & Risks, Research Publication No. 2018-6 September 25, 2018, Berkman Klein Center for Internet & Society at Harvard University, p. 5, Wachter, S., et al., Transparent, Explainable, and Accountable AI for Robotics, *Science Robotics*, Vol. 2(6), 2017, available at (PDF) https://www.researchgate.net/publication/318819126_Transparent_Explainable_and_Accountable_AI_for_Robotics and Cath, C., Governing Artificial Intelligence: Ethical, Legal and Technical Opportunities and Challenges, *Philosophical Transactions Royal Society A*, Vol. 376(2133), 2018, pp. 1–8. See also Zhang, B., et al., Ethics and Governance of Artificial Intelligence: Evidence from a Survey of Machine Learning Researchers, *Journal of Artificial Intelligence Research*, Vol. 71, 2021, pp. 591–666.

legal rules that are then binding for the entire society, enabling the enforcement by governments and the judiciary system.[602]

Conventions and norms may embody moral norms, but unless so embodied, moral norms are not usually associated with any sanction, that instead is present in conventions and laws with the intention to set a purpose, that is, to promote the sustainability of the group or society.[603] With the purpose of the law in mind, that is, the capability to regulate society, the way proper rules are set up will help in understanding which path society will undertake when dealing with AI systems, and it will help to answer the question posed by Douglas Rushkoff: if we want to manage the technology or if we want to be managed by it, that is, program it or be programmed.[604]

To answer this question a previous evaluation should be done on the human rights relevance when dealing with technology regulation considering the goal of technologies (what do we want to achieve with them): why did we want to have these technologies, and are these goals acceptable? Technologies are developed to avoid harm to human beings, to fulfil basic needs, to mitigate side effects of other technologies or to facilitate human beings in life projects, such as by making their lives easier or by helping them to be more successful in reaching their goals of action.[605] Therefore, "powerful AI systems should be developed only once we are confident that their effects will be positive, and their risks will be manageable".[606]

602 Nemitz, P., Constitutional Democracy and Technology in the Age of Artificial Intelligence, Vol. 376(2133), 2018, p. 10, available at https://royalsocietypublishing.org/doi/10.1098/rsta.2018.0089and Hagendorff, T., The Ethics of AI Ethics—An Evaluation of Guidelines, *Minds & Machines*, Vol. 30(1), 2020, pp. 99–120, and Weinberger, D., Don't Make AI Artificially Stupid in the Name of Transparency, Opinion: A Democracy Should't Leave It to Companies to Figure Out the Ethics of Artificial Intelligence, *WIRED*, 28 January 2018, available at https://www.wired.com/story/dont-make-ai-artificially-stupid-in-the-name-of-transparency/ (accessed 10 May 2022).

603 Bench-Capon, T. J. M., and Modgil, S., Norms and Value Based Reasoning: Justifying Compliance and Violation, *Artificial Intelligence and Law*, Vol. 25(1), 2017, pp. 29–63 and United Nations, The Guiding Principles on Business and Human Rights, Implementing the United Nations "Protect, Respect and Remedy" Framework, 2011, pp. 3–28, available at https://www.ohchr.org/sites/default/files/Documents/Publications/GuidingPrinciplesBusinessHR_EN.pdf. See also Australian Human Right Commission, Human Rights and Technology Issues Paper, July 2018, p. 23.

604 Astobiza Monasterio, A., Ética algorítmica: Implicaciones éticas de una sociedad cada vez más gobernada por algoritmos, *Dilemata*, Vol. 9(24), 2017, pp. 185–217 and Galzacorta, I., Hacer pública la red de las cosas. "Internet of Things" y "Dingpolitik", *Dilemata año 9*, no. 24, 2017, pp. 93–114. and Future of Life Institute, in its Pause Giant AI Experiments: AN Open Letter, 22 March 2023, pp. 1–2, available at https://futureoflife.org/open-letter/pause-giant-ai-experiments/.

605 Düwell, M., Human Dignity and the Ethics and Regulation of Technology, in *The Oxford Handbook of Law, Regulation and Technology* (eds. Roger Brownsword et al.), Oxford University Press, 2017, pp. 177–196.

606 Future of Life Institute, in its Pause Giant AI Experiments: AN Open Letter, 22 March 2023, pp. 1–2. See also García-Herrera Blanco, C., El uso del big data y la inteligencia artificial por las administraciones tributarias en la lucha contra el fraude fiscal. Particular referencia a los principios que han de regirla y a los derechos de los contribuyentes, Fiscalidad e inteligencia artificial: Administración tributaria y contribuyentes en la era digital / Fernando Serrano Antón (dir.), Aranzadi, 2020, pp. 297–318.

3 Processing juridical text with machine learning

Proof of concept

1 Introduction

This chapter will discuss the application of machine learning (ML) for the automated extraction of topics from summaries of legal texts. This application is the first step to perform for an artificial understanding of legal texts in an overall manner, thus allowing for their classification and categorization. Topics are meant to be clear, representative, segregated and meaningful. The chapter will present and evaluate a proof of concept and discuss potential deployment in larger scales based on results, with the aim to identify the usefulness of automated knowledge extraction methods driven by modern ML algorithms in the transfer pricing dispute field. The question posed is: *To what extent can ML help to extract knowledge from legal texts and how could this knowledge be useful for experts?*

Section 1 of this chapter presents research work, its application context and the reasons that motivate it, elaborating on the pursued goals and the methodology. It also depicts the structure of the next sections, where details of the experimental procedure will be presented.

1.1 Motivation

As we saw in the previous chapters, transfer pricing disputes are constantly arising and there are MAP procedures are constantly opened and closed on a yearly basis. However, currently, only statistical data is provided by the OECD (and currently, at the EU level, there are not enough closed cases, according to the new Directive[1]) with no possibility to access the decisions of the MAPs/arbitration's procedures. Therefore, the cases provided by the "TPcases.com" platform are used. This platform provides a free and fully searchable database of international tax and transfer pricing dispute resolution cases. In this large repository, documents are stored with summaries and indexed by means of tags and categories.

As a proof of concept, the aim of this chapter is to analyse the application of the most recent topic extraction techniques based on the Latent Dirichlet Allocation

1 European Union, Council Directive 2017/1852 of 10 October 2017.

DOI: 10.4324/9781003599814-3

(LDA) method proposed by Hoffman,[2] as well as the Latent Dirichlet Allocation with the Mallet approach, which uses collapsed Gibbs sampling[3] for efficient inference[4] and is commonly preferred for its better time performance and higher quality in topic segregation (see subsection 2.3.1). Although our experiments use a very limited number of documents and are based on summaries only, it will suffice to explore the potential of AI and to discuss its suitability as a tool to support law experts.

In few words, the way these algorithms work is by assuming that each document is composed of a mixture of topics, and they try to find out how strong a presence each topic has in each document. This is done by grouping together the documents based on the words they contain and noticing correlations between them.

It is important to emphasize at this point that, after receiving information from the TPcases.com technical team, they informed us of the following aspects:

- The attribution of "tags" and "categories" is a manual process. "Categories" were originally based on the chapters in the OECD Transfer Pricing Guidelines,[5] but later refined and increased. "Tags" are chosen during the process of reading the judgements and writing case summaries.
- The choice of taxonomies is important to guarantee the "accuracy of search and related post results".
- Automated algorithms tested to date do not generate adequate results.

1.2 Research questions and goals

The research carried out in this chapter aims to perform a proof of concept on the usefulness of automated knowledge extraction methods driven by modern ML algorithms in the transfer pricing dispute field. The question posed is: *To what extent can ML help to extract knowledge from legal texts and how could this knowledge be useful for experts?*

Being a proof of concept, the value of this research has an illustrative value; that is, it aims to give an example on a small scale of the potential of the application of such methods in the field, thus aligning with the central theme of the thesis; that is, the gradual impact that AI has on the transfer pricing disputes field. The aim

2 Hoffman, M., et al., Online Learning for Latent Dirichlet Allocation, *Advances in Neural Information Processing Systems*, Vol. 23, 2010, pp. 856–864. See also Kulshrestha, R., A Beginner's Guide to Latent Dirichlet Allocation (LDA), *Towardsdatascience, Blog*, 2019, available at https://towardsdatascience.com/latent-dirichlet-allocation-lda-9d1cd064ffa2 (accessed 9 July 2023).

3 The Gibbs sampler is an iterative simulation scheme for generating samples that converge to draws from a target distribution r(X) of a random variable X, see Jun, S. L., The Collapsed Gibbs Sampler in Bayesian Computations with Applications to a Gene Regulation Problem, *Journal of the American Statistical Association*, Vol. 89(427), 1994, pp. 958–966.

4 Griffiths, T. L., and Steyvers, M., Finding Scientific Topics, *Proceedings of the National Academy of Sciences (PNAS)*, Vol. 101(suppl_1), 2004, pp. 5228–5235.

5 OECD, *OECD Transfer Pricing Guidelines for Multinational Enterprises and Tax Administrations*, 2022.

of these experiments is to show that, although the application of AI in the field is progressing slowly, the medium- and long-term effects are set to drastically change both how legislation is provided and how legislation is managed and investigated, particularly in the field of double taxation cases.

1.3 Methodology

The methodology chosen for this proof of concept consists of the following steps:

- Showing how unstructured data related to real legal documents (texts) can be converted into pieces of information with a certain structure that can be handled in an automated way by ML tools (see subsection 3.3 with reference to the Text Manager function and functioning).
- Processing a small part of these texts (already converted into data structures) from a set of preselected documents related to legal documents on tax law to extract keywords that represent the overall topic as well as common topics among the documents, therefore allowing their classification and clustering. To carry out this process models obtained from two different approaches to the LDA inference technique are used.
- Study different visualization techniques on the LDA models to assess the congruence of the analyses and to be able to establish logical maps that allow the classification and the establishment of similarity and distance relationships between the documents contained in the studied corpus (i.e., in our case similarities among documents). This is done by projecting the documents captured by the models in multidimensional vector spaces (where topics become features or dimensions) in which feature reduction techniques can be subsequently applied for their visualization, such as multidimensional scaling (MDS), Principal Component Analysis (PCA) or t-distributed stochastic neighbour embedding (t-SNE). For this purpose, we also use the visualization methods for LDA provided by the pyLDAvis toolkit[6] (see subsection 3.4).
- Show examples of how classification by topics can be used to search for similar documents, to predict aspects of cases (e.g., resolutions) or to investigate possible biases in case resolutions based on common topics. That is, show examples of (i) advanced/smart search, (ii) prediction and (iii) hypothesis generation and testing.

1.4 Background

Topic modeling (also called topic detection, topic modeling or topic extraction) aims to reveal the underlying semantic structure contained in a set of documents, commonly a large corpus. The potential applications of topic modeling are multiple,

6 Khuyen, T., pyLDAvis: Topic Modelling Exploration Tool That Every NLP Data Scientist Should Know, *Neptune.AI, Blog*, 2023.

but basically, they are intended to help humans to extract meaning and key insights from large collections of unstructured text bodies.[7] In other words, topic modeling is a ML technique that organizes and understands large collections of text data, by assigning "tags" or "categories" according to each individual text's topic or theme. Common applications are document summarization, advanced navigation through categorized information, models for information retrieval, document segmentation and transformation, topic tracking in social media, sentiment analysis, event detection and so on. They are used in applications as diverse as analysing trending topics in social networks to exploring source code in software engineering or performing classification and feature extraction in biological data.[8]

To understand the process described in the following paragraphs of this chapter, the topic modeling algorithms will not deliver accurate packaged topics with labels such as "law" or "economics" or "politics" but rather, they provide collections of documents that the algorithm thinks are related, and specific terms that it used to infer these relations. It is then the expert's job (in our case the judge/arbitrator or tax expert) to figure out what these relations actually mean (see paragraph for the contextualization of the topic retrieved by the algorithms).

In the age of information, the legal and juridical environment comprises a large and growing accumulation of written documents. Therefore, it is a natural scientific and technological step that the most innovative AI techniques in text mining are gradually being incorporated in the field. Some recent precedents include the application of topic modeling for summarizing British legislation[9] or the classification of Brazilian Supreme Court lawsuits.[10] Results in such early approaches indicate an increment in the coherency and relevance of the obtained topics as well as in the classification quality.

1.5 Structure

The structure of the rest of the chapter is as follows:

- In Section 2 a review of the theoretical background and previous research, that is closely related to the theoretical framework of the experiments performed, will be carried out. As it will be described later, the proof of concept, different

7 Boyd-Graber, J., et al., Applications of Topic Models, *Foundations and Trends in Information Retrieval*, Vol. 20(20), Now, 2017, pp. 1–154, available at https://mimno.infosci.cornell.edu/papers/2017_fntir_tm_applications.pdf.

8 Liu, L., et al., An Overview of Topic Modeling and Its Current Applications in Bioinformatics, *SpringerPlus*, Vol. 5(1), 2016, pp. 1–22.

9 O'Neill, J., et al., An Analysis of Topic Modelling for Legislative Texts, *Proceedings of the Second Workshop on Automated Semantic Analysis of Information in Legal Texts, Co-located with the 16th International Conference on Artificial Intelligence and Law (ICAIL 2017)*, London, UK, 16 June 2016.

10 Luz De Araujo, P. H., and De Campos, T., *Topic Modelling Brazilian Supreme Court Lawsuits, Legal Knowledge and Information Systems*, IOS Press, 2020, pp. 113–122.

from other previous researchers, will be based on the analysis of decisions on cases from all over the world.

- Section 3 explains in detail the methods and methodologies used for the construction and application of the experiments, describing logical and functional blocks from the perspective of experiment development in computational, programming and algorithmic environments.
- In Section 4 the results obtained from the experiments are presented and discussed.
- The chapter closes with Section 5, in which conclusions are offered with an evaluation of the experiments from a more global perspective and framed in the central topics discussed in this thesis.

2 Theoretical background, previous research on AI applied to legal (tax) issues

2.1 AI for supporting tax legal issues

AI is progressively beginning to make its way into the legal and tax domains. For instance, in the tax domain, ML algorithms are used for predicting effective tax rates one year ahead as well as investigating which factors within financial statements and notes are the most suitable for making such predictions.[11] On the other hand, Abedin uses modern ML methods to address tax default prediction, noting that traditional statistically based methods are insufficient to consider "the appropriate data transformations and nonlinear relationships between early-warning financial indicators and tax default behavior".[12]

Regarding ML applied in trials and court judgements, Mumford[13] explores the use of ML to generate applications that aid in the task of deciding legal cases. Moreover, it is also worthwhile to emphasize the work of Medvedeva, in which authors use ML to predict decisions of the European Court of Human Rights, more specifically by applying NLP tools for text interpretation, obtaining by means of relatively simple algorithms an accuracy of 75% on predicting the violation of nine articles of the European Convention on Human Rights.[14]

In his recent article, Alarie foresees how AI will change the professional practice of taxation in all scopes, including analysis, planning and dispute resolution. In particular, he highlights two particularly promising areas for technological advancement: in his words, "the automation of legal research and the application of

11 Guenther, D. A., et al., How Useful Are Tax Disclosures in Predicting Effective Tax Rates? A Machine Learning Approach, *The Accounting Review*, Vol. 98(5), 2023, pp. 1–26.

12 Abedin, M. Z., et al., Tax Default Prediction Using Feature Transformation-Based Machine Learning. *IEEE Access*, Vol. 9, 2020, pp. 19864–19881.

13 Mumford, J., et al., Machine Learning and Legal Argument, in *Proceedings of the 21st Workshop on Computational Models of Natural Argument*, CEUR Workshop Proceedings, 2021, pp. 47–56.

14 Medvedeva, M., et al., Using Machine Learning to Predict Decisions of the European Court of Human Rights, *Artificial Intelligence and Law*, Vol. 28(2), 2020, pp. 237–266.

knowledge graphs".[15] While the application of knowledge graphs is already being used in current tax practice,

> (a)utomation of legal research is something that has been talked about for years and is only now starting to become a reality. It is likely to transform the way that legal services are provided, leading to greater efficiency and cost savings.[16]

Benjamin Alarie is CEO of Blue J Legal Inc.[17] (hereinafter also "Blue J"). Blue J regularly uses analysis based on modern ML techniques to predict the outcome of pending tax cases. In 2022, they published ten cases, of which only two did not have sufficiently discriminating and clear information to establish reliable predictions. These cases are available in the related literature, but we mention them briefly here:

- In *Olsen v. Commissioner*, T.C. Memo. 2021–41, aff'd, No. 21–9005 (10th Cir. 2022), related to "trade or business", the prediction was in favour of the government, and the final result confirmed the government as the prevailing party.[18]
- In *GSS Holdings (Liberty) Inc. v. United States*, No. 19–728T (Fed. Cl. 2021), related to "step transaction doctrine", the prediction was in favour of the government, and the final result is still pending in time of paper publication.[19]
- In *Tribune Media v. Commissioner*, T.C. Memo. 2021–122, related to "debt versus equity", the prediction was in favour of the government, and the result confirmed the government as the prevailing party.[20]
- In *Aspro Inc. v. Commissioner*, 32 F.4th 673 (8th Cir. 2022), related to "disguised corporate distributions", a significant uncertainty was found to establish a clear prediction. The final result is still pending in time of paper publication.[21]
- In *Reserve Mechanical Corp. v. Commissioner*, 34 F.4th 881 (10th Cir. 2022), related to "microcaptive insurance arrangement", the prediction was in favour of the government, and the final result confirmed the government as the prevailing party.[22]

15 Alarie, B., The Rise of the Robotic Tax Analyst, *Tax Notes Federal*, Vol. 178(1), 2023, p. 57.

16 Alarie, B., The Rise of the Robotic Tax Analyst, *Tax Notes Federal*, Vol. 178(1), 2023, p. 57.

17 Blue J. Legal Inc. it's a Canadian Based Company Which Operates as a Software Company. The Company offers a software that analyses data drawn from common law cases which will be useful in research. See https://www.bluej.com/.

18 Alarie, B., and Yan, C., Using Machine Learning to Evaluate the Existence of a Trade or Business: Olsen, *Tax Notes Federal*, 2022, p. 1231.

19 Alarie, B., and Di Giandomenico, S., Timing Is Everything: The Step Transaction Doctrine in GSS Holdings, *Tax Notes Federal*, 2022, p. 1849.

20 Alarie, B., and Gardhouse, K., The Debt-Equity Distinction and Tribune Media, *Tax Notes Federal*, 2022a, p. 593.

21 Alarie, B., and Yan, C., Disguised Distributions and Management Fees: Aspro Revisited, *Tax Notes Federal*, 2022b, p. 1401.

22 Alarie, B., and Xue Griffin, B., Reserve Mechanical: Microcaptive Insurance Arrangement Denied on Appeal, *Tax Notes Federal*, 2022a, p. 2037.

- In *Skolnick v. Commissioner*, T.C. Memo. 2021–139, related to "trade or business", the prediction was in favour of the government, and the final result confirmed the government as the prevailing party.[23]
- In *Mylan v. Commissioner*, 156 T.C. 137 (2021), related to "deductibility of legal expenses", the prediction was in favour of the taxpayer, and the final result confirmed the taxpayer as the prevailing party.[24]
- In *Cross Refined Coal LLC v. Commissioner*, 45 F.4th 150 (D.C. Cir. 2022), aff'g No. 19502–17 (T.C.2019) (bench op.), related to "existence of a partnership", the prediction was in favour of the taxpayer, and the final result confirmed the taxpayer as the prevailing party.[25]
- In *Chemoil Corp. v. United States*, Complaint, No. 1:19-cv-06314 (S.D.N.Y. July 8, 2019), related to "economic substance doctrine", a significant uncertainty was found to establish a clear prediction. The final result is still pending in time of paper publication.[26]
- In *Cashaw v. Commissioner*, T.C. Memo. 2021–123, related to "trust fund recovery penalty", the prediction was in favour of the government, and the final result is still pending in time of paper publication.[27]

These examples show that, in many cases, similarities and precedents with previous cases allow AI algorithms to make predictions about ongoing cases with a high degree of reliability. Furthermore, the algorithms themselves can estimate whether their predictions are sufficiently robust, providing not only the outcome but also the confidence that should be placed in such predictions. As Alarie points out, even if the information to make such predictions is available in archives, it is practically impossible for humans to objectively deal with and to contrast the immense corpus of past documents with their details and possible contradictions. Machines can perform these tasks in an automated and increasingly intelligent way, thus providing indispensable assistance to all parties and experts involved.[28]

Even more recently, Alarie goes further in the use of AI.[29] In *Skolnick v. Commissioner*, No. 22–1501 (3d Cir. 2023), aff'g, T.C. Memo. 2021–139, in which they had already established a correct prediction, the algorithms are addi-

23 Alarie, B., and Gardhouse, K., Situational Awareness: Accurate Financial Recordkeeping and Business Deductions, *Tax Notes Federal*, 2022b, p. 713.
24 Alarie, B., and Condon, K., Deducting Legal Expenses: Unpacking the IRS's Appeal in Mylan, *Tax Notes Federal*, 2022, p. 1419.
25 Alarie, B., and Xue Griffin, B., Tax Credits That Bond a Partnership: Revisiting Cross Refined Coal, *Tax Notes Federal*, 2022b, p. 2069.
26 Alarie, B., and Yan, C., Chemoil: Economic Substance, Tax Credits, and Unprofitable Ventures, *Tax Notes Federal*, 2022c, p. 719.
27 Alarie, B., and Velez, A., Cashaw: Conflicting Duties and the Trust Fund Recovery Penalty, *Tax Notes Federal*, 2022, p. 1257.
28 Alarie, B., The Rise of the Robotic Tax Analyst, *Tax Notes Federal*, Vol. 178(1), 2023, p. 57.
29 Alarie, B., et al., Unbridled Losses: Harnessing Machine Learning for Tax Analysis, *Tax Notes Federal*, 2023, p. 637.

tionally capable of weighting the relative weight of critical factors that affected or influenced the final decision. In this way, AI algorithms help to understand legal processes in more depth, revealing trends, possible failures, factors to improve or highly discriminating aspects.

2.2 Topic modeling by means of LDA

In Section 2.1 we saw how AI is starting to be applied in the prediction of legal decisions related to tax issues. As mentioned, a core part of such AI developments uses the family of ML algorithms that belong to natural language processing (NLP). Within the NLP sphere, perhaps the most resorted technique to extract meaning from text corpora is what is termed "topic modeling" or "topic inference".

In their survey, Kherwa and Bansal[30] define "topic modeling" as "the new revolution in text mining", and as a "statistical technique for revealing the underlying semantic structure in large collection of documents". Churchill and Singh[31] analyse the evolution of topic modeling, from the first algorithmic approaches back in to the 1990s to the present, discussing algorithms used and the success achieved in different fields. Applications of topic modeling are multiple and diverse, from fields related to scientific literature search and indexing, to bioinformatics, medicine, software engineering, analysis of social networks, source code analysis, requirements in engineering, business intelligence, communications and so on. Topic modeling applications are widely discussed and explored in multiple works.[32]

Explained intuitively, topic modeling techniques extract terms that human beings associate within the same context. In other words, they do not normally infer the topic itself but extract a series of terms that define it. This is easier to understand with simple examples. For example, in Figure 3.1, a topic modeling algorithm analyses tweet messages from a certain community. After processing all tweets, the algorithm extracts three main topics represented by three sets of keywords. Therefore, algorithm outputs are the three differentiated collection of terms, which can be easily interrelated by a human supervisor by a topic or a title that embraces each set. In the example of Figure 3.1,[33] such topics or titles could be "global warming", "the Champion's League" or "summer holidays".

Within ML techniques, topic modeling is considered unsupervised learning, since the learning process is not guided by any kind of ground truth or specific patterns or examples that should guide the learning itself, beyond dictionaries

30 Pooja, K., and Bansal, P., Topic Modeling: A Comprehensive Review, *ICST Transactions on Scalable Information Systems*, Vol. 7(24), 2018, pp. 1–15.

31 Churchill, R., and Singh, L., The Evolution of Topic Modeling, *ACM Computing Surveys*, Vol. 54(10s), 2022, pp. 1–35.

32 Abdelrazek, A., et al., Topic Modeling Algorithms and Applications: A Survey, *Information Systems*, Vol. 112, 2022, p. 102131 and Boyd-Graber, J., et al., Applications of Topic Models, *Foundations and Trends in Information Retrieval*, Vol. 20(20), now, 2017, pp. 1–154, available at 2017_fntir_tm_applications.pdf (cornell.edu).

33 Created by the author.

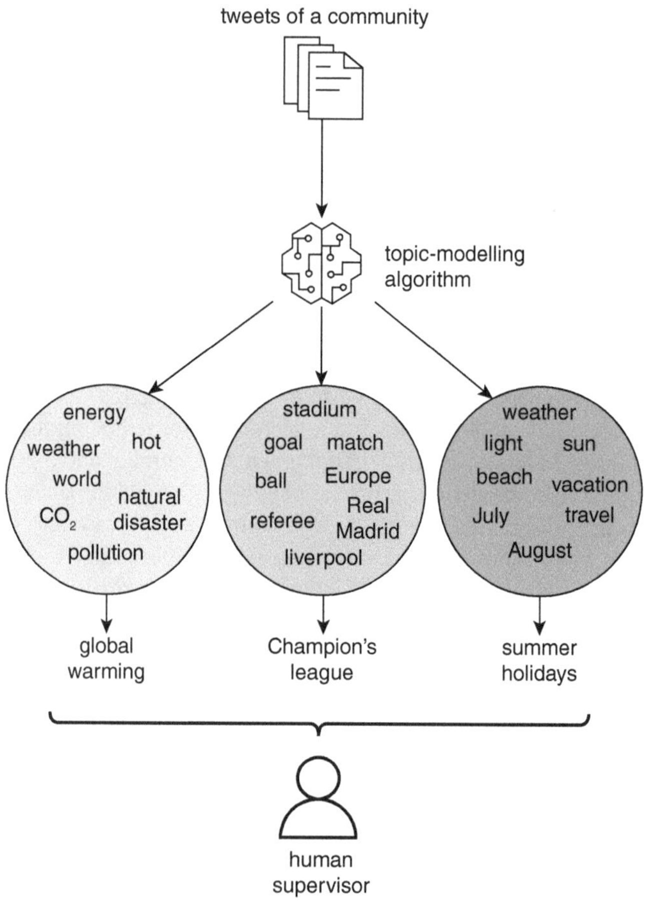

Figure 3.1 Example of a collection of tweets belonging to a community that are processed by a topic modeling algorithm.

or global resources that are specific to the language in which the documents under analysis are written. Therefore, being unsupervised learning, the difficulties encountered by topic modeling to be applied effectively and with impact in the social, commercial and technical context are linked to aspects of data accessibility and evaluation of results. This is precisely what Ramage concluded when studying topic modeling in social studies, highlighting "accessibility" and "trust" as the main barriers faced by experts (i.e., lack of proper structured and validated public available data).[34]

34 Ramage, D., et al., Topic Modeling for the Social Sciences, *Workshop on Applications for Topic Models, NIPS*, 2009, pp. 1–4.

2.3 *Types of topic models*

Before differentiating the types of topic models, it is important to clarify what some common terms refer to in the context of topic modeling. A "document" is a collection of "constructs" in a given field (i.e., in our case a "collection of words" when addressing textual data). A "topic" is a cluster of constructs that together describe a pure semantic meaning; that is, a collection of constructs that are strongly interrelated (i.e., in our case words that put together create a consistent and solid context). From a mathematical point of view, a topic can be described as a probability distribution over a series of constructs.[35]

Henceforth, we consider "documents" only as collections of textual data. Therefore, constructs are always words (or "terms", or connections of paired or connected words as "bigrams" or "trigrams"), a "word" becoming the essential unit of data, which is also defined as an item of an underlying vocabulary. In general, a document is expected to consist of a collection of constructs covering more than one topic, to varying degrees, but encompassing a not too large total number of topics. Given a corpus of documents, a topic modeling algorithm usually generates two structures (or internal models) in what is known as topic inference: (i) one referring to a number of topics X, each represented by Y constructs (words); and (ii) a second structure containing Z documents and distribution over the X topics or, to put it another way, the contribution of each topic X discovered in each document in Z (i.e., the distribution/contribution of a topic in a document).

In the related literature we find three main types of topic models:

- *Algebraic models—Latent Semantic Analysis (LSA).* Originally proposed by Deerwester,[36] algebraic models use singular-value decomposition (SVD) to transform a document-construct (or document-word) matrix into a set of orthogonal factors from which the original matrix can be approximated by linear combination. Thus, documents can be located in vectorial space that reflects the data corpus. LSA is the most popular algebraic topic modeling method.[37] The underlying rationale behind LSA is considering that the semantics of words can be inferred from the contexts in which they appear. The main weakness of these models is that they do not assume any distribution behind topics and documents, therefore generating less interpretable representations not supported by any statistical ground. On the other hand, the algebraic approach is straightforward and intuitive, not computationally exhaustive, and can cope properly with short text documents.

35 Hofmann, T., Probabilistic Latent Semantic Indexing, *ACM SIGIR Forum*, Vol. 51, 1999, pp. 211–218.

36 Deerwester, S., et al, Indexing by Latent Semantic Analysis, *Journal of the Association for Information Science*, Vol. 41(6), 1990, pp. 391–407.

37 Dumais, S. T., Latent Semantic Analysis, *Annual Review of Information Science and Technology*, Vol. 38(1), 2004, pp. 188–230.

- *Probabilistic models—LDA*. Similarly to algebraic approaches, probabilistic models also work considering that the meaning of two words should be similar if they are prone to appear in similar contexts. Models here are statistically grounded and assume that certain topics, which are distributed over words, can be used to generate the analysed documents. Note that both algebraic and probabilistic approaches do not consider syntactic aspects and see documents simply as bags of words. From a Bayesian perspective (in simple words, variable probabilistic perspective based on changes of believes/information), in probabilistic models the challenge is to disclose the posterior inference and find conditional distributions behind topics, their contribution and their assignment among documents. The most popular probabilistic model is LDA, whose working idea is that the distribution of topics in a document and the distribution of words in topics can be represented with Dirichlet distributions.[38] Due to its simplicity, naturalness and interpretability, LDA has been and is one of the most widely used methods in both scientific research and real applications. However, it is not without its problems, most notably the fact that inference becomes difficult as the complexity of the model increases.[39]
- *Neural topic models—Variational Auto Encoders (VAEs)*. Deep learning and neural networks have revolutionized the field of AI and ML in the last decade. There are many proposals for using multilayered neural structures in topic modeling, since deep learning creates complex internal maps capable of abstracting key information (i.e., feature extraction) from highly complex and unstructured input data. There are alternatives that use neural networks simply to transform texts into more manageable, less sparse and more meaningful structures, that is, word embeddings.[40] However, the most popular neural methods for topic modeling are those based on VAEs.[41] These approaches extend the generative process of probabilistic methods by using the type of unsupervised neural networks termed VAEs, thus avoiding the deviations typical of probabilistic models.

2.3.1 LDA

Since LDA is the topic modeling method used in our experiments, we expand on the technical details taken from the original work[42] and with the notation from

38 Blei, D. M., et al., Latent Dirichlet allocation, *Journal of Machine Learning Research*, Vol. 3, 2003, pp. 993–1022.

39 Abdelrazek, A., et al., Topic Modeling Algorithms and Applications: A Survey, *Information Systems*, Vol. 112, 2022, p. 102131.

40 Mikolov, T., et al., Efficient Estimation of Word Representations in Vector Space, *Proceedings of the International Conference on Learning Representations*, ICLR, 2013, pp. 1–12, available at https://arxiv.org/pdf/1301.3781.

41 Luyang, L., et al., Improving Neural Topic Modeling via Sinkhorn Divergence, *Information Processing & Management*, Vol. 59(3), 2022, p. 102864.

42 Blei, D. M., et al., Latent Dirichlet Allocation, *Journal of Machine Learning Research*, Vol. 3, 2003, pp. 993–1022.

Abdelrazek.[43] Before going into details, let's try to describe briefly the rationale behind the LDA functioning. It is assumed that a given set of documents are related to certain topics and such topics are represented by an (unknown) set of words (i.e., there are the topics that our set of documents cover, but we don't know what they are yet).

Therefore, the function of the LDA algorithm is to try to map all the (known) documents to the (unknown) topics in a way such that the words in each document are mostly captured by those topics. The assumptions behind this process are (i) documents with the same topic will use similar words, and (ii) every document is composed of a mixture of topics, and every word has a probability of belonging to a certain topic.[44]

For LDA, a given document—say document *i*—is a bag of words represented as a vector of length L (i.e., this *i*-document is formed by L words). LDA works assuming that the process that generates the *i*-document works iteratively as follows: (i) randomly selects a topic from the distribution of topics θ_i related to the document *i*; (ii) randomly selects a word w from this topic (a topic is a distribution of words). θ_i is a Dirichlet distribution in which topics are independent of each other. The connection of a topic to document *i* is expressed as z_i.

This way of modeling the generation of documents implies considering a joint probability distribution across the collection of documents under study and the hidden topics. Defining α and β as Dirichlet priors (which are external parameters in the algorithm implementations: α for the per-document topic and β for the per-topic word distributions respectively),[45] this probability takes the form:

$$p(\theta, z, w|\alpha, \beta) \quad \text{(V.1)}$$

In other words, assumed a reality consistent with α and β, there exists a probability distribution that represents the chances of getting the combinations of documents(z)-topics(θ)-words(w). By using the joint distribution and the collection of documents under analysis, we can infer the conditional distribution of the hidden topic structure as follows:

$$p(\theta, z\,|w, \alpha, \beta) = p(\theta, z, w|\alpha, \beta)\,/\,p(w|\alpha, \beta) \quad \text{(V.2)}$$

43 Abdelrazek, A., et al., Topic Modeling Algorithms and Applications: A Survey, *Information Systems*, Vol. 112, 2022, p. 102131.

44 Blei, D. M., et al., Latent Dirichlet Allocation, *Journal of Machine Learning Research*, Vol. 3, 2003, pp. 993–1022.

45 α (alpha) controls the similarity of documents where a low value will represent documents as a mixture of few topics, while a high value will output document representations of more topics making all the documents appear more similar to each other. β (beta) is the same but for topics, so it controls topic similarity. A low value will represent topics as more distinct by making fewer, more unique words belong to each topic. A high value will have the opposite effect, resulting in topics containing more words in common.

In other words, we want to know—given α, β and some words (w)—the probabilities of generating a document (z) with certain topics (θ). The denominator in Equation V.2 is the marginal probability of the observations, that is, simply the probability of seeing this set of words (w). This can be estimated by adding up the joint distribution along all possible topic structures. However, this represents such an extensive calculation that must be approximated by some kind of numerical method (e.g., Markov chain Monte Carlo).

This problem is faced by Pritchard,[46] who uses Gibbs sampling in Markov chain Monte Carlo approximation to estimate the immeasurable posterior distribution by continuously sampling from conditional distributions. In the context of topic modeling, it is only necessary to calculate the document-topic distribution θ and the topic-word distribution β. Taking this into account, Griffiths[47] simplified the process in what is called a collapsed Gibbs sampler.

2.3.2 Space visualization and feature reduction

Among data scientists and AI and ML experts, techniques of data interpretation, analysis results and model exploration are a major focus. It can be said that this issue cross-cuttingly covers all types of data analysis and AI applications in general, regardless of the field and methods used. More, data, results and models are understood by both the expert and the end user through visualization techniques, which are indispensable for the design of optimized pipelines, the selection of suitable methods and algorithms, for validation, evaluation and comparison, if not for the direct or final use of the results or predictions provided by the analysis tools.[48]

AI and ML represent reality through data, data that is processed and, in a great majority of cases, is converted into multidimensional vectors, so that the problem under study is reduced to understanding or explaining the shapes that this data creates in an input vector space, which we can call "problem space". This problem space is most often understood or explained in the form of patterns, clusters, anomalies, topologies or hierarchies. As the referee and judge of this process, the human being (AI and data analysis expert in this case) is not capable of visualizing spaces beyond three (or maybe four) dimensions. Therefore, techniques capable of projecting data, results and models on two- and three-dimensional maps while preserving as much as possible such patterns, clusters, anomalies, topologies or hierarchies (i.e., the intrinsic, discriminating and differentiating characteristics of those data, results and models) are highly necessary and required in the design,

46 Pritchard, J. K., et al., Inference of Population Structure Using Multilocus Genotype Data, *Genetics*, Vol. 155(2), 2000, pp. 945–959.

47 Griffiths, T. L., and Steyvers, M., Finding Scientific Topics, *Proceedings of the National Academy of Sciences (PNAS)*, Vol. 101(suppl_1), 2004, pp. 5228–5235.

48 Kaski, S., and Peltonen, J., Dimensionality Reduction for Data Visualization [Applications Corner], *IEEE Signal Processing Magazine*, Vol. 28(2), 2011, pp. 100–104.

research and application of AI. This challenge is commonly addressed as: *dimensionality reduction* or *feature reduction.*[49]

More specifically, in the field under study (i.e., topic modeling), feature reduction and visualization techniques allow us to create maps of LDA models, thus enabling the assessment of the topics discovered in terms of their diversity and discriminant power. In turn, these same techniques allow us to create maps in which our document collections are organized and segregated by topics, as well as located according to similarity estimates between documents.

Among the multiple options that exist for dimensionality reduction, the most popular are probably PCA, as a linear method that preserves global scale information, t-STNE and Uniform Manifold Approximation and Projection (UMAP) in terms of capturing the local similarity of the objects under analysis and being more suitable for high dimensionality and nonlinearity.[50] PCA is considered as the classical MDS technique.[51] For the interested reader, Anowar presents an extensive and recent comparison of different dimensionality reduction algorithms.[52] In this section we focus on the PCA and t-STNE algorithms due to their popularity, extension, complementary nature and the fact that they are the ones used in our experiments.

2.3.2.1 PCA

First presented at the beginning of the 20th century,[53] PCA is a simple unsupervised algorithm that performs a linear transformation of the data and projects them into a new subspace where the orthogonal axes are oriented in such a way that they point to the directions of maximum variance. Hence, the n-dimensions (or features) of the original space are projected (or transformed) into a new subspace of n-dimensions called Principal Components (PC), where the first feature shows the highest variance of all, followed by the second, the third and so on; that is, they are arranged in order of decreasing variance. In applications where PCA is used, it is usually considered that only the k-first dimensions are relevant or contain most of the information of the data and, therefore, the rest of the (n-k)-features are negli-

49 Dimensionality reduction, as explained in Chapter IV, refers to the process of reducing the number of input variables or features in a data set while preserving the relevant information. It is commonly used in machine learning and data analysis to address the curse of dimensionality, where data sets with a large number of features can lead to various challenges and inefficiencies.

50 Oskolkov, N., Dimensionality Reduction: Overview, Technical Details, and Some Applications, Applied Data Science in Tourism: Interdisciplinary Approaches, *Methodologies, and Applications*, 2022, pp. 151–167.

51 Hout, M. C., Papesh, M. H., and Goldinger, S. D., Multidimensional Scaling, *Wiley Interdisciplinary Reviews: Cognitive Science*, Vol. 4(1), 2012, 93–103.

52 Farzana, A., et al., Conceptual and Empirical Comparison of Dimensionality Reduction Algorithms (PCA, KPCA, LDA, MDS, SVD, LLE, ISOMAP, LE, ICA, t-SNE), *Computer Science Review*, Vol. 40, 2021, 100378, ISSN 1574–0137, available at https://www.sciencedirect.com/science/article/abs/pii/S1574013721000186?via%3Dihub.

53 Pearson, K., LIII. On Lines and Planes of Closest Fit to Systems of Points in Space, *Philosophical Magazine Series 1*, Vol. 2, 1901, pp. 559–572.

gible. In visualization applications, only 2 (or maximum 3) PCs are retained (i.e., $k = 2$ or $k = 3$).[54]

Considering the operational principle of the PCA algorithm, it is understandable intuitively that the projection of the data on a map where the 2 or 3 PCs are visualized captures a global perspective of the data, offering a coarse-grained and distant view where subtleties and details disappear or are masked.[55]

2.3.2.2 t-STNE

t-SNE is an algorithm for the visualization of high-dimensional data based on the Stochastic Neighbour Embedding proposed by Hinton and Roweis,[56] and later expanded in the t-Distributed variant by Van der Maaten and Hinton.[57] t-SNE is a nonlinear, unsupervised and manifold-based method where data are mapped in 2 or 3 dimensions while maintaining the structure of the original data from the perspective of local similarity; that means that it helps visualizing high-dimensional data in a lower-dimensional space. The operational principle of Stochastic Neighbour Embedding (SNE) is to transform Euclidean distances between points into conditional probabilities computed on each pair of points, so that similar points get high probabilities. Then, t-SNE creates a low-dimensional space in which it randomly scatters the points, but whose positions are fixed by a student t-distribution (to avoid the crowding problem) and optimized using the Kullback-Leibler divergence between the conditional probabilities.[58]

Thus, t-SNE is an algorithm that exhibits stochastic behaviour, meaning that, even using the same data and configuration parameters, the generated map may present notable differences from a global perspective due to random factors during the computation process. t-SNE strives fundamentally to preserve local information, tending to create maps that show cluster structures.

Different authors in their papers compared PCA and t-SNE,[59] where opposite or complementary nature makes their joint application recommended for a bet-

54 Jaadi, Z., A Step-by-Step Explanation of Principal Component Analysis (PCA), Built In, *Blog*, 2023 (accessed 9 July 2023).

55 Lee, W., Using Principal Component Analysis (PCA) for Machine Learning, Towards Data Science, *Blog*, 2022 (accessed 9 July 2023).

56 Hinton, G. E., and Roweis, S., Stochastic Neighbor Embedding, *NIPS'02: Proceedings of the 15th International Conference on Neural Information Processing Systems*, MIT Press, 2002, pp. 857–864.

57 Van der Maaten, L., and Hinton, G. E., Visualizing Data Using t-SNE, *Journal of Machine Learning Research*, Vol. 9(86) 2008, pp. 2579–2605.

58 Joyce, J. M., Kullback-Leibler Divergence, in *International Encyclopedia of Statistical Science* (ed. M. Lovric), Berlin, Heidelberg: Springer, 2011, pp. 720–722. In a few words, KL divergence is a way to compare distributions and see if they are similar or different.

59 Pareek, J., and Jacob, J., Data Compression and Visualization Using PCA and T-SNE, in *Advances in Information Communication Technology and Computing. Lecture Notes in Networks and Systems*, Vol. 135 (eds. V. Goar, M. Kuri, R. Kumar and T. Senjyu), Singapore: Springer, 2021, pp. 327–337.

ter and deeper understanding of the data. Different examples and representations show where PCA and t-SNE are used to visualize the popular MNIST data set.[60] Usually, the classes are differentiated by colour. In general, the t-SNE option is more suitable to visualize clusters and to establish searches for similar elements. Indeed, both PCA and t-SNE are dimensionality reduction techniques with the difference that PCA is a projection of the most variability in the data values (i.e., it maintains as much information from the original data set, or other said it identifies the underlying principal components in the data minimizing variance, and preserving large pairwise distances), while the tSNE is based on local similarities (i.e., it attempts to find the underlying structure of the data by taking into account the neighbours of a sample, so it prioritizes the neighbour points).[61]

3 Methodology

3.1 Overview—pipeline

The experiments conducted in this chapter are represented by the scheme in Figure 3.2,[62] which we discuss briefly and intuitively here. For our proof of concept, we have used a set of 105 documents on transfer pricing cases case decisions (TPcase law docs), freely available from the TPcases.com website. In our experiments, we did not use these documents, but the linked summaries provided by "TPcases.com" (TPcase summaries). Such documents are retrieved in an unstructured way and later pre-processed by the "Text Manager module" to comply structured data formats that make them tractable for analysis algorithms. From the documents as structured data objects, some specific fields are selected for the topic extraction with the "Topic Manager" module, which starts by inferring a dictionary, a corpus, and framed texts from the whole collection. Since there is no pre-knowledge or external imposition about the number of topics to discover, in the next step a set of topics-models with a different number of topics per model are generated. Models are generated by means of two different approaches based on the LDA algorithm: the native algorithm implemented in the Gensim package

60 MNIST stands for Modified National Institute of Standards and Technology database which is a large database of handwritten digits which is mostly used for training various processing systems. It is generally used for training and testing the data in the field of machine learning. In this respect, please see Kumar, B., PyTorch MNIST Tutorial, *PythonGuide.com, Blog*, 2022, available at https://pythonguides.com/pytorch-mnist/ (accessed 11 July 2023).

61 Shrivastav, N., PCA vs t-SNE: Which One Should You Use for Visualization, *Analytics Vidhya, Blog*, 2019, available at https://medium.com/analytics-vidhya/pca-vs-t-sne-17bcd882bf3d (accessed 31 July 2023) and Rohith, P., What Is the Difference Between T-SNE and PCA, *Medium, Blog*, 2020, available at https://medium.com/@rohith.phani7/what-is-the-difference-between-pca-and-t-sne-58589c81ae3e (accessed 31 July 2023) and Krilis, G., Comparison of t-SNE and PCA and Truncate SVD, *Data Science, Blog*, 2020, available at https://datascience.stackexchange.com/questions/66198/comparison-of-t-sne-and-pca-and-truncate-svd (accessed 31 July 2023).

62 Created by the author.

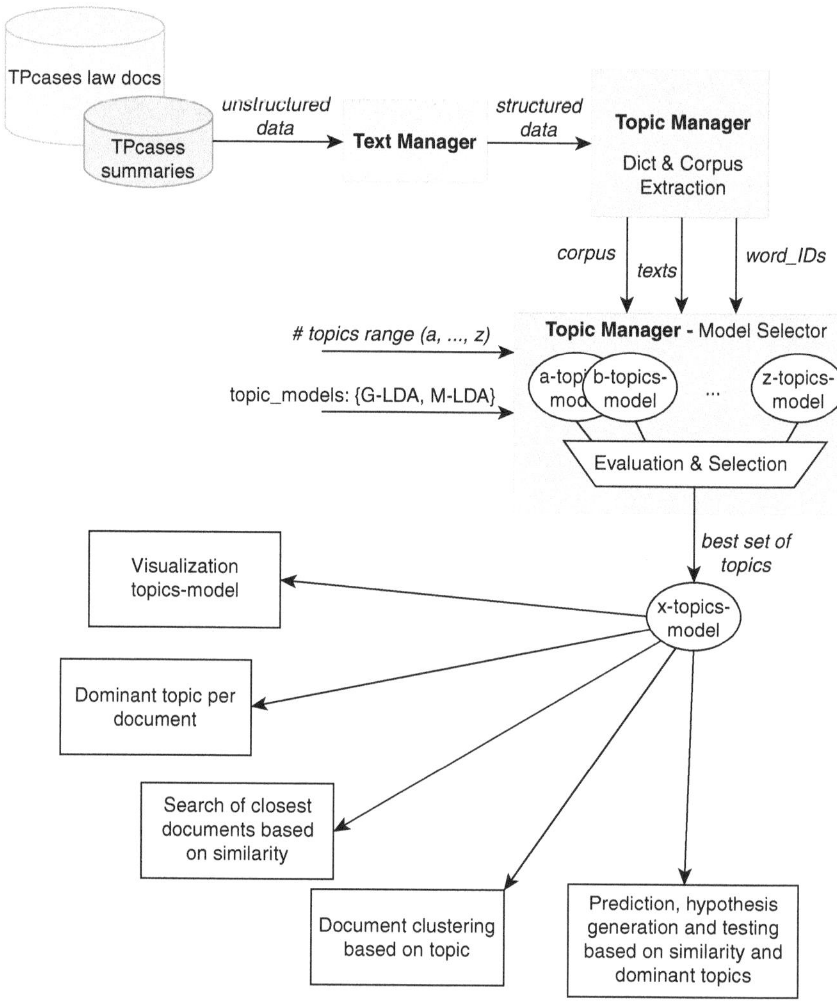

Figure 3.2 Overview of the experiment methodology.

(G-LDA), and the Mallet approach that uses collapsed Gibbs sampling (M-LDA). They are evaluated by means of a *Coherence* metric,[63] and the topics-model with the highest Coherence (either in the case of using G-LDA or M-LDA) is selected for subsequent phases. These operations are performed within the Model Selector of the "Topic Manager". From here, the best G-LDA and the best M-LDA models are compared in the subsequent evaluations. In the following part of our proof of concept we explore the topics-models in connection with the document collection by (i) analysing the topics and the main words representing each topic and the global collection of documents; (ii) visualizing the topics-model with pyLDAvis;[64] (iii) establishing the dominant topic in each analysed document; (iv) discovering the closest documents in the collection to each given document based on a topic comparison and examining the case resolution trend; (v) grouping documents based on discovered topics; and (vi) drawing a topic-based map of documents by using two alternative feature-reduction technique: PCA[65] and t-STNE.[66,]

The programming language used for our implementations and experiments is Python3,[67] since nowadays (April 2023) Python is globally accepted as one of the best options for Machine Learning and Data Science programming and software developments.[68]

3.2 Data

The data used for our proof of concept has been randomly selected and downloaded from "TPcases.com" with search criteria related to the terms: Countries: "All Countries" Categories: "Financial Transactions" "Royalty and License Payments" "Business Restructuring" "Comparability Analysis" and Keywords "Loans" (for the "Financial Transactions" case laws).

The common element among the cases is that they all refer to transfer pricing. Table 3.1 provides specific references for the identification of the cases used. The data selection aimed to identify, among the same topic "transfer pricing disputes", different arguments with the aim to then "feed" the algorithm and see the effectiveness for the identification and cluster of the different cases.

In Table 3.1 the full list of transfer pricing cases selected has been provided.

63 Mimno, D., et al., Optimizing Semantic Coherence in Topic Models, in *Proceedings of the 2011 Conference on Empirical Methods in Natural Language Processing*, Association for Computational Linguistics, 2011, pp. 262–272.

64 Sievert, C., and Shirley, K., LDAvis: A Method for Visualizing and Interpreting Topics, in *Proceedings of the Workshop on Interactive Language Learning, Visualization, and Interfaces*, Association for Computational Linguistics, 2014, pp. 63–70.

65 Abdi, H., and Williams, L. J., Principal Component Analysis. Wiley Interdisciplinary Reviews, *Computational Statistics*, Vol. 2(4), 2010, pp. 433–459.

66 Van der Maaten, L., and Hinton, G., Visualizing Data Using t-SNE, *Journal of Machine Learning Research*, Vol. 9(86), 2008, pp. 2579–2605.

67 https://docs.python.org/3/

68 https://dataconomy.com/blog/2022/11/17/best-language-for-machine-learning/

Table 3.1 Selected cases for our proof-of-concept experiments[69]

TP case			
Number	*Country*	*Case year*	*Case*
	Argentina		
1		2018	Argentina vs YPF S.A., May 2018, Supreme Court, Case No TF 29.205–1
	Australia		
2		2015	australia vs. chevron australia holdings pty ltd, october 2015, federal court of australia, case no. 3 and 4
3		2021	australia vs singapore telecom australia investments pty ltd, december 2021, federal court of australia, case no fca 1597
	Austria		
4		2019	austria vs shareholder, july 2019, bundesfinanzgericht, case no rv/1100628/2016
5		2022	austria vs "acq-group", february 2022, bundesfinanzgericht, case no rv/7104702/2018
6		2022	austria vs c-group, march 2022, bundesfinanzgericht, case no rv/7102553/2021
	Belgium		
7		2016	belgium vs. société a, march 2016, hof van cassatie, case no. f.14.0082.n
8		2021	belgium vs engie cc cv, january 2021, supreme court, case no f.18.0140.n
	Brazil		
9		2021	brazil vs natura cosmeticos s/a, august 2021, carf, case no. 16327.000738/2004–66
	Chile		
10		2020	chile vs wallmart chile s.a, october 2020, tax court, case n° ruc n° 76.042.014k
	Czech Republic		
11		2010	czech republic vs. daton technology, spol. s.r.o., august 2010, supreme administrative court, case no 2 afs 53/2010–63
	Denmark		
12		2012	denmark vs. swiss re., february 2012, supreme court, skm2012.92
13		2021	denmark vs. "h borrower and lender a/s", january 2021, tax tribunal, case no skm2021.33.lsr
14		2022	denmark vs. codan forsikring a/s, august 2022, eastern high court, case no bs-11370/2020
	El Salvador		
15		2021	el salvador vs corp, june 2021, tax court, case no 096–2021

(Continued)

69 Created by the author.

Table 3.1 (Continued)

TP case			
Number	*Country*	*Case year*	*Case*
	France		
16		1994	france vs baker international, april 1994, court of appeal, case no 92bx01109
17		1995	france vs. montlaur sakakini, oct 1995, administrative court of appeal, no 95ly00427
18		2014	france vs. bayerische hypo und vereinsbank ag, april 2014, conseil d'état, case no. fr:cessr:2014:344990.20140411
19		2014	france vs sté stryker spine, september 2014, administrative court of appeals, case no.12bx01182
20		2017	france vs general electric france, june 2017, conseil d état, case no 392543
21		2019	france vs st dupont, march 2019, administrative court of paris, no 1620873, 1705086/1–3
22		2019	france vs sas wheelabrator group, july 2019, conseil d'état opinion, no 429426
23		2020	france vs studialis, october 2020, administrative court of appeal, case no 18pa01026
24		2020	france vs bsa finances, december 2020, supreme administrative court, case no 433723
25		2020	france vs sté paule ka holding, december 2020, paris administrative court of appeal, case no 18pa02715
26		2020	france vs wb ambassador, december 2020, supreme administrative court, case no 428522
27		2022	france vs ferragamo france, june 2022, administrative court of appeal (caa), case no 20pa03601
28		2022	france vs sa tropicana europe hermes, august 2022, caa of douai, case no. 20da01106
29		2022	france vs sas oakley holding, may 2022, caa of lyon, no 19ly03100
30		2022	france vs sap france, september 2022, conseil d'état, case no. 461639
31		2022	france vs electricité de france, november 2022, conseil d'état, case no 462383 (ecli:fr:ce chr:2022:462383.20221116)
	Finland		
32		2014	finland vs. corp, july 2014, supreme administrative court, hfd 2014:119
33		2021	finland vs a oyj, may 2021, supreme administrative court, case no. kho:2021:66
34		2021	finland vs g oy, december 2021, supreme administrative court, case no. kho:2021:178
35		2021	finland vs d oy, december 2021, supreme administrative court, case no. kho:2021:179

(Continued)

Table 3.1 (Continued)

TP case			
Number	*Country*	*Case year*	*Case*
	Germany		
36		2006	germany vs "trademark gmbh", november 2006, fg münchen, case no 6 k 578/06
37		2014	germany vs license gmbh, february 2014, local tax court, case no 4 k 1053/11 e
38		2016	germany vs "x sub gmbh", december 2016, münster fiscal court, case no 13 k 4037/13 k,f
39		2017	germany vs "a investment gmbh", june 2017, tax court, case no 10 k 771/16
	Greece		
40		2019	greece vs "sh loan ltd", may 2019, court, case no a 1780/2019
41		2020	greece vs "lender corp", march 2020, court, case no a 638/2020
42		2021	greece vs cypriot company ltd., september 2021, tax court, case no 2940/2021
43		2022	greece vs "tin cup ltd", november 2022, tax court, case no 3743/2022
	Hungary		
44		2020	hungary vs "lender" kft, february 2020, budapest administrative court, case no. 16.k.33.691/2019/18
	Israel		
45		2022	israel vs ca software israel ltd, october 2022, tel aviv district court, case no 61226-06-17
	Italy		
46		2013	italy vs sgl carbon spa, september 2013, supreme court, 22010
47		2016	italy vs pdm d srl, february 2016, supreme court, case no. 6331–2016
48		2016	italy vs edison spa., supreme court, june 2016, no. 13387
49		2016	italy vs edison s.p.a., april 2016, supreme court, no 7493
50		2016	italy vs "lender spa", october 2016, regional tax commission, case no 17/10/2016 n. 308/2
51		2020	italy vs "lender" spa, february 2020, regional tax tribunal for umbria, case no 18/02/2020 n. 56/01
52		2021	italy vs gi group s.p.a., may 2021, supreme court, case no 13850/2021
53		2021	italy vs pompea s.p.a., october 2021, supreme court, case no 27636/2021
54		2022	italy vs arnoldo mondadori editore spa, february 2022, supreme court, cases no 3380/2022
55		2022	italy vs mauser s.p.a., february 2022, supreme court, case no 6283/2022
56		2022	italy vs basf italia s.p.a., june 2022, supreme court, cases no 19728/2022

(Continued)

Table 3.1 (Continued)

TP case			
Number	*Country*	*Case year*	*Case*
	Japan		
57		2022	japan vs universal music corp, april 2022, supreme court, case no 令和2(行ヒ)303
	Korea		
58		2021	korea vs "k-gas corp", november 2021, daegu district court, case no 2019구합22561
59		2022	korea vs "semicon-sales", june 2022, tax court, case no 2020-서-2311
	Luxembourg		
60		2007	luxembourg vs sa, october 2007, administrative court, case no 23053
61		2021	luxembourg vs "lux ppl sarl", july 2021, administrative tribunal, case no 43264
	Malaysia		
62		2022	malaysia vs keysight technologies malaysia, may 2022, high court, case no wa-144-03-2020
	Netherlands		
63		2003	netherlands vs "dutch low risk treasury b.v.", august 2003, district court, case no 01/04083, ecli:nl:ghams:2003:aj6865
64		2011	netherlands vs corp, 2011, dutch supreme court, case nr. 08/05323 (10/05161, 10/04588)
65		2020	netherlands vs zinc smelter b.v., march 2020, court of appeal, case no ecli:nl:ghshe:2020:968
66		2020	netherlands vs x b.v., july 2020, supreme court (preliminary ruling by the advocate general), case no ecli:nl:phr:2020:672
67		2022	netherlands vs "agri b.v.", september 2022, court of appeal, case no awb-16_5664 (ecli:nl:rbnho:2022:9062)
	Norway		
68		2007	norway vs. statoil angola, 2007, supreme court, no. rt 2007–1025
69		2018	norway vs. exxonmobil production norway inc., january 2018, lagsmanret, no lb-2016–160306
70		2022	norway vs conocophillips skandinavia as, march 2022, court of appeal, case no lg-2021–38180
71		2022	norway vs fortis petroleum norway as, march 2022, court of appeal, case no lb-2021–26379
72		2022	norway vs petrolia noco as, may 2022, court of appeal, case no lb-2022–18585

(Continued)

Table 3.1 (Continued)

TP case			
Number	*Country*	*Case year*	*Case*
	Peru		
73		2017	peru vs "holding s.a.", june 2017, tax court, case no 1308–2009
74		2021	peru vs. perupetro, june 2021, tax court, case no 05562-1-2021
75		2021	peru vs. "mining corp", december 2021, tax court, case no 11557-1-2021
	Poland		
76		2010	poland vs "f-inance. sp. z o.o.", october 2010, administrative court, case no i sa/kr 1188/10
77		2019	poland vs l s.a, june 2019, supreme administrative court, case no. ii fsk 1808/17—wyrok nsa
78		2019	poland vs "shopping centre developer sp.k.", may 2019, administrative court, case no iii sa/wa 1777/18
79		2021	poland vs q. f. sp. z o.o., january 2021, supreme administrative court, case no ii fsk 2514
80		2022	poland vs "x-tm" sp. z o.o., march 2022, administrative court, sa/po 1058/21
81		2022	poland vs "sport o.b. sa", march 2022, provincial administrative court, case no i sa/rz 4/22
82		2022	poland vs d. sp. z oo, april 2022, administrative court, case no i sa/bd 128/22
83		2022	poland vs "fertilizer licence sa", april 2022, provincial administrative court, case no i sa/po 788/21
84		2022	poland vs "shopping centre developer sp.k.", june 2022, supreme administrative court, case no ii fsk 3050/19
	Portugal		
85		2018	portugal vs "a infrastructure s.a.", november 2018, caad—administrative tribunal, case no: 70/2018-t
86		2021	portugal vs "b lender s.a", january 2021, supremo tribunal administrativo, case no jsta000p26984
87		2021	portugal vs "m fastfood s.a", april 2021, tribunal central administrativo sul, case no 1331/09
88		2021	portugal vs "welding mesh sa", december 2021, caad tax arbitration, case no 194/2021-t
89		2022	portugal vs "a sgps s.a.", march 2022, caad—administrative tribunal, case no: p590_2020-t
90		2022	portugal vs "a s.a.", march 2022, caad—administrative tribunal, case no: 213/2021-t
91		2022	portugal vs "l. . . . engenharia e construções, s.a.", june 2022, tribunal central administrativo sul, case 1339/13.0belra

(Continued)

Table 3.1 (Continued)

TP case			
Number	*Country*	*Case year*	*Case*
	Romania		
92		2020	romania vs impresa pizzarotti & c spa italia, october 2020, ecj, case c-558/19
93		2020	romania vs lender a. sa, december 2020, supreme court, case no 6512/2020
	Russia		
94		2014	russia vs continental tires rus llc, aug. 2014, russian court of appeal, case no a40- 251161/2015
	South Africa		
95		2018	south africa vs. crookes brothers ltd, may 2018, high court, case no 14179/2017 zagphc 311
	Spain		
96		2017	spain vs mcdonald's, march 2017, spanish tribunal supremo, case no 961–2017
97		2022	spain vs universal pictures international spain sl, december 2022, audiencia nacional, case no san 5855/2022—ecli:en:an:2022:5855
	Sweden		
98		2010	sweden vs. diligentia, june 2010, regeringsratten, case nr 2483-2485-09
99		2010	sweden vs. diligentia, june 2010, regeringsratten, case nr 2483-2485-09
100		2013	sweden vs cambrex, april 2013, administrative court, case no. 456–11
101		2016	sweden vs. nobel biocare holding ab, 2016, hfd, ref. 45
102		2021	sweden vs tele2 ab, january 2021, administrative court, case no 13259–19 and 19892–19
103		2022	sweden vs swedish match intellectual property ab, may 2022, supreme administrative court, case no mål: 5264–5267–20, 5269–20
	Switzerland		
104		2013	switzerland vs hotel x. sa, nov. 2013, courts of switzerland, case no. 2c_291/2013/2c_292/2013
	Turkey		
105		2008	turkey vs no-banker corp, november 2008, administrative court, e. 2006/3620 k. 2008/4633 t. 18.11.2008

For the proof of concept, we do not use the complete law resolution documents, but the overviews linked to such documents. An example of *Overview Document* for the case number 23 follows.

Example of raw *Overview Document* (case 23: norway vs petrolia noco—2022)

—

Norway vs Petrolia Noco AS, May 2022, Court of Appeal, Case No LB-2022–18585
Posted on May 31, 2022 | By Courts of Norway | No comments

Category: Financial Transactions, General Anti-Avoidance Rules (GAAR), Transfer Pricing Methods | Tag: Accurate delineation, Borrowing capacity, Cost plus method, CUP method, Discretionary assessment, Equity or Debt/Loan, Interest limitation, Intra-group loan, Loan, Oil and gas, Thin Capitalisation (Thin Cap)

In 2011, Petrolia SE established a wholly owned subsidiary in Norway—Petrolia Noco AS—to conduct oil exploration activities on the Norwegian shelf. From the outset, Petrolia Noco AS received a loan from the parent company Petrolia SE. The written loan agreement was first signed later on 15 May 2012. The loan limit was originally MNOK 100 with an agreed interest rate of 3 months NIBOR with the addition of a margin of 2.25 percentage points. When the loan agreement was formalized in writing in 2012, the agreed interest rate was changed to 3 months NIBOR with the addition of an interest margin of 10 percentage points. The loan limit was increased to MNOK 150 in September 2012, and then to MNOK 330 in April 2013.

In the tax return for 2012 and 2013, Petrolia Noco AS demanded a full deduction for actual interest costs on the intra-group loan to the parent company Petrolia SE.

An assessment was issued by the tax authorities for these years, where the interest deductions had been partially disallowed. The assessment for these years was later upheld in court.

For FY 2014, 2015 and 2016, Petrolia Noco AS had also claimed a full deduction for actual interest costs on the entire intra-group loan to the parent company. It is the assessment for these years that is the subject of dispute in this case.

The assessment was first brought to the Court of Oslo where a decision in favour of the tax authorities was issued in November 2021.

This decision was appealed by Petrolia Noco AS to the Court of Appeal.

Judgement of the Court

The Court of Appeal dismissed the appeal and decided in favour of the Norwegian tax authorities.

Excerpts

"The Court of Appeal also agrees with the state that neither the cost-plus method nor a rationality analysis can be considered applicable in this case. With the result the Court of Appeal has reached so far, the CUP method should be preferred—in line with the OECD guidelines.

After this, in summary, it appears clear that the interest margin on the intra-group loan is significantly higher than in a comparable and independent market and thus not an arm's length price. The higher interest implies a reduction in the appellant's income, cf. Tax Act section 13–1 first paragraph. The Court of Appeal cannot see that the adjustments claimed by the appellant change this. In the Court of Appeal's view, it is also clear that the reduction in income has its cause in the community of interest. Whether adjustments should be made to the basis of comparison at the time of the price change, the Court of Appeal comes back to when assessing the exercise of discretion.

Consequently, there was access to a discretionary determination of the appellant's income according to Section 13–1 first paragraph of the Tax Act, also with regard to the interest margin."

"In the Court of Appeal's view, additional costs that would have been incurred by independent parties, but which are not relevant in the controlled transaction, must be disregarded. Reference is made to the OECD guidelines (2020) point C.1.2.2, section 10.96:

In considering arm's length pricing of loans, the issue of fees and charges in relation to the loan may arise. Independent commercial lenders will sometimes charge fees as part of the terms and conditions of the loan, for example arrangement fees or commitment fees in relation to an undrawn facility. If such charges are seen in a loan between associated enterprises, they should be evaluated in the same way as any other intra-group transaction. In doing so, it must be borne in mind that independent lenders' charges will in part reflect costs incurred in the process of raising capital and in satisfying regulatory requirements, which associated enterprises might not incur.

The decisive factor is whether the costs or rights that the effective interest margin in the observed exploration loans between independent parties is an expression of, are also relevant in the intra-group loan.

As far as the Court of Appeal understands, the appellant does not claim that various fees or costs incurred in exploration loans from a bank have been incurred in the intra-group loan, and in any case no evidence has been provided for this. In the Court of Appeal's view, such costs and fees are therefore not relevant in the comparison. The appellant, on the other hand, has stated that the loan limit that Petrolia SE had made available, and the fact that the loan limit was increased, if necessary, means that a so-called "commitment fee", which accrues in loans between independent parties where an unused credit facility is provided, must be considered built into the agreed interest rate. In the Court of Appeal's view, Petrolia SE cannot be considered to have had any obligation to make a loan limit available or to increase the loan limit if necessary. It appears from the loan agreement point 3.2 that the lender could demand repayment of the loan at its own discretion. The appellant has stated that this did not entail any real risk for the borrower. It is probably conceivable that Petrolia SE did not intend for this clause to be used, and that the appellant had an expectation of this. In this sense, it was a reality in the loan framework. However, it is clear, and acknowledged by the appellant, that the point of financing the appellant through loans rather than higher equity was Petrolia SE's need for flexibility. Thus, it appears to the Court of Appeal that it is clear that the appellant had no unconditional right to the unused part of the loan limit. The Court of Appeal therefore believes that the Board of Appeal has not made any mistakes by comparing with nominal interest margins.

On this basis, the Court of Appeal can also see no reason why it should have been compared with the upper tier of the observed nominal interest margins in the exploration loans between independent parties. In general, an average such as the Appeal Board has built on must be assumed to consider both positive and negative possible variables in the uncontrolled exploration loans in a reasonable manner.

This Court of Appeal agrees with these assessments, which are considered relevant also for the income years 2014–2016.

The Court of Appeal cannot see that there is otherwise anything to indicate that the discretion is arbitrary or grossly unreasonable."

EG: Tax Authorities

Note that the last line (in bold type) has been manually added by the author in order to perform method evaluations.[70]

From the used Overview Documents, the extraction of topics conducted in our experiments and proof of concept only uses the part that we term "Summary", which, intuitively speaking, collects a short description of the case under study. Figure 3.3[71] shows specifically this part in a random example of Overview Document. Henceforth, the complete collection of 105 Summaries is referred as the "Summaries Database" or "Summaries-DB".

3.3 Text Manager

The aim of the Text Manager module is to parse unstructured texts and convert them into structured data objects that can be properly handled by analysis tools. In section 3.2 we have shown an example of a raw data document. Despite the independent content and particulars of each document, most of them show a similar pattern that can be used to structure and categorize text pieces. Figure 3.3 shows a scheme of such structure, which is used by the Text Manager module.

Hence, the core of the Text Manager module is the tDatabase class, which comprises the attributes and methods described next.

70 For each case, according to the court decision, it has been manually identified who has won between the taxpayer or the tax authority.

71 The author created the image. The variables have been designed while organizing the Text Manager, that is, they have been designed while structuring the data (it is a human decision).

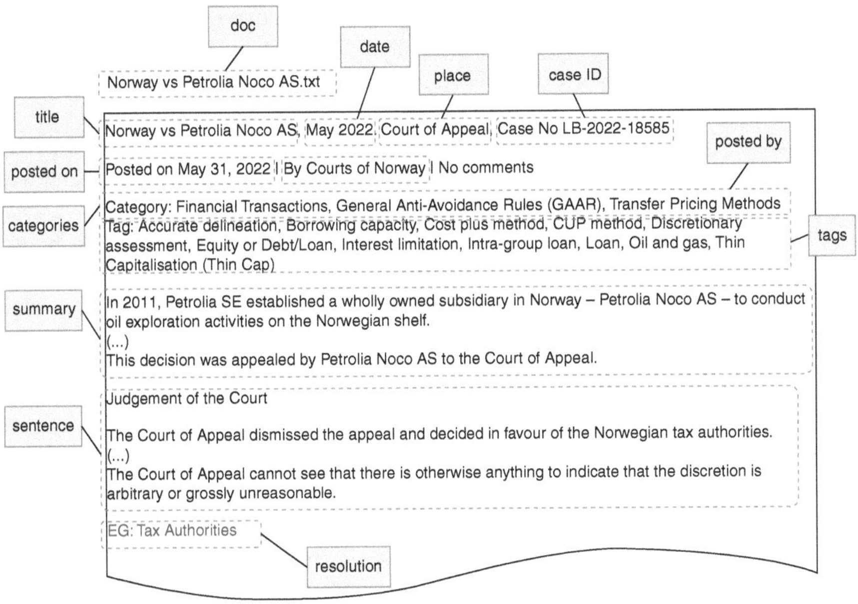

Figure 3.3 Example of parsing in the Text Manager module.

tDatabase class:

- Attributes:[72]
  - "docs" contains text file names.
  - "titles" stores the name of the TP case.
  - "dates" indicates the data linked to the case.
  - "places" shows the location of the case, type of court and so on.
  - "cases" contains the case identifier provided by the TP case document.
  - "posted_on" shows the date when each case was posted.
  - "posted_by" shows the institution that posted the case.
  - "categories" lists categories used by TPcases.com for indexing documents.
  - "tags" lists tags used by TPcases.com as keywords.
  - "summary" contains the parts of the documents describing the contents of each specific TP case. Any given summary (summary[i]) is a collection of tokenized words where *stopwords* have been removed (see the following section—the NLTK deployment Paragraph—for clarification on *stopwords*).

72 "Attributes" are lists of values in which each value corresponds to a different document in the collection. Henceforth, we term attr[i] as the i-element of the attribute named attr, which belong to the i-document.

- "sentence" contains the parts of the documents summarizing the resolution of the case. Any given sentence (sentence[i]) is a collection of tokenized words where *stopwords* have been removed (see the following section—the NLTK deployment Paragraph—for clarification on *stopwords*).
- "resolution" saves the identification of the part benefited by the sentence. This field is added by means of a human validation of the document and we use it for method evaluation.
- "puresum" saves summaries as retrieved from raw documents. Each puresum is a string variable.
- "puresen" saves sentences as retrieved from raw documents. Each puresen is a string variable.
- "all_words" contains all words used in each document.

- Methods:
  - __init__ initializes the class object and creates an empty data structure.
  - read_folder opens all txt files contained in a given folder and parses them according to the structure shown in Figure 3.4.
  - get_value retrieves the contents of a specific attribute of a tDatabase object given the desired attribute and its numerical index.
  - get_feature retrieves the complete aimed attribute of a tDatabase object as a list of values.
  - save_fields saves either raw summaries or raw sentences as independent text files in a specific folder by naming them consistently with values on docs plus a pertinent suffix.
  - save_topwords_struct outputs a structured summary (table) of the tDatabase collection by providing top-*k*-words (highest occurrence) in each summary[i] and sentence[i] with the corresponding count values. *k* is an input parameter.
  - save_entities saves "entities-files" for summary and sentence structures. An "entities-file" contains a matrix in which observed *words* (in summary or in sentence depending on the case) are rows and tags and categories are columns. Cells in a "entities-file" contains the number of occurrences of a given *word* in documents that are identified with a given tag[i] or category[i].

Our Text Manager module and the tDatabase class require some general purpose (general purpose libraries) Python packages as well as some libraries specific to NLP (Natural Language Processing). They are:

- numpy (general purpose), since it is a main package for scientific computing in Python and provides a wide assortment of functions for dealing with multidimensional arrays and objects.
- pandas (general purpose) to perform the manipulation of data structures and tables, allowing easy data values and format transformations, storage and retrieving.
- re (general purpose) is a library that provides functions to implement regular expression matching operations. This is necessary for parsing and splitting raw text files.

- os (general purpose) is used as interface for executing operating system instructions and manage file and folder searches, selections and operations.
- csv (general purpose) performs operations to load and save data to and from CSV (Comma Separated Values) format files. This is necessary for saving summary tables and results.
- sys (general purpose) implements functions that allow the control of parameters and arguments provided to the python scripts from the standard input environment (e.g., command terminal).
- nltk (NLP specific) from Natural Language Toolkit is the main existing python library to work with human language data. It provides interfaces for many lexical resources and a collection of text processing tools for classification, tokenization, stemming, tagging, parsing and semantic reasoning.[73]

NLTK deployment. The Text Manager module uses nltk in two specific ways:

- stopwords. *stopwords* are words that are very frequent in normal texts and do not add key meaning for the understanding and identification of sentences, so it might be preferable to remove them from texts to be processed. Some examples are "I", "and", "the", "is", "are", "a", "it". There is no global consensus for a *stopwords* collection, and they depend on the context, but nltk offers quite a comprehensive and general-purpose list of *stopwords*. Removing *stopwords* from texts before the analysis for topic extraction has become a common practice, even if some authors emphasize that the benefit of such practice is marginal.[74]
- word_tokenize is a function that takes a text (string) and returns a tokenized copy in the form of a list of words.

3.4 Topic Manager

Given a collection of documents in a structured format (e.g., a tDatabase object), the Topic Manager module is in charge of performing operations related to topic extraction, evaluation and visualization.

Topic Manager methods:

- create_dict_and_corpus is a method that transforms a collection of documents given as a set of lists of words (where each document is represented by a single list) in a set of *processed texts* (texts), a *word-ID-dictionary* (word_IDs) and a *corpus-count* (corpus). The *processed texts* are the same collection of documents after undergoing different transformations. These transformations include

73 Extensive information about this python package can be found in the book by Bird, S., et al., *Natural Language Processing with Python*, O'Reilly, 2009, p. 504.

74 Schofield, A., et al., Pulling Out the Stops: Rethinking Stopword Removal for Topic Models, in *Proceedings of the 15th Conference of the European Chapter of the Association for Computational Linguistics: Volume 2*, Short Papers, 2017, pp. 432–436.

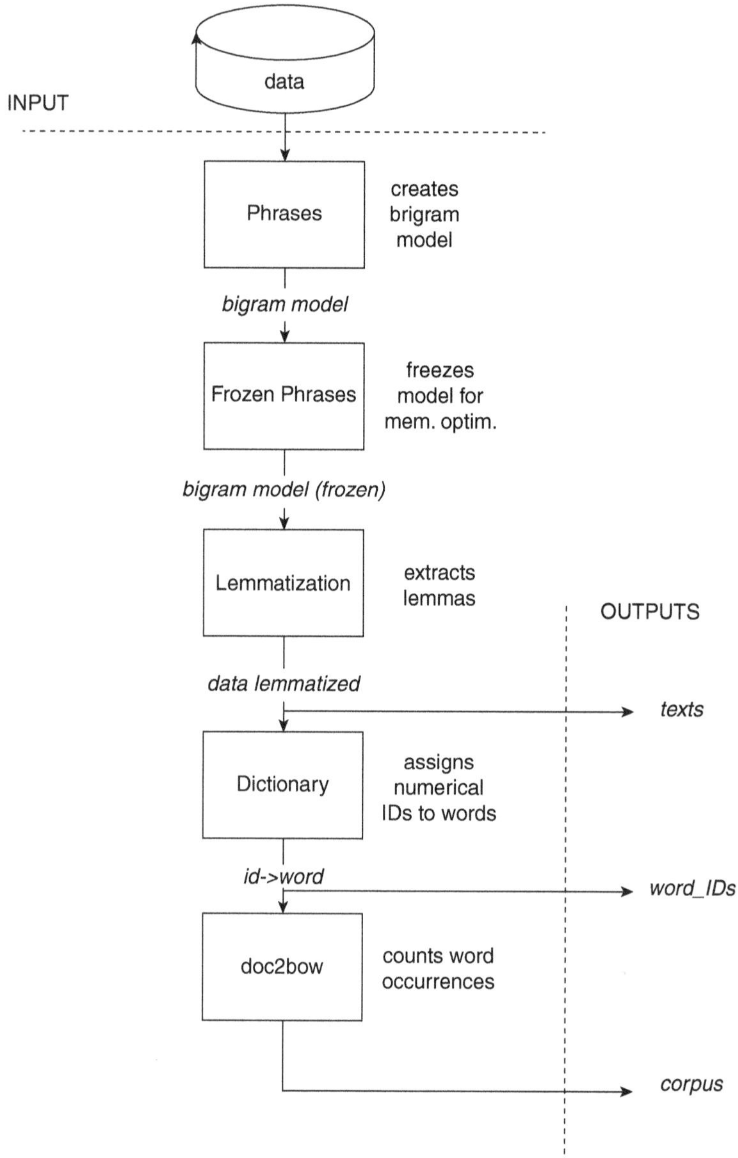

Figure 3.4 Scheme of the create_dict_and_corpus method.

removing stopwords (see remove_stopwords), extracting bigrams (bigrams are pairs of words that commonly appear together, see Phrases) and extracting lemmas (which are words in a "purest" form for the processing, see lemmatization). The *ID-dictionary* stores unique words (or bigrams) that appear in the *processed texts* and identify them with a numerical ID. Finally, the *corpus-count* contains the number of appearances of each entry from the *ID-dictionary* in the *processed texts.* Such data structures are required to enhance the algorithmic analysis and facilitate the automated management of unstructured texts. Figure 3.4[75] shows a scheme of the create_dict_and_corpus method.

- lemmatization is a method to perform *lemmatization*. The *lemmatization* process takes into account the complete vocabulary of a selected language (in our case: English) and performs morphological analysis to remove inflectional endings and retrieve the *lemmas* of a set of words. Taking the definition from Wikipedia:

> in lexicography a lemma (plural lemmas or lemmata) is the canonical form, dictionary form, or citation form of a set of word forms. In English, for example, break, breaks, broke, broken and breaking are forms of the same lexeme, with break as the lemma by which they are indexed. Lexeme, in this context, refers to the set of all the inflected or alternating forms in the paradigm of a single word, and lemma refers to the particular form that is chosen by convention to represent the lexeme.[76]

Lemmatization is required to reduce word diversity to units of meaning. It is a language modeling technique alternative to stemming but is considered to achieve better results.[77] Table 3.2 shows some examples comparing *lemmatization* (dictionary-based) and *stemming* (rule-based).

Table 3.2 Lemmatization versus stemming (examples)[78]

Word	*Stem*	*Lemma*
indices	indic	index
went	went	go
am	am	be
studying	stud	study
mice	mice	mouse

75 The image was created by the author.

76 Wikipedia—Lemma (Morphology), https://en.wikipedia.org/wiki/Lemma_(morphology).

77 Balakrishnan, V., and Lloyd-Yemoh, E., Stemming and Lemmatization: A Comparison of Retrieval Performances, *Lecture Notes on Software Engineering*, Vol. 2(3), 2014, pp. 262–267.

78 The list of examples was created by the author. Ff words appear in the text as in the example, the Stem identifies only the initial part of the word while the lemma determines how to find it in the vocabulary.

Python offers different methods for *lemmatization*. In our experiments we used the implementation provided by the spaCy implementation (see spaCy and spacy.load).

- check_and_save_model is a method that performs the following operations on a given *topic model*:
    1. It creates and saves the visualization environment.
    2. It computes model *perplexity*. "Perplexity" is an estimate of the quality with which a topic model is able to predict new data; that is, it represents its ability to generalize information. Thus, a model with high perplexity indicates uncertainty and lack of accuracy, while a low perplexity score tends to show a model with confident and accurate predictions. The calculation of the perplexity requires the contrast with a test set that has not been used for model training. For perplexity estimation, we use the log_perplexity method from the Gensim library.
    3. It computes model *coherence*. "Coherence" measures the degree to which a set of words is related to a topic; that is, it represents an attempt to assess whether a topic is consistent from a human perspective.[79] The automated calculation of coherence needs the support of an external corpus reflecting general knowledge about certain domains (e.g., Wikipedia). The coherence rating of a topic ranges from low scores for irrelevant and vague topics to high values for clear, solid and relevant topics. In our experiments, we use the CoherenceModel method (from the Gensim library) to obtain the coherence of topic models.
- compute_coherence_values is a method that, defined lower and upper bounds, extracts models with different number of topics from a collection of documents. Later, it evaluates the different models based on "coherence" (see check_and_save_model) and provides models and coherence estimations as outputs.
- format_topics_sentences builds a table in which each analysed document is assigned a topic from the model as *dominant topic*, with an estimation of its *contribution percentage* in the specific document as well as the *main words* that identify the dominant topic. It also contrasts such words with the targeted references/benchmarks (i.e., tags and/or categories of the studied law documents). Figure 3.5[80] shows an example of the tables generated by this method.
- topics_vectors creates a matrix of MxN dimensions, where "M" are documents, "N" are topics in the best model and cells contain *contribution percentage* values. Therefore, documents are expressed as vectors[81] that reflect their pertinence

79 Imagine that this activity could be done by a human being that will go through each document in order to identify similarities in such documents.

80 The image was created by the author.

81 Vectors represent numbers for machines to process and transform inputs. These are the coordinates within a dimensional space (e.g., x-axis and y-axis in a bi-dimensional space).

Document_No	Dominant_Topic	Topic_Perc_Contrib	Keywords	Target	IDs
0	10	0.4095	interest, rate, year, margin, lender, basis, point, court, set, fix	['comparability factors', ' cup method', ' intra-group loan', ' loan', ' oil and gas']	norway vs conocophillips skandinavia as
1	16	0.2826	profit, german, determine, fund, activity, gmbh, distribution, method, borrowing, argue	['burden of proof (onus)', ' hidden distribution of profits', ' license fee', ' license of trademark', ' royalties', ' trademark', ' vga (verdeckte gewinnausschüttung)']	germany vs "trademark gmbh"
2	15	0.21	financial, grant, independent, obtain, administration, present, condition, financing, demonstrate, constitute	['comparable data', ' interest rate', ' intra-group loan', ' loan']	france vs sas wheelabrator group
3	16	0.2018	profit, german, determine, fund, activity, gmbh, distribution, method, borrowing, argue	['cost plus method', ' credit rating', ' external comparables', ' hierarchy of methods', ' implicit support/guarantee', ' intra-group loan', ' loan', ' most appropriate method (mam)', ' netherlands']	germany vs "x sub gmbh"
4	13	0.336	agreement, loan, basis, parent, market, income, agree, term, change, section	['broad understanding of the notion of transaction', ' controlled transactions', ' definition of transaction', ' interest', ' intra-group loan', ' loan', ' obiter dictum', ' statute of limitation', ' zero-coupon bond']	denmark vs. swiss re.
5	2	0.3064	party, authority, issue, receive, audit, assessment, relate, income, deposit, make	['comparability', ' cup method', ' limited risk', ' limited risk distributors (lrd)', ' most appropriate method (mam)', ' royalty and license payments', ' tnmm', ' transfer pricing methods']	spain vs universal pictures international spain sl
6	8	0.2762	rate, bond, financial, risk, apply, determine, base, condition, credit, rating	['abnormal act of management', ' general electric', ' group rating', ' intra-group loan', ' loan', ' stand alone rating']	france vs general electric france
7	8	0.1531	rate, bond, financial, risk, apply, determine, base, condition, credit, rating	['comparable to a bank loan', ' interest rate', ' intra-group loan', ' ireland', ' legal status of tpg', ' loan', ' no control over risk', ' transfer pricing guidelines']	spain vs mcdonald's
8	12	0.3791	share, interest, acquisition, transfer, issue, correspond, sas_edfi, arrangement, conversion, difference	['bonds convertible into shares (oca)', ' convertible bonds', ' convertible note', ' interest rate', ' intra-group loan', ' loan', ' tsiveriotis and fernandes model']	france vs electricité de france
9	5	0.1123	tax, appeal, file, court, authority, assessment, issue, income, additional, administrative	['financial transactions', ' intra-group loan', ' loan', ' special purpose vehicle (spv)']	poland vs "f-inance. sp. z o.o."
10	5	0.1486	tax, appeal, file, court, authority, assessment, issue, income, additional, administrative	['burden of proof (onus)', ' interest rate', ' intra-group loan', ' loan', ' related parties']	italy vs "lender spa"

Figure 3.5 Example of a tabular output generated by the format_topics_sentences method.

to modelled topics, this way forming an input space and a problem representation that can be approached numerically.
- remove_stopwords removes *stopwords* from a given set of lists of words.

Our Topic Manager module requires some general purpose (general library) Python packages as well as some libraries specific to NLP (Natural Language Processing). They are:

- numpy, pandas, re (general purpose) and nltk (NLP specific).
- logging (general purpose) provides a set of methods and classes for the creation and management of log information, that is, diverse kinds of events, messages and notifications generated by the application. The main purpose of this library is to offer a standardized way to deal with log information, therefore allowing a smooth coexistence and consistency with log notification from third-party modules.
- Gensim (NLP specific) is a Python library for *topic modeling*, *document indexing* and *similarity retrieval* with large corpora, specifically designed to meet the requirements of the NLP and *information retrieval* (IR) communities.[82] Gensim has become extremely popular in recent years due to its scalability and ease of use, making a tooling environment that works properly regardless of the corpus size used for training. It implements versions of widely used algorithms for topic modeling and inference; for instance, Latent Semantic Analysis and Latent Dirichlet Allocation.
- spaCy: Industrial-strength NLP (NLP specific) is a library for advanced NLP designed for Python and Cython environments with the idea of being realistic and fully applicable to real products. SpaCy is fast and lightweight, incorporates tokenization and training for more than 70 languages and neural network models for tagging, parsing, named entity recognition, text classification and so on.
- pyLDAvis (NLP specific) is a Python library for interactively visualizing topic models in HTML formats, therefore allowing users to interpret the topics of a trained topic model when contrasted with training texts.[83]
- nltk

Deployment of NLP libraries. The Topic Manager module mainly uses the following NLP methods and functions from the cited libraries:

- Phrases/Phraser (Gensim) build topic models by optimizing memory usage.
- spacy.load (spaCy) with the en_core_web_sm argument provides a small, English pipeline pre-trained on web excerpts (blogs, news, comments, etc., including vocabulary, syntax and entities) for the lemmatization process.

82 Řehůřek, R., and Sojka, P., Software Framework for Topic Modelling with Large Corpora, *Proceedings of the LREC 2010 Workshop on New Challenges for NLP Frameworks*, ELRA, Valletta, Malta, 2010, pp. 45–50.

83 Mabey, B., pyLDAvis documentation, *Buildmedia, Blog*, 2021, available at https://readthedocs.org/projects/pyldavis/downloads/pdf/stable/ (accessed 11 July 2023).

- corpora.Dictionary (Gensim) creates an *ID-dictionary,* a data structure that links words with numerical identifiers.
- gensim_models (pyLDAvis) creates user-friendly visual representations of topic models.
- CoherenceModel (Gensim) allows and performs the coherence evaluation of topic models.
- LdaModel (Gensim) and LdaMallet (Gensim) are properly the builders of topic models by and for Latent Dirichlet Allocation in the traditional approach and via Mallet respectively.

3.5 Additional libraries and functions

In addition to the tools, libraries and functions used in Text Manager and Topic Manager, other Python libraries and tools have been used in our experiments. The most relevant ones are discussed here:

- matplotlib (general purpose) is a library oriented to the creation of figures, plots and graphs, in other words, for the visualization of static, dynamic and interactive data. Matplotlib creates the necessary environments for all kinds of configurations related to the display and export of figures in multiple formats. It is one of the basic libraries within the usual tools used by data experts in Python.
- seaborn (general purpose) is another library for the creation of statistical graphics in Python.[84] It is built on the top of matplotlib and is specially devised to work together with the data structures used in the pandas library. The idea behind seaborn is that users can create highly informative graphs with environments and functionalities that allow deep exploration of data and easy aggregation of features.
- scipy (scientific computing) is a library designed to provide mathematical algorithms and tools that are common in scientific and engineering environments. It is based on numpy and includes modules for optimization, linear algebra, integration and so on.
    - spatial.KDTree is a function of scipy that constructs a KD-Tree for the quick search of nearest-neighbours in data. A KD-Tree is a binary tree where nodes represent hyperrectangles aligned based on dimensional axis. Each node links to a different dimension and splits points based on if their values along that axis is above or below than a particular value.[85] In our experiments we use KD-Trees to quickly find the closest points (documents) to a given data point in our data structures.

84 Waskom, M. L., Seaborn: Statistical Data Visualization, *Journal of Open Source Software*, Vol. 6(60), 2021, p. 3021.

85 Maneewongvatana, S., and Mount, D. M., It's Okay to Be Skinny, If Your Friends Are Fat, *Center for Geometric Computing 4th Annual Workshop on Computational Geometry*, Vol. 2, 1999, pp. 1–8.

- scikit-learn (machine learning) is perhaps the most popular Python library for machine learning and data analysis applications, with a wide range of implementations for both supervised and unsupervised learning, as well as other forms of descriptive or predictive analysis. It is designed to coordinate seamlessly with numpy and scipy. In our experiments we primarily use two functions:
  - decomposition.PCA. It performs PCA, that is, a linear dimensionality reduction with singular value decomposition (SVD). Depending on the size and shape of the data and the number of final dimensions, it uses full SVD or a randomized truncated SVD approach.
  - manifold.TSNE. It implements t-SNE for the visualization of high-dimensional data in two- or three-dimensional maps. To construct a proper visualization, it converts distances between paired points into joint probabilities and minimizes the Kullback-Leibler divergence between the joint probabilities in the map embedding.

4 Results and discussion

4.1 Selection of best models

We approached the topic extraction of our Summaries-DB with two different algorithms: (i) the Gemsin' Latent Dirichlet Allocation (G-LDA) and (ii) the Mallet's Latent Dirichlet Allocation (M-LDA), which is used through a Gensim wrapper. In principle, M-LDA is expected to obtain more accurate topics.[86]

By using the "Text Manager" we processed the collection of law documents to create structured Overview Documents, from which we analysed the parts called Summaries-DB with the "Topic Manager" in order to obtain a set of *processed texts* (texts), a *word-ID-dictionary* (word_IDs) and a *corpus-count* (corpus). This is the required basis to create topics models.

In the next step, we generated a set of M-LDA and G-LDA with different numbers of topics (from 3 to 14)[87] and compared them based on Coherence scores. In the diagram shown for the "Text Manager" this corresponds to the Model Selector module. Results of these steps are shown in Figure 3.6,[88] List 1 and List 2.

86 Hongchen, G., et al., An Improved AD-LDA Topic Model Based on Weighted Gibbs Sampling, in *2016 IEEE Advanced Information Management, Communicates, Electronic and Automation Control Conference (IMCEC)*, Xi'an, China, 2016, pp. 1978–1982, https://doi.org/10.1109/IMCEC.2016.7867563.

87 During the process the machine was asked to identify three topics, then four, and so on . . . until 14. Indeed, before training the algorithm, the number of topics that the model will have was specified. The algorithm cannot decide this by itself, it needs to be told how many topics to find. Then, the output for every document will be the mixture of topics that each particular document has. This output is just a vector, a list of numbers that means "for topic 1, 0.2; for topic 2, 0.7; . . ." and so on. These vectors can be compared in different ways, and these comparisons are useful for understanding the corpus, to get an idea of its fundamental structures.

88 The image was created by the author.

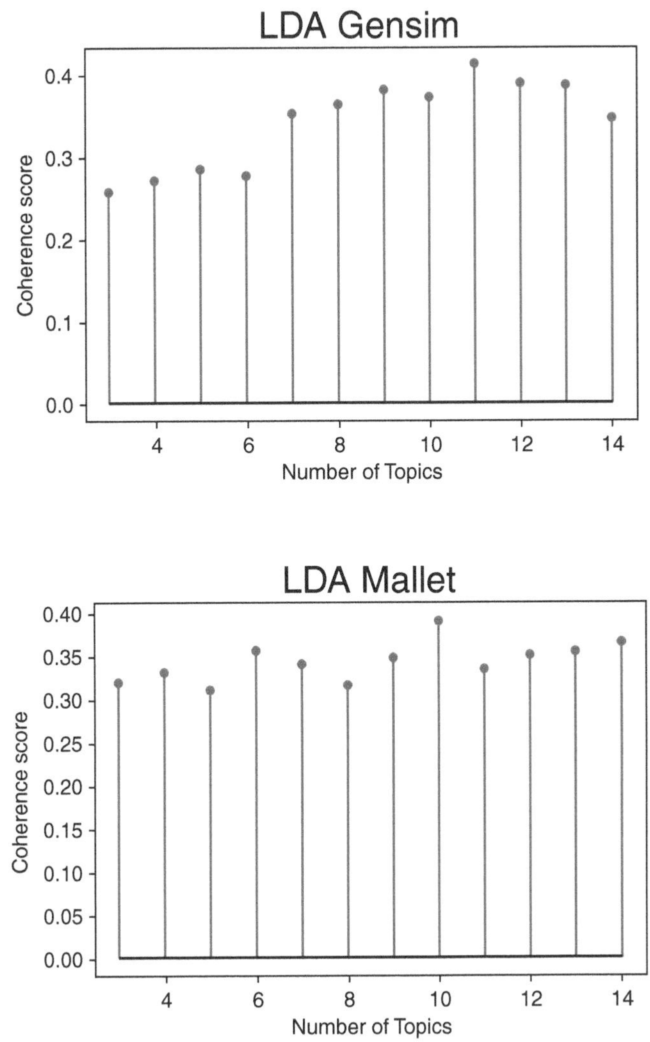

Figure 3.6 Stem plot for Coherence scores of G-LDA and M-LDA sets of models.

Thus, G-LDA models obtain models with the following Coherence scores (the bold ones identify better results in the analysis, that is, the machines when asked to identify 11 topics could create better clusters (distinct arguments):

Selected model: normal
Coherence score with 3 topics: 0.2587
Coherence score with 4 topics: 0.2724
Coherence score with 5 topics: 0.2872

Coherence score with 6 topics: 0.2771
Coherence score with 7 topics: 0.3531
Coherence score with 8 topics: 0.3660
Coherence score with 9 topics: 0.3818
Coherence score with 10 topics: 0.3733
Coherence score with 11 topics: 0.4147
Coherence score with 12 topics: 0.3932
Coherence score with 13 topics: 0.3896
Coherence score with 14 topics: 0.3498
List 1. Coherence scores of G-LDA models

On the other hand, M-LDA models obtain models with the following Coherence scores:

Selected model: mallet
Coherence score with 3 topics: 0.3217
Coherence score with 4 topics: 0.3345
Coherence score with 5 topics: 0.3142
Coherence score with 6 topics: 0.3589
Coherence score with 7 topics: 0.3411
Coherence score with 8 topics: 0.3192
Coherence score with 9 topics: 0.3515
Coherence score with 10 topics: 0.3930
Coherence score with 11 topics: 0.3374
Coherence score with 12 topics: 0.3542
Coherence score with 13 topics: 0.3577
Coherence score with 14 topics: 0.3687
List 2. Coherence scores of M-LDA models

If we focus on the *most coherent* G-LDA and M-LDA models (i.e., models with 11 and 10 topics respectively), we obtain sets of main keywords that identify each topic, as shown in List 3 for G-LDA and List 4 for M-LDA.

Topic number 0,

'0.067*"tax" + 0.032*"assessment" + 0.031*"interest" + 0.031*"authority" + '
'0.030*"cost" + 0.029*"group" + 0.029*"appeal" + 0.028*"issue" + '
'0.027*"file" + 0.025*"acquisition"'

Topic number 1,

'0.086*"loan" + 0.041*"tax" + 0.033*"authority" + 0.031*"capital" + '
'0.027*"issue" + 0.024*"income" + 0.022*"shareholder" + 0.021*"equity" + '
'0.019*"bind" + 0.016*"interest"'

Topic number 2,

‘0.012*”entity” + 0.010*”obtain” + 0.009*”independent” + ‘
‘0.008*”indebtedness” + 0.007*”report” + 0.007*”contract” + 0.006*”fastfood” ‘
‘+ 0.006*”amortization” + 0.006*”correction_rule” + 0.006*”result”‘

Topic number 3,

‘0.015*”appeal” + 0.013*”margin” + 0.013*”gmbh” + 0.012*”court” + ‘
‘0.011*”tax” + 0.011*”value” + 0.011*”decision” + 0.011*”sas_edfi” + ‘
‘0.010*”conversion” + 0.010*”share”‘

Topic number 4,

‘0.037*”company” + 0.021*”south” + 0.017*”transaction” + 0.014*”value” + ‘
‘0.014*”make” + 0.012*”article” + 0.012*”case” + 0.010*”consider” + ‘
‘0.010*”provision” + 0.010*”consideration”‘

Topic number 5,

‘0.067*”rate” + 0.061*”interest” + 0.046*”loan” + 0.040*”company” + ‘
‘0.033*”parent” + 0.023*”percent” + 0.021*”lender” + 0.019*”court” + ‘
‘0.017*”group” + 0.017*”condition”‘

Topic number 6,

‘0.030*”rate” + 0.030*”loan” + 0.027*”interest” + 0.022*”financial” + ‘
‘0.015*”bond” + 0.013*”condition” + 0.012*”company” + 0.012*”bank” + ‘
‘0.011*”rating” + 0.011*”apply”‘

Topic number 7,

‘0.051*”loan” + 0.039*”crookes_brother” + 0.039*”mml” + 0.032*”interest” + ‘
‘0.030*”agreement” + 0.028*”section” + 0.024*”basis” + 0.023*”income” + ‘
‘0.023*”tax” + 0.020*”requirement”‘

Topic number 8,

‘0.008*”salvatore” + 0.008*”italian” + 0.006*”remunerate” + ‘
‘0.006*”profitable” + 0.006*”luxury” + 0.005*”existence” + 0.005*”dismiss” + ‘
‘0.005*”indirect” + 0.003*”advantage” + 0.003*”judge”‘

Topic number 9,

‘0.023*”tax” + 0.021*”company” + 0.016*”administration” + 0.015*”branch” + ‘

'0.013*"pay" + 0.013*"charge" + 0.011*"decision" + 0.011*"article" + '
'0.010*"additional" + 0.010*"amount"'

Topic number 10,

'0.009*"remuneration" + 0.006*"zinc" + 0.006*"decision" + '
'0.005*"restructuring" + 0.003*"hearing" + 0.003*"settlement" + '
'0.003*"split" + 0.003*"smelter" + 0.003*"reach" + 0.003*"lay"'

List 3. Topics of the most coherent G-LDA model, relevant words and word impact

Topic number 0,

'0.060*"interest" + 0.050*"relate" + 0.044*"tax" + 0.042*"issue" + '
'0.041*"share" + 0.038*"deduction" + 0.028*"acquisition" + 0.022*"loss" + '
'0.021*"group" + 0.021*"debt"'

Topic number 1,

'0.184*"loan" + 0.056*"agreement" + 0.042*"party" + 0.041*"income" + '
'0.038*"authority" + 0.027*"capital" + 0.026*"provision" + '
'0.024*"shareholder" + 0.023*"arm_length" + 0.022*"agree"'

Topic number 2,

'0.108*"tax" + 0.079*"appeal" + 0.063*"authority" + 0.060*"assessment" + '
'0.059*"file" + 0.056*"issue" + 0.050*"court" + 0.038*"arm_length" + '
'0.036*"profit" + 0.026*"determine"'

Topic number 3,

'0.065*"case" + 0.042*"company" + 0.040*"tax" + 0.036*"price" + '
'0.028*"subsidiary" + 0.028*"expense" + 0.027*"increase" + '
'0.024*"assessment" + 0.022*"paragraph" + 0.022*"transfer_pricing"'

Topic number 4,

'0.128*"company" + 0.068*"transaction" + 0.047*"article" + 0.044*"rule" + '
'0.043*"parent" + 0.028*"establish" + 0.023*"hold" + 0.020*"market" + '
'0.019*"law" + 0.018*"fund"'

Topic number 5,

'0.045*"condition" + 0.038*"financial" + 0.032*"apply" + 0.028*"independent" '
'+ 0.028*"risk" + 0.028*"bond" + 0.025*"group" + 0.022*"bank" + '
'0.022*"credit" + 0.020*"rating"'

Topic number 6,

'0.147*"tax" + 0.099*"company" + 0.058*"authority" + 0.050*"grant" + '
'0.030*"carry" + 0.026*"amount" + 0.023*"german" + 0.022*"code" + ''
'0.019*"advantage" + 0.017*"favor"'

Topic number 7,

'0.057*"amount" + 0.046*"payment" + 0.044*"receive" + 0.040*"year" + '
'0.036*"audit" + 0.033*"financing" + 0.032*"business" + '
'0.028*"administration" + 0.027*"financial" + 0.026*"make"'

Topic number 8,

'0.064*"income" + 0.049*"pay" + 0.047*"cost" + 0.036*"taxable" + '
'0.032*"result" + 0.032*"service" + 0.026*"entity" + 0.025*"trademark" + '
'0.024*"transfer" + 0.022*"decision"'

Topic number 9,

'0.209*"interest" + 0.162*"rate" + 0.130*"loan" + 0.039*"base" + '
'0.038*"year" + 0.021*"court" + 0.020*"set" + 0.019*"margin" + 0.015*"high" '
'+ 0.014*"claim"'

List 4. Topics of the most coherent M-LDA model, relevant words and word impact

Note that in both cases there are some repeated terms that are common and relevant in most of the documents in the Summary-DB. From here we can infer a common context in which all documents are embraced. Figure 3.7[89] shows these terms, which are in both cases quite similar regardless of the model used.

G-LDA		M-LDA	
position	*term*	*position*	*term*
1st	loan	1st	tax
2nd	tax	2nd	loan
3rd	interest	3rd	interest
4th	company	4th	company
5th	rate	5th	rate
6th	issue	6th	authority

Figure 3.7 Most overall relevant terms in G-LDA and M-LDA models.

89 The image was created by the author.

4.2 Consistency of the global topic

Beyond the reader's intuition, to avoid the bias of the community to which this chapter is addressed, we used the Google search engine (Google) with the key terms to evaluate the consistency of the global topic revealed by the different models.[90] It has been inserted in Google the most relevant words to evaluate if the pages that are displayed in Google, after the insertion of such words, are related to the topic that we are dealing with (it is a common way to evaluate the models that came from the analysis).

It is clear in both cases (i.e., both models) that the fundamental issue addressed by the documents is "tax and double taxation issues relating to rates, interest and loans in business and between companies". Note the nuances provided by the differentiating terms "issue" (G-LDA model) and "authority" (M-LDA model), which suggest problems, difficulties or complications to be considered in the first case (G-LDA), and the intervention (perspective or scale) of national or international institutions in the second (M-LDA), for example, Austria, French, Switzerland, Singapore.

We can analyse the congruence of the results by referring to the Categories and Tags used by TPcases.com to index the analysed documents. Figure 3.8[91] shows the main ones and their number of occurrences in the identification of the documents selected for our experiments. It is important to remember here that our models only use a small extract obtained from the Summaries in the Overview Documents; on the other hand, the Categories and Tags provided by TPcases.com are established by experts by reading the full texts and are based on the OECD TPG 2022.

To sum up, remarkably, both models can abstract relevant terms to explain the global context representing all the documents selected for our experiments.

4.3 Comparing topic models with maps and metrics

We can continue to examine the models more closely. To do so, we can simply compare the visualizations provided by the pyLDAvis environment, with the aim to obtain more insights about both topic models. Figure 3.9[92] and Figure 3.10[93] show such visualizations for the G-LDA and M-LDA models respectively.

On the left side of Figure 3.9 and Figure 3.10 the pyLDAvis visualization shows topics and Intertopic Distances. Discovered topics are represented by circles, their size being correlated with the predominance among documents in the Summary-DB. Ideally, a good topic modeling should show big circles well separated (non-overlapping) sharing the whole available space. Therefore, even although Coherence scores are higher in the G-LDA case with 11 topics, the

90 We use Google with the most important words of the topic to find out if the pages that Google finds are related to the topic we are dealing with. It is a way to evaluate the discovered patterns.

91 The image was created by the author.

92 The image was created by the author.

93 The image was created by the author.

Categories	Occurrences
financial transactions	74
comparability analysis	18
disallowed deduction	11
general anti-avoidance rules (gaar)	9
tax avoidance schemes	9
transfer pricing methods	8
burden of proof	7
arm's length principle	5
services and fees	5
non-recognition and recharacterization	5
legality - legitimacy - constitutional	5

Tags	Occurrences
loan	73
intra-group loan	72
interest rate	25
burden of proof (onus)	14
interest free loan	14
equity or debt/loan	12
interest deduction	9
comparability factors	7
comparability	7
interest	7
comparable data	6

Figure 3.8 Main Categories and Tags used by TPcases.com for indexing the documents used in our experiments.

Intertopic Distances Map seems to be better in the M-LDA case, that is, big bubble sizes showing less overlap.

Also note another difference between both models regarding the size of the circles (or bubbles). In the M-LDA case they are quite similar to each other, whereas in the G-LDA case we have a greater variety of sizes. This directly expresses the topic dominance among documents. Figure 3.11[94] provides further details in this regard.

We can further investigate models and their suitability by using the topics_vectors function of the Topic Manager module. This will create a distance matrix when the distance of every document in the Summary-DB to each topic is computed (*Topic-to-Document Distances*). Later, we can use dimensionality reduction techniques to visually evaluate the consistency. pyLDAvis uses multidimensional

94 The image was created by the author.

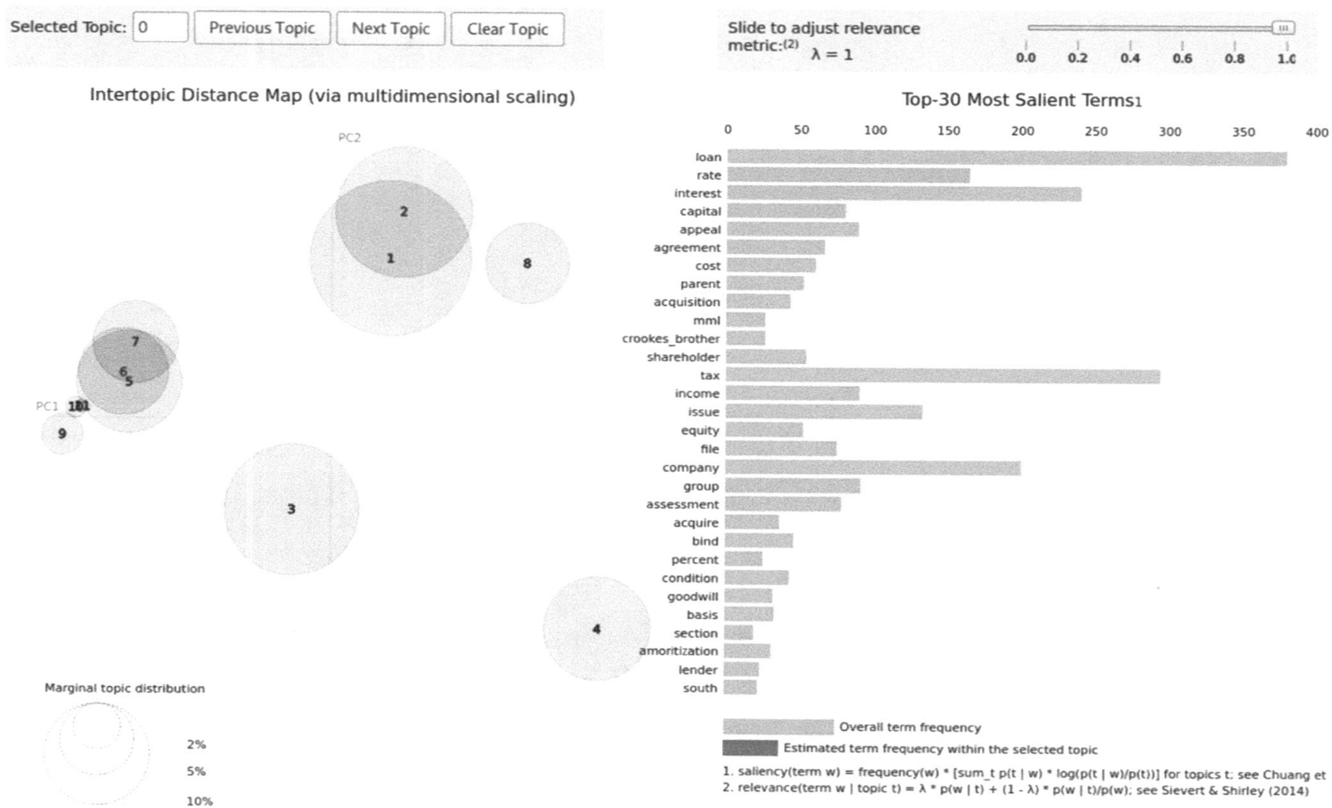

Figure 3.9 Visualization with pyLDAvis for the G-LDA model. On the left side, Intertopic Distances projected in a two-dimensional map by means of multidimensional scaling; on the right side, most salient topics in the model.

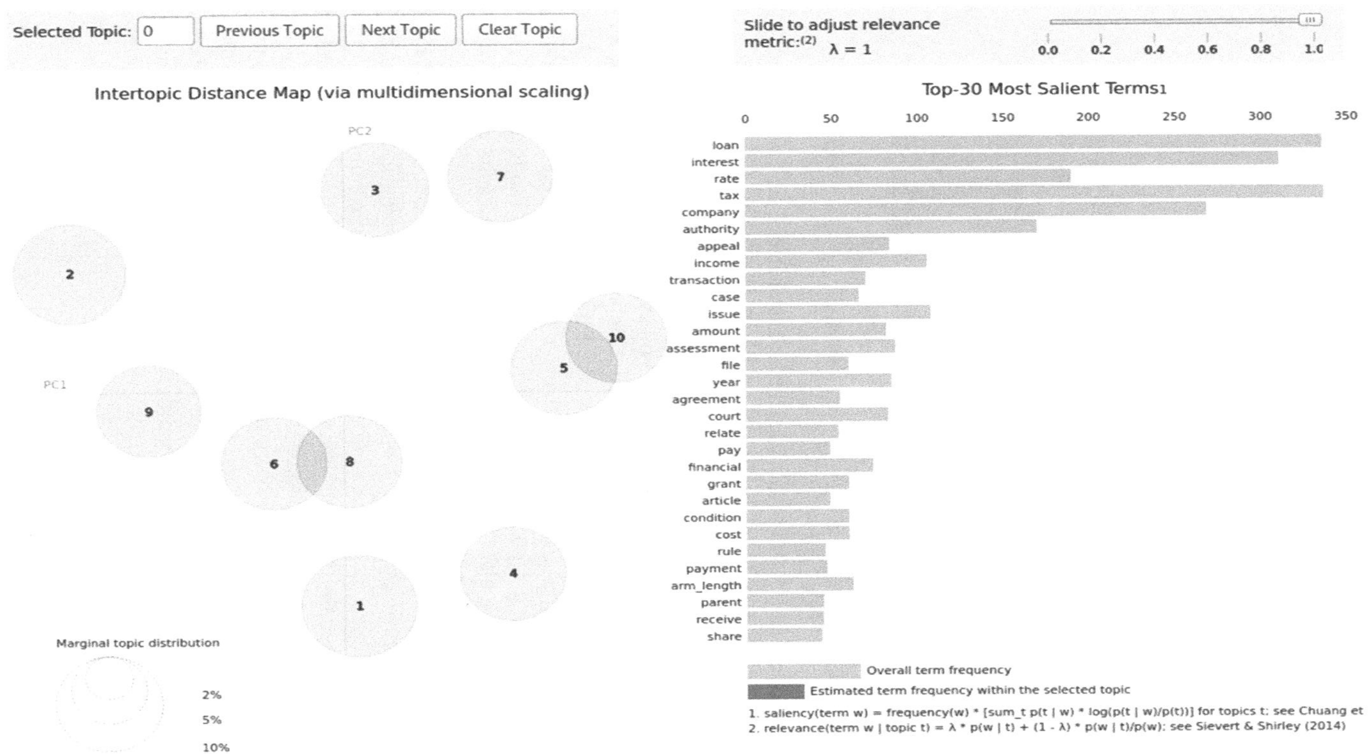

Figure 3.10 Visualization with pyLDAvis for the M-LDA model. On the left side, Intertopic Distances projected in a two-dimensional map by means of multidimensional scaling; on the right side, most salient topics in the model.

G-LDA topic	G-LDA dominance
1	0.236
2	0.169
3	0.164
4	0.104
5	0.101
6	0.073
7	0.065
8	0.064
9	0.016
10	0.004
11	0.002
sum	0.998
mean	0.091
median	0.073
std.dev	0.071

M-LDA topic	M-LDA dominance
1	0.116
2	0.111
3	0.102
4	0.098
5	0.098
6	0.097
7	0.097
8	0.097
9	0.095
10	0.089
sum	1.000
mean	0.100
median	0.098
std.dev	0.007

Figure 3.11 Topics in G-LDA and M-LDA models and their dominance over the studied documents (some rounding error is possible in the figures).

scaling to build its Intertopics Distances Maps; however, there are alternatives that can provide enhanced views of the data under analysis. Here we use PCA and t-STNE, since they offer complementary views of the data, that is, whereas PCA shows a projection from a global perspective by focusing on the most variable features, t-STNE draws a representation that tries to capture the local similarity among elements, keeping alike elements close to each other. Results are shown in Figure 3.12[95] and Figure 3.13.[96]

Results shown in Figure 3.12 and Figure 3.13 are quite revealing. The t-STNE representation is more interesting for our purposes of obtaining meaningful and well-differentiated topics, as it retains information about the most immediate similarity between individually selected documents. However, it is also important to consider the PCA perspective to obtain an overall assessment. In both cases, the G-LDA model obtains clearer and more differentiated maps. In the t-STNE map (Figure 3.12, left), documents can be linearly separated according to their most dominant topic, with a few exceptions. On the other hand, the PCA map shows two sets of documents that can be clearly differentiated from a general perspective (different colour dots in Figure 3.13, right), indicating that the dominant topics

95 The image was created by the author.
96 The image was created by the author.

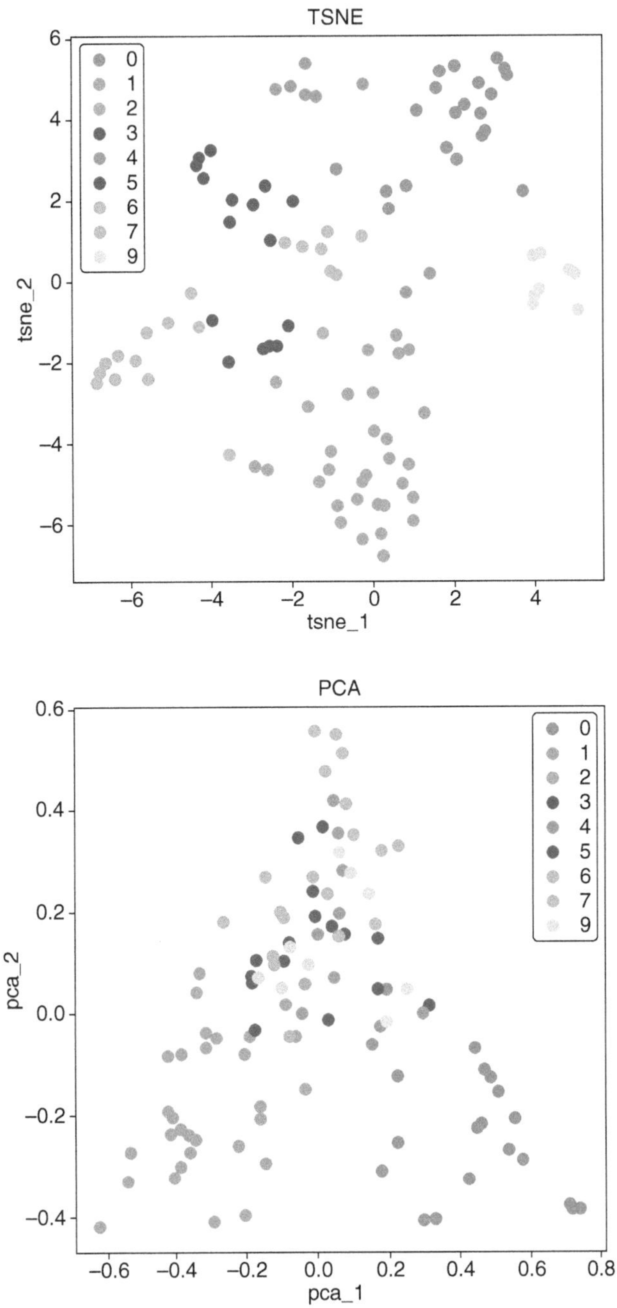

Figure 3.12 Visualizations of Topic-to-Document Distances obtained with the G-LDA model by means of PCA and t-STNE projections. Colours are established based on the dominant topic of each document.

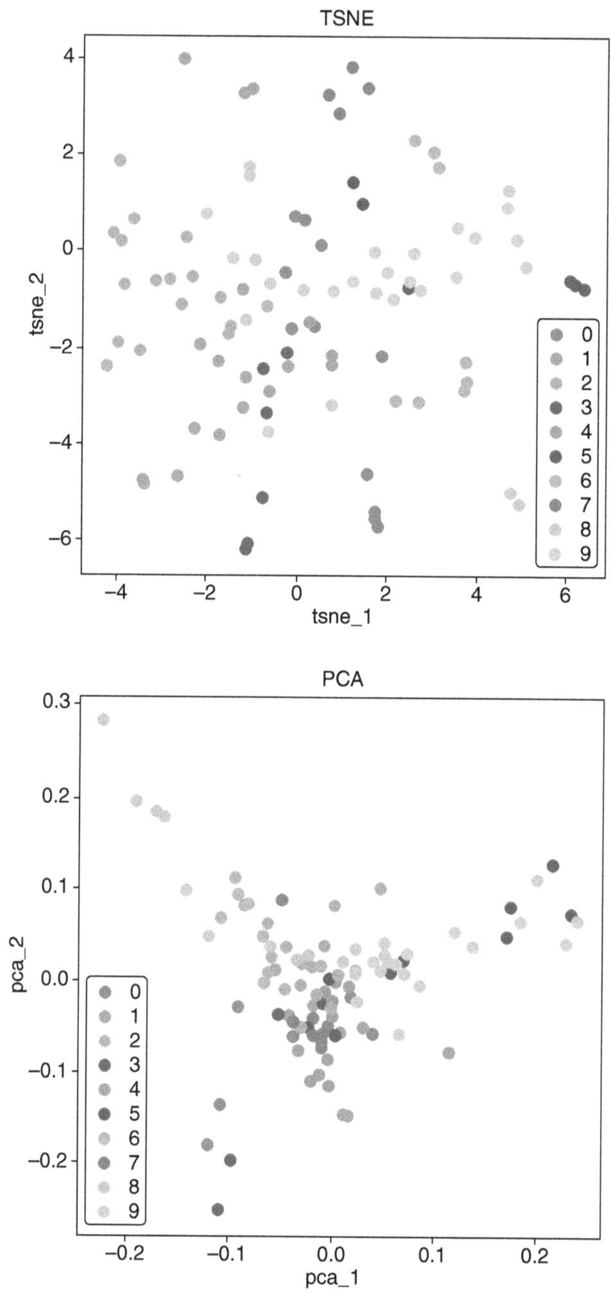

Figure 3.13 Visualizations of Topic-to-Document Distances obtained with the M-LDA model by means of PCA and t-STNE projections. Colours are established based on the dominant topic of each document.

and their respective documents are appropriate and clearly differentiable also in a coarse grain view. In contrast, the projections of the M-LDA model do not present such clear divisions. Again, it should be noted that the M-LDA model obtains more balanced topics, with the cardinality of the clusters established according to the most dominant topic being less variable. The t-STNE map continues to show well-differentiated, although less clear, zones, while the PCA map shows more overlap, although some documents are well grouped in the periphery.

In short, we find a certain divergence of criteria in the evaluation methods used to compare the G-LDA and M-LDA models. While the Coherence and Topic-to-Documents maps favour the G-LDA model, the interpretation of the Intertopic Distances maps provided by pyLDAvis tends to favour the M-LDA model.

4.4 Spread topics and discriminant terms

As mentioned before, the preselection of legal texts related to "financial transactions" means that many meaningful words from a semantic perspective (i.e., to define topics) are shared among all or most of the documents. Such words can be removed before the analysis, but we discarded this approach to keep potential term hierarchies in our Summary-DB collection. In other words, the preselection of documents to analyse poses some difficulties for the task as it establishes a common frame (i.e., a common overall topic) for which discovered topics are, in reality, sub-topics. If we reduce the *relevance* parameter in the pyLDAvis visualization, we remove the presence of such common terms and emphasize the relevance of discriminant (bottom-perspective) terms, which start emerging. Figure 3.14[97] and Figure 3.15[98] show such effect in both G-LDA and M-LDA models.

Besides, both models (particularly the G-LDA model) can be improved by merging overlapping topics (or very close topics) and removing topics with a minor relevance or low-representation along the collection. This can be done in an automatic way by, for instance, leveraging the Intertopic Distances map obtained from the pyLDAvis multidimensional scaling. Topic words collections can also be merged since models retain word importance in each case.

In any case, we continue our further exploration with the original G-LDA and M-LDA models. Documents can be easily related to each other and connected by means of the topic indexing and the problem space defined by the topics-to-documents contributions when interpreted as similarities (or distances). Figure 3.16 (for G-LDA) and Figure 3.17 (for M-LDA) show heatmaps where documents (rows) are expressed as N-dimensional vectors. Dimensions are topics, therefore feature values are contributions of topics in each document: 0-no contribution (dark colour), 1-maximal contribution (light colour). We call this matrix representation *Document-Topic matrix*, and the space defined by these vectors *Document-Topic space*.

97 The image was created by the author.
98 The image was created by the author.

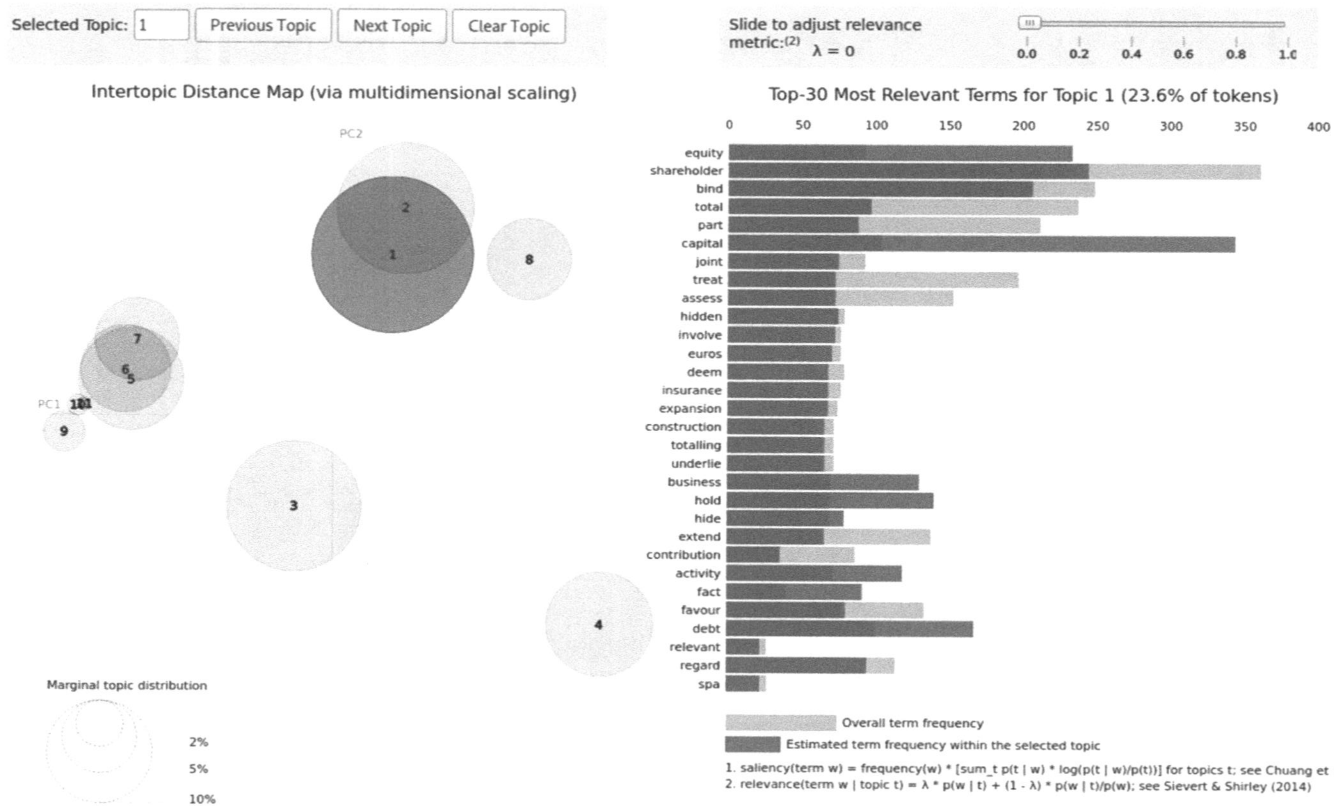

Figure 3.14 Visualization with pyLDAvis for the G-LDA model. On the left side, Intertopic Distances projected in a two-dimensional map by means of multidimensional scaling; on the right side, most salient topics in the model. The “relevance” metric has been reduced to show only discriminant terms in topic 1.

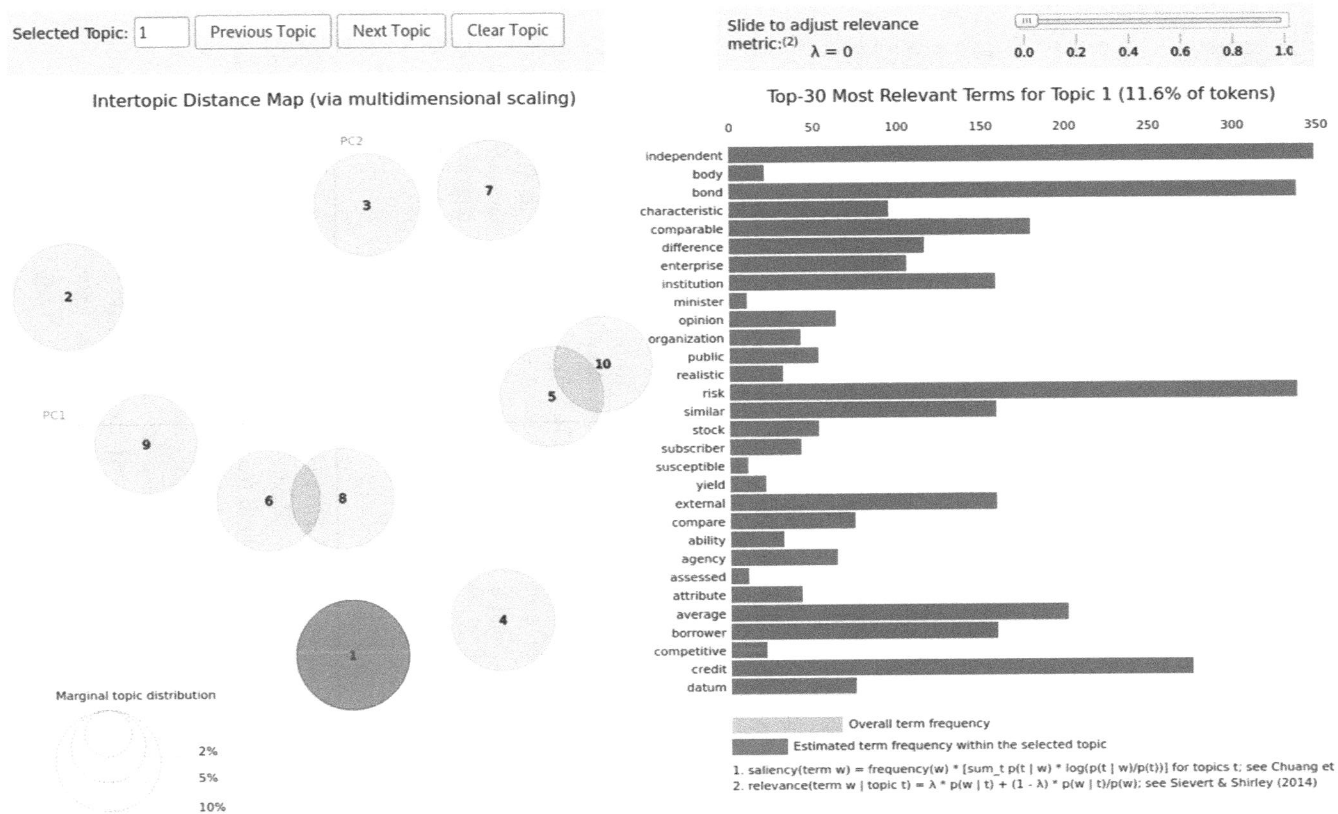

Figure 3.15 Visualization with pyLDAvis for the M-LDA model. On the left side, Intertopic Distances projected in a two-dimensional map by means of multidimensional scaling; on the right side, most salient topics in the model. The "relevance" metric has been reduced to show only discriminant terms in topic 1.

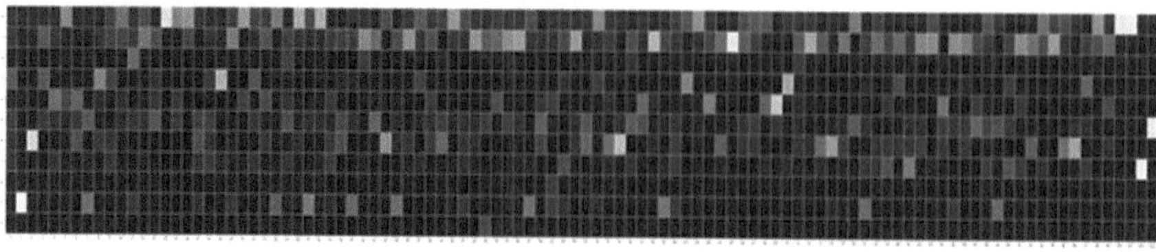

Figure 3.16 Document-Topic matrix of the G-LDA model. Documents of the Summary-DB represented as vectors in which features are topic contributions. Documents are columns and topics are rows. Colours follow a temperature scale from dark (0 value) to white (1 value).

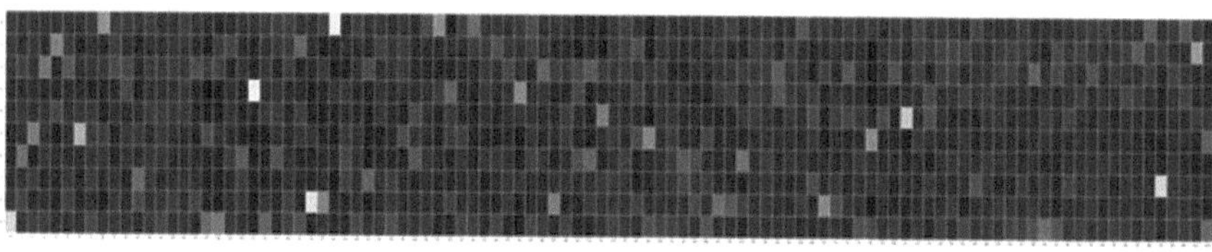

Figure 3.17 Document-Topic matrix of the M-LDA model. Documents of the Summary-DB represented as vectors in which features are topic contributions. Documents are columns and topics are rows. Colours follow a temperature scale from dark (0 value) to white (1 value).

When comparing Figure 3.16[99] and Figure 3.17,[100] one of the most striking aspects is the higher discriminant behaviour (lower entropy) of the G-LDA model, whereas topics in the M-LDA model seem to be present in more documents but with lower intensity (more entropy, less discriminant). A more discriminant and less entropic model is desired, but, as mentioned before, the tendency to create fewer clear topics must be due to the common context highly interrelated in the documents used.

4.4.1 Contextualization of topics

As explained earlier the general idea of the topic modeling and especially the LDA application, is that for every word in each document, the word frequency is counted and then the documents that have high frequencies of the same words are grouped together. Hence, just by looking at the words of a document, the topic can be detected, even if the actual message of the document doesn't come through. From the preceding models, 11 topics have been drawn from the 105 documents that are the base of the proof of concept developed. Each topic is related to ten keywords (relevant words and related word impact). To make the exercise more useful, that

99 The image was created by the author.
100 The image was created by the author.

is, identify what the topics are about to facilitate clarity for experts that among such documents certain themes are discussed, they have manually been contextualized (through the reading of the keywords of each topic a "differentiating title" has been found for each topic). To perform this exercise, the analysis of the "relevance metric" has been performed, that is, common words and discriminating words (these latter are exclusive word of a specific topic) to a given topic have been analysed in the two models. From this analysis the following titles have been allocated to each topic stemming from each model.

- Topics of the G-LDA model:

  Topic 1: Hidden capital distribution;
  Topic 2: Godwill amortization cost deduction;
  Topic 3: Credit rating and bond comparability yield;
  Topic 4: Interest rate of a loan provided by the parent company;
  Topic 5: Business restructuring;
  Topic 6: Branch funding;
  Topic 7: Tax assessment cash pooling arrangements;
  Topic 8: Arm's length intercompany interest rate;
  Topic 9: Determining the credit rating associated with the intercompany loan;
  Topic 10: Intangible and functions remuneration;
  Topic 11: Transfer pricing methods.

- Topics of the M-LDA model:

  Topic 1: Financial conditions in intercompany financing;
  Topic 2: Loan interest rates;
  Topic 3: Interest rate for share acquisition;
  Topic 4: Branch funding;
  Topic 5: Interest deduction allowance for intercompany loans;
  Topic 6: Proof of alternative means of financing;
  Topic 7: Appeal against tax authority tax assessment;
  Topic 8: License fee in an intercompany agreement;
  Topic 9: Arm's length in loan agreement between related parties;
  Topic 10: Creditworthiness in financial transactions.

It should be noted that this exercise could also be performed by the machine itself when implementing a proper algorithm but there would still be a need afterwards to perform a human analysis to be sure that the titles are really matching with the topic under discussion. Moreover, this manual exercise is even more important when, as in our case, the texts, object of the analysis, are too few and too similar to each other.

4.5 Searches and predictions based on topic similarity

In this section, we look at the resolutions of the most similar cases (i.e., the closest cases). In this way, we can try to predict the outcome of a resolution based on similar cases. Indeed, an expert can use both the models seen earlier to perform intelligent searches for similar documents based on the Document-Topic space.[101] The expert can also obtain an estimate of the norm, trend or expected value of any attribute in similar documents or those that are encompassed in the same topic. This is a very interesting application of the topic-modeling that can be highly helpful for law stakeholders. We have seen some examples before,[102] but we also see here some examples based on our proof-of-concept experiments.

For instance, considering that possible final resolutions of a given case are two: either the court decides in favour of the taxpayer, or the court decides in favour of the tax authorities. Given a case, we can search in our documents database similar cases in the past and try to predict the resolution-trend based on the topic. We label cases in favour of taxpayers with "1" and cases in favour of the tax authorities with "0".

We choose some random cases and check results in both models:

- Case "Norway vs Conocophillips Skandinavia AS"

—Case: norway vs conocophillips skandinavia as
Main topic: 3
Keywords: appeal, margin, gmbh, court, tax, value, decision, sas_edfi, conversion, share

101 It is the vector space created by representing the documents as vectors where the variables/features are topics. In the Document-topic map, it could be seen how far or close the documents are to each other.

102 Alarie, B., and Yan, C., Using Machine Learning to Evaluate the Existence of a Trade or Business: Olsen, *Tax Notes Federal*, 2022, p. 1231, Alarie, B., and Di Giandomenico, S., Timing Is Everything: The Step Transaction Doctrine in GSS Holdings, *Tax Notes Federal*, 2022, p. 1849, Alarie, B., and Gardhouse, K., The Debt-Equity Distinction and Tribune Media, *Tax Notes Federal*, 2022a, p. 593, Alarie, B., and Yan, C., Disguised Distributions and Management Fees: Aspro Revisited, *Tax Notes Federal*, 2022b, p. 1401, Alarie, B., and Xue Griffin, B., Reserve Mechanical: Microcaptive Insurance Arrangement Denied on Appeal, *Tax Notes Federal*, 2022a, p. 2037, Alarie, B., and Gardhouse, K., Situational Awareness: Accurate Financial Recordkeeping and Business Deductions, *Tax Notes Federal*, 2022b, p. 713, Alarie, B., and Condon, K., Deducting Legal Expenses: Unpacking the IRS's Appeal in Mylan, *Tax Notes Federal*, 2022, p. 1419, Alarie, B., and Griffin Xue, B., Tax Credits That Bond a Partnership: Revisiting Cross Refined Coal, *Tax Notes Federal*, 2022b, p. 2069, Alarie, B., and Yan, C., Chemoil: Economic Substance, Tax Credits, and Unprofitable Ventures, *Tax Notes Federal*, 2022c, p. 719, Alarie, B., and Velez, A., Cashaw: Conflicting Duties and the Trust Fund Recovery Penalty, *Tax Notes Federal*, 2022, p. 1257, Alarie, B., The Rise of the Robotic Tax Analyst, *Tax Notes Federal*, 2023, p. 57, Alarie, B., et al., Unbridled Losses: Harnessing Machine Learning for Tax Analysis, *Tax Notes Federal*, 2023, p. 637.

Tags: ["comparability factors", "cup method", "intra-group loan", "loan", "oil and gas"]
GT res: 0
P(res==1|topic): 0.3333333333333333
P(res==0|topic): 0.6666666666666667
Closest: (pos, ID, dom_topic, res) 0 norway vs conocophillips skandinavia as 3 0
Closest: (pos, ID, dom_topic, res) 1 norway vs petrolia noco as 3 0
Closest: (pos, ID, dom_topic, res) 2 germany vs "a investment gmbh" 5 0
Closest: (pos, ID, dom_topic, res) 3 denmark vs. codan forsikring a/s 3 1
Closest: (pos, ID, dom_topic, res) 4 poland vs "f-inance. sp. z o.o." 3 1

List 5. Case "Norway vs Conocophillips Skandinavia AS". Four closest cases and resolution prediction. Search based on the G-LDA model.

—Case: norway vs conocophillips skandinavia as
Main topic: 9
Keywords: interest, rate, loan, base, year, court, set, margin, high, claim
Tags: ["comparability factors", "cup method", "intra-group loan", "loan", "oil and gas"]
GT res: 0
P(res==1|topic): 0.38095238095238093
P(res==0|topic): 0.6190476190476191
Closest: (pos, ID, dom_topic, res) 0 norway vs conocophillips skandinavia as 9 0
Closest: (pos, ID, dom_topic, res) 1 germany vs "a investment gmbh" 9 0
Closest: (pos, ID, dom_topic, res) 2 australia vs. chevron australia holdings pty ltd 9 0
Closest: (pos, ID, dom_topic, res) 3 norway vs petrolia noco as 9 0
Closest: (pos, ID, dom_topic, res) 4 poland vs "shopping centre developer sp.k." 9 1

List 6. Case "Norway vs Conocophillips Skandinavia AS". Four closest cases and resolution preduction. Search based on the M-LDA model.

List 5 and List 6 show results for the G-LDA and M-LDA models respectively. In both cases, the first rows of the search show the "number of the dominant topic" in the model, the "keywords of the dominant topics" and the "Tags" associated to this document. The fourth row, named GT, shows the "resolution" of the case (i.e., 0, meaning that it was resolved in favour of the tax authorities). These first four rows are identical in both models. The fifth and the sixth rows show the probability of the resolution favouring the taxpayer (fifth row) and the probability of the resolution favouring the tax authority (sixth row) among cases that are dominated by the same topic. This is expressed as a conditional probability in Bayesian terms, pointing to the fact that knowing the dominant topic can have a determining effect on the probabilities. Note that, in a real-life working environment, we might be evaluating the possibilities of a case for which we do not yet have a resolution, estimating the possibilities simply based on the thematic similarity to other cases already evaluated in our database. It would not be strange to find that certain topics (here representing peculiarities common to certain cases) present a particular bias for reasons that are not obvious and that may prompt further investigation.

Coming back to the specific case, here the G-LDA model and the M-LDA model differ very slightly in the calculation of the result but estimate that the resolution tends to favour the tax authority in 67% and 62% of similar cases (respectively for the G-LDA and M-LDA model).

Rows 7 to 11 (named Closest) show the five most similar documents in our Summary-DB followed by the "dominant topic" and the "resolution", obviously being the first one the same case (this is added to keep a per-case evaluation of the model consistency). Note that the M-LDA model always shows cases with the same dominant topic (topic 9), while the G-LDA model shows a case that belongs mostly to another dominant topic (topic 5). This is possible (although ideally not desirable) since membership in topics is not exclusive, but diffuse; that is, a document may participate to a greater or lesser extent in different topics. In any case, both documents coincide in ranking the same two documents (i.e., the Germany vs "A Investment Gmbh" and the Norway vs Petrolia Noco AS cases) among the four most similar options to the case under analysis.

- Case "Netherlands vs Zinc Smelter B.V."

—Case: netherlands vs zinc smelter b.v.
Main topic: 1
Keywords: loan, tax, authority, capital, issue, income, shareholder, equity, bind, interest
Tags: ["burden of proof (onus)", "business restructuring", "cost plus method", "exit taxation", "pre- and post restructuring result", "pre-existing intangibles", "profit split method", "switzerland"]
GT res: 0
P(res=1|topic): 0.45161290322580644
P(res=0|topic): 0.5483870967741935
Closest: (pos, ID, dom_topic, res) 0 netherlands vs zinc smelter b.v. 1 0
Closest: (pos, ID, dom_topic, res) 1 netherlands vs corp 1 0
Closest: (pos, ID, dom_topic, res) 2 greece vs "sh loan ltd" 1 0
Closest: (pos, ID, dom_topic, res) 3 peru vs "holding s.a." 1 1
Closest: (pos, ID, dom_topic, res) 4 italy vs sgl carbon spa 5 0

List 7. Case "Netherlands vs Zinc Smelter B.V." Four closest cases and resolution preduction. Search based on the G-LDA model.

—Case: netherlands vs zinc smelter b.v.
Main topic: 2
Keywords: tax, appeal, authority, assessment, file, issue, court, arm_length, profit, determine

Tags: ["burden of proof (onus)", "business restructuring", "cost plus method", "exit taxation", "pre- and post restructuring result", "pre-existing intangibles", "profit split method", "switzerland"]
GT res: 0
P(res=1|topic): 0.4
P(res=0|topic): 0.6
Closest: (pos, ID, dom_topic, res) 0 netherlands vs zinc smelter b.v. 2 0
Closest: (pos, ID, dom_topic, res) 1 el salvador vs corp 2 0
Closest: (pos, ID, dom_topic, res) 2 korea vs "k-gas corp" 2 0
Closest: (pos, ID, dom_topic, res) 3 netherlands vs "agri b.v." 2 0
Closest: (pos, ID, dom_topic, res) 4 spain vs universal pictures international spain sl 2 1

List 8. Case "Netherlands vs Zinc Smelter B.V." Four closest cases and resolution prediction. Search based on the M-LDA model.

For this second case, again both models coincide in resolutions favouring the tax authority with a similar probability between documents of the same topic (55% and 60% for the G-LDA and M-LDA models respectively). However, the closest documents according to each of the models differ, with no match being found on this occasion. The M-LDA models seems to be more consistent when finding that similar documents share the same dominant topic.

- Case "France vs Sté Stryker Spine"

—Case: france vs sté stryker spine
Main topic: 4
Keywords: company, south, transaction, value, make, article, case, consider, provision, consideration
Tags: ["intra-group loan", "loan"]
GT res: 1
P(res=1|topic): 0.875
P(res=0|topic): 0.125
Closest: (pos, ID, dom_topic, res) 0 france vs sté stryker spine 4 1
Closest: (pos, ID, dom_topic, res) 1 france vs general electric france 4 1
Closest: (pos, ID, dom_topic, res) 2 france vs bsa finances 4 1
Closest: (pos, ID, dom_topic, res) 3 denmark vs. swiss re. 4 0
Closest: (pos, ID, dom_topic, res) 4 italy vs pdm d srl 4 1

List 9. Case "France vs Sté Stryker Spine". Four closest cases and resolution prediction. Search based on the G-LDA model.

—Case: france vs sté stryker spine
Main topic: 3

Keywords: case, company, tax, price, subsidiary, expense, increase, assessment, paragraph, transfer_pricing
Tags: [“intra-group loan”, “loan”]
GT res: 1
P(res=1|topic): 0.6666666666666666
P(res=0|topic): 0.33333333333333337
Closest: (pos, ID, dom_topic, res) 0 france vs sté stryker spine 3 1
Closest: (pos, ID, dom_topic, res) 1 russia vs continental tires rus llc 3 0
Closest: (pos, ID, dom_topic, res) 2 portugal vs “welding mesh sa” 0 1
Closest: (pos, ID, dom_topic, res) 3 netherlands vs “agri b.v.” 2 0
Closest: (pos, ID, dom_topic, res) 4 greece vs cypriot company ltd. 1 0

List 10. Case “France vs Sté Stryker Spine”. Four closest cases and resolution preduction. Search based on the M-LDA model.

Again, in this third example, both models show a bias coinciding with the resolution in question. In this case, the document resolution, also preferred in both topics of both models (88% and 67% for G-LDA and M-LDA respectively) favours the taxpayer. Note that this time it is the G-LDA model that finds the most similar cases within the same topic, while the M-LDA model diverges in this respect.

- Case “Italy vs Edison S.P.A.”

—Case: italy vs edison s.p.a.
Main topic: 1
Keywords: loan, tax, authority, capital, issue, income, shareholder, equity, bind, interest
Tags: [“burden of proof (onus)”, “ delineation”, “ delineation—substance over form”, “ equity or debt/loan”, “ interest free loan”, “ intra-group loan”, “ loan”, “ luxembourg”, “ non-interest-bearing loan”, “ shareholder loan”]
GT res: 0
P(res=1|topic): 0.45161290322580644
P(res=0|topic): 0.5483870967741935
Closest: (pos, ID, dom_topic, res) 0 italy vs edison s.p.a. 1 0
Closest: (pos, ID, dom_topic, res) 1 russia vs continental tires rus llc 1 0
Closest: (pos, ID, dom_topic, res) 2 norway vs. statoil angola 6 1
Closest: (pos, ID, dom_topic, res) 3 peru vs. perupetro 1 1
Closest: (pos, ID, dom_topic, res) 4 austria vs shareholder 1 1

List 11. Case “Italy vs Edison S.P.A.” Four closest cases and resolution preduction. Search based on the G-LDA model.

—Case: italy vs edison s.p.a.
Main topic: 1

Keywords: loan, agreement, party, income, authority, capital, provision, shareholder, arm_length, agree
Tags: ["burden of proof (onus)", " delineation", " delineation—substance over form", " equity or debt/loan", " interest free loan", " intra-group loan", " loan", " luxembourg", " non-interest-bearing loan", " shareholder loan"]
GT res: 0
P(res=1|topic): 0.23076923076923078
P(res=0|topic): 0.7692307692307692
Closest: (pos, ID, dom_topic, res) 0 italy vs edison s.p.a. 1 0
Closest: (pos, ID, dom_topic, res) 1 italy vs pompea s.p.a. 3 1
Closest: (pos, ID, dom_topic, res) 2 russia vs continental tires rus llc 3 0
Closest: (pos, ID, dom_topic, res) 3 greece vs "lender corp" 1 0
Closest: (pos, ID, dom_topic, res) 4 netherlands vs x b.v. 0 1

List 12. Case "Italy vs Edison S.P.A." Four closest cases and resolution preduction. Search based on the M-LDA model.

Again, in this fourth and last example, we can see that both models show a bias in the resolution within the group established by the dominant topic (55% and 77% for the G-LDA and M-LDA models respectively), which in this case favours the tax authority. At least one of the documents (the case "Russia vs Continental Tires RUS LLC") is shown in both models within the group of those most similar to the case under exploration.

It should be noted that, in our examples, the fact that the trends in resolutions within the documents grouped by the dominant topic coincide with the resolution of the document under analysis is an accidental fact. The opposite can and often does happen. In the same way, a document X grouped by dominant topic A in the G-LDA model could show an inverse trend to that of the dominant topic B of the M-LDA model to which document X belongs. This can and does happen. However, despite these possible drifts in our experiments, it is important to highlight the value of this proof of concept based only and simply on small excerpts of a couple of paragraphs on summaries of real court cases on a collection of only 105 cases. To sum up, the concept of proof here performed in the prediction of results demonstrates that the machine can help in grouping the cases that are more similar and that have been solved the same way, but this could be seen as a coincidence as also happens in real life when humans use precedents to try to solve future cases that have similar features. Indeed, in our experiments (which use very little information and documents) the fact that two cases are similar according to our model does not mean that they will get the same result/resolution (i.e., future cases that can be categorized under a common group by the machine, having similar features, can still be decided differently).

5 Summary

The experiments performed here as a simple game or approximation show the great potential that modern ML techniques have if applied on a relatively large corpus of documents and on the entire resolution documents. Not only as a replacement or aid to human inspection in aspects related to the indexing, the hierarchical organization and the establishment of taxonomies and interconnections of legal texts, but also in intelligent support in searches for similar cases, as well as in the detection of potential biases that could be due to flaws, blind spots or biased aspects of the laws or how they are applied. The extraction of topics is cross-cutting and intrinsically multi-perspective, that is, it is capable of being a source of hypotheses and conjectures that humans have not considered, as well as an effective way to evaluate hypotheses and conjectures that the expert has assessed or observed. At the same time, is also a powerful tool for prognosis.

In the first instance we have identified documents with mixture of topics, and where each topic is characterized by a distribution over words. Through the LDA algorithm, we have used such document collection as the initial input being each document represented as a bag-of-words (which is a vector of word frequencies or binary word indicators). Considering that LDA is based on the assumption that documents exhibit multiple topics, and each topic consists of a set of words that are more likely to co-occur (i.e., LDA enables the discovery of latent thematic structures in a collection of documents), a number of parameters has been provided (i.e., the number of topic as the basis to identify when more similarities among the documents are identified, i.e., more clear clusters are formed). Given such elements, the algorithm has been trained. The latter has randomly assigned each word in each document to a topic and in order to find the high percentage of convergence of the words in the documents the following steps have been iterated. For each word in each document: (i) the probability of the word belonging to each topic has been computed based on the current assignments and the overall topic-word distribution, (ii) reassigning the word to a new topic based on these probabilities, (iii) update the topic-word distribution and document-topic distribution based on the new assignments. From these iterated steps the following outputs have been generated: (i) topic-word distribution, where each topic has been represented as a distribution over words, hence being able to show the likelihood of each word occurring in a particular topic, and (ii) a document-topic distribution, where each document is represented as a distribution over topics. This distribution indicates the contribution of each topic to a given document, allowing us to interpret and analyse the resulting topics and their relationship to the original documents.

After this first analysis, a manual activity has been performed to identify which title could be attributed to each topic, with the aim to make it easier for the experts to understand which argument they could find in the proposal set of documents. If from one side this exercise can also be performed by the machine itself if provided a proper algorithm, it should be pointed out that a manual review will always be requested to avoid/reduce bias risks of misinterpretation. Moreover, a manual exercise will always be of help in cases where documents are too few and the themes too close to each other. Therefore, if we consider the MAPs/Arbitration decisions (if available), the eventual use of ML will always require human intervention in the interpretation when too many cases having the same topics are objects of the machine analysis.

This tool grants the possibility to definitely reduce the amount of time to search among tons of documents as the machine itself is able to cluster them already. This could be considered a first step in the document analysis, as it helps to make an initial skim. It could be seen as a time saving according to the fact that tax administrations or arbitrators (in the MAP procedures) could use an already identified number of cases to help perform their final decision of the case. This first analysis could even be improved by performing intelligent searches for similar documents based on the Document-Topic space, obtaining an estimate of the norm, trend or expected value of any attribute in similar documents or those that are encompassed in the same topic. Indeed, in the model it has been identified the probability that a case has a resolution in favour of the taxpayer or the tax authorities. This exercise, as described, can be of great help to group cases, according to common features, under the same final decision but it will still be considered that, even if the machine can help in doing that, it is not automatic to think that future cases or also past cases (if not inserted in the basket of documents to be analysed) will be or were decided the same way. Hence a proper further analysis to skim the documents should still be performed manually.

In our example, after setting manually per each document (i.e., court decision) who has obtained the favourable decision of the court, that is, taxpayer or tax administration, it has been shown how the machine can itself identify how the court decided and which are the related documents (out of the overall set provided initially to the machine) that have similarities with such sample decision. This could definitely be seen as a strong help in the rule of precedence, hence, to identify documents that have similarities in relation to the one that has to be decided.

However, notwithstanding the percentage of matches that are quite high, that is, the machine can identify who won in the previous cases, as showed in the previous paragraph, it should be noted that, even if this could be seen as a great help, human intervention is always needed and required. Indeed, it could always be the case that certain topics (representing peculiarities common to certain cases) present a particular bias for reasons that the machine itself cannot understand (i.e., is not obvious to the machine according to the parameters given), hence, further investigation is required. Human language is ambiguous and a false interpretation of it or of the commands given could be dangeroud for human beings.[103]

Indeed, the fact that a machine immediately provides a set of documents out of a myriad of documents should not lead automatically that this are always the perfect

103 Signorelli, A. D., È possibile dare i nostri valori a un'intelligenza artificiale?, *La Repubblica*, 8 Agosto 2023 (accessed 8 August 2023).

match for the resolution of a new case and other subjective factors/elements still need to be analysed as they probably were not part of the previous cases.

Lastly, it is important to mention that one of the most important elements in performing such machine experiments is the data availability, which should be quite extensive and of good quality. Indeed, this last chapter should be intended as a proof of concept, in other words, food for thought of the possibility to extend the use of ML to the MAP procedure but remembering that, at least at the OECD level, the document availability is missing, and it doesn't seem to be foreseen. At the EU level such a problem seems to be eliminated due to the obligation to publish the details of the decisions online. However, being this obligation only recently included by the Council Directive 2017/1852 the possibility to have enough data available could last some years.

To conclude, it could be inferred from this experiment that machines need to be fed with a great amount of data of a certain quality to be able to achieve better performance. Consequently, to take advantage of such technology a great level of transparency is needed, otherwise no achievements could be obtained in the next years. Such transparency should always safeguard the taxpayers' rights in a way not to jeopardize rights such as privacy or reputation. Therefore, as already discussed in Chapter 4 of this work, proper regulations should accompany the data availability. Indeed, it is still missing a so-called AI alignment where artificial intelligence is aligned with the values of human beings with the consequence that when an AI systems are left alone with the decision, or the decision is fully linked to the outcome of the AI system itself, there is a serious risk to jeopardize human rights.[104]

104 Signorelli, A. D., È possibile dare i nostri valori a un'intelligenza artificiale?, *La Repubblica*, 8 Agosto 2023 (accessed 8 August 2023) and Mitchell, M., What Does It Mean to Align AI With Human Values?, *Quantamagazine*, 13 December 2023. See also Gonfalonieri, A., Inverse Reinforcement Learning, *Towards Data Science*, 26 December 2018, available at I https://towardsdatascience.com/inverse-reinforcement-learning-6453b7cdc90d#:~:text=Inverse%20reinforcement%20learning%20(IRL)%20is,rewards%20by%20observing%20its%20behavior.

4 Conclusions

1 Double taxation: challenges and unresolved disputes

The issue of double taxation, whether legal or economic, not only causes difficulties in economic development and trade, but, once it occurs, generates increased costs for taxpayers, who will have to engage with the different tax administrations to find a solution or reach an agreement to eliminate or limit the effects of double taxation.

The issue is very relevant because, even if tax aspects should not be the reason for making an investment, they predominantly affect trade patterns. Consequently, the uncertainty of tax rules can influence decisions on where and how to invest as well as the tendency of countries to be cooperative with the needs of companies. This is particularly important when it comes to dispute settlement, which in practice ends up influencing companies' decisions on whether to invest in a country.

Therefore, there is a need for certainty between the parties that are involved in the tax collection, where taxpayers need not see taxes as a burdensome aspect while tax administrations need to invest their resources where they are really needed while gaining the right amount of taxes to be paid. Hence there is a need to build a cooperative relationship between these two subjects.

Indeed, the litigation phase, independently if at national or international levels, could cost years of uncertainty and affect the business of taxpayers that need to constantly set up provisions to cover possible future tax costs.

With the intention to achieve a better relationship between taxpayers and tax authorities, a cooperative compliance scheme has been built to create a cooperative environment. Such a scheme provides a series of instruments aiming at preventing disputes. Among these instruments some bring tax certainty (bilateral/multilateral APA, Simultaneous/Joint Audits) while others bring comfort in the relationship between the parties (Multilateral Risk Assessment—ICAP). The bilateral/multilateral set-up of such instruments can create a more favourable tax environment as it encompasses a wider number of subjects, whereas the unilateral measures provided by one state only could not achieve the expected tax certainty.

However, even if many instruments are at the disposal of the taxpayers/tax authorities there are many aspects that prevent their use or a positive outcome. In many cases, excessive costs, lengths of time and insecurity on the reaction of the

DOI: 10.4324/9781003599814-4

counterparty when proposing the start of the process (especially from a taxpayer point of view) limit or reduce the flourishing use of these systems and the persistence of situations of uncertainty and double taxation.

Both domestic remedies, which often fail to resolve double taxation on their own, and the shortcomings of the mutual agreement procedure mechanisms have demonstrated the need to find complementary methods that can assist in the resolution of international disputes. To support international tax dispute resolution, arbitration has been identified as a suitable method, even if improvements are needed for it to become optimal. It should however be noticed that, at the procedural level, in both the MAP and arbitration phases (both at international and EU level), shortcomings continue to exist that undermine the success of the processes. Indeed, despite the multitude of existing instruments at the international level to resolve international tax disputes, there is still uncertainty when bringing double taxation cases before the bodies designated to resolve them. In practice, multinational groups, when performing their internal evaluations about the possible resolution of disputes by the means currently available, are often not confident that the cases will be resolved or think that the time/costs needed for a possible solution may affect the smooth running of their businesses, thus opting for negotiation solutions with the authorities.

2 Artificial intelligence: common application, ethical issues and analogies in the disputes field

The change caused by new technologies make it important for our society to help daily activities while granting, among other things, a high task efficiency. This means reducing, when possible, the amount of time that humans need to dedicate to their jobs or increasing the possibility to have better cures against a wider range of illnesses, preventing the onset of diseases, or the possibility of accessing a mass culture.

However, the motor of these new disruptive technologies is still the human being, meaning people are needed to make AI work in a proper and to continue developing new systems. Indeed, computers are still considered to be plain machines, whereas AI, even if encompassing the term "intelligence", is a superficial approach of algorithms that are imagined and built by human minds.

The ongoing relationship between humans and machines shows that the functioning of these systems and models needs to be analysed not only from a mere technical point of view but also according to the way these can be controlled and the responsibilities that derive both at social and ethic levels when the existing and the new technologies become part of our society (considering that the algorithms receive, at least at an initial stage, inputs from humans).

Tax law and law in general has a strong argumentative element that could not be reduced to an analytic science. When putting together the scope of law and the application of AI we see that machines and computation systems do perform certain functions that provide certain benefits such as memory or logic induction compared to humans, but it would be necessary to separate positive law and the activities connected to it with the mere prediction which is not the aim of legal activity.

Legal reasoning is a complex activity. In the field of law, including tax law, when dealing with the decision functions performed by the courts and other decision bodies, such as the arbitration courts or the arbitration commissions, the implementation of AI systems has reached a supportive role, but still leaves the central functions for the final decision to humans. The role of AI and ML systems can find a substantive place when dealing with operational tax activities, such as those performed by the tax administrations and the tax departments among which the TP function.

Moreover, it is important to bear in mind that the use of AI systems and ML algorithms should be performed with respect for human rights, with the need to increase work on ethical discussion as a basis for further preparing, in a second phase, legal rules that will be binding on the whole society allowing their application by governments and the judicial system. It needs to be decided whether humanity wants to govern technology or if humanity wants to be governed by the technology.

3 Practical applications to AI to the (tax) law decision process field

The experiments performed with the aim of being a mere proof of concept or approximation show the great potential that modern ML techniques have if applied on a relatively large corpus of documents and on the entire body of resolution documents. Not only as a replacement or aid to human inspection in aspects related to the indexing, the hierarchical organization and the establishment of taxonomies and interconnections of legal texts but also in intelligent support in searches for similar cases, as well as in the detection of potential biases that could be due to flaws, blind spots or biased aspects. The extraction of topics is cross-cutting and intrinsically multi-perspective, that is, it is capable of being a source of hypotheses and conjectures that humans have not considered, as well as an effective way to evaluate hypotheses and conjectures that the expert has assessed or observed. At the same time, is also a powerful tool for prediction.

However, topic-modeling and machine learning solutions should not be regarded as the sacred grail. Indeed, we should consider that an overexcitement could bring us to overestimate the effect of a technology in the short run and underestimate the effect in the long run (Amara's Law). Do not forget that currently machines neither have the knowledge related to a specific topic, nor are they able to understand or make use of common sense.

The experiments themselves demonstrate the ability of machines to operate words' connections, however not being able to perform a proper semantic analysis that, instead remain in the hands of humans (i.e., judges, (tax) law experts, arbitrators). It is a matter of fact that machines are lacking a connection with reality, hence they remain locked in mere word analysis. Human beings, on the other hand, can associate what is written in a given text to reality; they link a text to something that is meaningful in reality.

Prediction from a set of documents has nothing to do with bringing language into reality, or otherwise said, one thing is the format of the language and the other is its functionality in society. Reasoning on the words cannot be easily replicated by applying a mere formal/statistical logic. Indeed, from the experiment it is inferred that it is one thing to speed up the work to assemble texts that are similar to each other, that is, they speak about the same argument, or the decisions are grouped together by arguments and winning party, but it is another to see how the outcome of such documents can be grounded in reality (i.e., the case to be decided).

Moreover, even if it can be argued that more data could produce a better result as the machine is fed with more fuel to work with, the incapability of the machines to reason will remain and eventually only clearer results on the still past documents will be achieved, but the interpretation of such outcomes will remain on the human beings' shoulders.

Indeed, the experiments showed that notwithstanding the percentage of matches being quite high, that is, the machine identifying who won in the previous cases, even so, human intervention is always needed and required. Indeed, it could always be the case that certain topics (representing peculiarities common to certain cases) present a particular bias for reasons that the machine itself cannot understand (i.e., is not obvious to the machine according to the parameters given), hence, further investigation is required. Indeed, the fact that a machine immediately provides a set of documents out of a myriad of documents should not get to the automatic conclusion that these are always the perfect solution for solving a new case and that it is still necessary to analyse other subjective factors/elements that were probably not part of the previous cases.

References

Abdelrazek, A., et al.: "Topic Modeling Algorithms and Applications: A Survey", *Information Systems*, Vol. 112, 2022.

Abdi, H. and Williams, L. J.: "Principal Component Analysis. Wiley Interdisciplinary Reviews", *Computational Statistics*, Vol. 2(4), 2010.

Abedin, M. Z., et al.: "Tax Default Prediction Using Feature Transformation-Based Machine Learning". *IEEE Access*, Vol. 9, 2020.

Access Now.: *Mapping Regulatory Proposal for Artificial Intelligence in Europe*, 2018, available at https://www.icnl.org/wp-content/uploads/mapping_regulatory_proposals_for_AI_in_EU.pdf.

Aghemo, R.: "Algoritmi e discriminazione: non veridicità della neutralità tecnologica", *Medium Blog*, 2021.

Akansu, A. N.: "The Flash Crash: A Review", *Journal of Capital Markets Studies*, Vol. 1(1), 2017.

Aker, C. and Kalkan, S.: "Using Deep Networks for Drone Detection", in *14th IEEE International Conference on Advanced Video and Signal Based Surveillance (AVSS)*, 2017, available at https://www.semanticscholar.org/paper/Using-deep-networks-for-drone-detection-Aker-Kalkan/64fcde870588026b026b16875fdad67df77d10f9.

Akinbo, R. S. and Daramola, O. A.: *Chapter 4—Ensemble ML Algorithms for Prediction and Classification of Medical Images*, IntechOpen Book Series, edited by Jaydip Sen, Vol. 7, 2021.

Alaire, B., et al.: "The Path of the Law: Towards Legal Singularity", *The University of Toronto Law Journal*, Vol. 66(4), 2016.

Alaire, B., et al.: "The Rise of the Robotic Tax Analyst", *Tax Notes Federal*, Vol. 178(1), 2023.

Alaire, B., et al.: "Unbridled Losses: Harnessing Machine Learning for Tax Analysis", *Tax Notes Federal*, 2023, p. 637.

Alaire, B., et al.: *Using Machine Learning to Predict Outcomes in Tax Law*, SSRN, 2017, available at SSRN: https://papers.ssrn.com/sol3/papers.cfm?abstract_id=2855977.

Alaire, B. and Condon, K.: "Deducting Legal Expenses: Unpacking the IRS's Appeal in Mylan", *Tax Notes Federal*, 2022, p. 1419.

Alaire, B. and Gardhouse, K.: "The Debt-Equity Distinction and Tribune Media", *Tax Notes Federal*, 2022a, p. 593.

Alaire, B. and Gardhouse, K.: "Situational Awareness: Accurate Financial Recordkeeping and Business Deductions", *Tax Notes Federal*, 2022b, p. 713.

Alaire, B. and Velez, A.: "Cashaw: Conflicting Duties and the Trust Fund Recovery Penalty", *Tax Notes Federal*, 2022, p. 1257.

Alaire, B. and Xue Griffin, B.: "Reserve Mechanical: Microcaptive Insurance Arrangement Denied on Appeal", *Tax Notes Federal*, 2022a, p. 2037.

Alaire, B. and Xue Griffin, B.: "Tax Credits That Bond a Partnership: Revisiting Cross Refined Coal", *Tax Notes Federal*, 2022b, p. 2069.

Alaire, B. and Yan, C.: "Chemoil: Economic Substance, Tax Credits, and Unprofitable Ventures", *Tax Notes Federal*, 2022c, p. 719.

Alaire, B. and Yan, C.: "Disguised Distributions and Management Fees: Aspro Revisited", *Tax Notes Federal*, 2022b, p. 1401.

Alaire, B. and Yan, C.: "Using Machine Learning to Evaluate the Existence of a Trade or Business: Olsen", *Tax Notes Federal*, 2022a, p. 1231.

Aletras, N., et al.: "Predicting Judicial Decisions of the European Court of Human Rights: A Natural Language Processing Perspective", *PeerJ Computer Science*, Vol. 2(2), 2016.

Aleven, V.: *Teaching Case-Based Argumentation through a Model and Examples*, Ph.D. Dissertation, University of Pittsburgh, 1997.

Aleven, V. and Ashley, K. D.: "Doing Things with Factors", *ICAIL '95: Proceedings of the 5th International Conference on AI and Law*, May 1995.

Alikhademi, K., et al.: *A Review of Predictive Policing from the Perspective of Fairness*, Springer, 2021.

Alpaydin, E.: *Lecture Slides for—Introduction to ML*, Third edition, The MIT Press, 2014.

Alpaydin, E.: *Machine Learning*, The MIT, Press Essential Knowledge Series, 2016.

Altman, Z.: *Dispute Resolution under Tax Treaties*, Chapter 5: Current Procedures and the need for change, On-Line Books IBFD, 2005.

Amnesty International: "Artificial Intelligence for Good", 2017, available at https://www.amnesty.org/en/latest/news/2017/06/artificial-intelligence-for-good/.

Amodei, D., et al.: "Concrete Problems in AI Safety", *arXiv*, 2016.

Anderson, M. and Leigh Anderson, S.: "Machine Ethics: Creating an Ethical Intelligent Agent", *AI Magazine*, Vol. 28(4), 2007.

Andrade, F., et al.: "Contracting Agents: Legal Personality and Representation", *Artificial Intelligence and Law*, Vol. 15(4), 2007.

Andreessen, M.: "Why Software Is Eating the World", *Wall Street Journal*, 2011, available at https://www.wsj.com/articles/SB10001424053111903480904576512250915629460.

Andreotta, A. J.: "The Hard Problem of AI Rights", *AI and Society*, Vol. 36(1), 2021.

Angwin, J., et al.: *Machine Bias: There's Software Used Across the Country to Predict Future Criminals. And It's Biased Against Blacks*, ProPublica, 2016.

Ankerst, M., et al.: "OPTICS: Ordering Points to Identify the Clustering Structure", *ACM Sigmod Record*, Vol. 28(2), 1999.

Antón, R. G.: "The 21st Century Multilateralism in International Taxation: The Emperor's New Clothes? ", *World Tax Journal*, Vol. 8(2), 2016.

Ash, E.: "The Making of International Tax Law: Empirical Evidence from Natural Language Processing", UC Irvine School of Law Research Paper No. 2019-02, 2019.

Ashley, K. D.: "An AI Model of Case-Based Legal Argument from a Jurisprudential Viewpoint", *Artificial and Law*, Vol. 10(1–3), 2002.

Ashley, K. D.: "Brief History of the Changing Roles of Case Prediction in AI and Law", *Law in Context*, Vol. 36(1), 2019.

Ashley, K. D.: "Reasoning with Cases and Hypotheticals in HYPO", *International Journal of Man-Machine Studies*, Vol. 34(6), 1991.

Astobiza Monasterio, A.: "Ética algorítmica: Implicaciones éticas de una sociedad cada vez más gobernada por algoritmos", *Dilemata*, Vol. 9(24), 2017.

Atkinson, K., et al.: "Toward Artificial Argumentation", *AI Magazine*, Vol. 38(3), 2017.

Ault, H. J.: "Improving the Resolution of International Tax Disputes", *Florida Tax Review*, Vol. 7(3), 2005.

Ault, H. J. and Sasseville, J.: "2008 OECD Model: The New Arbitration Provision", *Bulletin International Taxation*, Vol. 63(5), 2009.

Avery Jones, J. F.: *Arbitration and Publication of Decisions, International Arbitration in Tax Matters*, edited by Michael Lang and Jeffrey Owens, IBFD, 2015.

Baeldung: "What is the Difference Between Labeled and Unlabeled Data?", *Baeldung, Blog*, 5 May 2023.
Bagaria, S.: "The Nature and Purposes of Double Taxation Agreements and the Issues Which the Interpretation of Such Agreements May Give Rise", 2012, available at https://papers.ssrn.com/sol3/papers.cfm?abstract_id=2018859.
Balakrishnan, V., and Lloyd-Yemoh, E.: "Stemming and Lemmatization: A Comparison of Retrieval Performances", *Lecture Notes on Software Engineering*, Vol. 2(3), 2014.
Bantekas, I.: "The Mutual Agreement Procedure and Arbitration of Double Taxation Disputes", *ACDI, Bogotá, ACDI—Anuario Colombiano de Derecho Internacional*, Vol. 1, 2008.
Barbaro, C.: "The European Ethical Charter of the CEPEJ on the use of Artificial Intelligence (AI) in Judicial Systems and Their Environment", *European Expertise & Expert Institute (EEEI)*, 2019.
Barberá, P.: *Tweeting the Revolution: Social Media Use and the #Euromaidan Protests*, Huffpost, 2014.
Barmentlo, D. and Kraan, P.: "Safeguarding Taxpayer Rights", in *CFE Tax Advisers Europe 60th Anniversary—Liber Amicorum—Part II: Limits to Tax Jurisdiction and Taxpayer Rights*, edited by Servaas van Thiel, Piergiorgio Valente and Stella Raventós-Calvo, IBFD, 2019.
Barreno, M., et al.: "The Security of Machine Learning", *Machine Learning*, Vol. 81(2), 2010.
Bärsch, S. E. and Engelen, C.: "Ausländische Safe-Harbour-Regelungen bei Verrechnungspreisen und Mitteilungspflichten für Verrechnungspreisgestaltungen (DAC6)", *Internationale Steuer Rundschau.—Köln*, Vol. 10(5), 2021.
Barto, A. G.: "Reinforcement Learning: Connections, Surprises, Challenges", *AI Magazine*, Vol. 40(1), 2019.
Barto, A. G. and Fragkiadaki, K.: *Deep Q Learning*, Carnegie Mellon University, 2018.
Bartosik, A. and Whittinghamb, H.: "Chapter 7—Evaluating Safety and Toxicity", in *The Era of AI, ML, and Data Science in the Pharmaceutical Industry*, edited by Stephanie Kay Ashenden, Elsevier Science Publishing Co Inc., 2021.
Başaranyavaşlar, F.: "Tax Transparency—Part II: Instruments of Transparency towards the Tax Administration—Chapter 3", in *General Report—Instruments of Transparency towards the Tax Administration*, Edited by Funda Başaran Yavaşlar, Johanna Hey, EATLP International Tax Series, 2019.
Basuschoudhary, A, et al.: *Machine-Learning Techniques in Economics—New Tools for Predicting Economic Growth*, Springer, 2017.
Baumann-Larsen, S. and Giannelli, A.: "The Latest Generation of Tax Functions and the Role of Technology", *Bulletin for International Taxation*, Vol. 74(10), 2020.
Been, K. and Finale, D. V.: "Machine Learning Techniques for Accountability", *AI Magazine*, Vol. 42(1), 2021.
Bell, K., et al.: "The Recon Approach: A New Direction for ML in Criminal Law", *Berkeley Technology Law Journal*, Vol. 37, 2021.
Bellenger, G.: "Entering the Era of the Digital Tax Agency", in *Intra-European Organisation of Tax Administrations, in Applying New Technologies and Digital Solutions in Tax Compliance*, IOTA, 2020.
Bench-Capon, T. J. M.: "Eveline T. Feteris: Fundamental of Legal Argumentation", *AI Law*, Vol. 26, 2018.
Bench-Capon, T. J. M.: "The Need for Good-Old Fashioned AI and Law. In International Trends in Legal Informatics", in *Festschrift for Erich Schweighofer*, edited by W. Hötzendorfer, C. Tschol and F. Kummer, Bern: Editions Weblaw, 2020, pp. 23–36. See also Burri, T., *International Law and Artificial Intelligence (October 27, 2017). German Yearbook of International Law 2017* (Vol. 60), Berlin: Duncker & Humblot, 2019.
Bench-Capon, T. J. M.: "Special Issue in Memory of Carole Hafner: Editor's Introduction", *AI Law*, Vol. 24, 2016.

Bench-Capon, T. J. M. and Dunne, P. E.: "Argumentation in Artificial Intelligence", *Artificial Intelligence*, Vol. 171(10–15), 2007.

Bench-Capon, T. J. M. and Modgil, S.: "Norms and Value-Based Reasoning: Justifying Compliance and Violation", *Artificial Intelligence and Law*, Vol. 25(1), 2017.

Bengtsson, E.: "Image Processing and Its Hardware Support Analysis vs Synthesis—Historical Trends", in *Lecture Notes in Computer Science*, edited by P. Sharma and F. Bianchi, Vol. 10269, Cham: Springer, Image Analysis. SCIA 2017.

Berbari, A.: "The OECD/G20 Base Erosion and Profit Shifting (BEPS) Initiative and the Multilateral Convention to Implement Tax Treaty Related Measures to Prevent BEPS", *Bulletin for International Taxation*, Vol. 71(10), 2017.

Beretta, G.: "La giurisdizione sul diniego di acceso alla procedura arbitrale in tema di transfer pricing", *il fisco*, Vol. 1, 2016.

Berge, E.: "Introducing Anomaly/Outlier Detection in Python with PyOD", *Blog*, 27 December 2021.

Berman, D. and Hafner, C. D.: "Incorporating Procedural Context Into a Model of Case-Based Legal Reasoning", in *ICAIL '91: Proceedings of the 3rd International Conference on AI and Law*, May 1991.

Berman, D. and Hafner, C. D.: "Representing Teleological Structure in Case-Based Legal Reasoning: The Missing Link", in *ICAIL '93: Proceedings of the 4th International Conference on AI and Law*, August 1993.

Berman, D. and Hafner, C. D.: "Understanding Precedents in a Temporal Context of Evolving Legal Doctrine", in *ICAIL '95: Proceedings of the 5th International Conference on AI and Law*, May 1995.

Bex, F. and Prakken, H.: "On the Relevance of Algorithm Decision Predictors for Judicial Decision Making", in *Proceedings of the Eighteenth International Conference on AI and Law*, ACM Press, 2021.

Bhadri Naarayanan, P., et al.: "Comparing the Performance of Anomaly Detection Algorithms", *International Journal of Engineering Research & Technology (IJERT)*, Vol. 9(2), 2020.

Bhatia, S., et al.: "Analysis of Credit Card Fraud Detection Techniques", *International Journal of Science and Research (IJSR)*, Vol. 5(3). 2016.

Bibal, A., et al.: "Legal Requirements on Explainability in Machine Learning", *Artificial Intelligence and Law*, Vol. 29(2), 2021.

Biçer, R.: "The Effectiveness of Mutual Agreement Procedures as a Means for Settling International Transfer Pricing Disputes", *International Transfer Pricing Journal*, Vol. 21(2), 2014, pp. 83–84.

Biedermann, A., et al.: "Normative Decision Analysis in Forensic Science", *AI and Law*, Vol. 28, 2020.

Biggio, B., et al.: "Poisoning Attacks Against Support Vector Machines", in *International Conference on Machine Learning (ICML 2012)*, 2012.

Bird, S., et al.: *Natural Language Processing with Python*, O'Reilly, 2009.

Blasch, E., et al.: "Methods of AI for Multimodal Sensing and Action for Complex Situations", *AI Magazine*, Vol. 40(4), 2019.

Blei, D. M., et al.: "Latent Dirichlet Allocation", *Journal of Machine Learning Research*, Vol. 3, 2003.

Boellstorff, T.: "Making Big Data, in Theory", *First Monday*, Vol. 18(10), 2013.

Bolasco, D. M., et al.: "Understanding Text Mining: A Pragmatic Approach", in *Knowledge Mining*, Heidelberg: Springer, 2005.

Bommarito, J. M., et al.: *LexNLP: Natural Language Processing and Information Extraction for Legal and Regulatory Texts*, SSNR, 2018, available at https://ssrn.com/abstract=3192101 or http://dx.doi.org/10.2139/ssrn.3192101.

Borana, J.: "Applications of AI & Associated Technologies", *IDL—International Digital Library of Educational Research*, Vol. 1(6), 2017.

Bostrom, N.: *Superintelligence: Paths, Dangers, Strategies*, Oxford: Oxford University Press, 2014.

Bower, L. and Buitrago, C. J.: *Machine Translation and Global Research: Towards Improved Machine Translation Literacy in the Scholar Community*, First edition, Bingley: Emerald Publishing, 2019.

Branting, L. K.: "Data-Centric and Logic-Based Models for Automated Legal Problem Solving", *AI Law*, Vol. 25, 2017.

Branting, L. K., et al.: "Scalable and Explainable Legal Prediction", *AI and Law*, Vol. 29, 2021.

Bravo, N.: "Interpreting Tax Treaties in the Light of Reservations and Opt-Ins under the Multilateral Instrument", *Bulletin for International Taxation*, Vol. 74(4/5), 2020.

Bravo, N. and Dozsa, M.: "A Multilateral Convention to Implement Amount A of Pillar One", *Kluwer Tax Blog*, Vol. 31.2, 2021.

Breiman, L.: "Random Forest", *ML*, Vol. 45(1), 2001.

Brodley, C. E., et al.: "Challenges and Opportunities in Applied ML", *AI Magazine*, Vol. 33(1), 2012.

Brundage, M. et al.: *The Malicious Use of Artificial Intelligence: Forecasting, Prevention, and Mitigation*, Report of the Workshop Entitled Bad Actor Risks in Artificial Intelligence, Oxford, 2018.

Bruneault, F. and Sabourinlafamme, A.: "AI Ethics: How can Information Ethics Provide a Framework to Avoid Usual Conceptual Pitfalls? An Overview", *AI & Society*, Vol. 36(3), 2021.

Brüninghaus, S.: "Automatically Classifying Case Texts and Predicting Outcomes", *AI and Law*, Vol. 17(2), 2009.

Brüninghaus, S. and Ashley, K. D.: "Predicting Outcomes of Case Based Legal Arguments", in *ICAIL '03: Proceedings of the 9th International Conference on AI and Law*, 2003.

Bryson, J. J.: "Robots Should Be Slaves", in *Close Engagements with Artificial Companions: Key Social, Psychological, Ethical and Design Issues*, edited by Yorick Wilks, Amsterdam: John Benjamins Publishing Company, 2010.

Bryson, J. J. and Theodorou, A.: "How Society Can Maintain Human-Centric Artificial Intelligence", in *Human-Centered Digitalization and Services*, edited by Marja Toivonen and Eveliina Saari, Springer, 2019.

Burkart, N. and Huber, M.: "A Survey on the Explainability of Supervised Machine Learning", *Journal of Artificial Intelligence Research*, Vol. 70, 2021.

Burke, R., et al.: "Recommender Systems: An Overview", *AI Magazine*, Vol. 32(3), 2011.

Burrell, J.: "How the Machine "Thinks": Understanding Opacity in Machine Learning Algorithms", *Big Data & Society*, Vol. 3(1), 2016.

Burton, E.: "Ethical Considerations in Artificial Intelligence Courses", *AI Magazine*, Vol. 38(2), 2017.

Cai, Q. and Malamis, S. E.: "Digitalizations of International Tax Disputes Resolution: Reflecting in Light of the Covid-19 Pandemic", *Intertax*, Vol. 49(8&9), 2021.

Calderón Carrero, J. M.: "El encuadramiento legal y límites del uso de herramientas de inteligencia artificial con fines de control fiscal", in *Estudios financieros. Revista de contabilidad y tributación: Comentarios, casos prácticos*, ISSN 1138-9540, n. 444, 2020.

Calderón Carrero, J. M. and Quintas Seara, A.: "Introducción al modelo del cumplimento tributario cooperativo: estudio de los trabajos de la OCDE y principales experiencias internacionales", *Revista Española de Derecho Financiero*, Vol. 167, 2015.

Calderón Carrero, J. M. and Ribeiro, J. S.: "Fighting Tax Fraud through Artificial Intelligence Tools: Will the Fundamental Rights of Taxpayers Survive the Digital Transformation of Tax Administrations?", *European Taxation*, Vol. 60(6), 2020.

Carabantes, M.: "Black-Box Artificial Intelligence: An Epistemological and Critical Analysis", *AI & Society*, Vol. 35(7), 2020.

Carli, C. C.: voce "Cooperazione Internazionale Tributaria", in *Enciclopedia Giuridica Treccani*, Vol. IX.

Castagna, S.: "Essential Elements of Taxation—Investment Protection and Dispute Settlement", in *International Arbitration and EU Law*, edited by José R. Mata Dona and Nikos Lavranos, Elgar Arbitration Law and Practice Series, 2021.
Castellano, P. S.: "Inteligencia Artificial Y Valoración de la Prueba: las Grantías Jurídico-Constitucionales del Órgano de Control", *THĚMIS-Revista de Derecho*, Vol. 79, 2021.
Cath, C.: "Governing Artificial Intelligence: Ethical, Legal and Technical Opportunities and Challenges", *Philosophical Transactions Royal Society A*, Vol. 376(2133), 2018.
Cerioni, L.: "The Commission's Proposal for a Directive on Double Taxation Dispute Resolution Mechanisms: Overcoming the Final Hurdle of Juridical Double Taxation within the European", *European Taxation*, Vol. 57(5), 2017.
CFE—Fiscal Committee.: "Opinion Statement FC 15/2014 on Developing a Multilateral Instrument to Modify Bilateral Tax Treaties", *European Taxation*, Vol. 55(4), 2015.
CFE—Fiscal Committee.: "Opinion Statement FC 4/2017 on the Proposed Directive on Double Taxation Dispute Resolution Mechanisms in the European Union", *European Taxation*, Vol. 57(8), 2017.
Chatila, R. et al.: *Trustworthy AI, in Reflections on Artificial Intelligence for Humanity*, edited by Bertrand Braunschweig and Malik Ghallab, Springer, 2021.
Cheng, L.: "Socially Responsible AI Algorithms: Issues, Purposes, and Challenges", *Journal of Artificial Intelligence Research*, Vol. 71, 2021.
Cheng, P., et al.: "Humans' Invariance Assumption: Should Statistics and AI Adopt It?", *The Brain Blog*, 2021.
Chesney, B. and Citron, D.: "Deep Fakes: A Looming Challenge for Privacy, Democracy, and National Security", *California Law Review*, Vol. 107(1753), 2019.
Christians, A.: "Take MAP With a Grain of Salt: Sifto and the Legal Nature of Competent Authority Agreements", *Tax Notes International*, Vol. 86, 2017.
Chui, M. et al.: "What AI Can and Can't Do (yet) for Your Business", *Mckinsey Q.*, 2022.
Churchill, R. and Singh, L.: "The Evolution of Topic Modeling", *ACM Computing Surveys*, Vol. 54(10s), 2022.
Cirone, E.: "Big Data e Tutela dei Diritti Fondamentali, in Il ragionamento giuridico nell'era dell'intelligenza artificiale", *a cura di Stefano Dorigo, Pacini Giuridica*, 2020.
Clark, A.: *Natural-Born Cyborgs: Minds, Technologies, and the Future of Human Intelligence*, New York: Oxford University Press, 2003.
Cloudflare.: "What is Encryption? | Types of Encryption", *Blog*, available at https://www.cloudflare.com/learning/ssl/what-is-encryption/.
Cockfield, A. J.: "Tax Law and Technological Change", in *The Oxford Handbook of Law, Regulation and Technology*, edited by *Eoger Brwonsword* et al., Brwonsword, Oxford University Press, 2016.
Cohen, G.: "Israel Shoots Down Hamas Drone Over Gaza Strip", *Haaretz*, 2017.
Cohen, J. E.: "Affording Fundamental Rights: A Provocation Inspired by Mireille Hildebrandt", *Critical Analysis of Law*, Vol. 4(1), 2017.
Colaner, N.: "Is Explainable Artificial Intelligence Intrinsically Valuable?", *AI & Society*, Vol. 37(4), 2022.
Confédération Fiscale Européenne.: "Opinion Statement FC 15/2014 on Developing a Multilateral Instrument to Modify Bilateral Tax Treaties (BEPS Action 15)", *European Taxation*, Vol. 55(4), 2015.
Connors, J. y Delputte, B.: "Alternative Dispute Resolution in International Tax Law—The View of Business", in *International Arbitration in Tax Matters*, edited by M. Lang and J. P. Owens, IBFD, 2016.
Copus, R., et al.: *Credible Prediction: Big Data, ML and the Credibility Revolution, Forthcoming in Law as Data: Computation and the Future of Legal Analysis*, SFI Press, 2018.
Copus, R. and Hübert, R.: *Detecting Inconsistency in Governance*, SSRN, 2017, available at SSRN-id2812914.pdf.

Cowan, C., et al.: "Buffer Overflows: Attacks and Defences for the Vulnerability of the Decade", *Foundations of Intrusion Tolerant Systems, 2003 [Organically Assured and Survivable Information Systems]*, 2003.
Crawford, K. and Schultz, J.: "Big Data and Due Process: Toward a Framework to Redress Predictive Privacy Harms", *Boston College Law Review*, Vol. 55(1), 2014.
Cummings, M. L. and Stimpson, A.: "Identifying Critical Contextual Design Cues Through a ML Approach", *AI Magazine*, 2019.
Curry, E., et al.: *The Elements of Big Data Value*, edited by Edward Curry, Andreas Metzger, Sonja Zillner, Jean-Christophe Pazzaglia and Ana García Robles, Springer, 2021.
Custers, B.: "Using Sensitive Personal Data May Be Necessary for Avoiding Discrimination in Data-Driven Decision Models", *Artificial Intelligence and Law*, Vol. 24(2), 2016.
Cutting, J. E.: "Four Assumptions About Invariance in Perception", *Journal of Experimental Psychology Human Perception & Performance*, Vol. 9(2), 1983.
Dadgostari, F., et al.: "Modeling Law Search as Prediction", *AI and Law*, Vol. 29, 2021.
D'Alessandro, V. P.: "Improving the Resolution of International Tax Disputes", *Tax Notes International*, Vol. 55(13), 2009.
Datapred.: "Prediction and Prescription—Continuous Intelligence Twins (Part 1/2)", *Blog*, 23 September 2019.
Datta, A.: "Algorithmic Transparency via Quantitative Input Influence: Theory and Experiments with Learning Systems", in *Conference: 2016 IEEE Symposium on Security and Privacy (SP)*, 2016.
Debelva, F. and Luts, J.: "The European Commission's Proposal for Double Taxation Dispute Resolution: Turning the Tide?", *Bulletin for International Taxation*, Vol. 71(5), 2017.
De Bock, K. and Van Den Poel, D.: "Predicting Website Audience Demographics for Webadvertising Targeting Using Multi-Website Clickstream Data", *Fundamenta Informaticae*, Vol. 98(1), 2010.
De Carolis, D.: "The EU Dispute Resolution Directive (2017/1852) and Fair Trial Protection under Article 47 of the EU Charter of Fundamental Rights", *European Taxation*, Vol. 58(11), 2018.
De Fine Licht, K. and De Fine Licht, J.: "Artificial Intelligence, Transparency, and Public Decision-Making—Why Explanations Are Key When Trying to Produce Perceived Legitimacy", *AI & Society*, Vol. 35(4), 2020.
Del Campo, C.: "Dispute Resolution Procedures in International Tax Matters", *IFA General Report, Cahier 101a*, Madrid, 2016.
Del Federico, L.: "La tutela del contribuente nell'evoluzione del diritto tributario internazionale: dagli accordi amministrativi fra autoritá fiscali alle procedure arbitrali", *Rivista Semestrale di Diritto*, N. 2, 2020.
Delgado Guevara, B. and Leiva García, Y.: "El conocimiento jurídico. Una propuesta tecnológica para su gestión", *Revista Internacional de Gestión del Conocimiento y la Tecnología*, Vol. 1(1), 2013.
Dempsey, J. X.: *AI: An Introduction to the Legal, Policy and Ethical Issues*, Berkeley Center for Law & Technology, 2020.
Deng, L.: "A Tutorial Survey of Architectures, Algorithms, and Applications for Deep Learning", *APSIPA Transactions on Signal and Information Processing*, Vol. 3(e2), 2014.
Deotto, D. and Dorigo, S.: "I Sistemi Utilizzati per Motivare un Atto Vanno Resi Conoscibili al Cittadino", *IlSole24Ore*, Vol. 26, 2021.
Dertat, A.: "Applied Deep Learning—Part 1: Artificial Neural Networks", *towardsdatascience, Blog*, 2017.
De Ruiter, M.: "Supplementary Dispute Resolution", *European Taxation*, Vol. 48(9), 2008.
Desai, D. R. and Kroll, J.: "Trust but Verify: A Guide to Algorithms and the Law", *Harvard Journal of Law & Technology*, Vol. 31(1), 2017.

Diakopoulos, N.: "Algorithmic Accountability", *Digital Journalism*, Vol. 3(3), 2015.
Díaz Calvarro, J. M.: "Garantías de los derechos de los obligados tributarios. Los principios de seguridad y transparencia ante el uso de la informática decisional en la Administración tributaria", *Anuario de la Facultad de Derecho. Universidad de Extremadura*, Vol. 36, 2020.
Di Cesare, F.: "How to Revitalize the EC Arbitration Convention: The New Recommendations of the Joint Transfer Pricing Forum", *International Transfer Pricing Journal*, Vol. 17(4), 2010.
Dick, S.: "Artificial Intelligence", *Harvard Data Science Review*, (1.1), 2019.
Dickler, A. M., et al.: "Cross-Functional Collaboration and Change Management: The Key Ingredients for Tax Technology Transformation", *Bulletin for International Taxation*, Vol. 74(10), 2020.
Dimitropoulou, C. et al.: "Applying Modern, Disruptive Technologies to Improve the Effectiveness of Tax Treaty Dispute Resolution", *Intertax*, Vol. 46(12), 2018.
Dominici, R.: "Le regole per la risoluzione dei conflitti in materia di doppia imposizione internazionale", in AA. VV., *Corso di diritto tributario internazionale, a cura di V. Uckmar*, CEDAM, 2002.
Dorigo, S.: *Il ragionamento giuridico nell'era dell'intelligenza artificiale*, Pacini EditoreSrl, 2020.
Dorigo, S.: "Intelligenza artificiale e norme antiabuso: il ruolo dei sistemi "intelligenti" tra funzione amministrativa e attività giurisdizionale", *Rassegna Tributaria*, Vol. 4, 2019.
Dourado, A. P.: "Post-BEPS International Tax Arbitration", *Intertax*, Vol. 42(8&9), 2019.
Dourado, A. P. and Kostić, S.: "The MLI in Action", *Intertax*, Vol. 49(10), 2021.
Dourado, A. P. and Pistone, P.: "Some Critical Thoughts on the Introduction of Arbitration in Tax Treaties", *Intertax*, Vol. 42(3), 2014.
Drywa, A.: "Taxpayer's Right to Privacy?", *Intertax*, Vol. 50(1), 2022.
Duhigg, C.: "How Companies Learn Your Secrets", *The New York Times*, 2012.
Dung, P. M. and Tang, P. M.: "Modular Argumentation for Modelling Legal Doctrines in Common Law of Contract", *AI Law*, Vol. 17(3), 2009.
Düwell, M.: "Human Dignity and the Ethics and Regulation of Technology", in *The Oxford Handbook of Law, Regulation and Technology*, edited by Roger Brownsword et al., Oxford University Press, 2017.
Edelkamp, S. and Lomuscio, A.: "Model Checking and AI—4th Workshop", in *MoChArt IV Riva del Garda*, Italy, August 29, 2006 Revised Selected and Invited Papers, Lecture Notes in AI, edited by J. G. Carbonell and J. Siekmann, *Subseries of Lecture Notes in Computer Science*, Springer.
Elish, M. C.: "Letting Autopilot Off the Hook, Why Do We Blame Humans When Automation Fails?", *Slate*, 2016.
Esposito, E.: "Artificial Communication? The Production of Contingency by Algorithms", *Zeitschrift für Soziologie*, Vol. 46(4), 2017.
Ester, M., et al.: "A Density-Based Algorithm for Discovering Clusters in Large Spatial Databases with Noise", *(KDD)*. 1996, p. 96.
Ey.: "OECD's 2023 Mutual Agreement Procedure Statistics Show Continued Strength in the US Program", 2024, available at https://globaltaxnews.ey.com/news/2024-2149-oecds-2023-mutual-agreement-procedure-statistics-show-continued-strength-in-the-us-program.
Ey.: "Tax Administration Goes Digital", 2017, available at https://assets.ey.com/content/dam/ey-sites/ey-com/en_gl/topics/tax/tax-pdfs/ey-tax-administration-goes-digital.pdf#:~:text=Tax%20administration%20goes%20digital%20As%20more%20tax%20administrations,the%20IRS%E2%80%99%20information%20exchange%20program%2C%20told%20EY%20recently%2C.
Fagan, F.: "Natural Language Processing for Lawyers and Judges", *Michigan Law Review*, Vol. 119(6), 2021.

Farzana, A., et al.: "Conceptual and Empirical Comparison of Dimensionality Reduction Algorithms (PCA, KPCA, LDA, MDS, SVD, LLE, ISOMAP, LE, ICA, t-SNE)", *Computer Science Review*, Vol. 40, 2021.

Fast, A. F. and Funder, D. C.: "Personality as Manifest in Word Use: Correlations with Self-Report, Acquaintance Report, and Behavior", *Journal of Personality and Social Psychology*, Vol. 94(2), 2008.

Fazi, B. M.: "Can a Machine Think (Anything New)? Automation Beyond Simulation", *AI & Society*, Vol. 34(3058), 2019.

Ferguson, A. G.: "Policing Predictive Policing", *Washington University Law Review*, Vol. 94(5), 2017.

Ferraris, V., et al.: "The Impact of Profiling on Fundamental Rights", *SSRN*, 2013, available at SSRN: https://papers.ssrn.com/sol3/papers.cfm?abstract_id=2366753.

Fettke, P., et al.: "Anwendungspotenziale von Deep Learning im Process Mining—Prozessoptimierung in der Steuerabteilung am Beispiel von Henkel", *IM+io*, 4/2017.

Flowers, J. C.: "Strong and Weak AI: Deweyan Considerations", *AAAI Spring Symposium: Towards Conscious AI Systems*, 2019.

Foucard, A. and Grandfond, L.: "Arbitration of International Tax Disputes: A Move Towards Democratization? ", in *Contemporary Issues in International Arbitration and Mediation: The Fordham Papers 2014*, edited by Arthur W. Rovine, BRILL, 2015.

Fouzder, M.: "Artificial Intelligence Mimics Judicial Reasoning", *The Law Society Gazette*, 2016.

Future of Life Institute.: "Pause Giant AI Experiments: AN Open Letter", March 22, 2023.

Galparsoro, J. I: "Big Data y Psicopolítica. Vía de escape: de la vida calculable a la vida como obra de arte", *Dilemata*, año. 9(24), 2017.

Galzacorta, I.: "Hacer pública la red de las cosas. 'Internet of Things' y 'Dingpolitik'", *Dilemata*, año. 9(24), 2017.

Gantz, J., and Reinsel, D.: "Extracting Value from Chaos", *IDCIVIEW*, June 2011.

Garbarino, C. and Lombardo, M.: "Arbitration of Unresolved Issues in Mutual Agreement Cases: The New Paragraph 5, Art. 25 OECD Model Convention, A Multi-Tiered Dispute Resolution Clause", *Bocconi Legal Studies Research Paper No. 1628765*, 2010.

García-Herrera Blanco, C.: "El uso del Big data y la inteligencia artificial por las Administraciones tributarias en la lucha contra el fraude fiscal. Particular referencia a los principios que han de regirla y a los derechos de los contribuyentes", *Fiscalidad e inteligencia artificial: Administración tributaria y contribuyentes en la era digital/Fernando Serrano Antón (dir.)*, Aranzadi, 2020.

García-Herrera Blanco, C.: "The use of Artificial Intelligence by tax Administrations, a Matter of Principles", in *CIAT—Inter-American Center of Tax Administrations*, 2 March 2020.

Gary, M.: *Deep Learning: A Critical Appraisal*, Ithaca, NY: Cornell University, 2018.

Gillespie, T.: *The Relevance of Algorithms, in Media Technologies: Essays on Communication, Materiality, and Society*, edited by T. Gillespie, P. J. Boczkowski and K. A. Foot. Cambridge, MA: MIT Press, 2014.

Gonfalonieri, A.: *Inverse Reinforcement Learning*, Towards Data Science, 2018.

Goodman, B. and Flaxman, S.: "European Union Regulations on Algorithmic Decision Making and a "Right to Explanation"", *AI Magazine*, Vol. 38(3), 2016.

Gordon, J. S.: "AI and Law: Ethical, Legal, and Socio-Political Implications", *AI & Society*, Vol. 36(2), 2021.

Goumagias, N. D., et al.: "Using Deep Q-Learning to Understand the Tax Evasion Behavior of Risk-Averse Firms", *Expert Systems with Applications*, Vol. 101, 2018.

Govind, S.: "The New Face of International Tax Dispute Resolution: Comparing the OECD Multilateral Instrument with the EU Dispute Resolution Directive", *EC Tax Review*. Nr. 6, 2018.

Govind, S. and Monsenego, J.: "Chapter 11: Multilateralism in Dispute Resolution: Some Thoughts on the OECD Multilateral Instrument and the EU Dispute Resolution Directive", in *International and EU Tax Multilateralism: Challenges Raised by the MLI*, edited by Ana Paula Dourado, GREIT Series, 2020.

Govind, S. y Turcan, L.: "The Changing Contours of Disputes Resolution in the International Tax World: Comparing the OECD Multilateral Instrument and the Proposed EU Arbitration Directive", *Bulletin for International Taxation*, Vol. 71(3/4), 2017.

Govind, S. y Turcan, L.: "Cross-Border Tax Disputes Resolution in the 21st Century: A Comparative Study of Existing Bilateral and Multilateral Remedies", *Derivatives & Financial Instrument*, Vol. 19(5), 2017.

Graben, P. and Wright, J.: "From McCulloch–Pitts Neurons Toward Biology", *Bulletin of Mathematical Biology*, Vol. 73, 2011.

Grabmair, M.: *Modeling Purposive Legal Argumentation and Case Outcome Prediction Using Argument Schemes in the Value Judgement Formalism*, PhD thesis, University of Pittsburgh, PA, 2016.

Gray, S.: "Always On: Privacy Implications of Microphone-Enabled Devices", *Future of Privacy Forum*, 2016.

Greene, D., et al.: "Better, Nicer, Clearer, Fairer: A Critical Assessment of the Movement for Ethical Artificial Intelligence and Machine Learning", in *Proceedings of the 52nd Hawaii International Conference on System Sciences, Critical and Ethical Studies of Digital and Social Media*, 2019.

Griffiths, T. L. and Steyvers, M.: "Finding Scientific Topics", *Proceedings of the National Academy of Sciences (PNAS)*, Vol.101(suppl_1), 2004.

Grimmer, J.: "We Are All Social Scientists Now: How Big Data, ML, and Causal Inference Work Together", *PS: Political Science & Politics*, Vol. 48(1), 2015.

Groen, G.: "The Nature and Scope of the Mandatory Arbitration Provision in the OECD Multilateral Convention (2016)", *Bulletin for International Taxation*, Vol. 71(11), 2017.

Gronauer, S. and Diepold, K.: "Multi Agent Deep Reinforcement Learning: A Survey", *AI Review*, Vol. 55(6), 2022.

Grossman, L.: "How Computers Know What We Want—Before We Do", *Time*, 27 May 2010.

Gubelmann, R. and Hongler, P.: "Natural Language Processing—A Game Changer for Normative Reasoning in the Legal Discipline?", *IFF-HSG Working Papers*, Working Paper No. 2021-7, 2021.

Guenther, D. A., et al.: "How Useful Are Tax Disclosures in Predicting Effective Tax Rates? A Machine Learning Approach", *The Accounting Review*, Vol. 98(5), 2023.

Günther, M. and Kasirzadeh, A.: "Algorithmic and Human Decision Making: For a Double Standard of Transparency", *AI & Society*, Vol. 37(4), 2022.

Gupta, S., et al.: "Reshaping Public Finance: Digital Revolutions in Public Finance", *International Monetary Fund*, 2017.

Gutiérrez, D. M. E.: "Discutiendo la transparencia de las políticas de privacidad en la Era del Big Data. Hacia la "Norma Social" como nueva Regla de Derecho", *Dilemata*, año. 9(24), 2017.

Gutiérrez Tapia, A.: "Inteligencia Artificial", *Manual Formativo de ACTA*, Vol. 60, 2011.

Hadari, Y.: "Compulsory Arbitration in International Transfer Pricing and Other Double Taxation Disputes", 6 October 2009, available at https://papers.ssrn.com/sol3/papers.cfm?abstract_id=1483621.

Hadwick, D. and Lan, S.: "Lessons to Be Learned from the Dutch Childcare Allowance Scandal: A Comparative Review of Algorithmic Governance by Tax Administrations in the Netherlands, France and Germany", *World Tax Journal*, Vol. 13(4), 2021.

Hage, J.: "Theoretical Foundations for the Responsibility of Autonomous Agents", *Artificial Intelligence and Law*, Vol. 25(3), 2017.

Han, J., et al.: *Data Mining: Concepts and Techniques*, Third edition, Elsevier, 2011.

Haney, B. S.: "Applied Natural Language Processing for Law Practice", *Boston College Intellectual Property and Technology Forum*, 2020, available at https://ssrn.com/abstract=3476351 or http://doi.org/10.2139/ssrn.3476351.

Haney, B. S.: "The Perils and Promises of Artificial General Intelligence", *Journal of Legislation*, Vol. 45(2), 2019.
Harfoush, F. A.: *From Big Data to Intelligent Data—An Applied Perspective*, Springer Cham, 2021.
Heater, B.: "Cassie the Bipedal Robot Runs a 5k", *World Economic Forum*, 2021.
Hern, A.: "Partnership on AI Formed by Google, Facebook, Amazon, IBM and Microsoft", *The Guardian*, 28 September 2016.
Herrera, F., et al.: "Advances in AI, 18th Conference of the Spanish Association for AI", in *CAEPIA 2018 Granada, Spain, October 23–26, 2018 Proceedings*, Springer, 2018.
Hildebrandt, M.: "The Force of Law and the Force of Technology, in The Routledge International Handbook of Technology", in *Crime and Justice*, edited by M. R. P. McGuire and Holt, Routledge, 2017.
Hildebrandt, M.: "Law as Computation in the Era of Artificial Legal Intelligence Speaking Law to the Power of Statistics", *University of Toronto Law Journal*, Vol. 68(1), 2018.
Hinnekens, L.: "Different Interpretations of the European Tax Arbitration Convention", *ECTaxReview*, 1998/4.
Hinnekens, L.: "The Tax Arbitration Convention. Its Significance for the EC Based Enterprise, the EC Itself, and for Belgian and International Tax Law", *ECTaxReview*, 1992/2.
Hinton, G. E. and Roweis, S.: "Stochastic Neighbor Embedding", in *NIPS'02: Proceedings of the 15th International Conference on Neural Information Processing Systems*, 2002.
Hin-Yan, L.: "Refining Responsibility: Differentiating Two Types of Responsibilities Issues Raised by Autonomous Weapons Systems", in *Autonomous Weapons Systems: Law, Ethics, Policy*, edited by N. Butha, S. Beck, R. Geiß, H. Liu and C. Kreß, Cambridge: Cambridge University Press, 2016.
Hoffman, M., et al.: "Online Learning for Latent Dirichlet Allocation", *Advances in Neural Information Processing Systems*, Vol. 23, 2010.
Hofmann, T.: "Probabilistic Latent Semantic Indexing", *ACM SIGIR Forum*, Vol. 51, 1999.
Holmes, O. W.: "The Path of Law", *Harvard Law Review*, Vol. 110(5), 1997.
Hongchen, G., et al.: "An Improved AD-LDA Topic Model Based on Weighted Gibbs Sampling", in *2016 IEEE Advanced Information Management, Communicates, Electronic and Automation Control Conference (IMCEC)*, Xi'an, China, 2016.
Hoofnagle, C. J.: "Behavioural Advertising: The Offer You Cannot Refuse", *Harvard Policy & Law Review*, Vol. 6(2), 2012.
Hooker, J. and Tae Wan, K.: "Truly Autonomous Machines Are Ethical", *AI Magazine*, Vol. 40(4), 2019.
Hout, M. C., et al.: "Multidimensional Scaling. Wiley Interdisciplinary Reviews", *Cognitive Science*, Vol. 4(1), 2012.
Huang, Z., et al.: "Context-Aware Legal Citation Recommendation Using Deep Learning", in *ICAIL '21: Proceedings of the Eighteenth International Conference on AI and Law*, June 2021.
Hueso Cotino, L.: "Algunas cuestiones clave de protección de datos en la nube. Hacia una "regulación nebulosa", *Revista catalana de dretpúblic*, núm. 51, 2015.
Hueso Cotino, L.: "Big Data e inteligencia Artificial. Una aproximación a su tratamiento jurídico desde los derechos fundamentales", *Dilemata*, Vol. 9(24), 2017.
Hueso Cotino, L.: "Ética en el diseño para el desarrollo de una inteligencia artificial, robótica y big data confiables y su utilidad desde el derecho", *Revista catalana de dretpúblic*, Vol. 58, 2019.
Hurley, R.: *Data: A Guide to Big Data Trends, AI, Machine Learning, Predictive Analytics, Internet of Things, Data Science, Data Analytics, Business Intelligence, and Data Mining*, Ationa Publications, 2019.
Hyman, H., et al.: "A Process Model for Information Retrieval Context Learning and Knowledge Discovery", *AI and Law*, Vol. 23(2), 2015.
Hynek, N. and Solovyeva, A.: "Operations of Power in Autonomous Weapon Systems: Ethical Conditions and Socio-Political Prospects", *AI & Society*, Vol. 36(5), 2021.

Iacoviti, G: "How Technology Influences Information Gathering and Information Spreading", *Church, Communication and Culture*, Vol. 7(1), 2022.

Iannacone, A., "Doppia Imposizione Internazionale: approvata la Direttiva sui meccanismi di risoluzione delle controversie", *Corriere tributario*, 2018.

Iglesias Vazquez, F., et al.: "Clustering Refinement", *International Journal of Data Science and Analytics*, Vol. 12(4), 2021.

Iglesias Vazquez, F., et al.: "Outlier Detection Based on Low Density Models". in *Proceedings of the 18th IEEE International Conference on Data Mining Workshops ICDMW*, edited by J. Yu, Z. Li, H. Tong and F. Zhu, Vol. 2018-November, IEEE Press.

Innerarity, D.: "Making the Black Box Society Transparent", *AI & Society*, Vol. 36(4), 2021.

Introna, L. D. and Nissenbaum, H.: "Shaping the Web: Why the Politics of Search Engines Matters", *Information Society*, Vol. 16(3), 2000.

Iriarte Yanicelli, A. A.: "Derechos y garantías de los contribuyentes en la cuarta revolución industrial: aproximación desde las transformaciones de la relación jurídica tributaria en la era de la inteligencia artificial", *Fiscalidad e inteligencia artificial: Administración tributaria y contribuyentes en la era digital/Fernando Serrano Antón (dir.)*, Aranzadi, 2020.

Isinkaye, F. O., et al.: "Recommendation Systems: Principles, Methods and Evaluation", *Egyptian Informatics Journal*, Vol. 16, 2015.

Jaadi, Z.: "A Step-by-Step Explanation of Principal Component Analysis (PCA)", Built In, *Blog*, 2023.

Jain, S. A.: "Artificial Intelligence: A Threat to Privacy?", *Nirma University Law Journal*, Vol. 8(2), 2019.

Janasik, N.: *Reframing Autonomy: My Data, Our Data, and the Question of Human Dignity, in Human-Centered Digitalization and Services*, edited by MarjaToivonen and Eveliina-Saari, Springer, 2019.

Jannach, D., et al.: "Recommender Systems: Past, Present, Future", *AI Magazine*, Vol. 42(3), 2021.

Jattoni Dall'asèen.: "Evasione fiscale, ora in Francia un algoritmo andrà a caccia dei "furnetti" sui social network", *Corriere della Sera-Economia*, 19 February 2021.

Java T Point.: "Regression Analysis in ML", *Blog*, available at www.javatpoint.com/regression-analysis-in-machine-learning (accessed 15 July 2022).

Java T Point.: "Support Vector Machine Algorithm", *Blog*, available at https://www.javatpoint.com/regression-vs-classification-in-machine-learning (accessed 6 June 2022).

Jinyan, L., et al.: "Digitalization and International Tax Dispute Resolution: A Window of Opportunity for BRITACOM", *Osgoode Legal Studies Research Paper*, 2020.

Jirakunkanok, P., et al.: "Dynamic Epistemic Logic of Belief Changes in Legal Judgments", *AI and Law*, Vol. 26(3), 2018.

John, G. H. and Langley, P.: "Estimating Continuous Distributions in Bayesian Classification", in *Proceedings of the Eleventh Conference on Uncertainty in AI*, Morgan Kaufmann Publishers Inc., 1995.

Johnson, D. G.: "Computer Systems: Moral Entities but not Moral Agents", *Ethics and Information Technology*, Vol. 8(4), 2006.

Johnson, D. G.: "Difference Between Deep Learning and ML vs AI", *Guru99, Blog*, 2023.

Johnson, D. G. and Powers, T. M.: "Computer Systems and Responsibility: A Normative Look at Technological Complexity", *Ethics and Information Technology*, Vol. 7(2), 2005.

Jones, R. H.: *Reductionism: Analysis and the Fullness of Reality*, Lewisburg, PA: Bucknell University Press, 2000.

Jordan, M. I.: "AI—The Revolution Hasn't Happened Yet", *Harvard Data Science Review*, Issue 1 January 2019, available at https://hdsr.mitpress.mit.edu/pub/wot7mkc1/release/9 (accessed 12 December 2022).

Jun, S. L.: "The Collapsed Gibbs Sampler in Bayesian Computations with Applications to a Gene Regulation Problem", *Journal of the American Statistical Association*, Vol. 89(427), 1994.

Kalla, A.: "K Means Clustering", *Medium Blog*, 2019, available at https://medium.datadriveninvestor.com/k-means-clustering-4a700d4a4720 (accessed 15 July 2022).
Kaplan, J.: "Decision Theory and the Factfinding Process", *Stanford Law Review*, Vol. 20(6), 1968.
Karatzoglou, A., et al.: "Support Vector Machines", in *R, Research Report Series/Department of Statistics and Mathematics, 21. Department of Statistics and Mathematics*, WU Vienna University of Economics and Business, Vienna, 2005.
Kashyap, A., et al.: "An Evaluation of Digital Image Forgery Detection Approaches", *International Journal of Applied Engineering Research*, Vol. 12(15), 2017.
Kaski, S. and Peltonen, J.: "Dimensionality Reduction for Data Visualization [Applications Corner]", *IEEE Signal Processing Magazine*, Vol. 28(2), 2011.
Katsh, M. E. and Rabinovich-Einy, O.: *Digital Justice: Technology and the Internet of Disputes*, Oxford University Press, 2017.
Katz, D. M.: "Quantitative Legal Prediction-or-How I Learned to Stop Worrying and Start Preparing for the Data-Driven Future of the Legal Services Industry", *Emory Law Journal*, Vol. 62, 2013.
Katz, Y.: "Manufacturing and AI Revolution", *Harvard Medical School; Berkman Klein Center for Internet & Society*, 2017.
Kelleher, J. D. and Tierney, B.: *Data Science*, Cambridge, MA: The MIT Press Knowledge Series, 2018.
Khuyen, T.: "pyLDAvis: Topic Modelling Exploration Tool That Every NLP Data Scientist Should Know", *Neptune.AI, Blog*, 2023.
Kidd, K. and Saxena, B.: "NLP vs NLU: What's The Difference? ", *ML & Big Data, Blog*, available at https://www.bmc.com/blogs/nlu-vs-nlp-natural-language-understanding-processing/.
Kleist, D.: "The Multilateral Convention to Implement Tax Treaty Related Measures to Prevent BEPS-Some Thoughts on Complexity and Uncertainty", *Nordic Tax Journal*, Vol. 1, 2018.
Klingler, N.: "Deep Learning—What Is an AI Model? Here's What You Need to Know", *Blog*, 2023.
Klingler, N.: "The Ultimate Guide to Understanding and Using AI Models (2023)", *viso.ai, Blog*, 2023.
Klügl, F. and Bazzan, A. L. C.: "Agent-Based Modeling and Simulation", *AI Magazine*, Vol. 33(3), 2012.
Knoblock, C. A. and Szekely, P.: "Exploiting Semantics for Big Data Integration", *AI Magazine*, Vol. 36(1), 2015.
Koch, K.: "Mutual Agreement—Procedure and Practice", *IFA, Cahiers de droit fiscal International*, Vol. 66a, 1981.
Kofler, G.: "EU Tax Dispute Resolution Directive: The Deathblow to Double Taxation in the European Union", *EC Tax Review*, Vol. 28(6), 2019.
Kofler, G. and Potgens, F.: "—Article 23—Methods for Elimination of Double Taxation" in *IBFD Global Topics, Global Tax Treaty Commentaries* [Model articles and Issues], 2020.
Kolanovic, M. and Krishnamachari, R. T.: *Big Data and AI Strategies ML and Alternative Data Approach to Investing*, J.P. Morgan, 2017.
Komamizu, T., et al.: "Exploring Relevant Parts Between Legal Documents Using Substructure Matching", in New Frontiers in *AI, JSAI-isAI International Workshops, JURISIN, AI-Biz, LENLS, Kansei-AI Yokohama, Japan, November 10–12, 2019 Revised Selected Papers*, edited by Maki Sakamoto, Naoaki Okazaki, Koji Mineshima and Ken Satoh, Springer, 2020.
Komando, K.: "3 Gadgets That Are Always Listening and How to Stop Them", *USA Today*, 2015.
Kosinski, M., et al.: "Private Traits and Attributes Are Predictable from Digital Records of Human Behavior", *Proceedings of the National Accademy of Science*, Vol. 110(15), 2013.

Kotha, A. P.: "Baseball Arbitration Option under the EU Dispute Resolution Directive: How Well Does It Fare Against the Objectives?", *World Tax Journal*, Vol. 13(2), 2021.
Kovač, M.: *Judgement-Proof Robots and AI—A Comparative Law and Economics Approach*, Springer, 2020.
Kreutzer, R. T. and Sirrenberg, M.: *Understanding AI—Fundamentals, Use Cases and Methods for a Corporate AI Journey*, Springer, 2020.
Krilis, G.: "Comparison of t-SNE and PCA and Truncate SVD", *Data Science, Blog*, 2020.
Krishna, M. M., et al.: "Image Classification Using Deep Learning", *International Journal of Engineering & Technology*, Vol. 7(2.7), 2018.
Kritikos, M.: *What if Technologies Had Their Own Ethical Standards?, At Glance—Scientific Foresight: What if?*, European Parliament, Panel for the Future of Science and Technology (STOA), 2018.
Krupasnky, J.: "Untangling the Definitions of AI, Machine Intelligence, and ML", *Medium*, 2017.
Kuijper, B.: "Technology-Enabled Tax Compliance", *Bulletin for International Taxation*, Vol. 74(10), 2020.
Kulshrestha, R.: "A Beginner's Guide to Latent Dirichlet Allocation(LDA)", *towardsdatascience, Blog*, 2019.
Kumar, B.: "PyTorch MNIST Tutorial", *PythonGuide.com, Blog*, 2022.
Kumm, M.: "The Cosmopolitan Turn in Constitutionalism: An Integrated Conception of Public Law", *Indiana Journal of Global Legal Studies*, Vol. 20(2), Article 4, 2013.
Kuźniacki, B.: "How Constitutional Principles Pave the Way to eXplainable AI in Tax Law", *Kluwer International Tax Blog*, 2022.
Lang, M.: "ECJ and Mutual Agreement Procedures", *Intertax*, Vol. 42(3), 2014.
Lang, M. and Wiman, B.: "Conference on Arbitration in Tax Treaty Law—Uppsala University—22 August 2013", *Intertax*, Vol. 42(3), 2014.
Lanzing, M.: "Strongly Recommended Revisiting Decisional Privacy to Judge Hypernudging in Self-Tracking Technologies", *Philosophy & Technology*, Vol. 32(4), 2019.
La Quadrature du Net.: "le conseil constitutionnel autorise le Fisc à La Surveillance De Masse", *Blog*, 2019, available at https://gsell.tech/predicting-courts-decisions-is-lawful-in-france-and-will-remain-so/.
Largeanu, C.: "The Data Journey: from Reporting Obligations to Advanced Analytics", in *Intra-European Organisation of Tax Administrations, in Applying New Technologies and Digital Solutions in Tax Compliance*, IOTA, 2020.
Latonero, M.: "Governing Artificial Intelligence: Upholding Human Rights & Dignity", *Data & Society*, 2018.
Lawless, W. F. et al.: "Artificial Intelligence, Autonomy, and Human-Machine Teams: Interdependence, Context, and Explainable AI", *AI Magazine*, Vol. 40(3), 2019.
Lecun, Y., et al.: "Deep Learning", *Nature*, Vol. 521(7553), 2015
Lee, E. A. and Seshia, S. A.: *Introduction to Embedded Systems, A Cyber-Physical System Approach*, Second edition, MIT Press, 2017.
Lee, W.: "Using Principal Component Analysis (PCA) for Machine Learning", *Towards Data Science, Blog*, 2022.
Lieb, J. P.: "Chapter I—Introduction: Taking the Debate Forward", in *International Arbitration in Tax Matters, WU—Tax Law and Policy Series*, edited by Michael Lang and Jeffrey Owens, IBFD, 2016.
Liebwald, D.: "On Transparent Law, Good Legislation and Accessibility to Legal Information: Towards an Integrated Legal Information System", *AI and Law*, Vol. 23(3), 2015.
Liotti, B. F.: "Taxpayers' Data Protection: Do International, Regional, and Domestic Instruments Guarantee Adequate Rights in Tax (A)EoI?", *Intertax*, Vol. 50(2), 2022.
Liu, F. T., et al.: "Isolation Forest", in *ICDM '08. Eighth IEEE International Conference on Data Mining*, 2008.

Liu, H. Y. and Zawieska, K.: "From Responsible Robotics Towards a Human Rights Regime Oriented to the Challenges of Robotics and Artificial Intelligence", *Ethics and Information Technology*. Vol. 22, 2020.
Liu, L., et al.: "An Overview of Topic Modeling and Its Current Applications in Bioinformatics", *SpringerPlus*, Vol. 5(1), 2016.
Livermore, M. and Rockmore, D.: "France Kicks Data Scientists Out of Its Courts", *Slate*, 2019.
Locke, D.: "Case Law Retrieval: Accomplishments, Problems, Methods and Evaluations in the Past 30 Years", *ACM Computing Surveys*, Vol. 1(1), Article 1, 2022.
Loevinger, L.: "Jurimetrics: The Methodology of Legal Inquiry", *Law and Contemporany Problems*, Vol. 28(1), Duke University School of Law, 1963.
Loevinger, L.: "Jurimetrics—The Next Step Forward", *Minnesota Law Review*, Vol. 33(5), 1949.
Logility: "Descriptive, Predictive and Prescriptive Analytics Explained", *Blog*, 13 March 2020.
Lombardo, M.: "Il miglioramento della risoluzione delle controversia fiscali internazionali", *Bollettino Tributario*, Vol. 6, 2021.
Lovelace, R.: "Review of "The Data Revolution: Big Data, Open Data, Data Infrastructures & Their Consequences", *Rob Kitchin Journal of Regional Science*, Vol. 56(4), 2016.
Luchena Mozo, Mª. G.: "A Collaborative Relationship in the Resolution of International Tax Disputes and Alternative Measures for Dispute Resolution in a Post-BEPS Era", *European Taxation*, Vol. 58(1), IBFD, 2018.
Luchena Mozo, Mª. G.: "The Prevention and Resolution of Tax Conflicts within the Framework of International Exchange of Information", *European Taxation*, Vol. 52(5), IBFD, 2012.
Luchena Mozo, Mª.G.: "Procedimientos de resolución de controversias tributarias internacionales: Entre BEPS y la UE", *Aranzadi*, 2017.
Luyang, L., et al.: "Improving Neural Topic Modeling Via Sinkhorn Divergence", *Information Processing & Management*, Vol. 59(3), 2022.
Luz De Araujo, P. H. and DE CAMPOS, T.: "Topic Modelling Brazilian Supreme Court Lawsuits", in *Legal Knowledge and Information Systems*. IOS Press, 2020.
Lyons, J. B., et al.: "Certifiable Trust in Autonomous Systems: Making the Intractable Tangible", *AI Magazine*, Vol. 38(3), 2017.
Mabey, B.: "pyLDAvis Documentation", *Buildmedia, Blog*, 2021.
Mackaay, E. and Robillard, P.: *Predicting Judicial Decisions: The Nearest Neighbour Rule and Visual Representation of Case Patterns*, Band 3, Heft 3/4, 1974, Berlin, Boston: De Gruyter, 2020.
Macpherson, T. et al.: "Natural and AI: A Brief Introduction to the Interplay between AI and Neuroscience Research", *Neural Networks*, Vol. 144, 2021.
Maijdańska, A. and Pemberton Leigh, J.: "The OECD's International Assurance Programme (Part II)", *Linde, TPI*, Vol. 4, 2018.
Mandal, A., et al.: "Unsupervised Approaches for Measuring Textual Similarity between Legal Court Case Reports", *AI and Law*, Vol. 29(1), 2021.
Mandel, G. N.: "Legal Evolution in Response to Technological Change", in *The Oxford Handbook of Law, Regulation and Technology*, edited by Roger Brownsword, Oxford University Press, 2016.
Maneewongvatana, S. and Mount, D. M.: "It's Okay to Be Skinny, If Your Friends Are Fat", *Center for Geometric Computing 4th Annual Workshop on Computational Geometry*, Vol. 2, 1999.
Mani, G., et al.: "Artificial Intelligence's Grand Challenges: Past, Present, and Future", *AI Magazine*, Vol. 42(1), 2021.
Mantelero, A.: "AI and Big Data: A Blueprint for a Human Right, Social and Ethical Impact Assessment", *Computer Law &Security Review*, Vol. 34(4), 2018.

Markham, M.: "Litigation, Arbitration and Mediation in International Tax Disputes: An Assessment of Whether This Results in Competitive or Collaborative Relations", *Contemporary Asia Arbitration Journal*, Vol. 11(2), 2018, p. 278.

Marks, A.: "Automatic Justice? Technology, Crime, and Social Control", in *The Oxford Handbook of Law, Regulation and Technology*, edited by Roger Brownsword et al., Oxford University Press, 2017.

Marr, B.: "What Everyone Should Know About Cognitive Computing", *FORBES*, March 23, 2016.

Martin, F. J., et al.: "The Big Promise of Recommender Systems", *AI Magazine*, Vol. 32(3), 2011.

Martín Jiménez, A. J.: "Procedimiento Amistoso", en *Convenios fiscales internacionales y fiscalidad de la Unión" Europea*, coord. por Néstor Carmona Fernández and José Manuel Calderón Carrero, CISS, 2006.

Martín López, J.: "Inteligencia Artificial, Sesgos y No Discriminación en el Ámbito de la Inspección Tributaria", *Crónica Tributaria*, n. 182/2022.

Martín López, J. and Pérez Bernabeu, B.: "Inteligencia Artificial, Compliance Risk Management y Conflictividad Tributaria", en *Cumplimiento cooperativo y reducción de la conflictividad: hacia un nuevo modelo de relación entre la Administración tributaria y los contribuyentes*, coord. por José Angel Gómez Requena, Saturnina Moreno González (dir.) and Pedro José Carrasco Parrilla (dir.), Miguel Ángel Collado Yurrita (pr.), 2021.

Mattarelli, F.: "La sospensione del processo tributario: influenza del nuovo art. 39, D.Lgs. n. 546/1992 sulle procedure amichevoli internazionali in materia di transfer pricing", *Rassegna Tributaria*, n. 1, 2017.

Matthias, A.: "The Responsibility Gap: Ascribing Responsibility for the Actions of Learning Automata", *Ethics and Information Technology*, Vol. 6, 2004.

Mayer-Schonberger, C.: "Big Data. Una rivoluzione chet rasformerà il nostro modo di vivere e già minaccia la nostra libertà", *Garzanti*, 2013.

McCarty, L. T.: "An Implementation of Eisner v. Macomber". in *ICAIL '95: Proceedings of the 5th International Conference on AI and Law*. New York: ACM, 1995.

McCarty, L. T.: "Reflections on TAXMAN: An Experiment in AI and Legal Reasoning", *Harvard Law Review*, Vol. 90(5), 1977.

McCulloch, W. S., and Pitts, W.: "A Logical Calculus of the Ideas Immanent in Nervous Activity", *Bulletin of Mathematica Biology*, Vol. 52(1/2), 1990.

McGinnis, J. O. and Pearce, R. G.: "The Great Disruption: How Machine Intelligence Will Transform the Role of Lawyers in the Delivery of Legal Services", *Fordham Law Review/ Edited by Fordham Law Students*, Vol. 82(6), 2014.

McKinsey Global Institute.: "Notes from the AI Frontier Insights from Hundreds of Use Cases", 2018, available at https://www.mckinsey.com/west-coast/~/media/McKinsey/Featured%20Insights/Artificial%20Intelligence/Notes%20from%20the%20AI%20frontier%20Applications%20and%20value%20of%20deep%20learning/Notes-from-the-AI-frontier-Insights-from-hundreds-of-use-cases-Discussion-paper.pdf.

Medvedeva, M., et al.: "The Danger of Reverse-Engineering of Automated Judicial Decision-Making Systems", *ArXiv*, abs/2012.10301, 2020.

Medvedeva, M., et al.: "Rethinking the Field of Automatic Prediction of Court Decisions", *AI and Law*, Vol. 30(3), 2022.

Medvedeva, M., et al.: "Using Machine Learning to Predict Decisions of the European Court of Human Rights", *Artificial Intelligence and Law*, Vol. 28(2), 2020.

Mehl, L.: "Automation in the Legal World: From the Machine Processing of Legal Information to the "Law Machine". Mechanisation of Thought Processes", in *Proceedings of a Symposium Held at the National Physical Laboratory, 24–27 November 1958*, Vol. II, Her Majesty's Stationery Office, London, 1959.

Mehta, P., et al.: "DeepCatch: Predicting Return Defaulters in Taxation System Using Example-Dependent Cost-Sensitive Deep Neural Networks", in *2020 IEEE International Conference on Big Data (Big Data)*, 2020.

Merine, T.: *Quick Check: A Legal Research Recommendation System*, Published in NLLP @KDD 2020 Law, Computer Science, 2020.

Meya, M.: "La Inteligencia Artificial", *Revista Española de Lingüística*, Vol. 10(1), 1980.

Mikolov, T., et al.: "Efficient Estimation of Word Representations in Vector Space", in *Proceedings of the International Conference on Learning Representations, ICLR*, 2013.

Milano, S., et al.: "Recommender Systems and Their Ethical Challenges", *AI & Society*, Vol. 35(4), 2020.

Mimno, D., et al.: "Optimizing Semantic Coherence in Topic Models", in *Proceedings of the 2011 Conference on Empirical Methods in Natural Language Processing*, 2011.

Miron, M.: "Evaluating Causes of Algorithmic Bias in Juvenile Criminal Recidivism", *Artificial Intelligence and Law*, Vol. 29(1), 2021.

Mitchell, M.: "What Does It Mean to Align AI With Human Values?", *Quantamagazine*, 2023.

Mitchell, T. M.: "The Discipline of ML", *CMU-ML-06–108, School of Computer Science Carnegie Mellon University*, July 2006.

Mnih, V. et al.: "Human-Level Control Through Deep Reinforcement Learning", *Nature: International Journal of Science*, Vol. 518(1), 2015.

Mocchegiani, M.: "Algoritmi e diritto: I nuovi orizzonti (più o meno rassicuranti) della decisione robotica", *Cronache dal Convegno "Decisionerobotica" Accademia deiLincei*, forumcostituzionale.it, 2018.

Mohankumar, P.: "Big Data Analytics: A Framework for Unstructured Data Analysis", *International Journal of Engineering and Technology (IJET)*, Vol. 5(1), 2013.

Mohssen, M., et al.: *ML: Algorithms and Applications*, CRC Press, 2017.

Monsenego, J.: "Designing Arbitration Provisions in Tax Treaties: Reflections Based on the US Experience", *Intertax*, Vol. 42(3), 2014.

Montesinos López, O. A., et al.: *Multivariate Statistical Machine Learning Methods for Genomic Prediction*, Springer, 2022.

Morris, J.: "Issue-Based Prediction Basics", *GitHub, Blog*, available at https://gauntlet173.github.io/docassemble-openlcbr/docs/ibp_basics.html (accessed 3 September 2022).

Mosakas, K.: "Smart Technologies and Fundamental Rights: Brill's Interview with John-Stewart Gordon", *AI & Society*, Vol. 36(2), 2020.

Mumford, J. et al.: "Machine Learning and Legal Argument", in *Proceedings of the 21st Workshop on Computational Models of Natural Argument, CEUR Workshop Proceedings*, 2021.

Murugan, A., et al.: *Practical Text Analytics: Maximizing the Value of Text Data*, Springer International Publishing: Imprint: Springer, 2019.

Nadin, M.: "Machine Intelligence: A Chimera", *AI & Society*, Vol. 34(2), 2019.

Navarro Ibarrola, A.: "La eliminación de la doble imposición en la Unión Europea: el antiguo art. 293, competencias de la Unión y aspectos controvertidos de la Directiva de Arbitraje", en *La armonización de las normas contra la elusión fiscal relativas a la fiscalidad directa en la Unión Europea*, coord. por José Manuel Almudí, Jorge Alberto Ferreras Gutiérrez (aut.) and Pablo Andrés Hernández González-Barreda (aut.), Thomson Reuters Aranzadi, 2018.

Nemitz, P.: "Constitutional Democracy and Technology in the Age of Artificial Intelligence", *Royal Society Philosophical Transactions A*, Vol. 376(2133), 2018.

Nguyen, T., et al.: "Exploring the Filter Bubble: The Effect of Using Recommender Systems on Content Diversity", in *Proceedings of the 23rd International Conference on World Wide Web, WWW '14*, ACM, New York, USA, 2014.

Nielsen, K.: *Big Data and Sensitive Data, in Big Data for the Greater Good*, edited by Ali Emrouznejad and Vincent Charles, Springer International Publishing AG, 2018.

Nilsson, N. J.: *The Quest for AI: A History of Ideas and Achievements*, Cambridge, UK: Cambridge University Press, 2010.

Nissan, E.: "Digital Technologies and AI's Present and Foreseeable Impact on Lawyering, Judging, Policing and Law Enforcement", *AI & Society*, Vol. 32(3), 2017.

Nissenbaum, H.: "Accountability in a Computized Society", *Science and Engineering Ethics*, Vol. 2(1), 1996.
Nobles, C.: "The Cyber Talent Gap and Cybersecurity Professionalizing", *International Journal of Hyperconnectivity and the Internet of Things*, Vol. 2(1), 2018.
Noto La Diega, G.: "Against the Dehumanisation of Decision-Making—Algorithmic Decisions at the Crossroads of Intellectual Property, Data Protection, and Freedom of Information", *JIPITEC—Journal of Intellectual Property, Information Technology and E-Commerce Law*, Vol. 9(1), 2018.
Nurock, V. et al.: "What Does "Ethical by Design" Mean? ", in *Reflections on Artificial Intelligence for Humanity*, edited by Bertrand Braunschweig and Malik Ghallab, Springer, 2021.
Offermanns, R.: "Report on the Symposium, "Tax Digitization, Help or Obstacle to Legal Protection?"", *European Taxation*, Vol. 60(6), 2020.
Ofili, F.: "How to Tame the Tech Titans", *The Economist*, 2018.
O'Grady, J.: *Blue J Legal Tax Foresight Predictive AI for Tax Lawyers*, Dewey B Strategic, 2019.
Oliver, D.: "Law, Politics and Public Accountability. The Search for a New Equilibrium", *Public Law*, 1994.
Olson, D. L. and Wu, D.: *Predictive Data Mining*, Second edition, Springer. 2020.
Olson, M.: *The Logic of Collective Action—Public Goods and the Theory of Groups*, Cambridge MA: Harvard University Press, 1965.
O'Neill, J., et al.: (2016): "An Analysis of Topic Modelling for Legislative Texts", in *Proceedings of the Second Workshop on Automated Semantic Analysis of Information in Legal Texts, co-located with the 16th International Conference on Artificial Intelligence and Law, ICAIL*, London, UK, 2017.
Oskolkov, N.: "Dimensionality Reduction: Overview, Technical Details, and Some Applications", *Applied Data Science in Tourism: Interdisciplinary Approaches, Methodologies, and Applications*, 2022.
Ostalé García, J.: "Lucas y Penrose sobre los teoremas de Gödel", *Acontecimiento: Órgano de expresión del Instituto Emmanuel Mounier*, N. 120, 2016.
Ostendorff, M., et al.: "Evaluating Document Representations for Content-based Legal Literature Recommendations", in *Conference: ICAIL '21: Eighteenth International Conference for AI and Law*, 2021.
Owens, J.: "Resolving International Tax Disputes: The Role of the OECD", *OECD Observer*, Vol. 243, 2004.
Pablos Mateos, F.: "De las relaciones cooperativas al cumplimento cooperativo: las propuestas previas de tributación en el País Vasco", en *Documento de Trabajo 11/2019—VII Encuentro de Derecho Financiero y Tributario "Una estrategia global al servicio de la reducción de la conflictividad en materia tributaria*", coordinado por Cristina García-Herrera Blanco, 2019.
Pack Kaelbling, L., et al.: "Reinforcement Learning: A Survey", *Journal of AI Research*, Vol. 4, 1996.
Palmatier, R. W. and Martin, K. D.: *The Intelligent Marketer's Guide to Data Privacy, The Impact of Big Data on Customer Trust*, Palgrave Macmillan, 2019.
Paripally, G. and Controls, J.: "Artificial Intelligence Will Revolutionize Physical Security: Intelligent, Autonomous Systems That Prevent Incidents Are Coming", *SIA—Security Industry Association*, 2021, available at https://www.securityindustry.org/2021/11/09/artificial-intelligence-will-revolutionize-physical-security-intelligent-autonomous-systems-that-prevent-incidents-are-coming/.
Parker, P.: "What Is Identity Resolution and How Are Platforms Adapting to Privacy Changes?", *MarTech*, 2021, available at https://martech.org/what-is-identity-resolution-and-how-are-platforms-adapting-to-privacy-changes/.
Pasquale, F.: "A Rule of Persons, Not Machines: The Limits of Legal Automation", *George Washington Law Review*, Vol. 87(1), 2019.

Passagnoli, G.: "Il diritto civile al tempo dell'intelligenza artificiale: spunti per una problematizzazione", in *Il ragionamento giuridico nell'era dell'intelligenza artificiale, a cura di Stefano Dorigo*, Pacini Giuridica Srl, 2020.
Patroni Griffi, F.: "La decisione robotica e il giudice amministrativo, Intervento al Convegno "Decisione robotica", organizzato nell'ambito dei Seminari 'Leibniz' per la teoria e la logica del diritto—Roma", *Accademia dei Lincei*, Vol. 5 luglio 2018.
Pearson, K.: "LIII. On Lines and Planes of Closest Fit to Systems of Points in Space", *Philosophical Magazine Series 1*, Vol. 2, 1901.
Peng, L. L.: "Natural Language Processing", *Georgetown Law Technology Review*. Vol. 1, 2016, p. 98.
Pérez Bernabeu, B.: "El principio de explicabilidad algorítmica en la normativa tributaria española hacia un derecho a la explicación individual", *Civitas. Revista española de derecho financiero*, Vol. 192, 2021.
Pérez Bernabeu, B.: "Los contribuyentes ante las decisiones automatizadas de la administración tributaria", en *La digitalización en los procedimientos tributarios y el intercambio automático de información*, edited by Ana María Pita Grandal (dir.), Luis Alberto Malvárez Pascual (dir.), Carmen Ruiz Hidalgo (dir.) and Ernesto Eseverri Martínez (col.), Aranzadi, 2023.
Perrou, K.: "The Ombudsman and the Process of Resolution of International Tax Disputes—Protecting the "Invisible Party" to the MAP", *World Tax Journal*, Vol. 10(1), 2018.
Perrou, K.: *Taxpayer Participation in Tax Treaty Dispute Resolution—Part II: Private Parties in International Disputes: The Case of International Tax Disputes"Chapter 3: International Double Taxation Disputes as Disputes between the State(s) and the Taxpayer(s)*, IBFD Doctoral Series, 2014.
Perrou, K.: *Taxpayer Participation in Tax Treaty Dispute Resolution—Part IV: Summary and Conclusions—Chapter 8: Redesigning the International Tax Dispute Resolution Mechanism*, IBFD Doctoral Series 28, 2014
Pfeifer, R.: "Das ist immer noch ein Hype", *Tages-Anzeiger—Wissen*, 2018.
Picariello, S. and Chand, V.: "The Use of Country-by-Country Reporting for Tax Risk Assessment: Challenges and Potential Solutions", *International Tax Studies*, Vol. 3(1), 2020.
Pinto Nogueira, J. F.: *Tax Administration and Technology: From Enhanced to No-Cooperation? Digital Transformation of Tax Administrations*, SSRN, 2022, available at https://papers.ssrn.com/sol3/papers.cfm?abstract_id=4125999.
Pires de Oliveira, P. T.: "Action 14 of the OECD/G20 Base Erosion and Profit Shifting Initiative: Making Dispute Resolution More Effective—Did Action 14 "Piggyback" on the Initiative?", *Bulletin for International Taxation*, Vol. 71(1), 2017.
Pistone, P.: "Chapter I: General Report, in Tax Treaty Arbitration" in *Section 1.3*, edited by M. Lang et al., WU—Tax Law and Policy Series, IBFD, 2020.
Pistone, P.: "The Settlement of Cross-Border Tax Disputes in the European Union, in European Tax Law—Part 2", *B. Terra & P. Wattel*, edited by Peter J. Wattel, Otto Marres and Hein Vermeulen, Wolters Kluwer, 2018.
Pistone, P. and Ĉiĉin-Šain, N.: "Chapter 1: The Implementation and Lasting Effects of the Multilateral Instrument: General Report", in *The Implementation and Lasting Effects of the Multilateral Instrument*, edited by M. Lang et al., WU—Tax Law and Policy Series, IBFD, 2021.
Pit, H. M.: "Improving the Arbitration Procedure under the EU Arbitration Convention (1)", ECTaxReview, Vol. 1, 2015.
Pit, H. M.: "Improving the Arbitration Procedure under the EU Arbitration Convention (2)", *ECTaxReview*, Vol. 24(2), 2015, p. 81.
Polyakov, A.: "Seven Ways Cybercriminals Can Use Machine Learning", *Forbes*, 11 January 2018.
Pontin, J., et al.: "The Downsides to Deep Learning", *WIRED*, 2018.

Pooja, K. and Bansal, P.: "Topic Modeling: A Comprehensive Review", *ICST Transactions on Scalable Information Systems*, Vol. 7(24), 2018.
Pouyanfar, S. et al.: "A Survey on Deep Learning: Algorithms, Techniques, and Applications", *ACM Computing Surveys*, Vol. 51(5), 2018.
Prainsack, B.: "Logged Out: Ownership, Exclusion and Public Value in the Digital Data and Information Commons", *Big Data & Society*, Vol. 6(1), 2019.
Prakken, H. and Sartor, G.: "Law and Logic: A Review From an Argumentation Perspective", *AI*, Vol. 227, 2015.
Pretz, K.: "Stop Calling Everything AI, Machine-Learning Pioneer Says", *IEEE Spectrum*, 31 March 2021.
Pritchard, J. K., et al.: "Inference of Population Structure Using Multilocus Genotype Data", *Genetics*, Vol. 155(2), 2000.
Protto, C.: "Mutual Agreement Procedures in Tax Treaties: Problems and Needs in Developing Countries and Countries in Transition", *Intertax*, Vol. 42(3), 2014.
Pujara, J., et al.: "Using Semantics and Statistics to Turn Data into Knowledge", *AI Magazine*, Vol. 36(1), 2015.
Pupale, R.: "Support Vector Machines(SVM)—An Overview", *towardsdatascience, Blog*, 2018.
Quintarelli, S., et al.: "Intelligenza artificiale—cos'è davvero, come funziona, che effetti avrà", *A cura di Claudia Giulia Ferrauto*, Bollati Boringhieri, 2020.
Quiroga, A. F. P.: "Innovation of the Means of Tax Payment, a Tax Administration Challenge", in *CIAT—Inter-American Center of Tax Administrations*, 25 May 2021.
Rahman, M.: "Video Liveness for Citizen Journalism: Attacks and Defenses", *IEEE Transactions on Mobile Computing*, Vol. 16(11), 2017.
Rainey, B., et al.: *Jacobs, White and Ovey: the European Convention on Human Rights*, sixth edition, Oxford: Oxford University Press, 2014.
Ram, A., et al.: "A Density Based Algorithm for Discovering Density Varied Clusters in Large Spatial Databases", *International Journal of Computer Applications*, Vol. 3(6), 2010.
Ramage, D., et al.: "Topic Modeling for the Social Sciences", *Workshop on Applications for Topic Models*, NIPS, 2009.
Ramaki, A. A., et al.: "Credit Card Fraud Detection Based on Ontology Graph", *International Journal of Security, Privacy and Trust Management (IJSPTM)*, Vol. 1(5), 2012.
Raso, F. A., et al.: "Artificial Intelligence & Human Rights: Opportunities & Risks", *Berkman Klein Center for Internet & Society at Harvard University Research Publication*, no. 2018–6, 2018.
Řehůřek, R. and Sojka, P.: "Software Framework for Topic Modelling with Large Corpora", in *Proceedings of the LREC 2010 Workshop on New Challenges for NLP Frameworks*, ELRA, Valletta, Malta, 2010.
Reisman, D., et al.: "Algorithmic Impact Assessments: A Practical Framework for Public Agency Accountability", *AINOW Institute*, 2018.
Rentfrow, P. J. and Gosling, S. D.: "The Do Re Mi's of Everyday Life: The Structure and Personality Correlates of Music Preferences", *Journal of Personality and Social Psychology*, Vol. 84(6), 2003.
Ribes Ribes, A.: "La Inteligencia Artificial al Servicio del "Compliance Tributario"", *Revista Española de Derecho Financiero*, Vol. 188, 2020.
Ribes Ribes, A.: "La resolución de los conflictos tributarios en el ámbito internacional en la era post BEPS", in *Medios alternativos de solución de controversias en materia fiscal*, edited by Gómez Cotero, José de Jesús, Béjar Rivera and Luis José (coords.), Thomson Reuters, 2019, p. 147.
Risse, R.: "Digitalization and the Tax Function in Multilateral Enterprises", *Transfer Pricing International*, Linde, 6/2018.

Rissland, E. L.: “Book Review. An AI Approach to Legal Reasoning”, *Harward Journal Law Technology*, Vol. 1(Spring), 1988.

Rissland, E. L. and Skalak, B. D.: “Cabaret: Rule Interpretation in a Hybrid Architecture”, *International Journal Man-Machine Studies*, Vol. 34(6), 1991.

Rock, E.: “Accountability: A Core Public Law Value? ”, *Administrative Law Journal*, Vol. 24(3), 2017.

Roff, H.: “Meaningful Human Control, Artificial Intelligence and Autonomous Weapons”, *Briefing Paper for Delegates at the Convention on Certain Conventional Weapons (CCW) Meeting of Experts on Lethal Autonomous Weapons Systems (LAWS)*, 2016.

Rohan, N., et al.: “Unsupervised and Supervised Text Similarity Systems for Automated Identification of National Implementing Measures of European Directives”, *AI and Law*, Vol. 27(2), 2019.

Rohith, P.: “What Is the Difference between T-SNE and PCA”, *Medium, Blog*, 2020.

Romaní Sancho, A.: “La nueva relación Hacienda-contribuyente auspiciada por la OECD: La relación cooperativa. El Foro de Grandes Empresas y el Código de Buenas Prácticas Tributarias”, *Cuadernos de Formación 4/10*, Vol. 11, 2010.

Rosenblatt, F.: “The Perceptron: A Probabilistic Model for Information Storage and Organization in the Brain”, *Psychological Review*, 65(6), 1958.

Rothkopf, D.: “Unrestricted Internet Access a Modern Human Right?”, *Foreign Policy Magazine*, 2 February 2015.

Roy Rohatgi.: *Roy Rohatgi on International Taxation—Volume 1: Principles, Part 4: Interpretation and Application of Tax Treaties—Chapter 26: Tax Treaties and Dispute Resolution*, edited by Ola Ostaszewska and BelemaObuoforibo, IBFD, 2018.

Ryman-Tubb, N. and Krause, P. J.: “How AI and ML Research Impacts Payment Card Fraud Detection: A Survey and Industry Benchmark”, *Engineering Applications of AI*, Vol. 76, 2018.

Sagwan, S.: “The Discipline of ML”, *Medium, Blog*, 24 October 2017.

Saint-Amans, P. and Russo, R.: “The BEPS Package: Promise Kept”, *Bulletin for International Taxation*, Vol. 4(2), 2016.

Sakanyan, M.: “Big Data Analysis Towards the Future”, in *Intra-European Organisation of Tax Administrations, in Applying New Technologies and Digital Solutions in Tax Compliance*, IOTA, 2020.

Sandhya Madhuri, G. and Usha Rani, M.: “Statistical Approaches to Detect Anomalies”, *SSRN Electronic Journal*, 2018, available at https://www.researchgate.net/publication/325191790_Anomaly_Detection_Techniques.

Sandvig, C, et al.: “Uncovering Algorithms: Looking Inside the Facebook News Feed”, *Cyber Harvard Edu, Blog*, 2014.

Sandvig, C., et al.: “When the Algorithm Itself Is a Racist: Diagnosing Ethical Harm in the Basic Components of Software”, *International Journal of Communication*, Vol. 10, 2016.

Sarker, I. H.: “AI-Based Modeling: Techniques, Applications and Research Issues Towards Automation, Intelligent and Smart Systems”, *SN Computer Science*, Vol. 3, 2022.

Sarker, I. H.: “Data Science and Analytics: An Overview from Data Driven Smart Computing, Decision Making and Applications Perspective”, *SN Computer Science*, Vol. 2, 2021.

Sarker, I. H.: “Machine Learning: Algorithms, Real-World Applications and Research Directions”, *SN Computer Science*, Vol. 2, 2021.

Sartor, G.: *Human Rights and Information Technologies*, edited by Roger Brownsword et al., Oxford University Press, 2017.

Sartor, G. and Branting, L.: “Introduction: Judicial Applications of AI”, *AI and Law*, Vol. 6, 1998.

Saxena, K., et al.: “Towards Recommendations from User-specific Insights Based on Historical Legal Cases”. in *14th Innovations in Software Engineering Conference (Formerly Known as India Software Engineering Conference) (ISEC 2021)*, Bhubaneswar, Odisha, India. ACM, New York, NY, USA, 25–27 February 2021.

Scharre, P.: "Autonomous Weapons and Operational Risk", *Center for a New American Security*, 2016.
Scheutz, M.: "The Case for Explicit Ethical Agents", *AI Magazine*, Vol. 38(4), 2017.
Schneier, B. "The Internet of Things Is Wildly Insecure—and Often Unpatchable", *Wired*, 2014, available at https://www.wired.com/2014/01/theres-no-good-way-to-patch-the-internet-of-things-and-thats-a-huge-problem/.
Schneier, B. "Security and the Internet of Things", *Schneier on Security*, 2017, available at https://www.schneier.com/essays/archives/2014/01/the_internet_of_thin.html.
Schofield, A., et al.: "Pulling Out the Stops: Rethinking Stopword Removal for Topic Models", in *Proceedings of the 15th Conference of the European Chapter of the Association for Computational Linguistics: Volume 2*, Short Papers, 2017.
Schoueri, L. E. y Tomazela, R.: "The Influence of the BEPS Multilateral Instrument on Tax Treaties Concluded by Non-signatory Countries", *Intertax*, Vol. 49(10), 2021.
Schulz, W. and Dankert, K.: "Governance by Things' as a Challenge to Regulation by Law", *Internet Policy Review*, Vol. 5(2), 2016.
Schut, M. and Wooldrige, M.: "Intention Reconsideration in Complex Environments", in *Proceedings of the Fourth International Conference on Autonomous Agents*, 2000.
Scipione, J.: "Artificial Intelligence and Europe: Risks, Developments and Implications", *SSRN*, 2020, available at https://papers.ssrn.com/sol3/papers.cfm?abstract_id=3598543.
Serrano Antón, F.: "Artificial Intelligence and Tax Administration: Strategy, Applications and Implications, with Special Reference to the Tax Inspection Procedure", *World Tax Journal*, Vol. 13(4), 2021.
Serrano Antón, F.: "La Era Post BEPS o la Ejecución de su Plan de Acción: Convenio Multilateral vs. Implementación Unilateral", *Quincena Fiscal*, Vol. 12, junio 2016.
Serrat, M.: "Equality and AI. Bias and Discrimination". in *Artificial Intelligence and the Law*, edited by P. García-Mexía and F. Pérez Bes, Wolters Kluwer Legal & Regulatory Spain, S.A., 2021.
Seufert, E. B.: "in Chapter 3: Quantitative Methods for Product Management", in *Freemium Economics—Leveraging Analytics and User Segmentation to Drive Revenue*, Morgan Kaufmann, 2014.
Severt, N.: "An Introduction to Recommender Systems", (+9 Easy Examples), *Blog*, 2018.
Seymour, J. and Tully, P.: "Weaponizing Data Science for Social Engineering: Automated E2E Spear Phishing on Twitter", *Black Hat Conference*, 2016.
Shrivastav, N.: "PCA vs t-SNE: Which One Should You Use for Visualization", *Analytics Vidhya, Blog*, 2019.
Shulayeva, O., et al.: "Recognizing Cited Facts and Principles in Legal Judgments", *AI and Law*, Vol. 25(4), 2017.
Sidana, M.: "Types of Classification Algorithms in ML", *MEDIUM, Blog*, 2022.
Siekiersky, B. J.: "Deep Fake: What Can Be Done About Synthetic Audio and Video?", *Library of Parliament*, Ottawa, Canada, Publication No. 2019-11-E, 2019.
Sievert, C., and Shirley, K.: "LDAvis: A Method for Visualizing and Interpreting Topics", in *Proceedings of the Workshop on Interactive Language Learning, Visualization, and Interfaces*, Association for Computational Linguistics, 2014.
Signorelli, A. D.: "È possibile dare i nostri valori a un'intelligenza artificiale? ", La Repubblica, 2023.
Simon, E., et al.: *ASSYST—Computer Support for Guideline Sentencing*, ICAIL, 1989.
Simón Acosta, E.: "La doble imposición jurídica como obstáculo para la internacionalización de las empresas: el papel de las convenciones fiscales nacionales", *Nueva Fiscalidad*, Vol. 3, 2018.
Singer, P.: *Wired for War: The Robotics Revolution and Conflict in the 21st Century*, New York: Penguin, 2009.
Six, P.: "Ethics, Regulation and the New Artificial Intelligence, Part I: Accountability and Power", *Information Communication and Society*, Vol. 4(2), 2001.

Skilton, M. and Hovsepian, F.: *The 4th Industrial Revolution—Responding to the Impact of Artificial Intelligence on Business*, Palgrave Macmillan, 2018.
Smith, A.: "Franken-Algorithms: The Deadly Consequences of Unpredictable Code", *The Guardian*, 2018.
Smith, C. et al.: *The History of AI, History of Computing*, University of Washington, 2006.
Smuha, N. A.: "The EU Approach to Ethics Guidelines for Trustworthy Artificial Intelligence", *Computer Law Review International*, Vol. 20(4), 2019.
Socha, G.: "What Is An AI Model?", *revealdata, Blog*, available at https://www.revealdata.com/blog/what-is-an-ai-model (accessed 30 September 2022).
Soler Roch, M. T.: "Tax Administration Versus Taxpayer—A New Deal?", *World Tax Journal*, Vol. 4(3), IBFD, 2012.
Solomon, B.: "Witnessing an ISIS Drone Attack", *New York Times*, 2017.
Solon, O.: "Weavrs: The Autonomous, Tweeting Blog-Bots That Feed on Social Content", *WIRED*, 28 March 2012.
Somers, J.: "The Man Who Would Teach Machines to Think", *The Atlantic*, 2013.
Spiekermann, S.: "Ethical IT Innovation: A Value-Based System Design Approach", *Auerbach Publications*, 2015.
Stahl, B. C.: *Artificial Intelligence for a Better Future An Ecosystem Perspective on the Ethics of AI and Emerging Digital Technologies*, Springer, 2021.
Stephan, K. D. and Klima, G.: "Artificial Intelligence and Its Natural Limits", *AI and Society*, Vol. 36(1), 2021.
Stevens, S.: "Tax Transparency—Part II: Instruments of Transparency Towards the Tax Administration"in *Chapter 5: Thematic Report—Cutting-Edge Techniques to Collect Information from Taxpayers*, edited by Funda Başaran Yavaşlar and Johanna Hey, EATLP International Tax Series, 2019.
Stranieri, A. and Zeleznikow, J.: "Knowledge Discovery from Legal Databases", in *Springer Law and Philosophy Library*, Vol. 69, Springer Dodrecht, 2005.
Suay Belenguer, J. M.: "La mente mecánica, Naturaleza y Libertad", *Revista de estudios interdisciplinares*, Número 1, 2012.
Suliman, A. and Zhang, Y.: "A Review on Back-Propagation Neural Networks in the Application of Remote Sensing Image Classification", *Journal of Earth Science and Engineering*, Vol. 5, 2015.
Sun, H.: "The Fundamental Right to Technology", *Hofstra Law Review*, Vol. 48(2), 2020.
Surden, H.: "AI and Law: An Overview", *Georgia State University Law Review*, Vol. 35(4), 2019.
Surden, H.: "ML and Law", *Washington Law Review*, Vol. 89(87), 2014.
Susskind, R.: "Expert Systems in Law: A Jurisprudential Approach to AI and Legal Reasoning", *The Modern Law Review*, Vol. 49, 1986.
Susskind, R.: *Tomorrow's Lawyers—An Introduction to Your Future*, Second edition, Corby Northants: Oxford University Press, 2017.
Suthaharan, S.: "ML Models and Algorithms for Big Data Classification—Thinking with Examples for Effective Learning", *Integrated Series in Information Systems*, edited by Ramesh Sharda Stefan, Voß. 36, Springer, 2016.
Sutton, R. S., and Barto, A. G.: *Reinforcement Learning: An Introduction*, Second edition, Cambridge, MA, London: The MIT Press, 2017.
Swan, M.: "Connected Car: Quantified Self Becomes Quantified Car", *Journal of Sensor and Actuator Networks*, Vol. 4(1), 2015.
Szegedy, C. et al.: "Intriguing Properties of Neural Networks", in *2nd International Conference on Learning Representations, ICLR 2014*, Banff, Canada, 2014.
Taeho, J.: *Text Mining: Concepts, Implementation, and Big Data Challenge*, Springer International Publishing AG, ProQuest Ebook Central, 2018.
Taha, W. M.: *Cyber-Physical Systems: A Model-Based Approach*, First edition, Cham: Springer International Publishing: Imprint: Springer, 2021.

Tao, S.: "ML, Optimization, and Data Science", in *5th International Conference, LOD 2019 Siena, Italy, September 10–13, 2019 Proceedings*, edited by Giuseppe Nicosia, Panos Pardalos, Renato Umeton, Giovanni Giuffrida and Vincenzo Sciacca, Springer, 2019.
Taruffo, M.: "Judicial Decisions and AI", *AI and Law*, Vol. 6, 1998.
Tata, C.: "The Application of Judicial Intelligence and 'Rules' to Systems Supporting Discretionary Judicial Decision-Making", *AI and Law*, Vol. 6(2), 1998.
Taylor, M. E., and Stone, P.: "An Introduction to Intertask Transfer for Reinforcement Learning", *AI Magazine*, Vol. 32(1), 2011.
Taylor, S.: "Regression Analysis", *Corporate Finance Institute, Blog*, 2 May 2023.
Tegmark, M.: "Benefits & Risks of Artificial Intelligence", *Future of Life Institute*, 2015.
Teitelbaum, J. C.: "Analogical Legal Reasoning: Theory and Evidence", *American Law and Economics Review*, Vol. 17(1), 2015.
Terra, B. J. M. and Wattel, P. J.: "European Tax Law", *Kluwer Law International—Wolters Kluwer*, 2012.
Theobald, O.: "*ML: for Absolute Beginners: A Plain English Introduction*, Third edition, Independently Published, 2021.
Thomas, M.: *Safety Critical Systems*. Gresham Lectures: London, 2017, YouTube.
Thorén, E.: "Compliance by Design—Easy, Secure and Safe Business Systems", in *Intra-European Organisation of Tax Administrations, in Applying New Technologies and Digital Solutions in Tax Compliance*, IOTA, 2020.
Toledo Pires de Olivera, P.: "Action 14 of the OECD/G20 Base Erosion and Profit Shifting Initiative: Making Dispute Resolution More Effective—Did Action 14 "Piggyback" on the Initiative", *Bulletin for International Taxation*, Vol. 71(1), 2017.
Toro Icarte, R., et al.: "Reward Machines: Exploiting Reward Function Structure in Reinforcement Learning", *Journal of AI Research*, Vol. 73, 2022.
Tostes Neto, J. B. and Ferreira de Almeida, A. F.: "The Dilemmas of Digitalization", *CIAT*, 2022.
Tsamados, A., et al.: "The Ethics of Algorithms: Key Problems and Solutions", *AI & Society*, Vol. 37(3), 2022.
Turing, A. M.: "Computer Machinery and Intelligence", *Mind*, Vol. 59(236), 1950.
Turing, A. M.: "The Word Problem in Semi-Groups With Cancellation", *Annals of Mathematics Second Series*, Vol. 52(2), 1950.
Tuzet, G.: "Assessment Criteria or Standards of Proof? An Effort in Clarification", *AI and Law*, Vol. 28(2), 2020.
Tyriver, C.: "Part 1: Artificial Intelligence in Physical Security", *Security 101, Blog*, available at https://www.security101.com/blog/artificial-intelligence-in-physical-security.
UNSW: "Descriptive, Predictive & Prescriptive Analytics: What Are the Differences?", *Blog*, 29 January 2020.
Valcheva, S.: "5 Anomaly Detection Algorithms in Data Mining (With Comparison)", *Intellspot, Blog*, available at https://www.intellspot.com/anomaly-detection-algorithms/.
Valente, P.: "Advance Pricing Agreements; Optimal Tool—Optimal Framework?", *Intertax*, Vol. 48(1), 2020.
Valente, P.: "L'art. 25 del Modello di Convenzione OCSE: la procedura di composizione delle controversie internazionali", *il fisco*, Vol. 9, 2004.
Valente, P.: *Manuale del Transfer Pricing*, Ipsoa, 2012.
Valente, P.: "Nuovo Interpello Internazionale e Rapporti con le Verifiche Fiscali in Corso", *il fisco*, Vol. 42, 2016.
Valente, P.: "Procedure amichevoli, procedure arbitrali e rapporti Fisco-contribuente", *il fisco*, Vol. 5, 2017.
Valente, P., Alagna, C. and Mattia, S., *Controversie internazionali: procedure amichevoli e gestione delle relazioni*, IPSOA, 2013.
Valiant, L.: *Probably Approximately Correct*, Basic Books, 2013.

Van Den Brink, M. and Bakker, A. J.: "Technology: A Key Enabler for Tax Transformation", *Bulletin for International Taxation*, Vol. 74(10), 2020.
Van Den Hoogen, R.: "E-Justice", *Beginselen van Behoorlijke Elektronische Rechtspraak*, 2007.
Van Der Enden, E. M. E. and Bronzewska, K.: "The Concept of Cooperative Compliance", *Bulletin for International Taxation*, Vol. 68(10), 2014.
Van Der Enden, E. M. E. and De Groot, J.: "Two Missing Links: A Move Towards an Auditing Standard Specifically for the Tax Control Framework", *Bulletin for International Taxation*, Vol. 69(9), 2015.
Van Der Maaten, L. and Hinton, G. E.: "Visualizing Data Using t-SNE", *Journal of Machine Learning Research*", Vol. 9(86) 2008.
Van Haastert, H.: "Government as a Platform: Public Values in the Age of Big Data", *Policy & Internet*, Vol. 11(2), 2019.
Van Vlem, X., et al.: "The EU Arbitration Convention: Reinforcing the Procedure to Cope with an Expected Flood of Double Taxation Disputes", *International Transfer Pricing Journal*, Vol. 21(4), 2014.
Varma, A.: "Local Outlier Factor, GeeksforGeeks", *Blog*, 2022, available at https://www.intellspot.com/anomaly-detection-algorithms/ (accessed 3 September 2022).
Velicogna, M.: "Justice Systems and ICT-What Can Be Learned from Europe", *Utrecht Law Review*, Vol. 3(1), 2007.
Venkatachalam, M.: "About Adversarial Examples", *Towards Data Science, Blog*, 2019, available at https://towardsdatascience.com/about-adversarial-examples-2a7a7b4d2670.
Venkatachalam, S.: "Why 2017 Is The Year of Artificial Intelligence", *Forbes*, 27 February 2017, available at https://www.forbes.com/consent/ketch/?toURL=https://www.forbes.com/councils/forbestechcouncil/2017/02/27/why-2017-is-the-year-of-artificial-intelligence/.
Verheij, B.: "Artificial Intelligence as Law—Presidential Address to the Seventeenth International Conference on AI and Law", *AI as Law*, Vol. 28(3), 2020.
Verheij, B.: "Formalizing Value-Guided Argumentation for Ethical Systems Design", *AI and Law*, Vol. 24(4), 2016.
Verheij, B.: "Presidential Address to the Seventeenth International Conference on AI and Law", *AI as Law*, Vol. 28(3), 2020.
Verma, S.: "Weapons of Math Destruction: How Big Data Increases Inequality and Threatens Democracy—Book Review", *Vikalpa*, Vol. 44(2), 2019.
Vincent, J.: "The State of AI in 2019", *VERGE*, 2019.
Viola, L.: "Giustizia predittiva non equivale a Ia", *ItaliaOggi7*, Lunedì 24 Ottobre 2022.
Virgillito, A.: "Emerging Risks in Massive Data Analytics—A Data Scientist's Perspective", in *Intra-European Organisation of Tax Administrations, in Applying New Technologies and Digital Solutions in Tax Compliance*, IOTA, 2020.
Vozza, A.: "Intelligenza artificiale, giustizia predittiva e proceso tributario", *il fisco*, Vol. 32, 2019.
Wachter, S., et al.: "Transparent, Explainable, and Accountable AI for Robotics", *Science Robotics*, Vol. 2(6), 2017.
Waddell, K.: "How Big Data Harms Poor Communities", *The Atlantic*, 2016.
Wagner, B.: "Ethics as an Escape from Regulation: From Ehics-Washing to Ethics-Shopping?", in *Being Profiling: Cogitas Ergo Sum*, edited by M. Hildebrandt, Amsterdam: Amsterdam University Press, 2018.
Walmsley, J.: "Artificial Intelligence and the Value of Transparency", *AI & Society*, Vol. 36(2), 2021.
Walsh, T.: "Experiments in Social Media", *AI Magazine*, Vol. 40(4), 2019.
Walt, B., et al.: "Predicting the Outcome of Appeal Decisions in Germany's Tax Law", in *9th International Conference on Electronic Participation (ePart)*, St. Petersburg, Russia, 2017.

Walton, D., et al.: "An Argumentation Framework for Contested Cases of Statutory Interpretation", *AI Law*, Vol. 24(1), 2016.

Waskom, M. L.: "Seaborn: Statistical Data Visualization", *Journal of Open Source Software*, Vol. 6(60), 2021.

Waters, R.: "Why We Are in Danger of Overestimating AI", *Financial Times*, 2018.

Weinberger, D. "Don't Make AI Artificially Stupid in the Name of Transparency, Opinion: A Democracy Shouldn't Leave It to Companies to Figure Out the Ethics of Artificial Intelligence", *WIRED*, 2018.

Weinberger, D. "Optimization Over Explanation—Maximizing the Benefits of Machine Learning Without Sacrificing Its Intelligence", *Published in Berkman Klein Center Collection*, 2018.

Weizenbaum, J.: "On the Impact of the Computer on Society", *Science*, Vol. 176(4035), 1972.

Weller, A.: "Challenges for Transparency", Paper Presented at 2017 ICML Workshop on Human Interpretability in Machine Learning, WHI 2017, Sidney, NSW, Australia.

Westholm, H.: "Models of Improving e-Governance by Back Office Re-Organisation and Integration", *Journal of Public Policy*, Vol. 25(1), 2005.

Whittlestone, J., et al.: "Ethical and Societal Implications of Algorithms, Data, and Artificial Intelligence: A Roadmap for Research", *Nuffield Foundation*, 2019.

Winkels, R., et al.: "Towards a Legal Recommender System, Legal Knowledge and Information Systems", *JURIX 2014: The Twenty-Seventh Annual Conference, Frontiers in AI and Applications*, 2014.

Winston, P.: "Artificial Intelligence", Addison-Wesley Publishing Company, 1992.

Witten, I. H., et al.: *Data Mining—Practical ML Tools and Techniques*, Third edition, Morgan Kaufmann, 2011.

Wojciech, S. and Müller, K-R.: "Towards Explainable Artificial Intelligence", in *Explainable AI: Interpreting, Explaining and Visualizing Deep Learning*, edited by Wojciech Samek, Grégoire Montavon, Andrea Vedaldi, Lars Kai Hansen and Klaus-Robert Müller, Springer Cham, 2019.

Woolley, S. C. and Howard, P.: "Political Communication, Computational Propaganda, and Autonomous Agents", *International Journal of Communication*, Vol. 10(2016), 2016.

Yao, M.: "Chihuahua or Muffin? My Search for the Best Computer Vision API", *Blog*, October 12, 2017.

Yeung, K.: "Algorithmic Regulation: A Critical Interrogation", *Regulation & Governance*, Vol. 12(6), 2017.

Yeung, K.: "Design for Regulation", in *Handbook of Ethics, Values and Technological Design*, edited by M. J. Van Den Hoven, P. E. Varmaas and I. van de Poel, Dordecht: Springer, 2015.

Yeung, K.: "'Hypernudge': Big Data as a Mode of Regulation by Design", *Information, Communication & Society*, Vol. 20(1), 2017.

Yeung, K. and Weller, A.: "How Is "Transparency" Understood by Legal Scholars and the Machine Learning Community?", *Being Profiling. Cogitas Ergo Sum*, edited by E. Bayamlioglu, I. Baraluic, 2018.

Yildrim, S.: "K-Means Clustering—Explained", *towardsdatascience, Blog*, 2020.

Yin, T.: "Game of Drones: Defending Against Drone Terrorism", *Texas A&M University Law Review*, Vol. 2(4), 2015.

Zackrisson, M., et al.: "AI and Tax Administrations: A Good Match", *Bulletin for International Taxation*, Vol. 74(10), 2020.

Zalnieriute, M. and Bennett Moses, L.: "The Rule of Law and Automation of Government Decision-Making", *Modern Law Review*, Vol. 82(3), 2019.

Zeitzoff, T.: "How Social Media Is Changing Conflict", *Journal of Conflict Resolution*, Vol. 61(9), 2017.

Zeyen, G.: "When Taxation Meets Arbitration: Recent Initiatives to Introduce and Promote Arbitration in International and European Taxation", *Intertax*, Vol. 45(1), 2017.
Zhang, B., et al.: "Ethics and Governance of Artificial Intelligence: Evidence from a Survey of Machine Learning Researchers", *Journal of Artificial Intelligence Research*, Vol. 71, 2021.
Zhang, M. H. and Wu, J.: "Implementation of Rough Fuzzy k-Means Clustering Algorithm", in *Matlab, 2010 International Conference on ML and Cybernetics*, 2010.
Zhang, Z., et al.: "Hierarchical Cluster Analysis in Clinical Research with Heterogeneous Study Population: Highlighting its Visualization with R.", *Annals of Translational Medicine*, Vol. 5(4), 2017.
Zolfaghari, F.: "Hierarchical Cluster Analysis to Identify the Homogeneous Desertification Management Units", *PLoS One*, Vol. 14(12), 2019.
Zuboff, S.: "Big Other: Surveillance Capitalism and the Prospects of an Information Civilization", *Journal of Information Technology*, Vol. 30, 2015.
Züger, M.: "Arbitration Under Tax Treaties, Chapter 1: The Lack of Legal Protection in International Tax Law", *On-Line Books IBFD, Doctoral Series 5*, 2001.
Zuiderveen Borgesius, F., et al.: "Should We Worry About Filter Bubbles?", *Internet Policy Review Journal on Internet Regulation*, Vol. 5(1), 2016

Communications, declarations, directives, documents, reports and decisions of international bodies and organizations

Communications of the Commission to the Council, to the Parliament, to the Social and Economic Committee and to the Regional Committee

- Council of Europe, European Convention on Human Rights, Rome, 4.XI.1950.
- Proposal for a Council Directive on the elimination of double taxation in connection with the adjustment of transfers of profits between associated enterprises (arbitration procedure), COM(76)611 final, 25 November 1976.
- European Parliament, Directive 95/46/EC of the European Parliament and of the Council of 24 October 1995.
- Commission notice on the application of the State aid rules to measures relating to direct business taxation, (98/C 384/03), 1998.
- Commission of the European Communities, Commission Staff Working Paper—Company Taxation in the Internal Market, COM(2001) 582 final, 2001.
- Council of Europe, Recommendation CM/Rec(2012)4 of the Committee of Ministers to member States on the protection of human rights with regard to social networking services, Adopted by the Committee of Ministers on 4 April2012 at the 1139th meeting of the Ministers' Deputies.
- European Commission, Commission Staff Working Document, Impact Assessment Accompanying the Document Proposal for a Council Directive on Double Taxation Dispute Resolution Mechanism in the European Union, SWD(2016) 343 final 5, 2016.
- European Parliament and the European Council, Regulation (EU) 2016/679 of the European Parliament and of the Council of 27 April 2016.
- Council of Europe, Guidelines on the Protection of Individuals with regard to the Processing of Personal Data in a world of Big Data, 17 January 2017.
- European Parliament, Resolution of 14 March 2017 on fundamental rights implications of big data: privacy, data protection, non-discrimination, security and law-enforcement (2016/2225(INI)) (OJ C, C/263, 25.07.2018).
- European Parliament, Civil Law Rules on Robotics—European Parliament resolution of 16 February 2017 with recommendations to the Commission on Civil Law Rules on Robotics (2015/2103(INL).

- Council of Europe, Algorithms and Human Rights, Study on the human rights dimensions of automated data processing techniques and possible regulatory implications, prepared by the Committee of experts on internet intermediaries (MSI-NET), DGI(2017)12, 2017.
- European Commission, Directorate of the Human Rights, The CEPEJ European Ethical Charter on the use of artificial intelligence (AI) in judicial systems and their environment, Presentation Note, 4 December 2018.
- Council of Europe, European ethical Charter on the use of Artificial Intelligence in judicial systems and their environment, 2018.
- Council of Europe, European Commission for the Efficiency of Justice (CEPEJ), European Ethical Charter on the Use of Artificial Intelligence in Judicial Systems and their environment, Adopted at the 31st plenary meeting of the CEPEJ (Strasbourg, 3–4 December 2018).
- European Commission, Artificial Intelligence for Europe, Brussels, COM(2018) 237 final.
- European Commission, European Group on Ethics in Science and New Technologies, Statement on Artificial Intelligence, Robotics and 'Autonomous' Systems, 2018.
- European Commission, Communication from the Commission to the European Parliament, the European Economic and Social Committee and the Committee of the Regions—Coordinated Plan on Artificial Intelligence, Brussels, COM(2018) 795 final.
- European Commission, A Definition of AI: Main Capabilities and Scientific Disciplines, Definition developed for the purpose of the deliverables of the High-Level Expert Group on AI, 2018.
- Council of Europe, Consultative Committee of the Convention of the Protection of Individuals with regard to Automatic Processing of Personal Data—(Convention 108), Report on Artificial Intelligence, T-PD(2018)09Rev, Strasbourg, 25 January 2019.
- European Commission, Ethics guidelines for trustworthy AI, 2019.
- Council of Europe, Consultative Committee of the Convention of the Protection of Individuals with regard to Automatic Processing of Personal Data—(Convention 108), Report on Artificial Intelligence, T-PD(2018)09Rev, Strasbourg, 25 January 2019.
- Council of Europe, Committee of experts on human rights dimensions of automated data processing and different forms of artificial intelligence, Rapporteur: Yeung, Karen, A study of advanced digital technologies (including AI systems) for the concept of responsibility within a human rights framework, DGI(2019)05, 2019.
- Council of Europe, High-Level Conference Governing the Game Changer—Impacts of artificial intelligence development on human rights, democracy and the rule of law, Conference co-organised by the Finnish Presidency of the Council of Europe Committee of Ministers and the Council of Europe 26–27 February 2019.
- Council of Europe, Declaration by the Committee of Ministers on the manipulative capabilities of algorithmic processes, (Adopted by the Committee of Ministers on 13 February 2019 at the 1337th meeting of the Ministers' Deputies), Decl(13/02/2019)1.
- European Commission, An action plan for fair and simple taxation supporting the recovery strategy, COM(2020) 312 final, 2020.
- European Commission, White Paper On Artificial Intelligence—A European approach to excellence and trust, COM(2020) 65 final.
- European Commission, ANNEXES to the Communication from the Commission to the European Parliament, the European Council, the Council, the European Economic and Social Committee and the Committee of the Regions Fostering a European approach to Artificial Intelligence Brussels, 2021, COM(2021) 205 final.
- European Parliament, The Protection of Article 2 TEU Values in the EU, Fact Sheets on the European Union—2021.

Directives, recommendations and resolutions of the council

- Convention on the elimination of double taxation in connection with the adjustment of profits of associated enterprises n. 90/436/CEE.

- Revised Code of Conduct for the effective implementation of the Convention on the elimination of double taxation in connection with the adjustment of profits of associated enterprises (2009/C 322/01).
- Directive 2017/1852/EU on tax dispute resolution mechanisms in the European Union.

European Union Joint Transfer Pricing Forum (EU JTPF)

—EU JTPF, JTPF/007/2002/REV1/EN.

Organization for Economic Cooperation and Development—OECD

- OECD, Compliance Risk Management: Managing and Improving Tax Compliance (Guidance Note), 2004.
- OECD, Improving the Process for Resolving International Tax Disputes, version released for public comment on 27 July 2004.
- OECD, Improving the Process for Resolving International Tax Disputes (Report adopted by the Committee on Fiscal Affairs on 30 January 2007), 2007.
- OECD, Improving the Resolution of Tax Treaty Disputes (Report adopted by the Committee on Fiscal Affairs on 30 January 2007), February 2007.
- OECD, Study into the Role of Tax Intermediaries, Paris 2008.
- OECD, What is a competitive Tax System, OECD 50th Anniversary Challenges in designing competitive tax systems, 2011.
- OECD, Guidelines for Multinational Enterprises, 2011.
- OCDED, Dealing Effectively with the Challenges of Transfer Pricing, 2012.
- OECD, Action Plan on Base Erosion and Profit Shifting, 2013.
- OECD, Cooperative Compliance: A Framework—from enhanced relationship to cooperative compliance, 2013.
- OECD, Developing a Multilateral Instrument to Modify Bilateral Tax Treaties, Action 15: 2015 Final Report.
- OCDE, Hacer más efectivos los mecanismos de resolución de controversias, Informe final, 2015.
- OECD/G20 Base Erosion and Profit Shifting Project, Making Dispute Resolution Mechanisms More Effective, Action 14: 2015 Final Report, 2015.
- OECD, Explanatory Statement to the Multilateral Convention to Implement Tax Treaty Related Measures to Prevent Base Erosion and Profit Shifting, November 2016.
- OECD, Technologies for Better Tax Administration: A Practical Guide for Revenue Bodies, 2016.
- OECD, Advanced Analytics for Better Tax Administration, Putting Data to work, 2016.
- OCDE, Model Tax Convention on Income and Capital, 2017.
- OECD, Transfer Pricing Guidelines for Multinational Enterprises and Tax Administrations, 2017.
- OECD, International Compliance Assurance Programme Pilot Handbook—Working Document, 2018.
- OECD, Science, Technology and Innovation Outlook 2018.
- OECD, Scoping the OECD AI Principles—Deliberation of the Expert Group on AI at the OECD (AIGO), OECD Digital Economic Papers, n. 291, 2019.
- OECD, Artificial Intelligence in Society, 2019.
- OECD, Joint Audit 2019—Enhancing Tax Cooperation and Improving Tax Certainty—Forum on Tax Administration, 2019.
- OECD, International Compliance Assurance Programme Pilot Handbook 2.0, 2019.
- OECD, International Compliance Assurance Programme Pilot Handbook—Working Document, 2019.

- OECD, Tax Administration 2019: Comparative Information on OECD and other Advanced and Emerging Economies, 2019.
- OECD, Multilateral Convention to Implement Tax Treaty Related Measures to Prevent Base Erosion and Profit Shifting, Multilateral Instrument, Information Brochure, 2020.
- OECD, International Compliance Assurance Programme—Handbook for tax administrations and MNE groups, 2021.
- OECD, Forum on Tax Administration, International Compliance Assurance Programme—FAQs, 2021.
- OECD, OECD Framework for The Classification of AI Systems—OECD Digital Economy Papers, n. 323, 2022.
- OECD, Recommendation of the Council on OECD Legal Instruments Artificial Intelligence, 2022.
- OECD, Manual on the Handling of Multilateral Mutual Agreement Procedures and Advance Pricing Arrangements—Enhancing Tax Certainty, 2023.

Documents of the IMF (International Monetary Fund)/OECD

- 2017 Tax Certainty, IMF/OECD Report for the G20 Finance Ministers and Central Bank Governors, 2017.
- 2019 Progress Report on Tax Certainty, IMF/OECD Report for the G20 Finance Ministers and Central Bank Governors, 2019.

Others

- BOE, Convenio relativo a la supresión de la doble imposición en caso de corrección de los beneficios de empresas asociadas 90/436/EEC, fecha de la firma: 23/07/1990 en Bruselas.
- UN, General Assembly, Universal Declaration of Human Rights, 10 December 1948.
- UN, General Assembly (GA), International Covenant on Civil and Political Rights, 16 December 1966.
- United Nations, International Convention on the Protection of the Rights of All Migrant Workers and Members of Their Families, 18 December 1990.
- The Royal Academy of Engineering, Autonomous Systems: Social Legal and Ethical Issues, 2009.
- US: Dept. of Commerce, National Institute of Standards and Technology (NIST), The NIST Definition of Cloud Computing, 2011.
- FRA, European Union Agency for Fundamental Rights, Handbook on European law relating to access to justice, Luxembourg: Publications Office of the European Union, 2011.
- United Nations, The Guiding Principles on Business and Human Rights, Implementing the United Nations "Protect, Respect and Remedy" Framework, 2011.
- US Department of Defense, DoD Directive 3000.09: Autonomy in Weapon Systems, 2012.
- White House, Big Data: seizing opportunities, preserving values (Report for the President), Washington D.C., USA: Executive Office of the President, 2014.
- Stanford news, New Stanford research finds computers are better judges of personality than friends and family, 2015.
- UN, Coordinator's Rep. on Work of the Subcommittee on the Mutual Agreement Procedure—Dispute Avoidance and Resolution, Comm. of Experts on Int'l Cooperation in Tax Matters, Rep. on Its Twelfth Session, U.N. Doc. E/C.18/2016/CRP.4 (Oct. 11, 2016).

- United Nations, General Assembly, 2016 Report of the UN Special Rapporteur on the promotion and protection of the right to freedom of opinion and expression, David Kaye, to the Thirty-second session of the Human Rights Council (A/HRC/32/ 38).
- European Data Protection Supervisor (EPDS), Artificial Intelligence, Robotics, Privacy and Data Protection, Room document for the 38th International Conference of Data Protection and Privacy Commissioners, October 2016.
- White House Office of Science and Technology Policy (OSTP), Preparing for the Future of Artificial Intelligence, Report, 2016.
- The White House, Big Data: A report on Algorithmic Systems, Opportunity and Civil Rights, 2016.
- UK House of Commons—Science and Technology Committee, Robotics and artificial intelligence—Fifth Report of Session 2016–17, 13 September 2016.
- Federal Trade Commission—United States of America, Big Data—A Tool for Inclusion or Exclusions?, FTC Report, January 2016.
- Stanford University, One Hundred Year Study on AI (AI100), AI and Life in 2030, 2016 Report.
- The Association for the Advancement of Artificial Intelligence and the UK Computing Research Committee, Joint written evidence submitted by AAAI and UKCRC, April 2016.
- Agenzia delle Entrate, Circolare N. 16/E del 28/04/2016—Prevenzione e contrasto all'evasione—Indirizzi operativi, 2016.
- IEEE Global Initiative on Ethics of and Autonomous and Intelligent Systems, Ethically Aligned Design: A Vision for Prioritizing Human Well-Being with Autonomous and Intelligent Systems, (IEEE, 2017).
- International Committee of the Red Cross, Expert Meeting on Lethal Autonomous Weapon Systems, 2017.
- Noticias de actualidad, Nuevo sistema de resolución de litigios de doble imposición en el seno de la UE, Carta Tributaria, Revista de Opinión, Número 29–30, 2017.
- Guardia di Finanza, Circolare N. 1/2018, 27 November 2017, Volume 1, Chapter 6.
- EY, Tax Technology and Transformation, "Tax functions go digital", 2017.
- The Royal Society, Machine Learning: The power and promise of computers that learn by example, 2017.
- Centre for Strategic and International Studies (CSIS) and McAfee, The Economic Impact of Cybercrime report, written by James Lewis, 2018.
- Documentos de trabajo 7/2018, Problemas actuales sobre la residencia fiscal: perspectivas interna, comunitaria e internacional, Instituto de Estudios Fiscales, Director Isaac Merino Jara, Coordinador Antonio Vázquez del Rey Villanueva, 2018.
- Montréal Declaration Responsible AI, Montréal Declaration for a Responsible Development of Artificial Intelligence 2018.
- UK House of Commons—Digital, Culture, Media and Sport Committee, Disinformation and 'fake news': Interim Report, Fifth Report of Session 2017–19, 2018.
- European Union Agency for Fundamental Rights (FRA), #BigData: Discrimination in data-supported decision making, 2018.
- Australian Human Right Commission, Human Rights and Technology Issues Paper, July 2018.
- FAT/ML, FAT* '19: Conference on Fairness, Accountability, and Transparency in Machine Learning, FAT/ML, Association for Computing Machinery, New York, NY, United States, 2019.
- Stanford Encyclopedia of Philosophy, Moral Responsibility, October 16th, 2019.
- European Central Bank, Seventh report on card fraud, 2019.
- Conseil Constitutionnel, Décision n° 2019–796 DC du 27 décembre 2019, Loi de finances pour 2020.

- Microsoft, Fundamentals of AI—Student Guide Module 1, 2020.
- Rechtbank Den Haag, C-09–550982-HA ZA 18–388, 2020.
- History of Science: "AI Winter: The Highs and Lows of AI", Blog, 9 September 2021.
- Stanford University, Gathering Strength, Gathering Storms: The One Hundred Year Study on Artificial Intelligence (AI100), Study Panel Report 2021.
- Garante per la Protezione dei dati Personali (GPDP), Riconoscimento facciale: il Garante privacy sanziona Clearview per 20 milioni di euro. Vietato l'uso dei dati biometrici e il monitoraggio degli italiani, Press Release, 2022.
- Europa Press Islas Canarias, Marchena ve "indispensable" la inteligencia artificial pero sostiene que no puede sustituir al juez, europapress, published on 2022.
- Comisionado de Transparencia de Canarias, Manuel Marchena en el Parlamento de Canarias: "Hay que lograr que la Justicia siga siendo humana", YouTube, 2022.
- Wikipedia—Lemma (morphology).

Index

FSC
www.fsc.org
MIX
Papier | Fördert
gute Waldnutzung
FSC® C083411

Kolibri 360 GmbH
Ferdinand-Jühlke-Straße 7
99095 Erfurt, Deutschland
produktsicherheit@kolibri360.de